Alternative Modernities

A MILLENNIAL QUARTET BOOK

ALTERNATIVE MODERNITIES,

edited by Dilip Parameshwar Gaonkar

GLOBALIZATION, *edited by Arjun Appadurai*

MILLENNIAL CAPITALISM & THE

CULTURE OF NEOLIBERALISM, *edited*

by Jean Comaroff & John L. Comaroff

COSMOPOLITANISM, *edited by*

Carol A. Breckenridge, Sheldon Pollock,

Homi K. Bhabha, & Dipesh Chakrabarty

PUBLIC CULTURE BOOKS

Alternative Modernities

Edited by Dilip Parameshwar Gaonkar

DUKE UNIVERSITY PRESS * DURHAM & LONDON 2001

© 2001 Duke University Press   All rights reserved

Printed in the United States of America on acid-free paper ∞

Typeset in Adobe Minion by Tseng Information Systems, Inc.

Library of Congress Cataloging-in-Publication Data

appear on the last printed page of this book.

IN HONOR OF

Ramchandran Jaikumar

JUNE 18, 1944–FEBRUARY 10, 1998

FRIEND, BENEFACTOR, AND SCHOLAR

Contents

Acknowledgments

Alternative Modernities was originally published as a special issue of *Public Culture*. It was also the first volume in a *Public Culture* miniseries called the Millennial Quartet. The other three special issues in the Quartet, now in print, probe the thematics of globalization, millennial capitalism, and cosmopolitanism. My thanks to Carol A. Breckenridge for inviting me to edit the first volume of the Quartet and to the rest of the *Public Culture* editorial committee for reading and commenting on manuscripts at very short notice during that issue's assembly. As a special issue, *Alternative Modernities* placed extra demands on the staff of the *Public Culture* editorial office, including Robert McCarthy and Caitrin Lynch, who rose to the occasion, as always, with verve and imagination. Partial support for the special issue came through the generosity of the Division of Arts and Humanities of the Rockefeller Foundation.

Some of the essays in this volume were initially presented at two conferences on Alternative Modernities that I organized at Northwestern University (April 1996) and the India International Center, New Delhi (December 1997); my thanks to the School of Speech at Northwestern University, the India International Center, and the Center for Transcultural Studies for funding those two conferences. My thanks to Raheev Bhargava, who was co-organizer for the New Delhi conference, and Pratibe Gaonkar, who was my coordinator.

For conversations and comments that were useful in writing the introductory essay, I am grateful to Arjun Appadurai, Lauren Berlant, Carol A. Breckenridge, Dipesh Chakrabarty, Sally Ewing, Benjamin Lee, Claudio Lomnitz, Robert McCarthy, Thomas McCarthy, Elizabeth Povinelli, and Charles Taylor.

Finally, we dedicate this volume to the late Ramchandran Jaikumar, whose generous gift made the December 1997 New Delhi conference on Alternative Modernities possible. At the time of his untimely death, Jaikumar was Daewoo Professor of Business Administration at the Harvard Business School, a renowned authority on computer-integrated manufacturing, and a beloved mentor and friend. This volume is also a tribute to Jaikumar's family.

On Alternative Modernities

Dilip Parameshwar Gaonkar

To think in terms of "alternative modernities" is to admit that modernity is inescapable and to desist from speculations about the end of modernity. Born in and of the West some centuries ago under relatively specific sociohistorical conditions, modernity is now everywhere. It has arrived not suddenly but slowly, bit by bit, over the longue durée — awakened by contact; transported through commerce; administered by empires, bearing colonial inscriptions; propelled by nationalism; and now increasingly steered by global media, migration, and capital. And it continues to "arrive and emerge," as always in opportunistic fragments accompanied by utopic rhetorics, but no longer from the West alone, although the West remains the major clearinghouse of global modernity.

To think in terms of alternative modernities is to recognize the need to revise the distinction between societal modernization and cultural modernity. That distinction is implicated in the irresistible but somewhat misleading narrative about the two types of modernities, the good and the bad, a judgment that is reversible depending on one's stance and sensibility.

THE DILEMMAS OF WESTERN MODERNITY

For some, including contemporary neoconservatives like Daniel Bell, societal modernization, which involves a set of cognitive and social transformations, is both good and inevitable.[1] On this account, the cognitive transformations include or imply the growth of scientific

1. Daniel Bell, *The Cultural Contradictions of Capitalism* (New York: Basic Books, 1976).

consciousness, the development of a secular outlook, the doctrine of progress, the primacy of instrumental rationality, the fact-value split, individualistic understandings of the self, contractualist understandings of society, and so on. The social transformations refer to the emergence and institutionalization of market-driven industrial economies, bureaucratically administered states, modes of popular government, rule of law, mass media, and increased mobility, literacy, and urbanization. These two sets of transformations are seen as constituting a relatively harmonious and healthy package. This is the idealized self-understanding of bourgeois modernity historically associated with the development of capitalism in the West that called into existence not only a distinctive mode of production but also a new type of subject—an agent who was set free from constraints imposed by tradition to pursue its own private ends and whose actions were at once motivated by acquisitiveness and regulated by "this worldly asceticism."

Against this bourgeois order and orderliness, the other modernity—the cultural modernity—rose in opposition. It first appeared in the aesthetic realm led by different, sometimes competing, groups of avant-garde writers and artists starting with the Romantics in the late eighteenth century and was gradually absorbed and carried forward (with its critical edge dulled) by the popular medias of news, entertainment, and commercial arts and advertising. Thus cultural modernity came to permeate everyday life. By and large, the proponents of cultural modernity were repelled by the middle-class ethos—by its stifling conformities and banalities; by its discounting of enthusiasm, imagination, and moral passion in favor of pragmatic calculation and the soulless pursuit of money; and, more than anything else, by its pretensions, complacencies, and hypocrisies as represented by the figure of the philistine.

By contrast, cultural modernity, especially its aesthetic wing in the middle of the nineteenth century, turned its attention to the cultivation and care of the self. Self-exploration and self-realization were its primary concerns. In this quest for the self, a high premium was placed on spontaneous expression, authentic experience, and unfettered gratification of one's creative and carnal urges. Imagination was an ally, and reason was an obstacle. There were no aesthetic limits that could not be transgressed, no moral norms that could not be subverted. One must explore and experience anything—including the demonic, the artificial, and the fugitive—that would spur imagination, quicken sensibilities, and deepen feelings. Only those who would thus venture forth, such being the heroism of modern life, could expect glimpses of beauty, premonitions of happiness, and a modicum of wisdom.

This aesthetics of the self did not emerge and flourish in a social vacuum. It came to pass, ironically, in a world created by the bourgeois, a world of incessant change and deadening routine. Every authoritative vision of modernity in the West—from Marx to Baudelaire, from Nietzsche to Weber, from Simmel to Musil to Benjamin—is obliged to dwell and grapple with that twin matrix of change and routine in which the modern self is made and unmade. Each of those unforgettable figures of modernity—Marx's "revolutionary," Baudelaire's "dandy," Nietzsche's "superman," Weber's "social scientist," Simmel's "stranger," Musil's "man without qualities," and Benjamin's "flaneur"—is caught and carried in the intoxicating rush of an epochal change and yet finds himself fixed and formulated by a disciplinary system of social roles and functions. The accumulated tension and pathos of that condition so alluringly drawn in the psychological profile of those canonical "literary" figures—who are at once disengaged and embroiled, reflexive and blind, spectators and participants in every scene of life—finds its contemporary articulation, no longer confined to the West (nor confined to literature), in the idea/experience of "double consciousness," the poisoned gift of modernity for all who would be modern.

Marx unambiguously names the bourgeois as the author of those revolutionary changes that ushered in the modern age. "The bourgeois," writes Marx, "during the rule of scarce one hundred years, has created more massive and more colossal productive forces than have all preceding generations together." What intrigues Marx is not so much technological and industrial achievement but the manner in which the bourgeois has harnessed the productive powers that lay hitherto dormant in "the lap of social labor." They have instituted a mode of production that feeds on an unending cycle of competition, innovation, and destructive/creative change. There is no stability; "innovative self-destruction" is the order of the day.[2] For Marx, what distinguishes the bourgeois epoch from all earlier times is that "constant revolutionizing of production, uninterrupted disturbance of all social relations, everlasting

2. For an insightful reading of Marx and modernity, see Marshall Berman, *All That Is Solid Melts into Air: The Experience of Modernity* (New York: Penguin Books, 1982), 87–130.

uncertainty and agitation" that sweeps away "all fixed, fast-frozen rela-tionships, with their train of venerable ideas and opinions."[3]

What endures is the vortex of everyday life. With received tradi-tions of religion, philosophy, myth, and art in disarray, the "life-world" emerges from the shadow of those symbolic structures and begins to command attention as an autonomous domain of cultural practice. Charles Baudelaire, more than anyone else in the middle of the nine-teenth century, self-consciously sought to make the character and con-tents of everyday life the privileged object of aesthetic contemplation and cultural critique. But everyday life, as Baudelaire recognized, is an elusive object: it is concrete, but fragmentary; it is immediately present, but in flux. That recognition led him to search for modernity at the crossing where the fugitive materiality of the life-world impinges on a sharpened consciousness of the present. Nowhere is that crossing more vivid and dramatic than in the life and work of a modern city, such as Baudelaire's Paris. Here, in scenes of both "high" and "low" life, he finds the heroism of modern life and thus puts an end to what had by then become a tiresome *querelle des anciens et des modernes:*

> Modernity is the transient, the fleeting, the contingent, it is one half of art, the other being the eternal and the immovable. . . . You have no right to despise this transitory fleeting element, the metaphor-phoses of which are so frequent, nor to dispense with it. If you do, you inevitably fall into the emptiness of an abstract and undefinable beauty. . . . Woe betide the man who goes to antiquity for the study of anything other than ideal art, logic, and general method! By im-mersing himself too deeply in it, he will no longer have the present in his mind's eye; he throws away the value and privileges afforded by circumstance; for nearly all our originality comes from the stamp that time impresses upon our sensibility.[4]

Baudelaire is not content to treat modernity as a mere descriptive (and periodizing) term. Before specifying "the epic quality of modern life" and showing how "our age is no less rich than ancient times in sublime

3. All the quotes from Marx and Engels in this paragraph are from "Manifesto of the Communist Party," in *The Marx-Engels Reader,* ed. Robert C. Tucker (New York: W. W. Norton, 1972), 338–39.
4. Charles Baudelaire, "The Painter of Modern Life," in *Selected Writings on Art and Literature,* trans. P. E. Charvet (New York: Penguin Books, 1972), 403–5.

themes," which he does eloquently in his haunting sketches of Parisian life, Baudelaire insists in a distinctly historicist manner that "since every age and every people have had their own form of beauty, we inevitably have ours." That historicist dictum sets the stage for what Baudelaire considers "the main and essential question, which is to examine whether we have a specific kind of beauty, inherent in new forms of passion."

In exploring those "new forms of passion," Baudelaire calls into question the continuing relevance of yet another venerable opposition between the *vita contemplativa* and the *vita activa*. Neither pole of the opposition, from Aristotle to Renaissance humanism, had paid much attention to the struggles and pleasures of everyday life, which were relegated to the interiors of the household. Living in the midst of "everlasting uncertainty and agitation," Baudelaire does not anticipate "new forms of passion" to flow out of a pursuit of contemplative life. As for the French Republican ideal of active civic life, Baudelaire admits mockingly that we do have "our victories and our political heroism," but the artists who dwell on those "public and official subjects" do so reluctantly "with an ill grace because they are at the beck and call of the government that pays them." The heroism and beauty of modern life resides elsewhere — in private subjects or, more precisely, in civil society. New forms of passion are adrift here; they are not to be found around state-sponsored memories and monuments. Baudelaire was the first to offer a poetics of civil society: "Scenes of high life and of the thousands of uprooted lives that haunt the underworld of a great city, criminals and prostitutes, the Gazette des Tribunaux and the Moniteur are there to show us that we have only to open our eyes to see and know the heroism of our day. . . . The marvelous envelops and saturates us like the atmosphere; but we fail to see it."[5]

Baudelaire's summons to "open our eyes" entails more than learning to read and appreciate the scattered fragments of beauty and heroism amidst the barrage of ideas and images, moods and experiences, desires and fantasies routinely conjured up by metropolitan culture for its inhabitants. Baudelaire also wants us to awaken to the intimations of "the eternal and the immovable" in the new and as yet unnamed, ill-understood passions that begot those fragments, and to grasp therein

5. All the quotes by Baudelaire in this paragraph are from "Of the Heroism of Modern Life," in *Selected Writings on Art and Literature,* trans. P. E. Charvet (New York: Penguin Books, 1972), 104–7.

that which confers the status of the "classic" on what is temporally bound. Here modernity becomes normative. Prior to Baudelaire, and despite contextual variations, the term modern generally designates the consciousness of an age that imagines itself as having made the transition from the old to the new. This consciousness takes two different forms. In one version, the old representing venerable antiquity haunts and instructs the new. The old, as the custodian of the classical, sets the measures and models of human excellence that each new age must seek to emulate under altered conditions without ever hoping to surpass it. In the other version, which came into prominence with the Enlightenment, the modern is associated with the scientific superiority of the present over antiquity. With visions of the infinite progress of knowledge and continuous improvement in moral and material life, the modern at last frees itself from the spell of antiquity.

Against these two historically specific versions of modernity, Baudelaire, drawing on the Romantic theories of temporality, posits an abstract opposition between tradition and the present. By equating modernity with the present, Baudelaire opens "the paradoxical possibility of going beyond the flow of history through the consciousness of historicity in its most concrete immediacy, in its presentness."[6] "Presentness," in turn, is defined and marked by "the new," which is always in a state of disappearance, destined to be overcome and made obsolete through the novelty of the next fashion. One might interrupt the dialectic of novelty and disappearance by separating the "modern" from the fashionable: while the former endures the ravages of time, the latter erodes. Ironically, here one reverts to the notion of the classical—that is, that which endures in time—to recuperate the modern. But there is a crucial difference, as Jürgen Habermas notes: "The emphatically modern document no longer borrows this power of being a classic from the authority of a past epoch; instead, a modern work becomes a classic because it has once been authentically modern."[7] This is a double-edged gesture: Having deprived the tradition of its mediating function, the modern renounces its claim to instruct the future. Everything turns to

6. Matei Calinescu, *Five Faces of Modernity* (Durham, N.C.: Duke University Press, 1987), 50.

7. Jürgen Habermas, "Modernity—An Incomplete Project," trans. Seyla Benhabib, in *The Anti-aesthetic: Essays on Postmodern Culture,* ed. Hal Foster (Port Townsend, Wash.: Bay Press, 1983), 4.

the present, and that present, having broken out of the continuum of history, is caught in an unceasing process of internal ruptures and fragmentation. The modernist present, so conceived, is either ripe with danger and revelation, as with Walter Benjamin's notion of *Jetztzeit,* or devoid of hope and redemption, as with T. S. Eliot: "If all time is eternally present, All Time is unredeemable."[8]

What is "authentically" modern? Could the idea (or is it the rhetoric?) of the authentic rescue and secure the modern from a situation so poignant and divided? Clearly, one cannot find the modern by stepping outside the stream of the stylish and the fashionable. It is not an atemporal transcendental entity. To find "the eternal and the immutable" half of the modern, one must go by way of "the transient, the fleeting, the contingent"; to find the modern, one must go by the way of the fashionable. But fashion is not innocent of history; it continually scavenges the past for props, masks, and costumes. Perhaps one could make history lurk back through fashion, as Benjamin suggests that the (Robespierre-imagined) French Revolutionaries sought to do: "The French Revolution viewed itself as Rome incarnate. It evoked ancient Rome the way fashion evokes costumes of the past. Fashion has a flair for the topical, no matter where it stirs in the thickets of long ago; it is a tiger's leap into the past. This jump, however, takes place in an arena where the ruling class gives the commands. The same leap in the open air of history is the dialectical one, which is how Marx understood the revolution."[9] Perhaps that is how we should understand modernity: a leap in the open air of the present as history.

For those who would leap in the open air of the present, there is the sobering prospect of having to land in a Weberian "iron cage," a disenchanted world of shrinking freedom bereft of meaning.[10] The other side of flux and novelty is the routinization and standardization of vast sectors of people's lives, which follow societal modernization and which give rise to a pervasive sense of alienation and despair. Max Weber's dark vision of societal modernity, which undercuts the Enlightenment

8. T. S. Eliot, "Four Quartets," in *The Complete Poems and Plays 1909–1950* (New York: Harcourt, Brace and World, 1971), 117.
9. Walter Benjamin, "Theses on the Philosophy of History," in *Illuminations,* trans. Harry Zohn, ed. Hannah Arendt (New York: Schocken Books, 1969), 261.
10. Max Weber, *The Protestant Ethic and the Spirit of Capitalism,* trans. Talcott Parsons (New York: Scribner's, 1958).

project from within, is as compelling and influential as Baudelaire's vision of aesthetic modernity.

The eighteenth-century philosophers of the Enlightenment had limitless faith in the emancipatory potential of human reason. They believed that when reason is properly deployed, as exemplified in scientific inquiry, it will lead to steady progress in both the material and the moral condition of mankind. The former will be enriched through an explosive increase in productive powers that will accrue with the technological mastery of nature and with an efficient and planned administration of collective existence. As for the latter, the Enlightenment philosophers believed that the rationalization of cultural and social life resulting from the spread of scientific knowledge and attitude would lead, among other things, to the progressive eradication of traditional superstitions, prejudices, and errors, and to the gradual establishment of a republican form of government. This government would guarantee civil rights and promote political will formation through open and free debate, while a free and equitable economy would ensure general prosperity and growth by allowing individuals to energetically pursue their own interests as long as they do not impede the like pursuits of others.

Those anticipations and projections have been partially fulfilled, albeit in an uneven and distorted manner. More critically, the long march of reason has disclosed its essential character and its inherent limitations. According to Weber, the rationality that sustains and defines modernity is a purposive or means/ends rationality. Being value-neutral, purposive rationality is incapable of conferring meaning on the world it ushers into existence. At the same time, it works steadily to discredit and dissolve the traditional religious worldviews that, despite their errancy, give meaning and unity to life. As Habermas notes: "With cultural rationalization of this sort, the threat increases that the life-world, whose traditional substance has been already devalued, will become more and more impoverished."[11] Thus, in Weber's account, the triumph of reason culminates not in the establishment of a rational utopia imagined by the Enlightenment philosophers but in the forging of an "iron cage" of economic compulsion and bureaucratic control.

Such, briefly, is the tale of two intersecting visions of modernity in the West: the Weberian societal/cultural modernity and the Baudelair-

11. Habermas, "Modernity—An Incomplete Project," 9.

ian cultural/aesthetic modernity. Culture is the capacious and contested middle term. In the Weberian vision, societal modernization fragments cultural meaning and unity. The Baudelairian vision, which is equally alert to the effects of modernization, seeks to redeem modern culture by aestheticizing it. Each has a bright side and a dark side. The bright side of societal modernization anticipated by Enlightenment philosophers and analyzed by Weber refers to the palpable improvement in the material conditions of life as evident in economic prosperity, political emancipation, technological mastery, and the general growth of specialist knowledge. The dark side refers to the existential experience of alienation and despair associated with living in a disenchanted world of deadening and meaningless routine. This is the Sisyphean world of repetition devoid of a subjectively meaningful telos. The bright side of the Baudelairian vision draws on a different aspect of the experience of modernity. It focuses affectively on the cultural patina of modernity as a spectacle of speed, novelty, and effervescence. It finds aesthetic pleasure and creative excitement in treading the surface and is unencumbered by the hermeneutic temptation of having to find meaning and unity hidden beneath surface experiences. The dark side suggests the absence of moral constraints in a world of appearances where the aesthetic pursuit can deteriorate from a disciplined Nietzschean self-assertion against a seemingly meaningless and absurd world into narcissistic self-absorption and hedonism.

TWO RESPONSES TO THE DILEMMAS OF MODERNITY

My account of the divided, Janus-like character of modernity is only one among many narratives about its career in the West. However, despite the variations in the choice of key figures, seminal texts, and defining themes and concepts, virtually every scholar on modernity and its future feels compelled to address the dilemmas posed by its dual character. They also share an urge to imagine and propose a scenario that would attenuate and control the dark side while sustaining and enhancing the bright side. But that goal requires one to specify how the two sides are conceived and connected, which, in turn, leads one to make rather murky distinctions between what is necessary/unavoidable and what is optional/avoidable within the project of modernity. Here the responses to the dilemmas of modernity vary greatly. Consider, for instance, the strikingly different positions taken by two major thinkers on modernity: Jürgen Habermas and Michel Foucault.

For Habermas, modernity is an "incomplete" but redeemable project. In his numerous writings on the subject, Habermas pays particular attention to the Weberian argument about the disillusionment with the Enlightenment project of modernity and the resultant loss of faith in reason to direct our lives.[12] He does not question Weber's claim that modern society has witnessed a progressive erosion of meaning and freedom, and he concedes that some of this is the result of sociocultural rationalization. But Habermas firmly rejects the Weberian equation of reason with *Zweckrationalität* (purposive, instrumental rationality), along with the deeply pessimistic vein in which that equation is interpreted and elaborated by Max Horkheimer and Theodor W. Adorno in *Dialectic of Enlightenment*.[13] For Habermas, to construe sociocultural rationalization primarily in terms of reification (as in Georg Lukács) and techniques of administrative power and control (as in Foucault) is mistaken because it confuses the selective deployment of reason under capitalist modernization with the nature and telos of reason itself. Moreover, Habermas argues that reason is reduced to an instrumental mode only within the confines of subject-centered reason associated with the philosophy of consciousness. He believes that an alternative paradigm of reason such as the one enunciated in his *Theory of Communicative Action* would facilitate a balanced development of different dimensions of rationality necessary for understanding and living in a modern world.[14] While the details of Habermas's theory of communicative action are not germane here, it should be noted that he is committed to rehabilitating the project of modernity by revivifying reason as an agency with many forms and voices.

In contrast, Foucault's riveting accounts of how disciplinary society emerged from within the folds of the Enlightenment project of moder-

12. See Jürgen Habermas, *Legitimation Crisis,* trans. Thomas McCarthy (Boston: Beacon Press, 1975); Habermas, *The Philosophical Discourse on Modernity,* trans. Frederick Lawrence (Cambridge, Mass.: MIT Press, 1987); *Habermas and Modernity,* ed. Richard J. Bernstein (Cambridge, Mass.: MIT Press, 1985).

13. Max Horkheimer and Theodor W. Adorno, *Dialectic of Enlightenment,* trans. John Cumming (New York: Seabury Press, 1972).

14. Jürgen Habermas, *The Theory of Communicative Action,* vols. 1–2, trans. Thomas McCarthy (Cambridge, Mass.: MIT Press, 1987).

nity holds out little hope for rehabilitation.[15] In his genealogical critique of reason, Foucault shows how reason is not only embedded in sociocultural contexts and mediated by natural languages but also implicated in a complex network of power/knowledge, or what he calls each society's "regime of truth." Foucault's account of the "regime of truth" constitutive of Western modernity chronicles the inexorable march of reason, aided and abetted by the newly emergent human sciences, in setting up a social order geared to extend our mastery over both nature and culture. In that quest for mastery, reason is distilled as it becomes free of humanist trappings and reveals itself as an instrument of technical analysis, strategic calculation, and administrative control. Unlike Habermas, Foucault does not regard instrumental rationality as a disfiguration of reason that occurs under the compulsions of capitalist modernization or as a result of being subject-centered. For Foucault, reason, knowledge, and truth can never escape from relations and effects of power because they are constitutive of each other. As Foucault notes: "Truth isn't the reward of free spirits, the child of protracted solitude. . . . Truth is the thing of this world: it is produced only by virtue of multiple forms of constraint. And it induces regular effects of power."[16] Thus enmeshed with power, reason cannot disavow its strategic and instrumental character.

Even in his later writings, when he shifts the focus of his investigations from "coercive practices" and the technologies of subjectification associated with modern institutions to "practices of freedom" and the arts of self-formation in everyday life, Foucault continues to think of reason in terms of power and strategy. In those later writings, especially while discussing Kant's essay "What Is Enlightenment?," Foucault gives a positive reading of modernity—as "an attitude . . . a mode of relating to contemporary reality"—which is distinctively Baudelairian.[17] To add

15. See especially Michel Foucault, *Discipline and Punish*, trans. Alan Sheridan (New York: Pantheon Books, 1977).

16. Michel Foucault, *Power/Knowledge*, trans. Colin Gordon and others, ed. Colin Gordon (New York: Pantheon Books, 1972), 131.

17. See Foucault's two essays on Kant: "What Is Enlightenment?," in *Ethics: Subjectivity and Truth*, vol. 1 of *Essential Works of Foucault 1954–1984*, ed. Paul Rabinow (New York: New Press, 1997), 303–20, and "The Art of Telling the Truth," in *Critique and Power: Recasting the Foucault/Habermas Debate*, ed. Michael Kelly (Cambridge, Mass.: MIT Press, 1994), 139–48.

to the alchemy, the crossing of Kant and Baudelaire is mediated by the Greek notion of ethos, and one of the conceptual strands of ethos valorizes the practice of "asceticism": a practice that once forged the "iron cage" now instructs us how to resist, if not dismantle, it.

A central concern of these later writings on the "care of the self" is to explore strategies (both conceptual and practical) for keeping power relations mobile and symmetrical and preventing them from ossifying into states of domination. Here Foucault turns to the Greek asceticism. For Greeks, in Foucault's account, the care of the self is the ethical horizon within which one engages in "proper" practices of freedom. That care requires one to master one's desires and appetites and refuse to be a slave to popular opinions and passions. Ethos is the concrete form of "being and behavior" in which one's free self-possession is made visible to others: "A person's ethos was evident in clothing, appearance, gait, in the calm with which he responded to every event, and so on. For the Greeks, this was the concrete form of freedom. . . . A man possessed of a splendid ethos, who could be admired and put forward as an example, was someone who practiced freedom in a certain way."[18] The care of the self as the practice of freedom also involves complex relationships with others. Abuse of power is characteristic of one who is not in possession of himself. One who masters himself through self-knowledge is capable of properly exercising power over others and thus taking his rightful place in the city or the household or any other congregation.

A key move in Foucault's synthesis involves linking the Greek notion of ethos as "the concrete form of freedom" with Baudelaire's conception of modernity and Kant's answer to the question "What Is Enlightenment?," which inaugurates the philosophical discourse of modernity. What bridges the two concepts of modernity is the questioning of the present: "What is my present? What is the meaning of this present? And what am I doing when I speak of this present?"[19]

As for Baudelaire, Foucault argues that modernity entails both a form of relationship to the present and to oneself. This gives the task of discovering "the eternal and the immovable" in the midst of temporal flux a new inflection: "The deliberate attitude of modernity is tied to an indispensable asceticism. To be modern is not to accept oneself as one is

18. Foucault, "The Ethics of the Concern for Self as a Practice of Freedom," in *Ethics: Subjectivity and Truth,* 286.
19. Foucault, "The Art of Telling the Truth," 141.

in the flux of the passing moments; but it is to take oneself as the object of a complex and difficult elaboration: what Baudelaire in the vocabulary of his day, calls dandysme." [20] There is a striking similarity between the Greek view of the care of the self as summed up in the concept of ethos and "the asceticism of the dandy who makes his body, his behavior, his feelings and passions, his very existence, a work of art." [21] This is a crucial move because it undercuts the conservative critique of cultural modernity as a temperament that, by privileging individual self-realization and by promoting adversary culture, unleashes hedonistic impulses irreconcilable with the requirements of a well-ordered society. By foregrounding practices of freedom and the regimen of asceticism, Foucault gives the quest for and of the self an ethical dimension.

Similarly, Foucault finds in Kant's text "a new way of posing the question of modernity, not in the longitudinal relation to the Ancients, but in what might be called a 'sagital' relation to one's own present." [22] Kant, like Baudelaire, views modernity not as an epoch but as an attitude: "a mode of relating to contemporary reality." Moreover, that attitude or ethos of modernity finds its reflexive articulation in a distinctive "type of philosophical interrogation — one that simultaneously problematizes man's relations to the present, man's historical mode of being, and the constitution of the self as an autonomous subject" whose roots can be traced back to the Enlightenment. For Foucault's Kant, what is of enduring interest and what connects us to the Enlightenment is not its doctrinal substance, which is at any rate antiquated and fragmented, but rather its spirit of critique. The significance of the Enlightenment today, as always, is its call to those who would hear it to assume an attitude or to subscribe to "a philosophical ethos that could be described as a permanent critique of our historical era." [23]

ALTERNATIVE MODERNITIES

Assuming that modernity is best understood as an attitude of questioning the present, we might begin our explorations of alternative modernities by asking, What is the status of that attitude today? It seems

20. Foucault, "What Is Enlightenment?," 311.
21. Foucault, "What Is Enlightenment?," 312.
22. Foucault, "The Art of Telling the Truth," 141.
23. Foucault, "What Is Enlightenment?," 312.

to me that the attitude of questioning the present is both pervasive and embattled: it is pervasive because modernity has gone global, and it is embattled because it faces seemingly irresolvable dilemmas. In fact, the very idea of alternative modernities has its origin in the persistent and sometimes violent questioning of the present precisely because the present announces itself as the modern at every national and cultural site today.

That questioning sometimes, especially in the West, takes the form of proclaiming the end of modernity. One might be justified in pronouncing the end of modernity in a narrow and special sense, as Jean-François Lyotard does.[24] But to announce the general end of modernity even as an epoch, much less as an attitude or an ethos, seems premature, if not patently ethnocentric, at a time when non-Western people everywhere begin to engage critically their own hybrid modernities. To be sure, there is a widespread feeling that we are at some sort of a turning point in the trajectory of modernity. That sense of being at the crossroads might have less to do with the ending of an era than with the fact that modernity today is global and multiple and no longer has a governing center or master-narratives to accompany it. Besides, even if modernity were ending, its end, as in Samuel Beckett's *Endgame,* would turn out to be an eternal duration, an endlessly fading twilight.[25] In the meantime, we have to continue to think through the dilemmas of modernity, as the essays in this volume do, from a transnational and transcultural perspective.

However, to think in terms of alternative modernities does not mean one blithely abandons the Western discourse on modernity. That is virtually impossible. Modernity has traveled from the West to the rest of the world not only in terms of cultural forms, social practices, and institutional arrangements, but also as a form of discourse that interrogates the present. Whether in vernacular or cosmopolitan idioms, that questioning of the present, which is taking place at every national and cultural site today, cannot escape the legacy of Western discourse on modernity. Whoever elects to think in terms of alternative modernities

24. Jean-François Lyotard, *The Postmodern Condition: A Report on Knowledge,* trans. Geoff Bennington and Brian Massumi (Minneapolis: University of Minnesota Press, 1984).
25. Samuel Beckett, *Endgame* (New York: Grove Press, 1958).

(irrespective of one's location) must think with and also against the tradition of reflection that stretches from Marx and Weber through Baudelaire and Benjamin to Habermas, Foucault, and many other Western (born or trained) thinkers. This is evident, for instance, in the writings of Arjun Appadurai and Paul Gilroy, two scholars who have contributed significantly to the development of an "alternative modernities" perspective.[26] One can provincialize Western modernity only by thinking through and against its self-understandings, which are frequently cast in universalist idioms. To think through and against means to think with a difference — a difference that would destabilize the universalist idioms, historicize the contexts, and pluralize the experiences of modernity. But what is that difference? It is difficult to pin down.

To begin with, Western discourse on modernity is a shifting, hybrid configuration consisting of different, often conflicting, theories, norms, historical experiences, utopic fantasies, and ideological commitments. My portrait in the previous section is but one among many possible narratives of Western modernity, its dilemmas, and its future. Virtually every scholar on the subject has his or her own version of that narrative, and each version casts a different light on modernity. When viewed from different perspectives, modernity appears to have an almost iridescent quality; its contours shift depending on the angle of interrogation.

To think in terms of alternative modernities is to privilege a particular angle of interrogation. The obvious and common feature of the essays in this volume (except for those by Charles Taylor and Thomas McCarthy) is that they examine the career and dilemmas of modernity from a specific national/cultural site. What difference, if any, does a site-based reading of modernities make in our understanding and questioning of the present?

Certainly, a culture-specific and site-based reading complicates our understanding of the relationship between the two strands of modernity — societal modernization and cultural modernity. The tale of two modernities, however compelling it is for mapping the Western experience of modernity and its dilemmas, cannot be extended, without im-

---

26. Arjun Appadurai, *Modernity at Large: Cultural Dimensions of Globalization* (Minneapolis: University of Minnesota Press, 1996); Paul Gilroy, *The Black Atlantic: Modernity and Double Consciousness* (Cambridge, Mass.: Harvard University Press, 1993).

portant modifications, to cover other theaters of modernity. Although it is not a portable tale, neither is it wholly irrelevant, because the key elements in the narrative are present and active in a variety of combinations at different national and cultural sites. What a site-based reading decisively discredits is the inexorable logic that is assigned to each of the two strands of modernity. The proposition that societal modernization, once activated, moves inexorably toward establishing a certain type of mental outlook (scientific rationalism, pragmatic instrumentalism, secularism) and a certain type of institutional order (popular government, bureaucratic administration, market-driven industrial economy) irrespective of the culture and politics of a given place is simply not true. Nor does cultural modernity invariably take the form of an adversary culture that privileges the individual's need for self-expression and self-realization over the claims of the community. Still, many of the aforementioned cultural forms, social practices, and institutional arrangements do surface in most places in the wake of modernity. But at each national and cultural site, those elements are put together (reticulated) in a unique and contingent formation in response to local culture and politics. This is evident in Claudio Lomnitz's account of the checkered career of Mexican citizenship, one of the key tropes of modern subjecthood, which does not follow the progressivist logic of extending the promise and practice of citizenship to all eligible pueblo — "the good," "the bad," and the "abject." Instead, the discourse on citizenship is haphazardly "filled and emptied out of content" in response to contingent historical events and local politics pertaining to the stability of the central government, the state of the economy, external threats, and internal dissidence. Among other things, Lomnitz demonstrates that the rhetoric of citizenship is most intense and functions as an ideological glue in the era of national instability only to be pushed to the background with the strengthening and fetishization of the state (either in its "authoritarian" or "corporativist" guise), where the latter is the repository of rationality, order, and progress, and also, paradoxically, the guarantor of a massified and "debased" citizenship.

Therefore, a minimal requirement for thinking in terms of alternative modernities is to opt for what Taylor, in the essay included in this volume, characterizes as a "cultural" as opposed to an "acultural" theory of modernity. An acultural theory describes the transition to modernity in terms of a set of culture-neutral operations, which are viewed as "input" that can transform any traditional society: "On this view, modernity is not specifically Western, even though it may have started in the West. Instead it is that form of life toward which all cultures converge, as they go through, one after another, substantially the same changes." There are two basic errors in this theory. First, it fails to see that Western modernity itself is a "culture" with a distinctive moral and scientific outlook consisting of a constellation of understandings of person, nature, society, reason, and the good that is different from both its predecessor cultures and non-Western cultures. Second, it imposes a false uniformity on the diverse and multiple encounters of non-Western cultures with the allegedly culture-neutral forms and processes (science and technology, industrialization, secularization, bureaucratization, and so on) characteristic of societal modernization. In short, an acultural theory is a theory of convergence: the inexorable march of modernity will end up making all cultures look alike.

A cultural theory, in contrast, holds that modernity always unfolds within a specific cultural or civilizational context and that different starting points for the transition to modernity lead to different outcomes. Under the impact of modernity, all societies will undergo certain changes in both outlook and institutional arrangements. Some of those changes may be similar, but that does not amount to convergence. Different starting points ensure that new differences will emerge in response to relatively similar changes. A cultural theory directs one to examine how "the pull of sameness and the forces making for difference" interact in specific ways under the exigencies of history and politics to produce alternative modernities at different national and cultural sites. In short, modernity is not one, but many.

What Taylor proposes is not entirely new. It is implicit in a great number of site-specific studies of modernities, including those in this volume. To think productively along the lines suggested by the idea of alternative modernities, we have to recognize and problematize the unavoidable dialectic of convergence and divergence. It is customary to think about convergence in terms of institutional arrangements, such as a market economy, a bureaucratic state, modes of popular rule, and so on. Similarly, one thinks of divergence primarily in terms of lived experience and cultural expressions of modernity that are shaped by what is variously termed the "habitus," "background," or "social imaginary" of a given people. An alternative modernities perspective complicates this neat dichotomy by foregrounding that narrow but critical band of variations consisting of site-specific "creative adaptations" on the axis of convergence (or societal modernization).

This idea of creative adaptation requires further elaboration. It does not mean that one can freely choose whatever one likes from the offerings of modernity. It is delusional to think, as the neoconservatives in the West and the cultural nationalists in the non-West seem to do, that one can take the good things (i.e., technology) and avoid the bad (i.e., excessive individualism). To be sure, one can question (as McCarthy does in this volume) the scope and viability of creative adaptation in certain critical areas such as modern law where form and function (and the reflexive discourse about them) are tightly integrated. While coming up with indigenous and culturally informed "functional equivalents" to meet the imperatives of modernization is an important task of creative adaptation, that sort of institutional innovation does not exhaust its scope or reveal its true spirit. Creative adaptation (as the essays in this volume show) is not simply a matter of adjusting the form or recoding the practice to soften the impact of modernity; rather, it points to the manifold ways in which a people question the present. It is the site where a people "make" themselves modern, as opposed to being "made" modern by alien and impersonal forces, and where they give themselves an identity and a destiny. That is precisely what Michael Hanchard's essay so admirably demonstrates in the case of the Afro-diasporic peoples. No other peoples' accession to modernity was so driven and determined by unforeseen external events and forces. Violently captured and removed from home, brutally transported, and sold into slavery in the new world, they were deprived of a common tongue, tradition, and territory, elements so frequently associated with the onset of the "national modern." And yet the Afro-diasporic people, while forced to think through languages, religions, and political ideals of their oppressors, succeed in articulating their own distinctive vision of pan-African modernity. One strand of that vision, which Hanchard analyzes, concerns the strategies for overcoming the temporal disjunctions of "racial time" (which either denied their capacity for modernity altogether or kept them waiting their "turn" at modernity) — an overcoming that paved the way for imagining a "transnational imagined community" unhampered by the logic of territoriality.

Tejaswini Niranjana provides yet another intriguing account of a diasporic accession to modernity—that of Indian indentured laborers in Trinidad (taken there between 1845 and 1917) and their descendants—which runs counter to the logic of the "national modern." The transformations caused in the lives of indentured labor by displacement, the plantation system, the disparate sex ratio, and racial politics, destructive as they were, nevertheless signal an alternative route to modernity, a route viewed as "illegitimate" within the nationalist discourse back home in India. Niranjana shows how the struggle over the "proper" route to modernity gets played out on the body of the woman. The nationalist/reformist discourse in India "had already produced models of domesticity, motherhood, and companionate marriage," which would make the Indian women simultaneously modern and worthy of citizenship. It is hardly surprising that such a view of the "modern woman," implicit in the larger ideological project of the nation-in-the-making, would be severely unsettled by those Indian women who were becoming modern but in the context of indentureship where a disparate sex ratio and uneven wages (indentured women earned less than half of their male counterparts) forced women into paraconjugal arrangements with multiple male protectors, with all the attendant discord, jealousy, and violence. Such arrangements, along with other social practices such as drinking alcohol (invariably exaggerated), would elicit from the nationalists a condemnation of diasporic women as "the harlots of the Empire." According to Niranjana, the nationalists, as they fought to end indenture (while consolidating the "appropriate 'Indian' modes of sociosexual behavior"), were unable to entertain the possibility, as proposed by some colonial officers, that emigration, despite all its flaws, would give a chance for a new life to "abandoned and unfaithful wives." However, the experience of indenture and its openings to modernity were irreversible for those who stayed on in Trinidad after its end. Moving her analysis to the present, Niranjana shows how the struggle over "Indianness and modernity" continues to be played out in the Trinidadian popular culture over the participation of Indian women in a hybrid song and dance routine/genre called "Chutney-Soca" that mingles provocative dancing, salacious themes, and interracial mixing.

Andrew Wachtel's analysis of the theory and practice of translation, both literary and cultural, in nineteenth-century Imperial Russia provides another instance of an "alternative" route to cultural modernity.

According to Wachtel, unlike "the elites of other imperializing nations, whose explicit or implicit assumptions of cultural superiority caused them to view their own values as universal and as something to be imposed on others, members of the Russian cultural elite proposed a model that emphasized their nation's peculiar spongelike ability to absorb the best that other people had to offer as the basis for a universal, inclusive national culture." This unusual combination of imperialism and cultural hermeneutics within the fold of the Russian "national modern," while compensating for the perceived cultural inferiority vis-à-vis West European powers, also propagated an imaginary of Russia as a mediating civilization between East and West and of Moscow as "the third Rome," the fabled instance of a culture of translation. Such an imaginary, however fantastic and self-serving, did have two discernible material consequences: it inaugurated a massive translation project, something that was continued under the Soviet regime, and it truly cosmopolitanized the Russian literary elite.

The phrase "creative adaptation" has a positive ring to it, but it does not always succeed. Sometimes it is doomed to fail because one is looking for the impossible, as Elizabeth A. Povinelli shows (in this volume) in the case of the Australian quest to find that lost object called "native tradition" that would enable a modern "settler" nation to fulfill its moral and legal obligation to its indigenous population. The attempt at creative adaptation that one finds in that fantastic saga is not so much an instance of institutional innovation, although there is plenty of that, but one of a people struggling to find their moral footing. The creative adaptation, even when it succeeds as in Dipesh Chakrabarty's account of the *addas* of Calcutta, succeeds only in exposing the tensions inherent in learning to live with modernity. On Chakrabarty's account, *adda*— the practice of male "friends getting together for long, informal, and unrigorous conversations" in a variety of urban spaces ranging from *rawk* (elevated verandas), parlors, parks, and rooftops to book shops, tea shops, coffee houses, and college dormitories—has played a critical but contradictory role in the formation of Bengali modernity. On the one hand, it advances distinctly modernist values and practices—democratic speech, literary cosmopolitanism, enlarged ethical mentality, and discursive self-fashioning. On the other hand, it promotes an ethos inimical to work ethics and bourgeois domesticity by excluding women, neglecting work and family responsibilities, valorizing purposeless conversation, and seeking community in sheer orality. Chakrabarty offers an intriguing explanation of these contradictions by noting that the *adda,* despite all its flaws, serves as a site for the ceaseless "struggle to make a capitalist modernity comfortable for oneself, to find a sense of community in it," even though that community is largely male and exclusively middle-class. Here, as in every other site-based essay in this volume, we catch glimpses of a larger conception of creative adaptation as an interminable process of questioning the present, which is the attitude of modernity. Precisely in this sense, modernity is an incomplete project and necessarily so.

Creative adaptation is not necessarily an inward movement of mobilizing the resources of one's culture to cope with the seemingly irresistible cognitive and social changes that accompany modernity. Such a construction is too passive and suggests a mood of embattled resignation. Modernity is more often perceived as lure than as threat, and people (not just the elite) everywhere, at every national or cultural site, rise to meet it, negotiate it, and appropriate it in their own fashion. Pick any non-Western metropolis early in this century, such as Leo Ou-fan Lee's Shanghai in the 1930s or Dipesh Chakrabarty's Calcutta in the 1940s, and you see the rage for modernity. Everything in sight is named modern: "modern coffee house," "modern talkies," "modern bicycle shop," "modern tailor," "modern beauty salon," "modern bakery," a newspaper called *Modern Age,* a magazine for the "modern woman," an advertisement for the "modern kitchen," a call for "modern education," an agitation for "modern hygiene," and so on. Those who submit to that rage for modernity are not naive; they are not unaware of its Western origins, its colonial designs, its capitalist logic, and its global reach. In haphazardly naming everything modern, they are exercising one of the few privileges that accrue to the latecomer: license to play with form and refigure function according to the exigencies of the situation. This sense of the latecomer's license to play with the props of modernity is brilliantly captured in Leo Ou-fan Lee's descriptive essay on Shanghai in the 1930s, then known as "the Paris of Asia." In that treaty-port of divided territories (between the Chinese sections and the foreign concessions), one could find every concrete manifestation of advancing Western modernity—skyscrapers, Art Deco interiors, neon-lit advertisements, department stores with escalators, dance halls and rooftop bars, coffee houses and bookstores, luxury hotels and restaurants, cinemas and cabaret shows, race tracks and jai alai courts – a wealth of public sites that dazzlingly combined consumerism and entertainment. The Shanghai modernist elite, especially writers, artists, and political activists (including communists), could and did eagerly consume and appropriate those Western offerings. But they did so, according to Lee, not in the mode of "colonial mimicry" but in a cosmopolitan mode of dialogue and engagement. Even as they traversed the cityscapes, dazzled by and hungry for Western ideas, experiences, and cultural forms, they always remained certain of their own identity as "Chinese."

Thus, in the face of modernity one does not turn inward, one does not retreat; one moves sideways, one moves forward. All of this is creative adaptation. Non-Western people, the latecomers to modernity, have been engaged in these maneuvers now for nearly a century. Everywhere, at every national or cultural site, the struggle with modernity is old and familiar. In some places, as in Beatriz Jaguaribe's Rio de Janeiro, modernity is already in ruins. But modernist ruins are not just ruins; they are allegories that narrate the paradoxical crossing of "newness" and "nationhood." In a lyrical essay that concludes this volume, Jaguaribe reflects on the career of two state-sponsored architectural ventures: the Ministry of Education and Health (MES), built in the 1930s, and the campus of the Federal University of Rio de Janeiro, built between 1949 and 1962. These edifices, designed to convey a sense of the new and the ethos of a nation on a path to modernity, were constructed under the sign of the future. Now they stand in decrepitude, having "lost their newness not only because of their material erosion but also due to the fragmentation of the modernist national ethos that shaped them." On the surface, the modernist ruin alerts us to the fragility of utopian projections of an earlier modernity. It is an unsettling sign of an absence, the unraveling and disappearance of "what was once the future projection of our present." On a deeper level, the modernist ruin discloses a temporal paradox that agitates and propels all modernist cultural production. According to Jaguaribe, "The modernist ruin condenses the contradictions of how the objects of modernity, while positing themselves as the new, inevitably bear their own demise and yet deny their aging process." By expressing the "decrepitude of the new," the modernist ruin interrupts, however briefly, the breathless rhetoric of the new that conceals from our view the different notions of modernity (of our fathers and of our neighbors) and their ephemerality.

An alternative modernities perspective is equally vigilant in exploring the elusive and fragmentary band of similarities that surface unexpectedly on the axis of divergence. It is generally assumed that the lived experience and the embodied character of modernity vary vastly from site to site. This is not entirely correct. Though cultural modernity is conventionally seen as both the machinery and the optic for the limitless production of differences, such difference always functions within a penumbra of similarities, and such similarities may be seen in the style of the flaneur, the mystique of fashion, the magic of the city, the ethos of irony, or the anxiety of mimicry—all ineffable yet recognizable across the noise of difference. What is common to these strings of similarities is a mood of distance, a habit of questioning, and an intimation of what Baudelaire calls the "marvelous" in the midst of the ruins of our tradition, the tradition of the new. Whether these common intensities, which regularly find expression in popular media, especially in film and music, will one day pave the way for an ethic of the global modern remains to be seen.

Thus, just as societal modernization (the prime source of convergence theories) produces difference through creative adaptation or unintended consequences, so also cultural modernity (the prime source of divergence theories) produces similarities on its own borders. This double relationship between convergence and divergence, with their counterintuitive dialectic between similarity and difference, makes the site of alternative modernities also the site of double negotiations— between societal modernization and cultural modernity, and between hidden capacities for the production of similarity and difference. Thus, alternative modernities produce combinations and recombinations that are endlessly surprising. The essays in this volume chronicle the range of surprises and submit the following tentative conclusions: *everywhere, at every national/cultural site, modernity is not one but many; modernity is not new but old and familiar; modernity is incomplete and necessarily so.*

Settler Modernity and the Quest for an Indigenous Tradition

Elizabeth A. Povinelli

INTRODUCING (THE THING)

In the 1880 introduction of the ethnology *Kamilaroi and Kunai,* the Reverend Lorimer Fison described a sensation he experienced studying the "intersexual arrangements" of indigenous Australians. He described feeling "ancient rules" underlying the Kamilaroi's and Kunai's present sexual practices, catching fleeting glimpses of an ancient "strata" cropping up from the horrific given conditions of colonial settlement, sensing some "something else," "something more" Kamilaroi and Kunai than even the Kamilaroi and Kunai themselves, a some *thing* that offered him and other ethnologists a glimpse of an ancient order puncturing the present, often hybrid and degenerate, indigenous social horizon.[1] Fison pointed to this ancient order as the proper object of ethnological research and used the promised feelings this order produced to prod other ethnologists to turn its way. But Fison cautioned, even admonished, other researchers that in order to reach this order and to experience these feelings they had to be "continually on the watch" that "every last trace of white men's effect on Aboriginal society" was "altogether cast out of the calculation."[2] Only by stripping from their ethnological analysis the traumatic effect of settlement on indigenous social life could the researcher reach, touch, and begin to sketch the outline of that thing, which was not the present corrupted Aboriginal social body

---

1. Lorimer Fison, *Kamilaroi and Kunai* (Canberra: Australian Aboriginal Press, 1880). "[In] inter-sexual arrangements . . . as elsewhere, present usage is in advance of the ancient rules. But those rules underlie it, and are felt through it; and the underlying strata crop up in many places" (29).
2. Fison, *Kamilaroi and Kunai,* 29.

but an immutable form that predated and survived the ravage of civil society.

The emergent modern ethnological epistemology Fison promoted bordered on the paranoic. Every actual indigenous practice was suspect. All "present usages," even those seemingly "developed by the natives themselves" and seemingly untouched by "contact with the white man," might be mere mirages of the investigator's own society. They might be like the "present usages" of the "Mount Gambier blacks," the desperate social acts of men and women who had watched their society "reduced from 900 souls to 17" in thirty years and were "compelled to make matrimonial arrangements as [they could], whether they be according to ancient law or not." [3] But even "present usages" untouched by the ravages of British settlement were little more than mere chimera of the ancient thing Fison sought. They taunted him with glimpses of what he truly desired — a superseded but still signifying ancient society shimmering there just beyond him and them, settler time and emergent national history. [4]

The proper ethnological thing Fison sought would always just elude him, would always be somewhere he was not. Maybe this ancient order survived in the remote interior of the nation, but it was never where he was. Where he stood, the ancient rules were submerged in the horror of the colonial present and mediated by the faulty memory of a "few wretched survivors [who were] . . . obliged to take such mates as death has left them, whether they be of the right classes or not." [5] Or the ancient rules were heavily encrusted with the autochthonous cultural debris generated by the inexorable tectonic shifts called social evolution. Not surprisingly, a restlessness pervades Fison's ethnology. Irritation and humiliation punctuate the rational veneer of his text as he is forced to encounter his own intellectual limits and to account for his own conceptual failures. Time after time, Fison is forced to admit that

3. Fison, *Kamilaroi and Kunai*, 42.
4. "By present usage, I mean that which has been developed by the natives themselves, not that which has resulted from their contact with the white men. This is a factor which must be altogether cast out of the calculation, and an investigator on this line of research needs to be continually on watch against it" (Fison, *Kamilaroi and Kunai*, 29).
5. Fison, *Kamilaroi and Kunai*, 30.

what he feels and desires cannot be accounted for by what he sees, reads, and hears.[6]

Whatever Fison was chasing, Australians still seemed in desperate pursuit of a little over a hundred years after *Kamilaroi and Kunai* was first published. At the turn of the twentieth century, most Australians had the distinct feeling that some decisive national drama pivoted on their felicitous recognition of an ancient indigenous law predating the nation and all living indigenous subjects. In two crucial, nationally publicized and debated decisions, *Eddie Mabo v. the State of Queensland* (1992) and *The Wik Peoples v. the State of Queensland* (1996), the Australian High Court ruled that the concept of native title was not inconsistent with the principles of the Australian common law (*Mabo*) and that the granting of a pastoral lease did not necessarily extinguish native title (*Wik*). As a result, native title still existed where the state had not explicitly extinguished it, where Aboriginal communities still maintained its foundation — namely, the "real acknowledgement of traditional law and real observance of traditional customs" — and where those real traditions did no violence to common law principles.[7]

In the fantasy space coordinated by these two legal decisions, traditional and modern laws coexist without conceptual violence or producing social antagonism. The legitimacy of native title is granted; its authority is rooted in the ancient rules, beliefs, and practices that predate the settler nation. The object of native title tribunals is merely to judge at the "level of primary fact" if native title has disappeared "by reason of the washing away by 'the tide of history' any real acknowledgment of traditional law and real observance of traditional customs" and to judge whether any of these real ancient customs violate contemporary common law values.[8] This is why the *Wik* decision on pastoral property was so important: The vast hectares under pastoral lease were "the parts of Australia where [native] laws and traditions (important to sustain native title) are most likely to have survived." These places were the spaces perceived as least touched by modern society.[9]

6. Fison, *Kamilaroi and Kunai*, 59–60.
7. *The Wik Peoples v. the State of Queensland* (1996), 146, 176.
8. *The Wik Peoples v. the State of Queensland*, 146. See also an editorial written by the Chief Minister of the Northern Territory, Marshall Perron, "Sacred Sites — A Costly Token to a Dead Culture," *Northern Territory News*, 7 January 1989, 7.
9. *The Wik Peoples v. the State of Queensland*, 182.

The moral and legal obligation of the nation to its indigenous population was foregrounded in another well-publicized debate, namely, the moral and economic claim of "the Stolen Generation" on the Australian nation. The Stolen Generation refers to the 10 to 30 percent of Aboriginal children forcibly removed from their parents between 1910 and 1970 as part of the state's policy of cultural assimilation. Members of the Stolen Generation filed a federal class-action suit against the state, arguing it had violated their human and constitutional rights. A special Royal Commission was established to investigate the intent and effect of these assimilation policies. It found that past state and territory governments had explicitly engaged in what could most accurately be called a form of social genocide, a cultural holocaust as defined by the 1951 Genocide Convention on Nazi Germany — an analogy made more compelling by the age of the Aboriginal applicants, many of whom had been taken in the early 1940s. Australians looked at themselves in a ghastly historical mirror and imagined their own Nuremberg. Would fascism be the final metaphor of Australian settler modernity? In 1997 the High Court ruled that the 1918 Northern Territory Ordinance allowing Aboriginal and "half-caste" children to be forcibly removed from their mothers was constitutionally valid and did not authorize genocide de jure although, in retrospect, it was misguided and morally questionable.

This Australian drama would not surprise most liberal theorists of the global travails of liberal forms of nationalism. The works of Charles Taylor, Richard Rorty, and Jürgen Habermas, among others, pivot on the question of whether and how a multitude of modern liberal nation-states should recognize the worth of their interior ethnic and indigenous cultural traditions. This essay turns away, however, from the question of whether and how the settler nation should recognize the worth of indigenous customary law. Instead, it asks more fundamental questions: *What* is the state and nation recognizing and finding worthy when it embraces the "ancient laws" of indigenous Australia? What is this thing "tradition" which produces sensations; desires; professional, personal, and national optimisms; and anxieties? What is this thing which is only ever obliquely glimpsed and which resists the bad faith of the liberal nation and at the same time does no violence to good civil values, indeed crystallizes the best form of community "we" could hope for? What is this glimmering object the public support of which can produce, as if by magical charm, the feelings necessary for social harmony in the multicultural nation, for good trading relations with the Asian-Pacific, and for a new globally inspirational form of national cohesion?[10] How is this thing socially produced and politically practiced? Why must Aboriginal persons identify with it to gain access to public sympathy and state resources?

To understand what the nation is seeking to recognize, touch, feel, and foreground *through* its recognition of an ancient prenational order, this essay tracks (across multiple state and public domains) the public debates over the worth of ancient Aboriginal law, legal mandates on the form a native title and land claim case must take, and mass-mediated portraits of traditional indigenous culture. As it tracks the transformations of the object "traditional indigenous law" across these public, state, and commercial domains, this essay maps the political cunning and calculus of cultural recognition in a settler modernity. Almost ten years ago, Kaja Silverman noted the "theoretical truism that hegemonic colonialism works by inspiring in the colonized subject the desire to assume the identity of his or her colonizers."[11] Perhaps this is what fundamentally distinguishes the operation of power in colonial and (post)colonial multicultural societies. Hegemonic domination in the latter formation works primarily by inspiring in the indigenous subject a desire to identify with a lost indeterminable object—indeed, to be the melancholic subject of traditions.[12]

To understand this new form of liberal power, this essay examines how recognition is at once a formal acknowledgment of a subaltern group's *being* and of its *being worthy* of national recognition and, at the same time, a formal moment of being inspected, examined, and investigated. I suggest this inspection always already constitutes indigenous persons as failures of indigenousness as such. And this is the point. In certain contexts of recognition, Aboriginal persons must produce a detailed account of the content of their traditions and the force with which they identify with them—discursive, practical, and affective states that necessarily have a "more or less" relationship to the imaginary of a "real

10. Lisa Kearns, "Armbands Sell Like Hot Cakes," *Age*, Melbourne Online, 21 November 1997.
11. Kaja Silverman, "White Skin, Brown Masks: The Double Mimesis, or Lawrence in Arabia," *differences* 1 (1989): 3.
12. Sigmund Freud, "Mourning and Melancholia," in *Collected Papers, Vol. 4* (New York: Basic Books, 1959).

acknowledgment of traditional law and a real observance of traditional customs." What are the social consequences of the noncorrespondence between the object of national allegiance, "ancient tradition," and any particular Aboriginal person, group, practice, memory, or artifact?

I begin by reviewing the public debate over the state's recognition of indigenous traditional (native) title to Australian lands.

QUESTION (THEM)!

In 1993, in response to the *Mabo* decision, public pressure, and its own political strategy, the Labor government passed the federal Native Title Act legislating the mechanisms by which indigenous groups could claim land. A year later a conservative Liberal-National coalition, which promised to protect the interests of (white) miners, farmers, and land-owners from deleterious native title claims, defeated the Labor Party for the first time in nearly a quarter of a century. During the first session of the new Liberal parliament, Pauline Hanson, an independent minister from Queensland, vehemently attacked the basic tenets of the state's twenty-year-old multicultural policy, especially two of its central tenets: self-determination for indigenous Australians and increased Asian immigration. She claimed multiculturalism was a guilt-based ideological program doing little more than partitioning the country into drug- and crime-ridden Asian and Aboriginal enclaves. In what would provoke a national scandal, Hanson argued that self-determination was just another name for a massive and massively misconceived social welfare program, transferring through taxation national wealth generated by hardworking (white) Australians to socially irresponsible (black) Australians. It was time for white outrage. "Ordinary Australians" should reject "the Aboriginal industry's" insistence that they feel guilty for past colonial policies they were not responsible for and, instead, proudly embrace what was for her the obvious fact that white Australians made the modern nation — no matter that present-day white Australians had as little to do with past economic policies as they did with past colonial policies. In hailing what she often referred to as "ordinary Australians" Hanson constituted a political space for all who desired to be such and to have such define the motor of Australian settler modernity.

Hanson went to the heart of the traditional thing. In a series of public addresses and interviews, she argued "ordinary" Australians should ignore the romantic image of traditional Aboriginal society and instead examine what she believed were the real conditions of present-day indigenous social life: Third World health and housing conditions, dreadfully high infant mortality rates, rampant substance abuse, sexual disorder, and truncated life spans—namely, the horrific material conditions that, she claimed, indexed a tremendous "waste" of "our" tax dollars. What was this thing "Aboriginal tradition" which was never wherever anyone was? What did "self-determination" mean when so many Aboriginal communities and individuals would be destitute without massive governmental financial support? Indigenous social conditions had barely budged, she argued, in the thirty-odd years since Aboriginal men and women had been made citizens; been removed from ward rolls; and been given the rights to vote, receive social security benefits, and drink. Indeed, she and other conservative critics argued that indigenous social life had gotten worse since full citizenship had been extended to them. The availability of social security benefits increased drug and alcohol addiction and lessened the incentive for Aboriginal women and men to become working members of the national economy.

Most public and political spokespersons labeled Hanson and her followers "fringe" and "extreme," their views dangerously antiquated. They wrung their hands and rang warning bells, cautioning the nation that a line of tolerance was being approached that, if crossed, would bring grave social and economic consequences. But while Hanson was politically marginalized and her views historicized, mainstream political officials were also recorded as publicly questioning the value of an ancient indigenous law for a modern technological society. Just days before Liberal Prime Minister John Howard appointed Liberal Senator Ross Lightfoot to the backbench committee on Aboriginal Affairs, he forced the senator to apologize to Parliament for claiming that "Aboriginal people in their native state are the lowest colour on the civilization spectrum." [13] The Liberal Party's Aboriginal Affairs Minister, John Herron, nearly lost his portfolio after publicly supporting the assimilation policies of the 1950s, including the forced removal of indigenous children from their parents. [14] Herron argued forced assimilation had had positive social effects: "Half-caste" children had been given an eco-

13. Matt Price, "Lightfoot on Black Policy Committee," Australian, 11 June 1997, 4.
14. To lose one's portfolio in the Australian parliamentary system is somewhat equivalent to losing cabinet responsibilities in the U.S. system.

nomic and social head start over their "full-blood" cousins who were handicapped in the race to civil society by their adherence to outmoded beliefs and practices.[15]

In 1997, claiming the *Wik* decision on pastoral property threatened to ruin the moral, social, and economic health of the commonwealth, the Liberal government introduced federal parliamentary legislation exempting pastoral lands from native title claims and restricting native title rights in other contexts. Many public spokespersons and groups swiftly responded, couching their criticisms in a rhetoric of principle and passion, finance and freedom, modernity and its moral incumbences. Labor opposition leader Kim Beazley; two former prime ministers from opposing parties, Paul Keating (Labor) and Malcolm Fraser (Liberal); and church and business leaders urged the public to look beyond "simple property rights," beyond their pocketbooks, and beyond the actual social conditions of Aboriginal social life. They should consider, instead, the question of national honor, national history, and national shame looming just beyond these economic and social struggles. Recognizing the value of ancient indigenous law would finally free the settler nation from its colonial frontier and confirm its contemporary reputation as a model modern multicultural nation. So suggested Beazley in a nationally televised address explaining the Labor Party's support of existing native title legislation: "There's more bound up in this than simply property rights. We face here a question of our history and our national honour. We have a diverse and vibrant community which we will be putting on show in three year's time at the Sydney Olympics. We won that bid because nations around the globe believed rightly our better instincts lead us to co-exist effectively with each other in a way in which a torn world finds inspirational."[16]

In giving over the self-image of the nation to the world's aspirations,

15. See, for example, Patrick Lawnham, "Bush Reserves Judgment on Herron," *Australian,* 3 July 1996, 2; and Colin Tatz, "We Fail Aborigines if We Prune the Past," *Australian,* 3 July 1996, 13.

16. Kim Beazley, "Address to the Nation by the Leader of the Opposition, Kim Beazley," *Age,* Melbourne Online, 2 December 1997. See also Claire Miller, "Just Society at Risk, says Fraser," *Age,* Melbourne Online, 26 November 1997: "The former Liberal Prime Minister Mr. Malcolm Fraser yesterday added his voice to community pressure on the Federal Government over its handling of the Wik debate with a warning that a reputation of trying to build a fair and just society was at risk."

"Australia" would be reaffirmed, strengthened, and deepened by the very multicultural forces that Hanson thought threatened, weakened, and undermined it. Mourning a shared shameful past would do no more, and no less, than propel the nation into a new cleansed national form. Besides, Beazley reassured, native title was materially minor if not outright meaningless: "Native title will only ever be able to be claimed by a small minority of Aboriginal and Torres Strait Islander Australians — those who can evidence some form of ongoing traditional association with the land in question."[17] And "Native title itself will very often mean not much more than the right to access for hunting, fishing and traditional ceremonial purposes: only in a small minority of cases will it ever involve anything like rights of exlusive possession."[18]

Indeed, rather than subtracting from the nation's wealth, the primary purpose of native title legislation was to provide the symbolic and affective conditions necessary to garner financial investment in the new global conditions of late modern capital. In the global reorganization of finance, commerce, and trade, cultural intolerance was a market matter. The world, especially Asian and Southeast Asian financial and tourism industries, was listening into the national conversation about Asian immigration and Aboriginal human and native title rights. Moreover, Aboriginal traditions were a vibrant sector of the economy mark(et)ing the Australian difference to national and international cultural consumers. Major regional newspapers presented a daily tally of the political and financial stakes of Hansonesque rhetoric — lost trade, lost financial investment, lost international political influence and tourism, and lost jobs, all due to uncivil, intolerant talk.[19] These financial matters became more pronounced as regional financial markets began to collapse in the first half of 1998.

National spokespersons did not simply point to juridical principles of common law, abstract notions of national honor, or the public's pocketbooks. They also spoke of the pleasures produced by concentrating on the vibrant ancient laws found not only in isolated remote in-

17. Beazley, "Address to the Nation."
18. Beazley, "Address to the Nation."
19. Among these numerous reports, see Michael Millet, "Race Row: Tourists Cancel Trips," *Sydney Morning Herald*, 1 November, 1996, A1; and Peter Switzer, "Hansonism Feeds on Economy's Failings," *Weekend Australian*, 21–22 June 1997, 54.

terior indigenous communities but also on cable channels; in concert halls and art galleries; and in the glossy magazines leafed through on airplanes, couches, and toilets. An ancient law was now thoroughly intercalated in public, intimate, even scatological spaces of the nation. If the good Australian people could look past the current bad material conditions of much of Aboriginal Australia, if they could strip away the encrustations of two hundred years of engineered and laissez-faire social neglect and abuse, they would catch a glimpse of the traditional values that remained, persisted, and survived state and civil society. Shimmering off this traditional mirage, they would catch a glimpse of their own best selves.

In 1998 a coalition of Labor and Democratic senators refused to pass the Howard government's new native title legislation. As a result, Howard threatened to dissolve both houses of Parliament and call a new election. If he did so, the Australian government would be decided in large part on the basis of its citizens' belief about the extant value to the modern nation of an enduring ancient prenational tradition. What did the public and its politicians think they were recognizing or rejecting?

ENJOY (THEM)!

We can begin to answer this question by examining the difference between the traditions to which a cacophony of public voices pledge their allegiance and the indigenous people who are the alleged sociological referent of these traditions. Simply put, what does "indigenous tradition" refer to and predicate? What does the nation celebrate? Answering this question entails examining the relationship between indigenous tradition, identity, and subjectivity and their discursive, affective, and material entailments. Let me begin with a set of commonplaces — in other words, with the hegemonic status of "indigenous traditions" in Australia.

Most people would probably not spontaneously describe indigenous subjectivity, or other social subjectivities, as a passionate attachment to a point in a formally coordinated system or the regimentation of ongoing semiotic practices — as people, consciously or unconsciously, articulating gaps and differences in an unfolding relational network itself part of the "historical reality of the intertextual, multimedia and multimediated modern public sphere."[20] But most Australians would have a strong sense that indigenous subjects are more or less like other social subjects as a result of shared or differing beliefs, characteristics, and practices (often experienced as characterological essentialisms) and that the loss of certain qualities and qualifiers would narrow the difference between contemporary social groups. For instance, they might not be able to say why, but they would "feel" ethnic and indigenous identities share the common qualifiers "race" and "tradition-culture." And they would feel these qualifiers somehow differentiate their social location from the other social positions, or identities, crowding the symbolic space of the nation — say, whites, homosexuals, women, and the disabled. But an indigenous identity would not be considered the same as an ethnic identity because traditional indigenous culture has a different relationship to nation time and space.[21]

Indigenous modifies "customary law," "ancient tradition," and "traditional culture," among others, by referring to a social practice and space that predates the settler state. Commonsensically, *indigenous people* denotes a social group descended from a set of people who lived in the full presence of traditions. I would hazard that in contrast to *unicorn* most Australians believe that to which *tradition* refers existed at some point in time and believe some residual part of this undifferentiated whole remains in the now fragmentary bodies, desires, and practices of Aboriginal persons if in a modified form. And I would also hazard most non-Aboriginal Australians think indigenous people are distinguished not only by their genealogical relation to the nation-state but also by their affective, ideational, and practical attachment to their prior customs. To be truly Aboriginal, Aboriginal persons must not just occupy a place in a semiotically determined social space; they must also identify with, desire to communicate (convey in words, practices, and feelings), and, to some satisfactory degree, lament the loss of the ancient customs that define(d) their difference.

I mean the awkward "that to which" and the seemingly vague "experienced" to evoke the strategic nonspecificity of the discursive and affective space of "indigenous tradition" in the contemporary Australian

20. Benjamin Lee, "Textuality, Mediation and Public Discourse," in *Habermas and the Public Sphere,* ed. Craig Calhoun (Cambridge, Mass.: MIT Press, 1993), 414–15.
21. See, for instance, William Kymlicka, *Multicultural Citizenship* (New York: Oxford University Press, 1995).

nation, a point I will elaborate later. And I mean my constant conditioning—"to some satisfactory degree," "some . . . part," "if in a modified form"—to mimic the juridical, public, and political conditioning of an authentic Aboriginal subjectivity. And, finally, I intend these mimetic provisos to suggest how the very discourses that constitute indigenous subjects *as such* constitute them as failures *of such*—of the very identity that identifies them (differentiates their social locality from other social localities) and to which they are urged to establish an identification (affectively attach).

In their discursive passage into being, then, indigenous people are scarred by temporal and social differences. These scars are the difference between any actual indigenous subject and the full presence promised by the phrase "indigenous tradition" and thus the identity "indigenous." At its simplest, no indigenous subject can inhabit the temporal or spatial location to which indigenous identity refers—the geographical and social space and time of authentic Ab-Originality. And no indigenous subject can derive her being outside her relation to other social identities and values currently proliferating in the nation-state. Because the category of indigenousness came into being in relation to the imperial state and the social identities residing in it and continues to draw its discursive value in relation to the state (and other states) and to other emergent national subjects (and other transnational subjects), to be indigenous requires passing through, and, in the passage, being scarred by the geography of the state and topography of other social identities. Producing a present-tense indigenousness in which some failure is not a qualifying condition is discursively and materially impossible. These scars are what Aborigines are, what they have. They are their true difference; the "active edge" where the national promise of remedial action is negotiated.[22] Legal and popular questions coagulate there: Is the scar small or large, ancient or recent, bleeding or healed, breeded out or passed on? What institutional suturing was and is necessary to keep this lacerated body functional? For whom? For what?

The gap existing between the promise of a traditional presence and the actual presence of Aboriginal persons is not simply discursive. It also produces and organizes subaltern and dominant feelings, expectations,

22. Jacques Lacan, "Agency of the Letter in the Unconscious or Reason since Freud," in *Écrits*, trans. Alan Sheridan (New York: Norton, 1977), 146–78.

desires, disappointments, and frustrations—sometimes directed at a particular person or group, sometimes producing a more diffuse feeling. For instance, as early as 1951, while advocating the forced assimilation of "half-castes"—to make them "white" by forcibly removing them from their Aboriginal mothers—the conservative Liberal Party leader Paul Hasluck counseled the nation to tolerate but, better, to take full "enjoyment" of the traditions of its indigenous "full-bloods."[23] Likewise, mid-century liberal educational films like *Art of the Hunter* promoted traditional Aboriginal "culture" as a critical contribution to the production of a unique, distinct Australian nationalism and, thus, to the global relevance of the nation—its "artistic and social contribution to the history of mankind."[24]

By the 1990s the nation seemed to have fully incorporated Hasluck's suggestion. In certain commercial and cultural domains the Australian public took pleasure from representations of brightly smiling Aboriginal persons forgetting the trauma of three decades of Aboriginal activism. Businesses took advantage of this shift in public attitudes, regularly using images of traditional Aborigines to establish an identification between consumers and commodities. Citations of nonabrasive indigenous "traditional culture" saturated the mass-mediated public sphere. In Coke, Telecom, and Qantas commercials, Hasluck's command, "enjoy their traditions" was translated: Enjoy our product *like* you enjoy their traditions. And as the public consumed indigenous traditions in the form of art, music, and cultural tourism, the national economy came to rely increasingly on the popularity of the simulacra of indigenous culture to fuel its internal combustion.

The listening public probably needed little urging to imagine the ancient traditions of Aboriginal people as a powerful, pleasurable, persisting force that predated the nation and defined its historically specific difference in modernity's global diaspora. A generation of popular books, musical groups (Midnight Oil, Yothu Yindi), and film (*Walkabout* [1971], *Picnic at Hanging Rock* [1975], *The Last Wave* [1977], *The*

23. Geoffrey Partington, *Hasluck versus Coombs: White Politics and Australia's Aborigines* (Sydney: Quaker Hill Press, 1996).
24. *Art of the Hunter: A Film on the Australian Aborigines,* produced and directed by John Endean, with the assistance of A. P. Elkin (Canberra: Australian Institute of Aboriginal Studies, ca. 1950).

Adventures of Priscilla, Queen of the Desert [1993]) refigured Australian modernity through an archetypical ancient law, sensual and perduring, lying under the physical and social space of the nation and gestating in the bodies and practices of Aboriginal people living in remote bush, in fringe communities, and in urban centers. Traditions were a level, a layer, a strata, existing before, but now thoroughly intercalated in the present symbolic and material conditions of the multicultural nation. EcoFeminism, EcoTourism, and New-Agism, along with mass popular books like *Mutant Message Down Under* (1994), *Crystal Woman* (1987), and *The Songlines* (1987), elaborated and plowed into the national consciousness a commonsense feeling that this ancient order made Australia a special country.

But if for non-Aboriginal Australian subjects indigenous tradition is a nostalgic memory-trace of all that once was and now is only partially, for Aboriginal subjects ancient law is also a demand: You, Aborigine, establish an identification with a lost object. Strive after what cannot be recovered. Want it badly. We do. See us celebrating it. Embracing its shameful frontier history would allow the nation to begin bit by bit to unbind itself from the memories and hopes once associated with that history; would allow the nation to get on with its business as it finds new ideals and images to identify with. But something very different happens with the indigenous subject. For not only are indigenous people scarred by loss in their discursive passage into being, the historical and material pressures on them to identify with the name of this passage (tradition) affectively constitutes them as melancholic subjects,[25] and the more an Aboriginal person identifies as a traditional person, the more he or she believes public incitements that the nation is embracing them. This melancholia acts as a communicative vehicle for distributing, and confusing, the relationship between an identity, ideas, and *feelings* about who is responsible for present-day social maladies— for the state's failure to curb the excess of capital and to provide equitable health, housing, and education. Non-Aboriginal Australians enjoy ancient traditions while suspecting the authenticity of the Aboriginal subject. Aboriginal Australians enjoy their traditions while suspecting the authenticity of themselves.

25. Freud, "Mourning and Melancholia."

Given this public commotion and commercial promotion, it might surprise us to learn most Australians know very little about the actual social conditions of indigenous Australia. Many Australians acquire a sketchy outline of Aboriginal "culture" in school and from mass and multimediated images — glimpses of traditional culture garnered from popular books, movies, television talk shows, commercials, audiotapes, and compact disks. But while many Australians have heard Peter Garrett of the rock band Midnight Oil sing the lyrics from "The Dead Heart" ("we carry in our heart the true country and that cannot be stolen, / we follow in the steps of our ancestry and that cannot be broken") few know to what these musically moving evocations of "ancestry" refer.[26] Likewise, after the *Wik* decision, the Body Shop stores in Melbourne began selling armbands bearing the message "Coexistence, Justice, Reconciliation." Most Australians knew the colors of the armband (red, black, and yellow) referred to the Aboriginal flag. But few Australians knew much about what the nation was reconciling itself to, nor knew how specific legislative, juridical, or constitutional principles had already figured "tradition" as a rights-bearing sign in a series of federal, state, and territory land rights, social welfare, and cultural heritage acts.[27] Still fewer had any sense of the local, national, and transnational political and social struggles entextualized in law and legislation.[28]

Most people did not know, for instance, that the federal Aboriginal Land Rights (Northern Territory) Act of 1976 defined "Aboriginal traditions" as "the body of traditions, observances, customs and beliefs of Aboriginals or of a community or group of Aboriginals, and includes those traditions, observances, customs, and beliefs as applied in relation to particular persons, sites, areas of land, things or relationships."[29] Or

26. Peter Garrett, *Diesel and Dust* (New York: Columbia Records, 1988).
27. The first land rights statute was passed in 1966 in South Australia — The Aboriginal Land Trusts Act 1966 (SA). Since then there have been a series of statutes: Pitjantjatjara Land Rights Act 1981 (SA), Maralinga Tjarutja Land Rights Act (SA), Aboriginal Land Rights Act 1983 (NSW), Local Government (Aboriginal Lands) Act 1978 (Qld), Land Act (Aboriginal and Islander Land Grants) Amendment Act 1982 (Qld).
28. Elizabeth A. Povinelli, "The State of Shame: Australian Multiculturalism and the Crisis of Indigenous Citizenship," *Critical Inquiry* 24 (1998): 575–610.
29. Aboriginal Land Rights (Northern Territory) Act 1976 (Canberra: Government Printer).

that this definition became the blueprint for most major legislative references to "Aboriginal traditions." Nor would most people know that if they are to be successful claimants, Aboriginal persons must provide evidence not only of the enduring nature of their customary law but also of their "degree of attachment" to these ancient laws and lands. Likewise, while they might know the federal Native Title Act of 1993 stipulates that an Aboriginal group must continue to observe "traditional laws" and "traditional customs," most Australians would not know that the content of these traditional laws and customs are left undefined even as others are altogether excluded from legal recognition. Still fewer Australians have had the chance to appreciate the breathtaking rhetorical skill with which the High Court in *Mabo* and *Wik* simultaneously castigated previous courts for their historically and morally laden refusal to recognize the value of Aboriginal beliefs and customs and, nevertheless, reconfirmed the function of dominant morality in deciding issues of cultural recognition: "The incidents of particular native title relating to inheritance, the transmission or acquistion of rights and interests in land and the grouping of persons to possess rights and interests in land are matters to be determined by the laws and customs of the indigenous inhabitants, provided those laws and customs are not so repugnant to natural justice, equity and good conscience that juridical sanctions under the new regime must be withheld." [30]

Never defining the content of "the repugnant" or "the good," the court nevertheless relied on the commonsense notion that they were formally distinct and discernible states in order to establish a limit to internal national cultural alterity. The repugnant and the good are "to be debated" in the open forum of the public sphere. What cannot be debated is where the repugnant lies in relation to the common law. Moral codes change, but the repugnant, whatever it is, is always a stranger to the real being of the common law. Thus, in any given moment of history, if an indigenous law is felt to be "repugnant" the repugnancy is seen to emanate from it—no matter if the court itself cites the vast historical trail of its own mistaken bigotry and malice or that in its hands the common law becomes little more than a reminder of a constant process of continual self exile. *Still* natural justice remains the common law's private property.

30. *Eddie Mabo v. the State of Queensland,* 107 *ALR* 44.

Why, then, should we be surprised to learn that Pauline Hanson knew little more about indigenous traditions than the average non-Aboriginal Australian when she urged the public to avert their eyes from the mesmerizing image of indigenous tradition and to wake up from the spell cast by a materially motivated "Aboriginal industry"? (Neither Howard's ministers, who questioned the value of Aboriginal traditions, nor Beazley, who supported them, knew much more.) Hanson should make us pause—but not, however, for the usual suspects lurking in her rhetoric: spectres of racism, intolerance, and bigotry. We should pause because unlike Fison, Fraser, Keating, and Beazley, Hanson insists "ordinary Australians" look at the real conditions of Aboriginal social life.

What if we were to do the unthinkable and agree with Hanson that there is something fishy about the nation's enjoyment of ancient Aboriginal traditions? About the national celebration of a social law preceding the messiness of national history? About the tacit silences surrounding the content of Aboriginal traditions? About legislation written to support an ancient law predating anything present-day non-Aboriginal Australians are responsible for and anything present-day Aboriginal Australians could know about? To appreciate Hanson's uncanny insight while refusing her political or social analysis necessitates taking seriously the claims of many public spokespersons and ordinary Australians that they are honestly celebrating the survival of indigenous traditional culture. When they think about it, many Australians are truly deeply moved by the miraculous persistence of an Aboriginal law in the face of centuries of traumatic civil onslaught. There in the distance, although never wherever an actual Aboriginal subject stands and speaks, the public senses a miracle of modern times: an impossible to define but truly felt sublime material, an immutable and indestructible thing, predating and surviving civil society's social and corporeal alterations. *The Last Wave, Picnic at Hanging Rock,* and numerous other mass media films and mass-marketed books strive to evoke this affective state. The nation truly celebrates this actually good, whole, intact, and somewhat terrifying *something* lying just beyond the torn flesh of present national social life. And it is toward this good object that they stretch their hands. What is the object of their devotion?

In part, this object is the easily recognized wounded subject of the modern liberal state.[31] The political drama of an ancient law's battle for recognition is refigured as a series of personal traumas suffered by innocent citizens. In the Australian edition of *Time Magazine,* a psychiatrist rather than a politician or constitutional lawyer explained the social meaning and import of the Stolen Generation's moral claim to the nation: "The grief echoes through generations. With no experience of family life themselves, many find parenthood difficult—one woman told how she had to be taught how to hug her children."[32] This individualized traumatic subject is then elevated to archetype, the holocaust survivor. Not surprisingly, given the ages of the plaintiffs, in its investigation of the forcible removal of Aboriginal children from their parents, the Royal Commission likened the Australian liberal state's final plan for Aborigines, cultural assimilation, to the German fascist state's final plan for European Jews, physical annihilation. The Royal Commission and many Aboriginal men and women noted the irony that as Australians were fighting fascism abroad they were perpetuating it at home.

The Royal Commission was not alone in raising the specter of a creeping fascism secreted in the heart of Australian nationalism. It was widely feared that popular support for Hanson's xenophobic political party, One Nation, signaled a potentially apocalyptic failure of historical consciousness and memory of the social costs of the infamous mid-century white immigration policy. While commenting on the need for federal recognition of indigenous native title, former Labor Prime Minister Keating explicitly figured opposition to native title in the common-sense formula of antifascism: First they came for the . . . , finally they came for me: "If we start wiping out indigenous common law rights, when do we start wiping out non-indigenous common law rights? This is what this game is about."[33]

This *is* what the game is really about or, at least, is *also* about—the rightness and authority of "our" common law, its defense, and in its de-

31. See Wendy Brown, "Wounded Attachments," in *States of Injury: Power and Freedom in Late Modernity* (Princeton, NJ: Princeton University Press, 1995). Also Lauren Berlant, "The Subject of True Feeling," in *Cultural Pluralism, Identity Politics, and the Law,* ed. Austin Sarat (Ann Arbor: University of Michigan Press, 1997).
32. Lisa Clausen, "The Cruelty of Kindness," *Time,* 9 June 1997, 46.
33. Laura Tingle, "Keating Attacks Wik Plan as Racist," *Age,* Melbourne Online, 12 November 1997.

fense the defense of the liberal subject of rights. Another wounded subject stands behind the scarred indigenous body: the liberal subject who wielded the frontier blade and near fatally wounded itself in the process. Explicit ongoing intolerance of the indigenous population threatened to reopen the wound. Mitigating the ongoing failures of the liberal common law through acts of public contrition and atonement simply provides a means of building a newer, deeper form of national self-regard and pride, a form freed from its tragic siblings, imperialism, totalitarianism, fascism. Beazley, Keating's successor in the Labor Party, put it succinctly:

> I love our history. It is one of greatness, of struggle and survival. Like all nations, it contains elements for which we must atone and disagreements for which we must reconcile.
>
> But the issue here is not our history. The High Court settled that. The fact is that we are making history—this Parliament, those of us in political life, and you working hard to understand and contribute to this debate. As we write history in the coming days, the question is this—will it be one for which our grandchildren and great-grandchildren will have to atone, or will it be one in which we make them proud of this generation?[34]

In short, national subjects are not pretending to celebrate the survival of indigenous traditions while secretly celebrating their necessary discursive and affective failures, returning again and again to wound and worship the wound. Liberal supporters of indigenous traditions really want them to have survived. They want to worship a traditional order stripped of every last trace of bad settlement history. This real desire makes it even more difficult for Aboriginal men and women not to see the failure of cultural identity as their own personal failure rather than a structure of failure to which they are urged to identify. Aboriginal persons often turn their critical faculty on themselves or become trapped between two unanswerable questions: Were my traditions taken from me? and Did I, my parents, or my children abandon them?

An ancient law wiped clean of the savage history of modernity simul-

34. Beazley, "Address to the Nation." Tasmanian Green Party Senator Bob Brown said, "It would embarrass Australia internationally at the Olympics in Sydney, besides the Aboriginal people would not accept it, nor should they." Paul Daley, "Wik Poll Gives Liberals a Shock," *Age*, Melbourne Online, 7 December 1997.

taneously purifies the liberal subject. First, the survival of good indigenous traditions transforms liberalism's bad side into a weak, inconsequential historical force. The very social weakness of Aboriginal people
reinforces this fantasy. If even *they* could survive liberalism's bad side,
this bad side must be weak indeed. Second, when good traditions appear
before the nation, liberalism's good side also appears as a strong supporting force. The trauma of imperial history is revealed to have been an
unfortunate transition on the long road to a new triumphant national:
"We cannot really celebrate the triumphs of our history if we're not also
prepared to acknowledge the shame of our history."[35] Of course, much
depends on Aboriginal persons censoring "those laws and customs . . .
repugnant to natural justice, equity and good conscience" so that the
nation does not have to experience its own continuing intolerance, its
own failures to achieve a truly multicultural national formation without
recourse to discipline and repression. Third, resilient Aboriginal traditional law provides a fantasy space for non-Aboriginal subjects to imagine their own resilience in the face of the brutal conditions of liberal
capital and to hope things will get better without the painful process
of social transformation. Fourth and finally, the survival of some Aboriginal traditions confuses the question of who or what is responsible
for the loss of other traditions. If some Aborigines were able to resist
the "tides of history," why weren't most? Responsibility for the continuity of native title is shifted from the state to the "activities and will
of the indigenous people themselves."[36] The social conditions in which
Aboriginal subjects must maintain their law is materially extraneous to
law and nation.

As the nation stretches out its hands to an ancient Aboriginal law
in order to embrace its own ideal body, indigenous subjects are called
on to perform a complex set of sign functions in exchange for the good
feelings of the nation and the reparative legislation of the state. Indigenous subjects must transport to the present ancient prenational meanings and practices in *whatever* language and moral framework prevails
at the time of enunciation. For these rights and resources are really intended for the indigenous subject — that imaginary prenational subject
haunting the actions of every actual Aboriginal person. If this were not

35. Lisa Clausen, "Cruelty of Kindness."
36. *Wik People v. the State of Queensland* (1996) 176.

an arduous enough semiotic odyssey, Aboriginal men and women are also called on to give national subjects an experience of being transported from the present to the past, including transportation past the nation's failed promise to the very persons carrying them along. The demand for this dual transportation is captured in the most banal of public queries, "Tell us what was it like before us."

Aboriginal subjects should, in short, construct a sensorium in which the rest of the nation can experience the sensations Fison described. They should model a national noumenal fantasy. But every determinate content of Aboriginal culture forecloses the imaginary fullness of ancient law. No matter how strongly Aboriginal persons identify with these now lost but once fully present customary practices, all Aboriginal subjects are always being threatened by the categorical accusation, "You are becoming (just) another ethnic group" or "You are becoming a type of ethnic group whose defining difference is the failure to have maintained the traditions that define your difference." They are always falling away from their identity because their identity is the temporal unfurling of an indeterminable ideal of national good.

So?

What I am saying is hardly news, nor do I mean it to be. In their nature as socially produced and negotiated abstractions, all identities fail to correspond fully with any particular social subject or group and are propped up or undermined by their relation to other social identities and institutions. But all failures of identity are not the same; they are not related to state and capital institutional structures in the same way, and they do not produce the same discursive and affective results. Each one arises from and is situated in a particular set of social practices and relations; constitutes a particular set of social problems; and organizes a particular set of social desires, horrors, and hopes.

My ultimate interest is not in these discursive and affective aspects of indigenous subjectivity. The goal of understanding the necessary failure of indigenous identity is to understand what national work is being done through its recognition and to understand better how power operates and is configured in multicultural settler nations like Australia. The abstraction "indigenous tradition" is a critical relay point through which immanent critiques of dominant social formations, institutions, values, and authorities are transformed into identifications with these same forms, institutions, values, and hierarchies. This socially practiced *idea* translates national failures to provide even basic economic and social justice into local failures of culture and identity. It organizes commonsense notions of who (or what) is responsible for the social inequalities characteristic of the late liberal Australian nation.

And so, in this last section, I examine an all too clear calculus, coordinating the material stakes of an Aboriginal person's or group's claim to be traditional and the determinate content and passionate attachment that they must produce to support their claim. When capital resources are only indirectly at stake, the content of the "ancient order" often remains vaguely defined. But when the material stakes increase, particular indigenous persons and groups are called on to provide precise accounts of local social structures and cultural beliefs that necessarily have a "more or less" relationship to the ideal referent of "traditional customs and laws" and to anything actually occurring in their day-to-day lives. At some "to be announced" boundary, the "less" becomes "too little" and the special rights granted to indigenous persons give way to the equal rights granted all groups in the multicultural nation.

SPECIFY (THEM)!

Managing this discursive gap is clearly the semiotic challenge and dilemma of urban Aborigines. How does an urban Aboriginal person become a convincing indigenous subject and thus secure the social, discursive, and affective resources available through this convincing performance? We find a clue in an ordinary article published in the *Sydney Morning Herald* on 7 August 1997, ironically, citing Hanson's One Nation Party. The story featured Lydia Miller, "a very modern manifestation of Aboriginality . . . a city power broker . . . in charge of nine staff and an annual $3 million budget." Miller is described as an Aboriginal activist from "one of Australia's best-known indigenous families," a family composed of lawyers, activists, artists, and actresses. What makes Miller's Aboriginality compelling is not, or not simply, her biological heritage but that heritage plus her identification with the "diplomatic protocol of ancient Australia." She becomes authentically Aboriginal only at the moment she willingly alienates her discourse and identity to the fantastic claim that she is able to transport an ancient practice from the past:

Lydia Miller, until recently the head honcho of indigenous arts fund-ing in Australia, and current Olympic events organiser, has a par-ticularly Aboriginal view of the political geography of this nation. "I think of it as something like 301 nations—300 indigenous nations and one nation called Australia." This view of the world makes life infinitely more complex for Miller than for your common or garden variety bureaucrat. For example, during her two and a half years as director of the Australia Council's indigenous arts board and now, as a project head with the Olympic Festival of the Dreaming, she has meticulously followed the diplomatic protocol of ancient Australia.[37]

Some readers probably passed over the strange passage, "she has meticulously followed the diplomatic protocol of ancient Australia," without much thought. Others might have imagined sun-drenched, clay-painted *black* bodies dancing a sacred corroboree or sacred ritual objects passing from *black* hand to *black* hand. If they did, they imagined bodies and hands whose color coding is otherwise than Miller's own. Still other readers might have smirked, believing the entire article to be a product of public relations machinery. If she said anything like what was quoted, Miller might have thought she was donning an "ideological mask" for a variety of political reasons.[38] In any case, the *Sydney Morn-ing Herald* does not elaborate what "the diplomatic protocol of ancient Australia" refers to.

This referential nonspecificity is not the result of a lack of knowl-edge or a failure to report it. Rather "ancient protocol" is experienced as maximally symbolic at exactly the moment when it is minimally de-terminate. This semiotic hinge allows readers to fantasize a maximal variety of images of the deserving indigenous subject at the very mo-ment the description of the content of the social geography approaches zero. Nineteenth-century social models of a male-dominated family and clan walk side by side with twentieth-century models featuring crystal woman, and ad infinitum. This proliferation of possible pro-tocols of ancient Australia fits neatly in the consumer-driven logic of

37. Debra Jopson, "One Nation or 301 Nations?" *Sydney Morning Herald,* 9 August 1997, 15s.

38. Peter Sloterdjik, *Critique of Cynical Reason* (Minneapolis: University of Minne-sota Press, 1987) and Slavoj Žižek, "How Did Marx Invent the Symptom?" in *The Sublime Object of Ideology* (New York: Verso, 1992), 28–33.

late capital and, especially, the modern protocols of global tourism (of which we can now understand the Olympics to be a part).

Of course, the seemingly simple statement, "the diplomatic protocol of ancient Australia," projects national and state forms and practices into this empty geography (diplomatic, protocol, an ancient *Australia*). A landscape actually emptied of all meanings derived from settlement history is the real, unimaginable, unrepresentable ground of "indigenous." All *representations* of this ground must pass through whatever narratives of national history exist at the time. But it is this fantastic, unrepresentational, felt social ground where the truly deserving Aboriginal subject(s) stand(s) — the social state against which the legal apparatus and the jury of public opinion measure whether contemporary Aboriginal persons are deserving of national sympathy and special state ameliatory legislation. Every actual Aboriginal subject produces personal and national optimisms and antagonisms because they *stand in the way of* this unrepresentable good object in the dual sense of being merely metonyms of and material barriers to them.

When material resources are directly at stake, the distance between unknowable prenational social geographies and present social, linguistic, and cultural practices are more closely scrutinized in the press and are more precisely measured in law. In these instances, nation and law demand Aboriginal subjects produce maximally concrete cultural referents, diminishing the symbolic range and potency of every particular contemporary practice. For example, in the midst of the Kenbi Land Claim in the Northern Territory, Rupert Murdock's *Northern Territory News* featured an interview titled "Topsy Secretary — Last of the Larrakia." This interview came amid a stream of editorials detailing the large cost of the Kenbi Land Claim (to white Australians) and the amount of land that would be taken out of the (white) "Territory's future." A breezy setting piece, the article pivots on a series of racial, cultural, and ideological differences between the ancient Aboriginal past and the unfolding Aboriginal present. The interview begins by describing Topsy Secretary as "the last full-blooded Larrakia." Other Larrakia exist, but they are "fair-skinned descendents."

Although the article describes Topsy Secretary as a "pure" Larrakia in a racial sense, it suggests she is not a pure Larrakia in her material and cultural desires. Her desires mark her as just another hybrid cultural subject, undermining the political cause she is cast as a symbol of.

The article is able to undermine the Kenbi Land Claim by suggesting that this last real Larrakia is *really* not different from the average Australian citizen. Topsy Secretary only retains "knowledge about traditional foods," an enthusiasm shared by many white Australians. Her other pastime pleasures are on par with many middle-brow "white" pleasures — sitting on her veranda and watching *Days of Our Lives* and *The Young and the Restless.* The hallmark of Aboriginal high culture, men's ceremonies, are now " 'All forgotten,' she said. 'No old men — they're gone — no-one to teach.' " Finally her political views, the very fact she has political views, differentiate her from her own parents: "Topsy said her father never worried about land rights. He accepted the Europeans as friends and never wished them to go away. But Topsy had lived to see her country shrink with the passing of generations. She wanted to see freehold title over the Kulaluk land and was hopeful the Larrakia would be successful in the long-awaited Kenbi land claim." [39]

A knot of speculative enjoyment is captured in this interview, inciting questions about the *deserving* Aboriginal subject: Who should receive the benefits of reparative legislation? How do we measure the line between the polluted and diluted present and the pure ancient past? What line demarcates an Aboriginal subject from a national ethnic subject? The article does not answer these questions; it simply raises the stakes of any particular decision a land commissioner might make regarding what will constitute legally felicitous cultural difference.

All major pieces of cultural heritage and land legislation in some way mandate such felicitous cultural differences and promote to some degree the paranoid epistemology of Fison's modern ethnology. Most land legislation restricts claims to (or produce the necessity to produce) "traditional Aboriginal owners." And they demand that these owner-claimants demonstrate a genealogical connection between their present and past customary beliefs and practices (the more specifically the better) and, further, that they identify with those customs (the more passionately the better). Those few pieces of legislation based on history, or a combination of tradition and history, reaffirm as "unchallengeable" the commonsense notion that tradition provides the true economic and cultural value of Aboriginal society to Aborigines and to the nation. In

39. Genny O'Loughlin, "Topsy Secretary—Last of the Larrakia," *Northern Territory News,* 10 December 1989, 16.

New South Wales, for instance, land rights legislation is not restricted to traditional owners. It allows Aboriginal groups to claim land on the basis of their historical attachment. But the goal of the legislation is the "regeneration of Aboriginal culture and dignity, and at the same time laying the basis for a self-reliant and more secure economic future for our continent's Aboriginal custodians."[40]

When Aboriginal persons disrupt the fantasy of traditional identity by rejecting it as the authentic and valuable difference of their person and group or insisting on its alterity to common law values, they not only risk the material and symbolic values available to them through this *idea* but also jeopardize the ability of future generations to stake a claim based on its semiotic remainders. The following few interlocutions between lawyers and their Aboriginal clients drawn from the Kenbi Land Claim suggest the microdiscursive nature of these subjective struggles. The first example is taken from a proofing session held right before the claim was first heard in 1989; the second is from a videotape I made with two younger claimants during a lull in a young men's ceremony; the third comes from public testimony given during the second hearing in 1995–96. In the second sequence, Raelene Singh, Jason Singh, Nathan Bilbil, and I tease each other about the basis of the Belyuen claim: conception relationships (*maruy*) with the Belyuen waterhole and by extension a spiritual tie to other sacred sites in the claim area, a physical relationship to each other and the claim area by the fact of a shared substance (sweat or *ngunbudj*), and a familial relationship with the spirits and graves of deceased ancestors (*nguidj*) throughout the claim area.

KENBI LAWYER: What was it like before the white man?

TOM BARRADJAP: I don't know mate, I never been there.

KL: Yeh, right, ha, ha, ha. But what was the traditional law for this place? We need to know: What was the traditional law for this place?

BETH POVINELLI: Hn, what you? Are you for this country?

RAELENE SINGH: He taping for pretend report.

BP: Ngambin (cousin's daughter), you for this country?

RS: Yes. This is my country. It's like my life.

40. Linda Pearson, "Aboriginal Land Rights Legislation in New South Wales," *Environmental and Planning Law Journal* 10 (1993): 398–422, esp. 399 and 400.

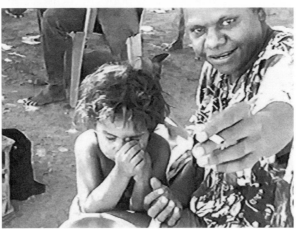

BP: Oh, it's like your life from the Dreamtime ancestors?

RS: Yeh, and I come out of that Belyuen waterhole.

BP: Oh, you been born from there now?

RS: Yeh, that's the dam. That old man Belyuen gave this mob kid here now—us here now—like today where we walk around.

BP: Yeh, walk around.

RS: It's like a gift from God.

BP: From which one? From on top way?

RS: Yeh, well, we got our own; we got our own thing—gift. Ah, we got our own father, see.

BP: We got him from here now?

RS: From Belyuen, from our ancestors.

BP: And do you believe that?

RS: Yes.

BP: Oh, you do?

RS: Yes. That is true.

BP: And are you teaching your kids?

RS: Yes.

BP: Oh, which ones?

RS: I am teaching my niece, there, Chantelle.

BP: You call her daughter, isn't it?

RS: Yeh, my daughter from my little sister.

JASON SINGH: I'm from Daly River.

BP: Wait now, I'm shifting from sun. Daly River?

JS: Yeh.

BP: I don't know, you look like Belyuen. You got the same Belyuen nose.

JS: Nah, but you look here. I staying at Peppi.

BP: Let me look. Ah, you been live there.

NATHAN BILBIL: I always come here for just once in a while.

JS: Keep going.

BP: Ah, yeh? You smell like a Belyuen again.

JS: Oooh, ha ha ha.

ROBERT BLOWES: Right. And when you were talking to Mr. Howie here, you said that's the native way to call him brother?

TOPSY SECRETARY: Yes.

RB: Yes. Was that really brother?

TS: Well, in your way it's cousin brother, but my way we call him brother, and sister.

RB: So he had a different father and different mother?

TS: Yes, but it's still, we call him brother and sister.

RB: And he's still Larrakia?

TS: Yes.

RB: And he's still the same country?

TS: Yes.

RB: Okay. And what about your father and Tommy Lyons? Is that the same way, then? Your father Frank . . .

TS: Yes, it's the same way.

RB: So he's not really "brother."

TS: Well, they all brothers.

RB: That native way.

TS: Real brothers.[41]

In this case, as in other land claim cases, lawyers and the anthropologists who help them practice the law as if knowing that their asking an Aboriginal witness to embody an imaginary and discursive impossibility were irrelevant to the very organization and operation of power they intend to be challenging. Keeping with *local* speech practices, Barradjap uses humor to jolt the Kenbi lawyer back into "reality" — to think about what he is asking. But speaking the "truth" to fantasy (such as Barradjap tries to do) or creating an ironic hypertext about law and identity (as Raelene, Jason, and I do) does not upset the practice of primarily valuing Aboriginal subjects in relation to their ability to afford for national subjects a language and experience of "before all this." It only shifts the register — only sets into motion a string of signs whose object is to forestall the collapse of the fantasy: OK, right, but what about "before the white man," about "traditional law," about the "real Aboriginal way"?

The Kenbi lawyer is no fool. It is not a lack of knowledge that prompts his query. He knows he is asking the impossible of Tommy Barradjap. He and I laughed about these types of questions. Yet he asks anyway. The lawyer desires, *if only for a moment,* for reality to be torn, for what he knows is true not to impede what he wishes for *nevertheless,* for the

41. Kenbi Transcripts (Indooroopilly, 1995), 2990–2991.

social consequences of violent settler history to be suspended *even if only for this private moment,* especially in this *intimate interpersonal moment.* And in this movement from knowledge to its refusal, we see the contours of the desires and suspicions constantly circulating around Aboriginal men and women, an affective topology in which they are formed and to which they must respond. These personal and national needs, desires, and demands disturb every Aboriginal enunciation. In the logic of fantasy, Barradjap's insistence that the Kenbi lawyer "get real" is reinterpretable as Barradjap withholding from the lawyer the *real* truth, a form of truth existing somewhere beyond this fragmented and corrupted social reality. In the linguistic fragment "yeh, right, ha, ha, ha. But," the lawyer marks the unresolvable tension between a barred desire (his desire to refuse knowledge and gain entry to a traditional land) and a barring agent (Barradjap's refusal to act as a discursive passage to that land).

Like the Kenbi lawyer, Robert Blowes is very knowledgeable about Aboriginal social relations. Among numerous land claim cases, he was counsel assisting in the presentation of *Wik* before the High Court. Yet, again, something intrudes and interrupts this knowledge. If the Kenbi lawyer desired for history not to bar his access to the prehistorical, Blowes wanted his support of difference not to bar his desire for a form of difference that remains skin deep, just a matter of words. Although Topsy Secretary refuses to orient her understanding of family to Blowes, Blowes's micromanagement of the truth value of various kinship systems is an example, and just an example, of the historical and still pervasive microdiscursive disciplines that produced in Raelene, Topsy Secretary's brother's granddaughter, the (mis)recognition of her daughter as her niece. Moreover, the evidence of Topsy Secretary suggests how any determinate content of local traditions upsets the fantasy of "ancient law" as a form of otherness that is deeply recognizable and that does not violate core subjective or social values. Jason, Raelene, Nathan, and I may pun the micromanagement of discourse necessary to maintain the core fantasy of land and native title claims, but our discursive play also marks the migration of this fantasy. My own reminder to Raelene to describe Chantelle as "daughter" rather than "niece" provides further evidence of the microdisciplinary tactics constantly operating within an Aboriginal social field.

The desires and suspicions circulating around Aboriginal women and men are not confined to formal legal hearings. In now numerous commercial venues commodifying Aboriginal traditional culture, national and international consumers approach indigenous men and women expectant, optimistic, and cynical. They hope *this time* traditional culture will appear before them (which it always does, *more or less*) and that *this time* they are buying sight unseen the real thing (which they always are, *more or less*). But before they have even purchased their ticket, every consumer of culture is already disappointed by what they know: What they are about to see is a commercial product. They, like Fison, leave the scene of cultural performance frustrated. Why aren't traditions wherever I am? Who is withholding them from me? I bet there are none here. Who is to blame for their disappearance?

This is why the "real law man" and, to a lesser extent, the "real law woman" fix the attention of the nation—law and commerce, publican and politician. Law men and women are simultaneously what the nation viciously ghosted and where it hopes it can recover a previously unstained image. The nation looks not at but through contemporary Aboriginal faces, past where every Aboriginal and non-Aboriginal Australian meet, wanting the spirit of something promised there: "Tell us something we do not, cannot, know *from here*—what it was (you and we were) like before all this. What our best side looks like." In the moment before any particular answer, ears and eyes are transfixed by the potential of indigenous knowledge—by what might be unveiled and by a more general possibility of experiencing the new, the ruptural, the truly transformative. This moment is filled with horror, anticipation, and excitement. Of course, no Aboriginal person can fulfill this desire, be truly positively alterior; nor if they could would they *make sense* to the institutional apparata necessary to their livelihood. This "first speaker, the one who disturbs the eternal silence of the universe" would in fact be experienced as a stereotypical psychotic.[42]

Legal practitioners may hope to disambiguate themselves from these other cultural markets, but economic and symbolic logics articulate them, as do the Aboriginal subjects who move between them. Aboriginal subjects field similar desire-laden questions from tourists, anthro-

---

42. Mikhail M. Bakhtin, "The Problem of Speech Genres," in *Speech Genres and Other Late Essays* (Austin: University of Texas Press, 1990), 68.

pologists, and lawyers: Is this how it was done before white people? And they hear legal and commercial consumer reports—satisfied consumers grateful to be shown a part of real traditional culture; dissatisfied consumers grumbling that what they heard and saw didn't seem real *enough*. As did their ancestors, Tommy Barradjap, Topsy Secretary, and Jason and Raelene Singh must orient themselves to the multiple symbolic and capital economies of "traditional law" if they are to gain the personal and material values available through them—if they are to alleviate to some extent the social conditions Hanson alluded to. They navigate among mass- and multimediated fragments of public discourses—not only on the value of Aboriginal traditions but also on the limits of cultural alterity. What constitutes too much otherness? Aboriginal men and women like Topsy Secretary, Nathan Bilbil, and Jason and Raelene Singh are left to grapple with how to present a form of difference that is maximally other than dominant society and minimally abrasive to dominant values. The hot potato of nation-building in multicultural formations is dropped into their laps.

The ever-widening stretch of history never seems to soothe the desires or irritating suspicions of white subjects that somewhere out there in archives or within a withholding Aboriginal subject is the knowledge that would fill the fantasy space of "tradition." At the time Fison wrote *Kamilaroi and Kunai,* one hundred years had passed since the settlement of Sydney. At the time Tom Barradjap spoke, over two hundred years had passed and Aboriginal traditions had long since become a politicized and commodified form of national identity. Raelene and Jason Singh had literally grown up under the shadow of the Kenbi Land Claim. For the entire span of their lives, Raelene and Jason had heard their grandfather, grandmother, and mother publicly valued primarily for their traditional knowledge and role. Now they and their sister must be that impossible thing of national desire. And if the Kenbi Land Claim were ever to end, other land claims, native title claims, and cultural heritage claims are ever over the southern horizon. The external suspicion that somewhere out there someone is withholding a valuable thing is transformed into an internal local anxiety: Which of "our" old people is withholding information from us? What will they say or not say? How will the lives of the next generation be altered on the basis of a speaking or withholding relative? What if someone reveals a "real tradition" repugnant to the common law?

As if conspirators in a political intrigue whose measure is yet to be determined, we huddled around my small tape recorder under the veranda of the Belyuen women's center: Marjorie Bilbil, Alice Djarug, Alice's daughter Patsy-Ann, Ruby Yarrowin, Ruby's daughter Linda, Ester Djarim, and myself. Betty Billawag was too sick to join us. Ruby, Ester, Marjorie, and Alice are the critical remainders of language and history in the community, their daughters trying to "pick it up" in the local colloquial creole. And I use "remainders" advisedly. What was once the nation's cultural debris is now the local's cultural mines. These women are the last fluent speakers of Emmiyenggal, Mentha, and Wadjigiyn, the languages of the region.

In the center of our loose circle lies a sound-tape of a funeral rite (*kapuk,* rag-burning) held at Belyuen in 1948 when the older women were young adults—my age, Patsy's age, Linda's age.[43] The 1948 *kapuk* was held for Mabalang, Ester Djarim's deceased husband's first wife. An ethnomusicologist found the recording in the archives of the Australian Institute of Aboriginal and Torres Strait Islander Studies in Canberra and informed lawyers at the Northern Land Council that, on it, the now-deceased Mosec, Mabalang's elder brother, sings a *Belyuen wangga* (a regional song genre). The ethnomusicologist thought that the *wangga* might prove useful to the Belyuen community's land claim if it and other *wangga* on the tape could be translated. The Belyuen community had just recently decided to put themselves forward as "traditional Aboriginal owners" for the Kenbi Land Claim even though doing so placed them in a potentially antagonistic relationship with other Aboriginal persons and groups who also claimed to be the traditional Aboriginal owners of the land. Ruby Yarrowin, Ester Djarim, Alice Djarug, and Marjorie Bilbil were eager to listen to the tape, as was I. They remembered Mosec as a *djewalabag,* a "cleverman," a man steeped in sacred law. They remembered national and international celebrities and media traveling to Belyuen to record his singing and dancing.[44]

This is why the women and I had gathered: We were looking for tra-

43. *Australian Walkabout Show,* "Death Rite for Mabalang," 1948 Program, ABC Radio.
44. Collin Simpson (on tape) announces to the radio audience: "Mosec is dancing solo around the old man, and I don't know if I have ever seen finer dancing in my

ditional evidence that would link these women and their families to this land. I was the senior anthropologist for their claim. And so Northern Land Council lawyers told me about the tape, and I told the women. We were hoping we would find their tradition in this archived sound fragment. At least for the moment, they desperately desired to be the traditional thing immanent in this material thing, to be propped up by the traditional, to be its object, to become the archival. And these desires organized their talk about the living and the dead, the remembered, loved, and disappointing.

As we waited for tea to boil and for the tape to rewind, the women meditated on the consequences of failing in this discursive quest, of "being wrong," of "not fitting the law," of their parents and themselves having made "mistakes," having lost their culture while busy living their lives. Marjorie Bilbil asked me whether, in the event that they failed to convince the judge that they were the traditional owners of the land, the entire community would be uprooted and sent to southern countries. From these women's historical perspective, this seemingly fantastic communal apocalypse is not so far-fetched. Soon after the Japanese bombing of Darwin in 1942, the war government transported the community to war camps in Katherine. Closer to the present, these women have watched other communities displaced in the wake of lost or disputed land claims. The Wagait dispute, the Kamu and Malakmalak dispute, the Kungwarakang and Maranunggu dispute: These are the well-known names of current bitter intra-Aboriginal arguments over what constitutes a "traditional attachment" to country, arguments battled in courts and bush camps. I had no idea what to reply when Marjorie Bilbil asked me,

What if we are wrong?

---

life. He is comparable with a dancer like Le Shine — the art of a faun ballet. Really, but don't take my word for it: Ask Ted Shaun, the American dancer who toured Australia and visited Delissaville and who said that Mosec would be a sensation in London or New York." "Death Rite for Mabalang."

Translation, Imperialism, and National Self-Definition in Russia

Andrew Wachtel

The Russian empire entered the age of nationalism in unusual circumstances. Elsewhere in Europe, the elites who worked to create the horizontal feeling of national kinship that slowly came to replace more traditional forms of social identification operated either in consolidated states with a long native secular cultural tradition (such as Britain, France, and Spain), in territories with a similar cultural history but without a contemporary unified state (such as the German- and Italian-speaking lands), or in culturally marginalized and politically subordinated areas (such as the various potential nations within the Hapsburg empire).

Russia was a politically united and powerful state; indeed, after the defeat of Napoleon in 1812 it was arguably the leading power in continental Europe. It was also an imperializing state, and it had been so at least since Ivan IV's conquest of the Tatar khanate of Kazan in 1553. In the course of the nineteenth century, as the European powers collected ever greater numbers of overseas colonies, Russia proceeded with its expansionist efforts into contiguous territories, swallowing up such non-Russian lands as Poland (divided among Russia, Prussia, and Austria in 1795), Georgia (annexed between 1800 and 1810, although wars in the Caucasus against mountain tribesmen continued into the 1860s), Finland (1809), and Bukhara and Khiva (which became Russian protectorates in 1868 and 1873, respectively), and receiving a serious case of imperial indigestion into the bargain. At the same time, in sharp contrast to other politically strong imperializing modern states, Russia found herself in a culturally subordinate, one might even say colonialized, position entering the nineteenth century.

The reasons for this anomaly are well known. In the wake of the Mongol invasions of the thirteenth century, Russia had been essentially cut off from European cultural developments for four centuries. Consumed by the projects of national salvation and unification, Russia underwent no renaissance, no secularization of culture, no development of a middle class or a civil society. In the course of the first quarter of the eighteenth century, however, Peter the Great forcibly reoriented his society (at least its elites) toward Western Europe, mandating wholesale borrowing of European forms. The modernization and Europeanization of the Russian elites was successfully completed during the reign of Catherine the Great in the last quarter of the eighteenth century. Ultimately, this cultural reorientation laid the groundwork for the great Russian literary, musical, and artistic achievements of the nineteenth and twentieth centuries, but it also produced a strong case of culture shock and a nagging sense of inferiority. And it was in this matrix of political power and cultural inferiority that Russian nationalist thought crystallized in the first decades of the nineteenth century.[1]

Many studies have focused on the Russian reaction to modernity, a reaction that is generally seen as having taken the form either of a wholesale acceptance of European forms (the position of the "Westernizers") or an equally wholesale rejection of them (by the "Slavophiles").[2] As different as these groups may have appeared on the surface, however, Westernizers and Slavophiles had a great deal in common, particularly

---

1. In both cases, by the way, the feelings were exaggerated. Russia was not nearly as militarily powerful as Russians thought, although this was not generally recognized until the humiliating defeat in the Crimean War of 1853–55. Nor was her cultural production as negligible as many Russians feared—after all, by the 1830s Russian literature had already produced Pushkin and Gogol, and in music Mikhail Glinka. What counts, however, is contemporary perception, for it is from these attitudes that national images are formed.

2. Classic treatments of the clash between Westernizers and Slavophiles include Isaiah Berlin, "A Remarkable Decade," in *Russian Thinkers,* ed. Henry Hardy and Aileen Kelly (New York: Penguin Books, 1978), 114–209 (the essay dates from 1955, however), and Andrzej Walicki, *The Slavophile Controversy,* trans. Hilda Andrews-Rusiecka (Oxford: Oxford University Press, 1975). More recent work that places this conflict in the context of Russian national definition includes Liah Greenfeld, *Nationalism: Five Roads to Modernity* (Cambridge, Mass.: Harvard University Press, 1992), 189–274; Andrew Wachtel, *An Obsession with History: Russian Writers Confront the Past* (Stanford, Calif.: Stanford University Press, 1994); and Amy C. Singleton, *No Place Like Home: The Literary Artist and Russia's Search for Cultural Identity* (Albany: State University of New York Press, 1997).

in their attitudes to Russia's position in time.[3] Although they disagreed in their interpretation of Russia's past (Westernizers regarded the pre-Petrine period as a wasteland while Slavophiles saw it as a paradise), both groups agreed that there was something seriously wrong with Russia's present position, and both were convinced that a most glorious future awaited their nation. Their shared opinion of Russia's present encouraged a feeling of ressentiment toward the West that Liah Greenfeld has identified as the characteristic feature of Russian modern thought.[4]

Although it is easy to agree that ressentiment has been prevalent in Russian thought since the late eighteenth century, it is less clear that it provided a basis for Russian nationalism. I would argue, pace Greenfeld, that neither Westernizers nor Slavophiles provided a productive blueprint for Russian national ideology. And their inability to do so stemmed from the same cause; neither group was able to recognize that a viable national project would have to take into account that an imagined Russian nation was inextricably linked to the imperial state formation in which Russians lived. The same problem, by the way, dogged the project of so-called official nationalism that was proposed by Czar Nicholas I and his coterie.[5] This view of the nation, which was eventually codified under the trinitarian formula "orthodoxy, autocracy, and nationality," was clearly designed to emphasize Russia's difference from Western European nations. But given the actual composition of the Russian empire, as well as its imperial aspirations, none of these categories was unproblematic. For one thing, large numbers of the czar's subjects were not orthodox Christians. For another, devotion to autocracy as a

---

3. This similarity, by the way, helps explain the fact that many Slavophiles started out as Westernizers, and vice versa.

4. According to Greenfeld's analysis, after an initial period of optimism, cultured Russians came to recognize "their absolute impotence in the competition with the West" by the late eighteenth century. At the same time, "unable to tear themselves away from the West, to eradicate, to efface its image from their consciousness, and having nothing to oppose to it, they defined it as the anti-model and built an ideal image of Russia in direct opposition to it. Russia was still measured by the same standards as the West (for it defined Western values as universal), but it was much better than the West. For every Western vice it had a virtue, and for what appeared as a virtue in the West, it had a virtue in reality" (*Nationalism*, 254–55).

5. For the classic study of this ideological formation, see Nicholas Riasanovsky, *Nicholas I and Official Nationality in Russia* (Berkeley: University of California Press, 1959).

basis for citizenship was, to say the least, not a modern concept. Finally, nationality, which "was at the time and has remained the most obscure, puzzling, and debatable member of the official trinity,"[6] assumed the existence of precisely what needed to be defined by any nationalist project—that is, the nation itself.

There was, however, a loosely defined group of cultural figures that did attempt to create a viable Russian national identity, one that was not merely a reaction (either positive or negative) to Western European national forms and one that took the imperial nature of the putative Russian nation seriously. This is not to say that they did not continue to look over their shoulders at the West; certainly, the alternative view of the nation and its culture they proposed appeared in the context of Western European views. But Russians did develop—and this is what needs to be emphasized—a genuinely alternative view and not merely a transvaluation of Western European signs. This group recognized that Russianness could not successfully be defined by ethnicity, religion, or political traditions. Rather, the nation was to be imagined on the basis of a few carefully chosen qualities of Russian culture and the Russian language in particular. As opposed to the elites of other imperializing nations, whose explicit or implicit assumption of cultural superiority caused them to view their own values as universal and as something to be imposed on others, members of the Russian cultural elite proposed a model that emphasized their nation's peculiar spongelike ability to absorb the best that other peoples had to offer as the basis for a universal, inclusive national culture. As we will see, the basis for this national image lay in a novel interpretation of the imperial project as a project of translation of world culture into and through Russia.

The connection between imperialism and translation has been the focus of a great deal of recent scholarship.[7] Always with reference to Western European practices, it has been claimed that they are linked in one of two ways. Either the imperializing power simply assumes the worthlessness of the languages spoken by those it conquers and imposes its own voice, ignoring or marginalizing native discourse, or it learns

6. Riasanovsky, *Nicholas I,* 124.
7. For good examples of analyses of this kind, see Eric Cheyfitz, *The Poetics of Imperialism: Translation and Colonization from* The Tempest *to* Tarzan (New York: Oxford University Press, 1991), and Edward Said, *Culture and Imperialism* (New York: Knopf, 1993).

the local language but only in order to force its own ideas even more effectively on the local population. On this view, imperializing powers generally sponsor translation not into their own languages but out of them, producing a one-way trade by which the products of the mind are exported in order to ensure a cultural and ideological dependence that mirrors the political and economic relations between themselves and the dominated.[8] In this nexus, the cultural capital of "inferior" countries is reduced at best to a series of exotic fragments (usually from the realm of visual culture) which may, from time to time, enrich the "finished products" of the dominating power's culture, but which are never allowed to speak fully in their own voice. At worst, the local culture is simply destroyed. When translation into the dominating language does occur, translators tend to lack respect for the very works they are translating, even when those works come from a culture that may well be far older and sophisticated than their own. Typical in this regard are the remarks of Edward Fitzgerald, Victorian translator of the *Rubáiyát of Omar Khayyám:* "It is an amusement for me to take what Liberties I like with these Persians who (as I think) are not Poets enough to frighten one from such excursions, and who really want a little Art to shape them."[9]

If we examine Russian views of translation, however, we see a very different picture. For while Russia has unquestionably been and remains an imperialist power, it has also been a country in which translation has been held in high regard and consistently practiced, not only by professional translators but also by most major authors. It is rare to find a major Russian poet who did not translate extensively—and not only from Western European languages. Poets generally include these translations together with their original verse when selecting poetry for publication, and, surprising as it might seem to an American poetry enthusiast, standard Russian one-volume anthologies of the work of famous poets always contain a section of translations. Now it might be thought that the coexistence of an imperialist foreign policy and a culture based on translating into Russian from foreign languages was accidental. We

8. The attitude can be best seen, perhaps, in Thomas Babington Macaulay's flippant comment that "a single shelf of a good European library is worth the whole native literature of India and Arabia." Quoted in Benedict Anderson, *Imagined Communities: Reflections on the Origin and Spread of Nationalism* (London: Verso, 1983), 86.
9. André Lefevere, *Translating Literature* (New York: Modern Language Association, 1992), 119.

might imagine that the pure cultural strivings of individual writers had no connection with the imperializing tactics of the state. After all, it is well known that Russian writers have frequently formed what Aleksandr Solzhenitsyn called a "second government," so it is tempting (from our academic multicultural perspective) to ascribe an oppositional motive to all this translation. Could it be that writers translated in order to oppose government policy, albeit surreptitiously? When we examine the situation more closely, we see that this was not the case.[10] Indeed, writers and other members of the intelligentsia were precisely in the vanguard of those who developed a peculiarly Russian cultural theory that insists that imperialism and translation not only can but must be connected for they are the basis of the national definition. After all, if Russia's manifest destiny was to absorb other civilizations rather than destroy them, it followed logically that they all had to be translated into Russian, to be made available for the grand synthetic project whose realization was to occur in the future.

The origins of this belief in modern Russian culture are obscure, but it is most probable that they lie in certain vestiges of pre-Petrine national identity (not, by the way, ones that the Slavophiles tended to emphasize) that were retained in the post-Petrine period. In particular, they appear to reside in a cultural pun, if one can use this expression. As early as the sixteenth century certain Russians had developed the political-theological notion of Moscow as the Third Rome. That theory, articulated most succinctly by the monk Philopheus, expressed the idea that Muscovite civilization would be the world's final one: "Two Romes have fallen, but a third stands fast; a fourth there cannot be."[11] Although the formulation was specifically designed to link Moscow to Constantinople and Rome as centers of Christianity, it could also serve to link Russian power to the pre-Christian power of the Roman empire.[12] This link-

10. In the Soviet period, of course, there were times when certain writers, notably Boris Pasternak, Anna Akhmatova, and Joseph Brodsky, were allowed to publish only translations and did so in order to survive. Although such cases are famous, they mark the exception rather than the rule, particularly because, at least in the case of Pasternak, translation was clearly of central creative import for the poet as well.

11. Quoted in Frederick T. Griffiths and Stanley Rabinowitz, *Novel Epics: Gogol, Dostoevsky and National Narrative* (Evanston, Ill.: Northwestern University Press, 1990), 1.

12. This connection was explicit in the Muscovite period in the belief codified in the

age invited a search for various analogies, but most important for us is that the cultural-political position of the first Rome (particularly in its pre-Christian period) was quite similar to that of Russia in the modern period. That is to say, it combined political power with a feeling of cultural weakness (in the case of Rome this was vis-à-vis ancient Greece). Roman culture was, quite openly, a culture of translation, and in aligning themselves with ancient Rome, Russian cultural figures had a justification for identifying their national project in the present with that of ancient Rome in a way that modern Western European imperial cultures did not. The extent to which the link between Russia and pre-Christian Rome was felt by Russian cultural leaders in the period of the formation of the modern Russian national identity can perhaps be sensed in the number of translations Russian poets made of Horace's famous thirtieth ode from his book 3, "Exegi monumentum"; we find versions by Mikhailo Lomonosov, Gavrila Derzhavin, Konstantin Batiushkov, and Aleksandr Pushkin in a period of some seventy years.

In any case, whatever the origins, it became a given that Russia's manifest destiny was built not on any inherent quality of Russian culture itself but rather on its ability to absorb and perfect what it had taken from outside.[13] This universality resides, first and foremost, in the language itself. Thus, according to Lomonosov, Russia's greatest eighteenth-century poet:

> The Holy Roman Emperor Carl the Fifth used to say that one should speak Spanish with God, French with one's friends, German with

spurious genealogy provided by Metropolitan Makarius that "the rulers of Moscow were heirs of an imperial line that extended all the way back to the Emperor Augustus." Richard Pipes, *Russia under the Old Regime* (New York: Scribner's, 1974), 233.

13. In this context it is worth noting that a certain paradoxical combination of respect for the languages of other cultures with an inability to find any worth in the cultures themselves is characteristic of orthodox Christianity. As opposed to the Roman Catholic Church, which insisted until very recently that liturgy was to be in sacred languages (Latin, Greek, or Hebrew), the Eastern Orthodox branch generally tolerated the use of the local language. When the Russian church itself became a missionary church, this same practice was followed. Thus, for example, St. Stephen, who converted the Permians (a Finnic tribe), is praised in his vita as "writer of books" and "the creator of Permian letters" (Serge Zenkovsky, *Medieval Russia's Epics, Chronicles, and Tales* [New York: Dutton, 1963], 208), although there was no question of those "letters" being put to use to preserve or advance Permian culture itself.

one's enemies, and Italian with the fair sex. But had he been skilled in Russian, he would, of course, have added that it would be appropriate to speak with all of these in it, for he would have found in it the greatness of Spanish, the liveliness of French, the force of German, the tenderness of Italian, and, in addition, the richness and strong terse descriptiveness of Greek and Latin.[14]

The important point here is not merely that Russian is conceived as the universal language (for many other languages have conceived of themselves as universal), but that it includes within itself the best qualities of the world's major languages. This lends the language a flexibility and capaciousness that makes it an ideal vehicle for universal cultural translation. And, perhaps in analogy to Lomonosov's claims, in a verse *ars poetica* loosely translated from Nicolas Boileau-Despréaux, Aleksandr Sumarokov exhorted Russian poets to make all of European literature their own:

> All is praiseworthy — dramas, eclogues, odes
> Write whatever your nature inclines you to.
> Just let the enlightened writer go to work
> Our sublime language is up to everything.[15]

Despite an obvious lack of original native work, most Russian critics of the early nineteenth century continued to believe that the Russian language had the ability to do everything. Their faith rested, first and foremost, on the quality of translations into Russian. Thus, Nikolai Polevoi called Nikolai Gnedich's translation of the *Iliad,* "a treasure house of language . . . [that] exposes the richness, power, and resources of our own language." [16] And in his description of Vasily Zhukovsky's truly brilliant translation of the *Odyssey,* Nikolay Gogol went even further: "Now a translation of the greatest poetic work has been accomplished in the fullest and richest of all the European languages. . . . This is not a translation but rather a recreation, rebuilding, resurrection of Homer.

14. Mikhail Lomonosov, *Rossiiskaia grammatika: Izbrannye proizvedeniia v dvukh tomakh,* vol. 2 (Moscow: 1986), 195. Translation mine. The work was written in 1754–55.
15. "Epistola o stikhotvorstve," in *Russkaia poeziia 18ogo veka,* ed. G. Makogonenko (Moscow: 1972), 173. Translation mine. The "Epistle" dates from 1747.
16. Quoted in Griffiths and Rabinowitz, *Novel Epics,* 7.

The translation seems to lead us more deeply into antiquity than does the original itself."[17] Gogol doesn't quite say so, but he apparently believes that Zhukovsky's translation is better than the original, a position that many Russian readers and even some critics have taken.[18]

It was precisely in the 1820s and 1830s that the leaders of Russian cultural opinion began to recognize that their views on the qualities of the Russian language could be projected onto the culture as a whole, and that Russia's national project could be defined by Russia's ability to synthesize both European and non-European cultures. We can see hints of a realization of this kind in an article on Romantic poetry (1823) by the writer and critic Orest Somov:

> But how many diverse peoples have merged under the single name of Russians or depend on Russia, separated neither by the expanse of alien lands nor by wide seas! There are so many diverse appearances, mores, customs which present themselves to the searching eye in the one volume of aggregate Russia! . . . And thus, Russian poets, without leaving the boundaries of their motherland, can fly across from the stern and somber legends of the North to the opulent and brilliant fancies of the East; from the educated mind and taste of Europeans to the crude and unaffected mores of hunting and nomadic peoples.[19]

No doubt, a recognition of the essentially synthetic nature of the Russian national project during this period was aided by the highly improbable but nevertheless true circumstance that practically none of Russia's major Romantic writers was a pure ethnic Russian. Zhukovsky, Russia's first Romantic poet and a major translator from German, English, and ancient Greek, was the son of a Turkish woman. Pushkin was descended from an Ethiopian prince on his mother's side, a fact that played

---

17. Nikolay V. Gogol, *Sobranie sochinenii v semi tomakh*, vol. 6 (Moscow: 1984), 193, 194. It is quite ironic, of course, that the translation Gogol praised so highly was done from a German translation of the *Odyssey* rather than from the Greek. But since Gogol himself was unacquainted with Greek, he was ill-equipped to perceive the irony.

18. See, for example, S. S. Averintsev, "Razmyshleniia nad perevodami Zhukovskogo," in *Zhukovskii i literatura kontsa XVIII–XIX veka*, ed. V. Iu. Troitskii (Moscow: 1988), 255–74.

19. Quoted in Katya Hokanson, "Literary Imperialism, *Narodnost'* and Pushkin's Invention of the Caucasus," *Russian Review* 53 (1994): 34.

a central role in his personal biographical myth and in his poetic persona.[20] Gogol's father was Ukrainian, and so, like Zhukovsky, he was only half Russian. And, finally, Lermontov's ancestry was Scottish on his father's side.

In any case, the connection between the culture's peculiar synthetic essence and Russia's manifest destiny was already made clear in Gogol's essays on Pushkin and translation written only a decade or so after Somov's essay. Gogol emphasized what he saw as Pushkin's protean nature, declaring him to have been a perfect instrument for poetic translation and, as a result, the model Russian:

> In Spain he is a Spaniard, with a Greek, a Greek — in the Caucasus —
> a free mountaineer, in the full sense of the term; with an older person he breathes the passage of time in olden days; should he glance toward a peasant in his hut — he is completely Russian from head to toe: all the features of our nature were echoed in him. . . . Our poetry has tried all the chords, was nurtured by the poetry of all the peoples, listened to the lyres of all the poets, attained some sort of world-wide language, so that it could prepare everyone for a more meaningful service.[21]

The most vigorous attempt to create an explicit national ideology by linking the national project with an ethos of translation, however, was performed by Fyodor Dostoyevsky, who knew well both the Russian religious culture that had spawned the theory of Moscow as the third Rome and the secular imperial culture of post-Napoleonic Russia. He argues his case frequently in the course of his *Diary of a Writer,*

20. In his youth, Pushkin was called "the African" by his school chums. Later in life, he mentioned the fact of his African ancestry in his poetry and wrote (but never finished) a prose work entitled "The Blackamoor of Peter the Great" about his maternal great-grandmother.

21. Hokanson, "Literary Imperialism," 20, 21. It is worth mentioning that the desire expressed by Gogol to identify a national poet whose work would somehow stand for the entire country's spiritual strivings was a typical one for European romantic culture. It was precisely in this period that one finds the creation of the cult of Shakespeare in England and of Goethe in Germany. Less-developed countries tended, in this as in other areas, to follow suit; thus, the 1840s and 1850s saw the apotheosis of Mickiewicz in Poland, Petöffi in Hungary, and Njegoš in Serbia. Only in Russia, however, was the national poet praised for his ability not to epitomize but to transcend his native culture.

a heterogeneous work concerned primarily with two central and related historical themes: the development of European civilization and Slavdom's (read Russia's) relation to that development in the past, the present, and (most important) the future. Both themes are discussed within a millenarian framework. As Gary Saul Morson puts it:

> The central—and certainly the most frequently repeated—theme of the monthly Diary [is] . . . that the apocalypse is literally imminent. In countless articles, the author argues that social "fragmentation," "dissociation," and "isolation" have reached such an extreme that the "final battle" is almost certainly near. And as promised in the Revelation to St. John, he contends, that battle will be followed by the millennium—which, for him, means a worldwide utopia headed by Russia and based on the Russian Orthodox faith.[22]

The millennium is not merely a miraculous promise to be accepted on faith; it is fully historicized and will issue forth directly and logically from the nation's past.

Contemporary Europe, in Dostoyevsky's view, was on the verge of collapse. Of course, this had been the contention of the Slavophiles as early as the 1830s. But Petr Kireevsky, Aleksei Khomiakov, and Ivan and Konstantin Aksakov, for all their idealization of the Russian past and Russia's potential, realized that Russia had a great deal of internal work to do before it could even fantasize about a place on the world-historical stage. As a result, their discussions of Europe's senescence were meant primarily to show Russians the bankruptcy of a European-style modernity rather than as clarion calls for national glory in the here and now. As far as Dostoyevsky was concerned, however, the Russians were ready to take the leading, world-historical role from a faltering Europe in his own day.

And what is the "word" that the Russians possess and which will allow theirs to become the ultimate word? "Our mission and our role are not at all like those of other nations, for there each separate people lives exclusively for itself and in itself, while we will begin, now that the time has come, precisely by becoming the servants of all for universal peace-making. And this is in no way something to be ashamed of; on

22. Gary Saul Morson, *The Boundaries of Genre* (Austin: University of Texas Press, 1981), 33.

the contrary, this constitutes our greatness because it all leads to the ultimate unity of humankind."[23] Here Dostoyevsky's historical system takes a definite turn toward millenarianism; for if the meaning of history is the harmonious union of all humankind and if the Russian Orthodox ideal (which is about to be realized) is identical to it, then it follows that history is about to come to an end.

Necessarily, Dostoyevsky followed two strategies to convince himself and his readers of the soundness of his views. On the one hand, he eagerly scanned the periodical press for signs of Europe's imminent demise. On the other hand, he sought for evidence in Russia of the ripening of the Russian ideal. As far as the demise of Europe went, evidence seemed abundant, and Dostoyevsky gleefully pointed out trends indicating the decay of the rational West.[24] On the positive side, Dostoyevsky finds his strongest evidence for his claim of Russia's universality in literary history. Clearly building on Gogol's theories, Dostoyevsky finds the Russian ideal expressed most strongly in the works of Pushkin (and, to a lesser extent, Lev Tolstoy).

Dostoyevsky's ultimate statement of this belief was in the speech he delivered at the unveiling of the first monument to Pushkin in 1880. "In fact," the author claimed,

> in European literatures there were artistic geniuses of immense magnitude—Shakespeares, Cervanteses, Schillers. But point to even one of these geniuses who could have possessed such an aptitude for universal responsiveness as our Pushkin. And this very capability, the major capability of our nationality, he precisely shares with our people, and by virtue of this he is preeminently a national poet. Even

23. "Utopicheskoe ponimanie istorii," *Diary of a Writer,* June 1876 (F. M. Dostoyevsky, *Polnoe sobranie sochinenii v tridtsati tomakh,* vol. 23 [Leningrad: 1972–1990], 47). Translations are mine.

24. See, for example, the following quote from the August 1880 *Diary:* "The fourth estate is coming, it is knocking and banging on the door, and if the door is not opened, it will break it down. It does not want the former ideals and rejects all previously existing law. It will not make compromises or concessions and buttresses will not save the building. Concessions only make them more fired up and they want everything. Something is coming that no one can imagine. All their parliamentarism, all the governmental theories now professed, all the riches that have been accumulated, the banks, science, the yids—all of this will crash irreversibly in a moment" (Dostoyevsky, "Dve polovinki," 167–68).

the greatest of the European poets themselves were never able to embody with such strength as Pushkin the genius of an alien, perhaps neighboring people—its spirit, all the repressed depth of this spirit and all its longing for its mission, as Pushkin could show it. On the contrary, turning to foreign nations, the European poets usually reincarnated them in their own nationality, and understood them in their own way. Even in Shakespeare, his Italians, for example, are almost everywhere the very same Englishmen. Pushkin alone of all world poets has the virtue of reincarnating himself wholly into an alien nationality.[25]

The idea that Russian self-definition in the nineteenth century was closely tied with the idea of translation is not entirely new.[26] In what follows, however, I shall attempt to extend these notions into new territory, trying to explain certain seemingly disparate phenomena relating to the continued popularity of translation in the broad sense in twentieth-century Russian culture. The connection between these phenomena and the better known situation of the nineteenth century has not been made, I believe, because it has seemed to scholars that the objective reasons for the existence of a translation culture had by and large disappeared in Russia by the end of the nineteenth century. After all, by the beginning of the twentieth century Russia appeared to have achieved a balance of cultural trade with Western Europe: This was the time when Ivan Turgenev, Dostoyevsky, and Tolstoy took the European literary scene by storm; and the popularity of Sergey Diaghilev's *Ballets Russes* indicates that Russia was playing a central role in contemporary European culture as well. Nevertheless, Russian culture retained the synthesizing impulses it had developed as a reaction to the long years of cultural dependence. By the early twentieth century, however, the synthesizing urge expressed itself in some unexpected ways. In particular, Russian cultural theory began to link the cult of the future to a cult of the past.

Already in the nineteenth century there had been a tendency to search for the bases of Russia's manifest destiny, not merely in her future

25. Quoted in Hokanson, "Literary Imperialism," 23–24.
26. See, for example, Katya Elizabeth Hokanson, "Empire of the Imagination: Orientalism and the Construction of Russian National Identity in Pushkin, Marlinskii, Lermontov, and Tolstoi" (Ph.D. diss., Stanford University, 1994).

potential but in some objective past. In his article on Zhukovsky as translator of the *Odyssey,* for example, Gogol closed by saying that

> the *Odyssey* will have an affect on those suffering from their European perfection. It will recall to them much from that sublime infancy which has (alas!) been lost, but which humankind must recreate for itself as its rightful heritage. Many will be forced to think about much. And meanwhile, much from patriarchal times with which there is such a strong connection in the Russian nature will waft invisibly across the face of the Russian land.[27]

Russia's unique potential, Gogol claimed, grows from the fact that Russians are the only modern nation to have retained a sense of their idyllic childhood.[28] This thought is the inchoate expression of a complex of ideas that will eventually link primitivism and utopianism in an attempt to overcome the mundane present. Russians, it will be claimed, can be universal translators not simply because they will be able to sum up world culture but because they can still access a universal past.

In *Diary of a Writer,* Dostoyevsky, characteristically, makes the Gogolian equation even clearer, practically inviting others to search for signs of universality in earlier times, as well as in the present: "I dare to state that the fact that Russia will be able to say the word of living life to humankind in the future lies in the foundations of the Russian nation."[29] It was precisely this invitation that was taken up by a number of linguistic thinkers who sought to create, through Russian, a universal language for mankind.

Of course, universal language theories are by no means unique to Russia. The desire to overcome the problems that resulted from the confusion of tongues at Babel occupied many of the best European philo-

27. Gogol, *Sobranie,* 200.

28. It is curious that Gogol's metaphorical appeal to the existence of an idyllic national childhood appears before any expression of a Russian ideology of actual childhood. When the Russian view of childhood crystallized, however, it agreed exactly with Gogol's version. Andrew Wachtel, *The Battle for Childhood: Creation of a Russian Myth* (Stanford, Calif.: Stanford University Press, 1990), provides more details.

29. Dostoyevsky, "Nechto o Peterburgskom Baden-Badenstve," *Diary of a Writer,* July–August 1876 (vol. 23, 58).

sophical minds from the seventeenth century.[30] Russia, however, has been a major source of such theories, which have ranged from scientifically responsible (albeit usually quixotic) attempts to reconstruct protolanguages or build ideal communications systems, to insane and sometimes sinister parodies of such efforts. What is more, in Russia, theories of this sort easily take on a political dimension, since they jibe so well with the peculiar character of Russian imperialist thought. This is true even in those cases, which are in fact rather frequent, when the theories in question have clear utopian tendencies.

The most energetic proponent of universal language theories in the first decades of the century was the futurist poet Velimir Khlebnikov, a distinctive genius but a man whose linguistic thought can be taken as representative of at least one branch of Russian modernist cultural thinking. Echoes of his personal universalist mythology can be seen in his self-chosen first name, which means "world ruler," as well as in the titles bestowed on him by his fellow futurist poets — "first president of the globe" and "king of time." Of course, the titles point to Khlebnikov's utopian dreams of conquering both space and time. Politically, Khlebnikov was a devout Russian nationalist. Indeed, the impetus for his theorizing was his personal feeling of shame at Russia's humiliation in the Russo-Japanese War of 1904–5.

Khlebnikov's 1919 declaration "To the Artists of the World!" marks the apotheosis of his linguistic thinking. The poet begins the manifesto with the announcement that his long-sought (and now achieved) goal has been the creation of "a common written language . . . that can be understood and accepted by our entire star [sic]." It turns out that this language is not so much a creation as a rediscovery, however. There was once a time, in the prehistoric past, when "words served to dispel enmity and make the future transparent and peaceful, and when languages, proceeding in stages, united the people of (1) a cave, (2) a settlement, (3) a tribe or kinship group, (4) a state, into a single rational world. . . . One savage caveman understood another and laid his blind weapon

30. For the best short treatment of this subject, see George Steiner, *After Babel: Aspects of Language and Translation,* 2d ed. (New York: Oxford University Press, 1992), 207–15. See also Marina Yaguello, *Lunatic Lovers of Language: Imaginary Languages and Their Inventors,* trans. Catherine Slater (Rutherford, N.J.: Fairleigh Dickinson University Press, 1991), 15–22.

aside."[31] The goal of poetic creation and historical/linguistic research is to rediscover this protolanguage. The poet must therefore abandon linguistic history in favor of linguistic prehistory; the historian of language becomes its archeologist. Poetic creation in this new/old language will lead to universal understanding and the re-creation of paradise lost. "Mute graphic marks will reconcile the cacophony of languages,"[32] and humankind in general.

The rest of Khlebnikov's manifesto explains what he believes to be the inherent meaning of each letter of the alphabet. The specifics of these claims are not of interest to us here, but their main thrust is to discover a connection between the shapes of the graphemes of Russian consonants (vowels play no role here) and the types of words they begin. Thus for example, because of its shape the grapheme "X" is seen naturally to begin words that define things that "protect the point of man from the hostile point of bad weather, cold, or enemies."[33] The fact that twenty such words in Russian do in fact begin with "X" is taken as proof of the theory's validity. It is curious that Khlebnikov's theory implies the priority of written over oral language (or at least their simultaneity), making him something of a precursor to Jacques Derrida. The theory is also synesthetic; that is, sounds are linked to the hieroglyphs that should be used to represent them, and to appropriate colors, thus allowing for the creation of works of art that could transcend media boundaries.[34]

At the end of the manifesto, Khlebnikov presents his own version of a sentence in Russian "translated" into his proposed universal "zaum" ("transsense" or "beyondsense" language). The sentence he chose to translate is in itself extremely suggestive, because it illustrates the close ties between the types of historical events that interested the poet and the language proper for describing them. Of all possible sentences, Khlebnikov provides the following for the purposes of illustration.

31. Velimir Khlebnikov, "To the Artists of the World!" in *The King of Time,* trans. Paul Schmidt, ed. Charlotte Douglas (Cambridge, Mass.: Harvard University Press, 1985), 146.
32. Khlebnikov, *King of Time,* 147.
33. Khlebnikov, *King of Time,* 149.
34. In this area Khlebnikov's utopian project overlaps with that of the Russian composer and mystic Scriabin, who attempted to create an instrument to link musical sounds with appropriate colors. Khlebnikov was enamored of Scriabin.

Соединившись вместе, орды гуннов и готов, собравшись кругом Аттилы, полны боевого воодушевления, двинулись далее вместе, но, встреченные и отраженные Аэцием, защитником Рима, рассеялись на множество шаек и остановились и успокоились на своей земле, разлившись в степях, заполняя их пустоту.[35]

[Having linked up and gathered around Attila, the hordes of Huns and Goths, filled with martial enthusiasm, moved forward together. But having been engaged and repulsed by Aetius, the defender of Rome, they scattered into a multitude of bands. They halted and settled down peacefully on their own land, spilled out into the steppes, and filled their emptiness.]

Khlebnikov gives two "zaum" versions of the sentence, which are presumably meant to be synonymous:

Ша + со (гуннов и готов), *вэ* Аттилы, *ча по, со до*, но *бо + эо* Аэция, *хо* Рима, *со мо вэ + ка со, ло ша* степей + *ча*

Or, alternatively,

Вэ со человеческого рода *бэ го* языков, *пэ* умов *вэ со ша* языков, *бо мо* слов *мо ка* разума *ча* звуков *по со до лу* земли *мо со* языков *вэ* земли.

It will be noted, of course, that both "universal" texts are written in Cyrillic letters and that, in addition to monosyllables, they contain recognizable Russian words. But a recognition of the Russocentric bias at the basis for his universal language seems to have eluded Khlebnikov.

Then, and this is far more surprising and significant, Khlebnikov provides what a professional would call a back translation from "zaum" into Russian. It is, of course, well known that a back translation is unlikely to reproduce the original sentence, since the initial translation was merely an approximation of the original, and the back translation is an approximation of an approximation. In this particular case, however, the back translation is not so much a distant echo of the original as an interpretation of its "true" meaning. Presumably (since Khlebni-

35. The Russian text for this section of the manifesto is cited from Khlebnikov, *Tvoreniia* (Moscow: 1991), 623. The English translation is mine.

kov provides no information as to how the translation process works, we are forced to presume), although this new sentence does not much resemble the original on the surface, we are meant to believe that they are equivalent—that is, that their semantic deep structures are identical. Far from being a random nonsense language, then, "zaum" appears to be a sort of deep structural code that mediates between different versions of the same thought, allowing the poet/seer to decode the hidden meaning of ordinary linguistic signs.

Думая о соединении человеческого рода, но столкнувшись с горами языков, бурный огонь наших умов, вращаясь около соединенного заумного языка, достигая распылением слов на единицы мысли в оболочке звуков, бурно и вместе идет к признанию на всей земле единого заумного языка.

[Thinking about the unification of humankind but running up against the mountains of languages, the energetic flame of our minds turns to the unity of beyondsense language, achieving the scattering of words into thought units cloaked in sound, and energetically and in concert moves toward the acceptance of a single beyondsense language for the entire world.]

The wars between Rome and the barbarians, the conflicts between East and West, turn out to have been signs of humankind's ultimate desire for unity. A specific historical event had within itself the latent seeds of utopia, but their presence could only be divined by the poet through his "translation" of the words used to describe them. Through translation, Khlebnikov claims to have apprehended the hidden meaning of history.

Khlebnikov's linguistic research, striving as it does to recognize in modern Russian the outline of a universal language (one that had existed in the past and would do so again in the future), had, as we will see a bit later, numerous and extremely diverse followers in the Soviet Union. Before examining them, however, we must pause to consider for a moment the local historical events Khlebnikov uses to make his universalist point, because his choice for translation purposes of a sentence describing an attack on Western civilization by hordes from the East was by no means accidental. For nineteenth-century advocates of the synthetic nature of Russian civilization such as Gogol and Dostoyevsky,

Russia would be the civilization of the future, in part because she was not part of the rational, individualistic, now-decadent West. Instead, Russia was perceived as the heir to the Christian church's spiritual tradition, embodied in Byzantine and Hellenic culture. This version of universalism was still Eurocentric, however; after all, Homer has generally been seen as a foundation of West European civilization as well. Therefore, it was only natural for later thinkers to reason that if Russia's distance from Western Europe was an asset, then her connection with the civilizations of the East was at least as important as her Byzantine heritage. Starting with the thought of the Russian religious philosopher Vladimir Solov'ev at the end of the nineteenth century and culminating in the so-called Eurasian historical theories of Nikolay Trubetskoy, a view developed that saw Russian civilization as a counterweight to that of Europe. Russia, it was asserted, was at least as much Asian as she was European. As Trubetskoy put it:

> The political unification of Eurasia was first accomplished by the Turanians in the person of Genghis Khan; these Turanian nomads were the first bearers of the idea of a common Eurasian state system. Later the Turanians' statist zeal degenerated as a national religious revival spread rapidly among the Russians, and the idea of a common Eurasian state passed from the Turanians to the Russians, who became its inheritors and bearers. It was now possible for Russia-Eurasia to become a self-contained cultural, political, and economic region and to develop a unique Eurasian culture.[36]

And while Trubetskoy himself was no imperialist (his goal, rather, was to oppose what he saw as the imperialism of Romano-German thought), others were far more willing to refigure the old Russian claim to universalism in a Eurasian key. This ideology is transparent in one of the last poems of Aleksandr Blok, entitled "Scythians" (1918?). The poem starts with an epigraph by Solov'ev, lines which in their original context expressed an ambivalent acceptance of what Solov'ev predicted to be the coming destruction from the East: "Panmongolism! Uncouth name, but music to my ear." Blok's own poem begins as follows:

36. Nikolai Trubetskoy, *The Legacy of Genghis Khan* (Ann Arbor: University of Michigan Press, 1991), 221.

You have your millions. We are numberless,
numberless, numberless. Try doing
    battle with us! Yes, we are Scythians! Yes,
Asiatics with greedy eyes slanting!

    For you, the centuries; for us, one hour.
We, like obedient lackeys, have held up
    a shield dividing two embattled powers —
the Mongol hordes and Europe!

·   ·   ·   ·   ·   ·   ·   ·   ·   ·

    Russia is a sphinx. Grieving, jubilant,
and covering herself with blood
    she looks, she looks, she looks at you — her slant
eyes lit with hatred and with love.

·   ·   ·   ·   ·   ·   ·   ·   ·   ·

    All things we love — the mystic's divine gift,
the fever of cold calculus;
    all we appreciate — the Frenchman's shaft
of wit, the German's genius . . .[37]

The idea that Russia is a mediating civilization between East and
West — and the belief that she has a special ability to appreciate all cultures, to absorb them without actually being a part of them — is, as we
have seen, a typical component of modern Russian nationalist thought.
The new concern for the East and Russia's new self-definition as — at
least in part — an Asiatic country, naturally brought in its wake a re-
doubling of translation efforts. For while the eighteenth and nineteenth
centuries had seen the assimilation of European literary culture into
Russian through translation, the literary heritage of the East had been of
relatively minor importance. Now, practically every major Russian poet
turned his attention to the poetry of peoples stretching from the Caucasus through central Asia and to the far East. In 1916, for example, Valery
Briusov edited a large and excellent anthology of Armenian poetry
(*Poezii Armenii s drev-neishikh vremen do nashikh dnei* [The Poetry of
Armenia from Ancient Times to Today]), a work for which he enlisted

37. Aleksandr Blok, *The Twelve and Other Poems*, trans. Jon Stallworthy and Peter
France (New York: Oxford University Press, 1970), 161–62.

the help of what amounts to a who's who of Russian poetry. The Russian symbolist poet Konstantin Bal'mont was himself practically a one-man translation factory, both in Russia before the revolution and in emigration afterward, producing translations from Georgian, Armenian, Mongolian, Japanese, and Hindi. Bal'mont was dubbed by Osip Mandelshtam "a translator by calling, by birth, even in his most original works ... the rare case of a typical translation without an original."[38] Nor was a fascination with the East limited to the symbolist poets, who saw it as a source of apocalyptic energy. The acmeist Nikolay Gumilev produced an entire book of free translations of Chinese poetry, and Mandelshtam and Pasternak both translated from the Georgian, as well as from European languages.

Of course, at this stage it may well be argued that there is a big difference between the theoretical outlook of poets and the activities of the Soviet state. Just because poets believed that Russia's destiny was to put an end to Western civilization by incorporating it into her own Eurasian synthesis does not mean that the government endorsed such a project. Nevertheless, it is not difficult to see a debased version of the same mentality in the statements of the leading Bolshevik spokesman on the nationalities question: Joseph Stalin. In an article entitled "The October Revolution and the National Question," Stalin sounded a prosaic theme that, except for a Marxist overlay, does not differ all that much from the poetic version advanced by Blok at about the same time: "The October Revolution [used throughout the article as a metonym for Soviet Russia] by establishing a tie between the peoples of the backward East and of the advanced West, is ranging them in a common camp of struggle against imperialism."[39] Naturally, this is not to say that Blok influenced Stalin, or vice versa; merely that such views of Russia were common currency at about this time, available for use in stunning poetry or practical prose, for utopian projects or imperialist designs.

In this context, it is not surprising that the Soviet state turned out to be an extremely active sponsor of translations.[40] Considering that

38. Osip Mandelshtam, "On the Nature of the Word," in *The Complete Critical Prose and Letters,* trans. Jane Gary Harris and Constance Link (Ann Arbor, Mich.: Ardis, 1979), 125.
39. Joseph Stalin, *Works,* vol. 4 (Moscow: 1953), 168.
40. According to the American scholar Lauren G. Leighton: "Translations outnumber original works in Soviet publishing. . . . According to official statistics cited by

in its early days the new state espoused a typically Russian universalist policy (worldwide "permanent" revolution advanced theoretically by Parvus and Trotsky) based on a doctrine imported from Europe, it was probably inevitable that Soviet imperialism would replay the moves that were characteristic of Russian nationalist thought at the beginning of the nineteenth century.[41] Rather than imposing the Russian language on all the peoples of the Soviet Union (and those beyond her borders who would eventually join the communist fold), the Soviet leadership developed a nationalities policy that called for the development of cultures which would be "socialist in content, national in form." Such a policy, naturally, required extensive translation of Russian-language materials into the literally hundreds of languages that were spoken in the territory of the U.S.S.R. (which also entailed the provision of alphabets for previously illiterate peoples), as well as translation into Russian of the cultural monuments of these peoples. One of the cornerstones of this policy was the founding by Maksim Gorky (at Lenin's behest) of the publishing house World Literature. In his manifesto-like statement of purpose introducing the series to be published by this house, Gorky announced that, although the first group of works translated were to be from Western European languages, "in the future 'World Literature' intends to acquaint the Russian reader with the literature of the middle ages, the literature of Russia and other Slavic countries, as well as the exemplary thought and verbal creations of the East — with the belles lettres of India, Persia, China, Japan, and the Arabs."[42] And indeed, the

---

Antokolsky in a speech on Soviet translation, 44.6% of all books produced in 1953 [a fairly xenophobic year, it might be added] were translations of foreign fiction. . . . A. Leytes once surveyed the leading journal *Novyi mir* (New World) for the year 1953 and found that its issues contained twenty-five original poems and forty-nine poems translated from eighteen languages" (*Two Worlds, One Art* [Dekalb: Northern Illinois University Press, 1991], 17–18).

41. Even though the idea of permanent revolution was later denounced in favor of the concept of "a revolution in one country," the belief that the whole world would eventually follow Russia's path to communism was never abandoned. Nor could it have been, because to have done so would have been to abandon the basic historical belief of Marxism — that all societies must inevitably pass through the same stages on the way to communism, the final and most perfect one.

42. Quoted in *Russkie pisateli o perevode*, ed. Iu. Levin and A. Fedorov (Leningrad: 1960), 588. As Leighton puts it: "Gorky's World Literature belongs among the most ambitious Soviet Great Projects. The goal of the newly founded Soviet school was the

World Literature series did eventually come to include works from all these national traditions.[43]

At the same time, gigantic efforts were made to develop the languages and literatures of minority groups within the U.S.S.R. Of course, this work was generally carried out at the behest of a state whose capital was Moscow and whose elite was heavily Russian. But although it is easy to say that such efforts were made cynically, primarily in order to make possible more effective propaganda, the fact remains that the work was done in this way and not by simply ignoring the local languages and cultures as is the standard practice of other imperialist powers. Much of the work was done from a Russocentric viewpoint, however, as the following account (originally published in *Pravda*) makes clear. In a speech given in 1949, S. K. Kenesbayev, a member of the Kazakh Republic Academy of Sciences, is reported to have said that

> The Kazakh people, resurrected by the great October [revolution], have become one of the socialist nations endowed with its own Soviet statehood and its own rich culture, national in form and socialist in content — thanks to the correct realization of the Leninist-Stalinist national policy. As a result of the historic successes attained in the years of the Soviet rule by the Kazakh people in both the economic and cultural spheres, the Kazakh language is beginning to develop rapidly. Its vocabulary, grammar and phonetics are being perfected, and standards for the literary language have been set. The speaker noted that the Russian language has exercised and is exercising a beneficial influence on the growth and development of the Kazakh literary language. Arabic writing was a force of oppression in the hands of reactionary forces — the beys and the Moslem clergy. The contemporary Kazakh alphabet and orthography are built mainly on the correct principle of completely borrowing the Russian alpha-

---

translation of all world literature — every world classic in all languages of all times, peoples and cultures" (*Two Worlds*, 7).

43. Ironically enough, although the ostensible purpose of translation was propagandistic, at certain periods translated literature was the one area in which Russians could avoid reading socialist realism. Thus, for example, the translation of J. D. Salinger's *Catcher in the Rye* (Boston: Little, Brown, 1959) opened the door for an entire generation of Russian experimental writers in the early 1960s.

bet while taking into account the peculiarities of the contemporary Kazakh language.[44]

Here is a perfect recipe for the Soviet combination of imperialism and translation. The Kazakh language was allowed to develop, even flourish, but only as a vehicle for the expression of Soviet (read Russian)– dominated content, and even the language's external form was brought as close as possible to that of Russian. What is not noted by *Pravda* and what is even more striking was the tendency, in republics of this sort, for the Soviet government to send eager young Russian poets to compose heroic epics (presumed to be the proper first stage of literary development) for such peoples. Thus, it sometimes happened that the great epic of, say, the Kazakh or Tatar peoples appeared in print for the first time not in the original but in a Russian translation, a translation that, needless to say, might have corrected any mistakes that lurked in the original, if, indeed, any original existed. The philosophy underlying such corrections was accepted, publicly at least, by the major translators themselves. Certainly, their formulations are a perfect statement of the ways in which imperialism and translation were reconciled by Soviet culture. This is what Semen Lipkin, a major translator from Central Asian languages, had to say on the subject: "An artistic translation can no longer confine itself to the noble aim of 'acquainting peoples with peoples.' It now has an aim even more fine, an even more difficult and distinguished aim . . . to establish the community of socialist nations."[45]

The most striking example of this sort concerns the "poetry" of the Kazakh bard Dzhambul Dzhabaev. In a sense, Dzhabaev was a twentieth-century Ossian, the creation of a Russian poet and journalist who claimed to have written down and translated a few poems of a Kazakh folk singer. The party leader of Kazakhstan saw the poems, realized the potential they had for currying favor with the center, and ordered an ode to Stalin by this great poet. The problem was that there was no original poet. As reported in the putative memoirs of Dmitry Shostakovich:

---

44. *The Soviet Linguistic Controversy,* trans. John V. Murra, Robert M. Hankin, and Fred Holling (New York: King's Crown Press, 1951), 7.
45. Quoted in Leighton, *Two Worlds,* 19.

Dzhambul Dzhabaev existed as a person, and the Russian texts of his poems existed too, the translations that is. Only the originals never existed. Dzhambul Dzhabaev may have been a good man, but he was not a poet. I suppose he might have been, but no one cared, because the so-called translations of the nonexistent poems were written by Russian poets and they didn't even ask our great folk singer for permission. And if they had wanted to ask they couldn't have, because these translators didn't know a word of Kazakh and Dzhambul didn't know a word of Russian.[46]

In the area of linguistics, developments in the Soviet Union paralleled those in literature. Responsible Soviet and Russian linguists were fascinated by questions regarding the origins of human language, as well as the possibility of creating universal languages. Such theoretical interests led to careful study of many unusual languages of the Soviet Union and ingenious attempts to reconstruct a "Nostratic" which connects proto–Indo European with a number of other language groups. In less scrupulous hands, however, these same theories easily became instruments for a specifically Russian-style imperialism—one that translates from and into such languages with the goal of incorporating them, one way or another, into the future universal Russian state.

The paradoxical union of translation and imperialism can be found most clearly in one of the most notorious episodes in the history of Soviet science: the Soviet cooptation of the linguistic theories of Nikolai Marr. Marr, it must be emphasized, was half Georgian and half Scottish, and he made no attempt to advance the candidacy of Russian either as the former universal language or as the basis for some future one. However, Marr's version of linguistic universalist thought clearly reflected the Russian scholarly and amateur linguistic traditions in which he was trained. He pushed for the recognition of the so-called Japhetic languages—including Georgian, Basque, and a few others—as the world's oldest (while rejecting, by the way, any theories of a former univer-

46. Dmitry Shostakovich, *Testimony: The Memoirs of Dmitri Shostakovich*, ed. Solomon Volkov, trans. Antonina W. Bouis (New York: Harper and Row, 1979). This book itself, by the way, may be a similar type of mystification, for it is uncertain that Volkov ever really interviewed Shostakovich for it. However, like many of the other anecdotes in the book, the story about Dzhambul appears to be true even if Shostakovich never told it.

sal language). At the same time, he insisted that in the utopian future humankind would develop a single language:

> No individual language, however widespread its use as an instrument of imperialism, is fit to be this single language of the future. All the languages which were at one time international are now dead; all languages, whatever their spread, whether they are minor or major in terms of the number of their speakers, whether they emanate as class languages from the upper strata of society or, on the contrary, are more vigourous productions of the masses — they will perish in like manner; nor will they be replaced by any of these ersatz human languages — the Esperantos, Idos and the like — which are sprouting up nowadays like mushrooms, nor by any of the languages which individual acts of creation may offer us in the future. This common language of future mankind will have to contain all the richness, all the qualities of dead languages as well as of languages living at this moment, but destined to die. The omni-expressive, single language of the future is the inevitable concomitant of a future human society without classes or nationalities.[47]

The utopian quality of Marr's work, plus his hostility to Indo-European linguistics (rejected as "the purest expression of decadent bourgeois society founded on the oppression of the peoples of the East beneath the yoke of a savage European colonial policy")[48] and perhaps their common Georgian origin, was probably what attracted Stalin to his work. Very cleverly, Stalin used Marrism as "a cover-up for a policy of Russification which was intensified at the end of the thirties."[49] Although continuing to insist that local languages were of primary importance, Stalin organized state linguistic policy in such a way that if the universal language of the future were to have arisen from worldwide socialist culture (as the theory predicted), its primary parent would have to have been Russian. While it might appear that Soviet policies in literature and linguistics were preferable to the arrogant dismissal practiced by other imperializing cultures, it should be noted that those policies, by their very openness, at least provoked oppositional practices. The Soviet

47. Quoted in Yaguello, *Lunatic Lovers,* 176.
48. Yaguello, *Lunatic Lovers,* 70.
49. Yaguello, *Lunatic Lovers,* 79.

approach, by contrast, was far more invidious, creating the literatures of the cultures that it was destroying, practicing translation and imperialism simultaneously. In this respect, nothing can surpass the odes to Stalin composed in most of the Soviet national languages and translated into Russian.[50] This sort of publication, praising in Russian translation the Georgian despot who spouted a dogma of European origin, surely marks the perfection of a vision of Russia as a universal imperium.

In a broader sense, the entire Soviet cultural project represents merely an extension of the universalizing translation project that had already been felt intuitively as Russia's mission in the nineteenth century. But now this project moved from the utopian dream of a Dostoyevsky to a state-sponsored enterprise guided by the knowledge that history had come to an end. In its maximalist formula,

> socialist realism was proclaimed the heir to all progressive art of all periods of world history. As to the reactionary art of each period, it was to be forgotten and stricken from the annals of history; the only possible reason for preserving anything at all was to illustrate the forces hostile to genuine, progressive art. Thus, since socialist realism shared the "historical optimism," "love of the people," "love of life," "genuine humanism," and other positive properties characteristic of all art expressing the interests of the oppressed and progressive classes everywhere in all historical periods, it acquired the right to use any progressive art of the past as a model.[51]

One might have assumed that the collapse of the Soviet imperial project would have sounded the death knell for theories of Russian universalism. But what is beyond the realm of possibility in practice nevertheless dies hard in the cultural sphere. The continuing resonance of theories combining Russian imperialist dreams with claims of linguistic universality as seen through translation can be seen in a curious article published recently in the Russian nationalist newspaper *Za Russkoe Delo*

50. See, for example, the collection entitled *Tvorchestvo narodov SSSR* (Moscow: 1937), which includes Russian versions of poems dedicated to the "Stalin Constitution" translated from Armenian, Lezgian, Georgian, Kazakh, Farsi, Belorussian, Ukrainian, and Uzbek. Also included in the same volume are excerpts from Kazakh, Kirgiz, Kalmyk, and Kurdish epics.

51. Boris Groys, *The Total Art of Stalinism*, trans. Charles Rougle (Princeton, N.J.: Princeton University Press, 1992), 46.

(No. 5, 1994, pp. 2–3). The author, one Petr Oreshkin (whose surname, by the way, means "nut" in English), announces that his linguistic researches have proved that the unitary language spoken by the builders of the tower of Babel was proto-Slavic. He then goes on to show that Etruscan was a Slavic language, as was the language of ancient Egypt. And what follows from the discovery that the world's original language was Slavic, a fact that has been proven through a complicated process of translation? It is quite simple and, in the context of this essay, not surprising—translation leads directly to imperialism: "We were given 'THE CRUCIAL WORD.' It was broken up and we have been running around in its shards—the 'guinea pigs' of a global tragi-comic experiment. But had our language remained unified, had it not been purposely broken up—in our place today there might have been the experimenters themselves." The author's promised book, no doubt, will explain to the modern-day Russians just what they need to do to reconstitute their language. The editor's afterword to this publication makes the connection between linguistic and political matters clear. After attacking specialists who claim that Old Church Slavic was an invented language, the editor adds: "They need to humiliate, to trample on the soul of the Russian people, and thus paralyze their will to national revival."

Shanghai Modern: Reflections on Urban Culture in China in the 1930s

Leo Ou-fan Lee

By 1930, Shanghai had become a bustling cosmopolitan metropolis, the fifth largest city in the world, and China's largest harbor and treaty-port—a city that was already an international legend ("the Paris of Asia") and a world of splendored modernity set apart from the still tradition-bound countryside that was China.[1] Much has been written about Shanghai in Western languages, and the corpus of "popular literature" that contributed to its legendary image bequeaths a dubious legacy. For aside from perpetuating the city's glamour and mystery, it also succeeded in turning the name of the city into a debased verb in the English vocabulary: To "shanghai" is to "render insensible, as by drugs [read opium], and ship on a vessel wanting hands" or to "bring about the performance of an action by deception or force," according to *Webster's Living Dictionary*.[2] At the same time, the negative side of this popular portrait has been in a sense confirmed by Chinese leftist writers and latter-day communist scholars who likewise saw the city as a bas-

---

1. H. J. Lethbridge, introduction to *All about Shanghai: A Standard Guidebook* (1934–35; reprint, Hong Kong: Oxford University Press, 1983), x.

2. An old version of the dictionary was translated and published in Shanghai around this time by the Commercial Press. A representative account of the Shanghai legend for Western tourists can be found in the following: "In the twenties and thirties Shanghai became a legend. No world cruise was complete without a stop in the city. Its name evoked mystery, adventure and licence of every form. In ships sailing to the Far East, residents enthralled passengers with stories of the 'Whore of the Orient.' They described Chinese gangsters, nightclubs that never closed and hotels which supplied heroin on room service. They talked familiarly of warlords, spy rings, international arms dealers and the peculiar delights on offer in Shanghai's brothels. Long before landing, wives dreamed of the fabulous shops; husbands of half an hour in the exquisite grip of a Eurasian girl." Harriet Sargeant, *Shanghai* (London: Jonathan Cape, 1991), 3.

tion of evil, of wanton debauchery and rampant imperialism marked by foreign extraterritoriality—a city of shame for all native patriots. It would not be too hard to transform this narrative into another discourse of Western imperialism and colonialism by focusing on the inhuman exploitation of the urban underclasses by the rich and powerful, both native and foreign.

Although I am naturally drawn to the "political correctness" of such a line of interpretation, I am somewhat suspicious of its totalizing intent. Mao Dun, the avowed leftist writer and an early member of the Chinese Communist Party, inscribes a "contradictory" message even on the very first page of his first novel, *Midnight* [*Ziye*], subtitled *A Romance of China, 1930*. Whereas Shanghai under foreign capitalism has a monstrous appearance, the hustle and bustle of the harbor—as I think his rather purple prose seeks to convey—also exudes a boundless energy, as summed up by three words on a neon sign: LIGHT, HEAT, POWER![3] These three words, together with the word NEON, were written originally in English in the Chinese text of *Midnight,* which obviously connotes another kind of "historical truth," the arrival of Western modernity whose consuming power soon frightens the protagonist's father, a member of traditional Chinese gentry from the country, to death. In the first two chapters of the novel, in fact, Mao Dun gives prominent display of a large number of material emblems of this advancing modernity: cars ("three 1930-model Citroens"), electric lights and fans, radios, "foreign-style" mansions (*yang-fang*), sofas, guns (a Browning), cigars, perfume, high-heeled shoes, beauty parlors (in English), jai alai courts, "Grafton gauze," flannel suits, 1930 Parisian summer dresses, Japanese and Swedish matches, silver ashtrays, beer and soda bottles, as well as all forms of entertainment—dancing (fox-trot and tango), "roulette, bordellos, greyhound racing, romantic Turkish baths, dancing girls, film stars."[4] Such modern conveniences and commodities of comfort and consumption were not fantasy items from a writer's imagination; on the contrary, they were part of a new reality which Mao Dun wanted to portray and understand by inscribing it onto his fictional landscape. They are, in short, emblems of China's passage to modernity to which

3. Mao Tun [Dun], *Midnight: A Romance of China, 1930,* trans. Sidney Schapiro, 2d ed. (Beijing: Foreign Languages Press, 1979), 1.
4. Mao Dun, *Ziye* (reprint, Hong Kong: Nanguo, 1973), 1–66.

Mao Dun and other urban writers of his generation reacted with a great deal of ambivalence and anxiety. After all, the English word "modern" (and the French "moderne") received its first Chinese transliteration in Shanghai itself: In popular parlance, the Chinese word *modeng* has the meaning of being "novel and/or fashionable," according to the authoritative Chinese dictionary, *Cihai*. Thus in the Chinese popular imagination, Shanghai and "modern" are natural equivalents. So the beginning point of my inquiry will have to be: What makes Shanghai modern? What made for its modern qualities in a matrix of meaning constructed by both Western and Chinese cultures?

Politically, for a century (from 1843 to 1943) Shanghai was a treaty-port of divided territories. The Chinese sections in the southern part of the city (a walled city) and in the far north (Chapei district) were cut off by the foreign concessions—the International Settlement (British and American) and the adjacent French Concession—which did not come to an end until 1943 during the Second World War, when the Allied nations formally ended the concession system by agreement with China. In these "extraterritorial" zones, Chinese and foreigners lived "in mixed company" (*huayang zachu*) but led essentially separate lives. The two worlds were also bound together by bridges, tram and trolley routes, and other public streets and roads built by the Western powers that extended beyond the concession boundaries. The buildings in the concessions clearly marked the Western hegemonic presence: banks, hotels, churches, cinemas, coffeehouses, restaurants, deluxe apartments, and a racecourse. They served as public markers in a geographical sense, but they were also the concrete manifestations of Western material civilization in which were embedded the checkered history of almost a century of Sino-Western contact.[5] As a result of Western presence, many of the modern facilities of Shanghai's urban life were introduced to the concessions starting in the mid-nineteenth century: These included banks (first introduced in 1848), Western-style streets (1856), gaslight (1865),

5. For studies of the concessions histories, see Shanghai Shi Ziliao Congkan, ed., *Shanghai gonggong zujie shigao* [History of Shanghai's International Settlement] (Shanghai: Shanghai Renmin Chubanshe, 1980); Louis des Courtils, *La concession française de Changhai* (Paris: Libraire du Recueil Sirey, 1934); and Ch. B.-Maybon and Jean Fredet, *Histoire de la concession française de Changhai* (Paris: Librairie Plon, 1929).

electricity (1882), telephones (1881), running water (1884), automobiles (1901), and streetcars (1908).[6] Thus by the beginning of the twentieth century the Shanghai concessions already had the "infrastructure" of a modern city even by Western standards. By the 1930s, Shanghai was on a par with the largest cities of the world.

What made Shanghai into a cosmopolitan metropolis in cultural terms is difficult to define, for it has to do with both "substance" and "appearance" — with a whole fabric of life and style that serves to define its "modern" quality. While obviously determined by economic forces, urban culture is itself the result of a process of both production and consumption. In Shanghai's case, the process involves the growth of both socioeconomic institutions and new forms of cultural activity and expression made possible by the appearance of new public structures and spaces for urban cultural production and consumption. Aspects of the former have been studied by many scholars,[7] but the latter remains to be fully explored. I believe that a cultural map of Shanghai must be drawn on the basis of these new public structures and spaces, together with their implications for the everyday lives of Shanghai residents, both foreign and Chinese. In this essay, I would like first to give a somewhat descriptive narrative so that I can map out what I consider to be significant public structures and places of leisure and entertainment. This will serve as the "material" background for further interpretations of Shanghai's urban culture and of Chinese modernity.

6. Fredet, *Histoire de la concession française*, 13. See also Tang Zhenchang, ed., *Jindai Shanghai fanhua lu* [The splendor of modern Shanghai] (Hong Kong: Shangwu Yinshu Guan, 1993), 240. The first automobile was imported by a Hungarian named Lainz.

7. See Wen-hsin Yeh, "Shanghai Modernity: Commerce and Culture in a Republican City" (unpublished manuscript). I am most grateful to Professor Yeh for her criticism and advice in my writing of this chapter. Another useful guide is Frederic Wakeman and Wen-hsin Yeh, eds., *Shanghai Sojourners* (Berkeley: Institute of East Asian Studies, University of California, Berkeley, 1992). See also Mark Elvin and G. William Skinner, eds., *The Chinese City between Two Worlds* (Stanford, Calif.: Stanford University Press, 1974); Marie-Claire Bergère, *The Golden Age of the Shanghai Bourgeoisie* (Cambridge: Cambridge University Press, 1989); and Christian Heriot, *Shanghai, 1927–1937: Municipal Power, Locality, and Modernization* (Berkeley: University of California Press, 1933).

Architecture and Urban Space "There is no city in the world today with such a variety of architectural offerings, buildings which stand out in welcome contrast to their modern counterparts."[8] This statement implies that Shanghai itself offered a contrast of old and new, Chinese and Western. However, it does not mean that the Chinese occupied only the old sections of the city and the Westerners only the modern. The notorious regulation that barred Chinese and dogs from Western parks was finally abolished in 1928, and the parks were opened to all residents.[9] In fact, the population in the foreign concessions was largely Chinese: more than 1,492,896 in 1933 in a total city population of 3,133,782, of which only about 70,000 were foreigners.[10] But the contrast nevertheless existed in their rituals of life and leisure, which were governed by the ways in which they organized their daily lives. For the Chinese, the foreign concessions represented not so much "forbidden zones" as the "other" world—an "exotic" world of glitter and vice dominated by Western capitalism, as summed up in the familiar phrase *shili yangchang* (literally, "ten-mile-long foreign zone"), which likewise had entered into the modern Chinese vocabulary.[11]

The central place of the *shili yangchang* is the Bund, a strip of embankment facing the Whampoo River at the entrance of the harbor. It is not only the entrance point from the sea but also, without doubt, the window of British colonial power. The harbor skyline was dotted

8. Tess Johnston, *A Last Look: Western Architecture in Old Shanghai* (Hong Kong: Old China Hand Press, 1993), 9.

9. See Robert A. Bickers and Jeffrey N. Wasserstrom, "Shanghai's 'Dogs and Chinese Not Admitted' Sign: Legend, History and Contemporary Symbol," *China Quarterly* 142 (1995): 443–66.

10. Lethbridge, *All about Shanghai,* 33–34. The Chinese population in the International Settlement alone grew from 345,000 to 1,120,000 between 1900 and 1935; see Frederic Wakeman, "Licensing Leisure: The Chinese Nationalist Regulation of Shanghai, 1927–1949," *Journal of Asian Studies* 54 (1995): 22, n. 1.

11. *Yangchang* is defined in one recent Chinese-English dictionary as a "metropolis infested with foreign adventurers (usu. referring to preliberation Shanghai)"; the same book defines *yangchang e'shao* as a "rich young bully in a metropolis (in old China)." See Beijing Foreign Languages Institute, *The Pinyin Chinese-English Dictionary,* ed. Wu Jingron (Beijing: Commercial Press, 1979), 800.

with edifices of largely British colonial institutions,[12] prominent among which were the British Consulate, the Shanghai Club (featuring "the longest bar in the world"), the Sassoon House (with its Cathay Hotel), the Customs House, and the Hong Kong and Shanghai Bank.[13] The imposing pomposity of these buildings represent perfectly British colonial power. Most of these British edifices on the Bund were built or rebuilt in the neoclassical style prevalent in England beginning in the late nineteenth century, which replaced the earlier Victorian Gothic and "free style" arts and crafts building and was essentially the same style that the British imposed on its colonial capitals in India and South Africa. As the dominant style in England's own administrative buildings, neoclassical style consciously affirms its ties to imperial Rome and ancient Greece. As Thomas Metcalf has stated, "the use of classical forms to express the spirit of empire was, for the late-Victorian Englishman, at once obvious and appropriate, for classical style, with their reminders of Greece and Rome, were the architectural medium through which Europeans always apprehended Empire."[14] However, by the 1930s, the era of Victorian glory was over: England was no longer the unchallenged master of world commerce. A new power, the United States of America, began its imperial expansion into the Pacific region, following its conquest of the Philippines. The merger of the British and U.S. concessions into one International Settlement had occurred earlier, when U.S. power had been dwarfed by the might of British imperialism. But by the 1930s, Shanghai's International Settlement was the site of competing architectural styles: Whereas British neoclassical buildings still dominated the skyline on the Bund, new constructions in a more modern style that exemplified the new U.S. industrial power had also appeared.

Since the late 1920s, some thirty multistoried buildings taller than

12. See Jon Huebner's two articles, "Architecture on the Shanghai Bund," *Papers on Far Eastern History* 39 (1989): 128–63; and "Architecture and History in Shanghai's Central District," *Journal of Oriental Studies* 26 (1988): 209–69.
13. See Lai Delin, "Cong Shanghai gonggong zujie kan Zhongguo jindai jianzhu zhidu" [The institutions of modern Chinese architecture as seen from Shanghai's International Settlement], *Kongjian* [Space magazine], nos. 41–43 (1993).
14. Thomas R. Metcalf, *An Imperial Vision: Indian Architecture and Britain's Raj* (Berkeley: University of California Press, 1989), 177–78.

the colonial edifices on the Bund had already begun to emerge as a result of the invention of modern construction materials and techniques in America.[15] These were mainly bank buildings, hotels, apartment houses, and department stores—the tallest being the twenty-four-story Park Hotel designed by the famous Czech-Hungarian architect Ladislaus Hudec, who was associated with the American architectural firm of R. A. Curry before he opened his own offices in 1925.[16] Hudec's "innovative and elegant style added a real flair to Shanghai's architecture," as evidenced by the many buildings he designed: in addition to the Park Hotel, the twenty-two-story building of the Joint Savings Society, the Moore Memorial Church, several hospitals and public buildings, and three movie theaters, including the renovated Grand Theater.[17] The exteriors and interiors of some of these modern buildings—the Park Hotel, the Cathay Hotel/Sassoon House, and new cinemas such as the Grand Theater, the Paramount Ballroom and Theater, the Majestic Theater, and many apartment houses—were done in the prevalent Art Deco style. According to Tess Johnston, "Shanghai has the largest array of Art Deco edifices of any city in the world."[18] The combination of the high-rise skyscraper and the Art Deco interior design style thus inscribed another new architectural imprint—that of New York City, with which Shanghai can be compared.[19]

15. See Muramatsu Shin, *Shanhai toshi to kenchiku 1842–1949 nen* [The metropolitan architecture of Shanghai] (Tokyo: Parco, 1991), esp. chap. 3, on skyscrapers.

16. See Johnston, *Last Look,* 86. See also *Men of Shanghai and North China* (Shanghai: University Press, 1935), 269. The Park Hotel remained the tallest building in East Asia for some thirty years. See *Jinadai Shanghai jianzhu shihua* [Historical accounts of modern Shanghai architecture] (Shanghai: Shanghai Wenhua Chubanshe, 1991), 91–99.

17. Johnston, *Last Look,* 86. "Wudake jiangzhushi xiaozhuan" [Brief biography of Hudec, the architect], *Jianzhu zazhi* [Architecture magazine], 1 (1933): 13.

18. Johnston, *Last Look,* 70; see also the photos of the cinemas, 88–89. Photos of the old and renovated Grand Theater and the Majestic Theater can also be found in Chen Congzhou and Zhang Ming, eds., *Shanghai jindai jianzhu shigao* [Draft history of modern Shanghai architecture] (Shangha: Sanlien, 1988), 207–9.

19. For New York skyscraper architecture and Art Deco, see Robert Stern et al., *New York 1930: Architecture and Urbanism between the Two World Wars* (New York: Rizzoli, 1987); Cervin Robinson and Rosemarie Bletter, *Skyscraper Style: Art Deco New York* (New York: Oxford University Press, 1975); Don Vlack, *Art Deco Architecture in New York, 1920–1940* (New York: Harper and Row, 1974); and Robert Messler, *The Art Deco Skyscraper in New York* (New York: Peter Lang, 1986). For a recent, ingenious analy-

New York remained in many ways the prototypical metropolis for both the skyscraper skyline and the Art Deco style. Its tallest buildings—those of Rockefeller Center, the Chrysler Building, and, above all, the Empire State Building—were all constructed only a few years before Shanghai's new high-rise buildings. Although dwarfed in height, the Shanghai skyscrapers bear a visible resemblance to those in New York. This U.S. connection was made possible by the physical presence of U.S. architects and firms. Another likely source of American input is Hollywood movies, especially musicals and comedies, in which silhouettes of skyscrapers and Art Deco interiors almost became hallmarks of stage design.[20] The Art Deco style may be said to be the characteristic architectural style of the interwar period in Europe and America; it was an architecture of "ornament, geometry, energy, retrospection, optimism, color, texture, light and at times even symbolism." When transplanted into the American cities—New York in particular—Art Deco had become an essential part of "an architecture of soaring skyscrapers—the cathedrals of the modern age."[21] The marriage between the two synthesizes a peculiar aesthetic exuberance that was associated with urban modernity and which embodied the spirit of "something new and different, something exciting and unorthodox, something characterized by a sense of *joie de vivre* that manifested itself in terms of color, height, decoration and sometimes all three."[22]

When "translated" into Shanghai's Western culture, the lavish ornamentalism of the Art Deco style becomes, in one sense, a new "mediation" between the neoclassicism of British imperial power, with its manifest stylistic ties to the (Roman) past, and the ebullient new spirit of American capitalism. In addition to—or increasingly in place of—

sis, see Jeffrey Wasserstrom, "Comparing the 'Incomparable' Cities: Postmodern Los Angeles and Old Shanghai," *Contention: Debates in Society, Culture, and Science* 5 (1996): 69–90.

20. For examples, the musical *Broadway Melody* (1938) with Eleanor Powell and the comedy, *The Magnificent Flirt* (1928), in which Loretta Young "bedded down in Art Deco comfort." See Richard Striner, *Art Deco* (New York: Abbeville Press, 1994), 9, 72. At the same time, the Art Deco style is supposed to evoke the fantasy and charm of the movies, rather than real life. See Robinson and Bletter, *Skyscraper Style*, 40.

21. Patricia Bayer, *Art Deco Architecture: Design, Decoration and Detail from the Twenties and Thirties* (New York: Harry N. Abrams, 1992), 8.

22. Bayer, *Art Deco Architecture*, 12.

colonial power, it signifies money and wealth. At the same time, the Art Deco artifice also conveys a "simulacrum" of the new urban lifestyle, a modern fantasy of men and women living in a glittering world of fashionable clothes and fancy furniture. It is, for Chinese eyes, alluring and exotic precisely because it is so unreal. The American magazine *Vanity Fair,* perhaps the best representation of this image in print, was available in Shanghai's Western bookstores and became a favorite reading matter among Shanghai's modernist writers. One need only glance through a few issues of the magazine to discover how some of its visual styles (Art Deco, in particular) crept into the cover designs of the Chinese magazines in Shanghai, even reworked in the design of the Chinese characters themselves.

Whereas this gilded decadent style may be a fitting representation of the "Jazz Age" of the "Roaring Twenties" in urban America, it remained something of a mirage for Chinese readers and filmgoers—a world of fantasy that cast a mixed spell of wonder and oppression. The Chinese term for skyscrapers is *motian dalou*—literally, the "magical big buildings that reach the skies." As a visible sign of the rise of industrial capitalism, these skyscrapers could also be regarded as the most intrusive addition to the Shanghai landscape, as they not only tower over the regular residential buildings in the old section of the city (mostly two- or three-story-high constructions) but offer a sharp contrast to the general principles of Chinese architecture in which height was never a crucial factor, especially in the case of houses for everyday living. No wonder that it elicited responses of heightened emotion: In cartoons, sketches, and films, the skyscraper is portrayed as showcasing socioeconomic inequality—the high and the low, the rich and the poor. A cartoon of the period, titled "Heaven and Hell," shows a skyscraper towering over the clouds, on top of which are two figures apparently looking down on a beggarlike figure seated next to a small thatched house.[23] A book of aphorisms about Shanghai has the following comment: "The neurotic thinks that in fifty years Shanghai will sink beneath the horizon under the weight of these big, tall foreign buildings."[24] These reactions

23. Xiao Jianqing, *Manhua Shanghai* [Shanghai in cartoons] (Shanghai: Jingwei Shuju, 1936).
24. Xiao Jianqing, *Xianhua Shanghai* [Random talks about Shanghai] (Shanghai: Jingwei Shuju, 1936), 2, 8.

offered a sharp contrast to the general pride and euphoria accorded to New Yorkers, as described in Ann Douglas's recent book.[25]

To the average Chinese, most of these high-rise buildings are, both literally and figuratively, beyond their reach. The big hotels largely catered to the rich and famous, and mostly foreigners. A Chinese guidebook of the time stated: "These places have no deep relationship to us Chinese . . . and besides, the upper-class atmosphere in these Western hotels is very solemn; every move and gesture seems completely regulated. So if you don't know Western etiquette, even if you have enough money to make a fool of yourself it's not worthwhile."[26] This comment reveals at once a clear sense of alienation as it marks an implied boundary, drawn on class lines, between the urban spaces possessed by Westerners and Chinese. The upper-class solemnity of the Western hotels and dwellings may be disconcerting, but it does not prevent the author of the guidebook, Wang Dingjiu, from talking ecstatically about the modern cinemas and dance halls and, in its section on "buying," about shopping for new clothes, foreign shoes, European and American cosmetics, and expensive furs in the newly constructed department stores. It seems as if he were greeting a rising popular demand for consumer goods by advising his readers on how to reap the maximum benefit and derive the greatest pleasure.

Department Stores   Whereas the deluxe Western hotels catered mainly to a Western clientele (although a Chinese crowd of thousands greeted the opening of the Park Hotel), a number of multistoried department stores in the International Settlement—in particular the "Big Four" of Xianshi (Sincere), Yong'an (Wing On), Xinxin (Sun Sun), and Daxin (Sun Company), all built with investment from overseas Chinese businessmen—had become great attractions for the Chinese. With their escalators leading to variegated merchandise on different floors—together with dance halls and rooftop bars, coffeehouses, restaurants, hotels, and playgrounds for diverse performances—these edifices of commerce combined the functions of consumerism with entertainment.

25. Ann Douglas, *Terrible Honesty: Mongrel Manhattan in the 1920s* (New York: Farrar, Straus, Giroux, 1995), 434–36.
26. Wang Dingjiu, *Shanghai menjing* [Keys to Shanghai] (Shanghai: Zhongyang Shudian, 1932), chap. on living [*zhu de menjing*], 11–12.

That all these department stores were located on or near Nanking Road, the main thoroughfare of the International Settlement, was no surprise. If the Bund was the seat of colonial power and finance, Nanking Road, which stretched westward from the Bund, was its commercial extension: "Nanking Road was Shanghai's Oxford Street, its Fifth Avenue."[27] The natives still called it *Damalu*—the Number One Street (with a premodern reference to its days of horse-drawn carriages, or *malu*)—in honor of its privileged status. Since the late 1910s, its eastern portion had already become the most prosperous commercial area. The street's legendary reputation could only be further enhanced by the addition of the new department stores. For the out-of-towners visiting Shanghai, shopping for modern luxury items at the department stores on Nanking Road had become a necessary and desirable ritual.

An index to the role of material consumption in Shanghai's modern life can be found in the omnipresent advertisements that appeared as signs lit up with neon lights, as written posters in front of street stores, and, above all, as printed words and pictures in newspapers and journals. They add up to what may be called a "semiotics" of material culture. For instance, an advertisement for Wing On Department Store in a page of the *Liangyou* [The young companion] pictorial presents a mosaic of the following items: Conklin fountain pen, various kinds of cotton cloth, Swan brand silk stockings and cotton socks, Pilsner Art Export Beer, and a copy of *Liangyou*. From this we can easily compile a list of daily necessities and luxuries for the modern urban household, as gathered from the ubiquitous ads in the *Liangyou* magazine: sundry food products (Quaker Oats, Momilk), laundry detergent (Fab), medicine and health products ("Dr. Williams' Pink Pills for Pale People"), electric cooking pots and automatic gas burners (the ad noted that "recently Chinese people have largely replaced coal burners with gas burners" which is especially suitable for Chinese houses in winter for the sake of "hygiene for the whole family"), medicine, perfume, cigarettes, cameras, gramophones and records (Pathe, RCA), and many more. Needless to add, advertisements for automobiles are everywhere,[28] since

27. Nicholas R. Clifford, *Spoilt Children of Empire: Westerners in Shanghai and the Chinese Revolution of the 1920s* (Hanover, N.H.: Middlebury College Press published by University Press of New England, 1991), 61.
28. A special "automobile Edition" of *Shen Bao* (August 1923), features photos of such

the number of privately owned automobiles between 1922 and 1931 had increased from 1,986 to 4,951.[29] Such a picture of modern consumption set in urban Shanghai must have struck any Chinese of the time who lived in the rural hinterland as nothing short of a "wonderland" — a brave new world stuffed with foreign goods and foreign names.

Consumption is also linked with leisure and entertainment. And the institutions of the latter equally deserve our equal attention: in particular, cinemas, coffeehouses, theaters, dance halls, parks, and the racecourse. Whereas Westernstyle hotels were beyond the pale of Chinese life, cinemas, cafes, and dance halls were an entirely different matter. In a way, they provided an alternative to the traditional places of leisure and entertainment for native residents: local opera theaters, restaurants, and teahouses in the old city, as well as houses of prostitution, which continued to hold sway in the Chinese sections of the city. Together, these places of leisure and entertainment that sprang from the foreign concessions had become the central sites of Shanghai's urban culture.

Coffeehouses and Dance Halls   As a public place fraught with political and cultural significance in Europe, especially France, the coffeehouse proved likewise extremely popular in 1930s Shanghai. Like the cinema, it became one of the most popular leisure spots—decidedly Western, to be sure—a prerequisite site for men and women sporting a modern lifestyle, particularly writers and artists. Habits and styles generally grew out of Shanghai's French Concession. While the British-dominated International Settlement was the site for skyscrapers and deluxe mansions and department stores, the scenery underwent a sudden transformation in the French Concession. The farther one followed the tram route into the concession along its main street, Avenue Joffre (named after the French general who stemmed the German invasion during the First World War), the more serene and atmospheric the place became. Trees imported from France (the Chinese called them French "wutong") flanked both sides of the street, fronting fine "suburban"

---

cars as the British Steyr and Austin, and three Ford models: the Hudson, Essex, and Ford Car, the last being advertised as the cheapest car in which one could "drive all over the world"—the slogan is still used for Fords in Taiwan.

29. Tang Weikang and Du Li, eds., *Zujie yibainian* [One hunded years of the treaty concessions] (Shanghai: Shanghai Huabao Chubanshe, 1991), 128.

residences built in various styles. As one local aficionado observed, on Avenue Joffre "there are no skyscrapers, no specially large constructions" but "every night there are the intoxicating sounds of jazz music coming from the cafes and bars that line both sides. This is to tell you that there are women and wine inside, to comfort you from the fatigue of a day's toil."[30]

The special allure of French culture was perpetuated by a number of Chinese Francophile writers, notably the Zengs, father and son—Zeng Pu and Zeng Xubai. Although Zeng Pu, author of the famous late Qing novel *Niehai hua* [A flower in a sea of retribution] (1905), had never set foot on French soil, he lost no time in creating his own French world at his bookstore residence at 115 rue Massenet, in the heart of the French Concession. Zeng Pu intended to make his bookstore—called "Truth, Beauty, and Goodness" (Zhen-mei-shan)—a library of French literature and a cultural salon in which he would gather his guests and disciples around him and discuss his favorite French authors: Victor Hugo, Anatole France, Leconte de Lisle, George Sand, and Pierre Loti.[31] The guests and friends at Zeng's bookstore/salon had all become Francophiles themselves.

Although it is doubtful that the Chinese Francophiles succeeded in turning their literary salon into something approaching Jürgen Habermas's notion of "public sphere," there is no denying that Shanghai writers indeed used the coffeehouse as a place for friendly gatherings. From both contemporary accounts of the time and latter-day memoirs, this French institution was combined with the British custom of the afternoon tea to become a highlight of their daily rituals. The choice of the hour for "high tea" was often necessitated by economic considerations, since some of the cafes most frequented by impoverished writers and artists were housed in restaurants that offered a cheaper afternoon price for coffee, tea, and snacks. Zhang Ruogu, an avid Francophile, named several as his favorite spots: Sun Ya (Xinya) on Nanking East Road across from the Xinxin department store, for tea and snacks; Sulli-

30. Zhongguo tushu bianyi guan, ed., *Shanghai chunqiu* [Shanghai annals] vol. 2 (Hong Kong: Nantian Shuye Gongsi, 1968), 88.

31. Heinrich Fruehauf, "Urban Exoticism in Modern and Contemporary Chinese Literature," in *From May Fourth to June Fourth: Fiction and Film in Twentieth-Century China*, ed. Ellen Widmer and David Der-wei Wang (Cambridge, Mass.: Harvard University Press, 1993), 145.

van's, a justly famous chocolate shop; Federal, a German-style cafe at Bubbling Well Road; Constantine's, a Russian cafe; Little Man (Xiao nanren), across the street from the Cathay Theater (where "the decor is splendid and the waitresses young and pretty"); D. D.'s Cafe; and Cafe Renaissance on Avenue Joffre.[32] But his real favorite was the Balkan Milk Store, another Russian-run cafe in the French Concession that offered coffee at cheaper prices and where he and his friends could spend long hours undisturbed by the waiters.

Zhang concluded that there were three kinds of pleasures that could be derived from going to the coffeehouse: first, the stimulus of the coffee itself, with an effect "not inferior to that of opium and wine"; second, the space provided by the coffeehouse for long talks among friends, "the most pleasurable thing in life"; and, last but not least, the charming presence of the coffeehouse waitress — a literary figure first introduced to Chinese writers by Yu Dafu's translation of a story by George Moore[33] and made more famous by their knowledge of Japanese waitresses in Tokyo bars and coffeehouses before the 1923 earthquake.[34] Zhang considered the coffeehouse to be one of the crucial symbols of modernity, together with the cinema and the automobile; and more than the latter two, it had an enormous impact on modern literature. He proudly mentioned some of his favorite French writers — Jean Moreas, Theophile Gautier, Maxime Rudé, and Henri de Regnier — as diehard cafe addicts.

At the time of Zhang Ruogu's writing (1929), literary Shanghai seemed to be caught in a "coffeehouse craze" — celebrated not only in Zhang's essays and Yu Dafu's translations but also in Tian Han's play *One Night in a Cafe* [*Kafei guan de yiye*] and numerous fictional works. Tian Han also advertised for a new bookstore run by his Nanguo (Southern China) dramatic society with a coffeehouse attached where "wait-

32. Zhang Ruogu, "Cha, kafei, maijiu" [Tea, coffee, ale], *Furen huabao* [Women's pictorial] (1935): 9–11.

33. Zhang Ruogu, "Xiandai duhui shenghuo xiangzeng" [The symbol of modern urban life], in *Kafei zuotan* [Cafe forum] (Shanghai: Zhenmeishan Shudian, 1929), 3–11.

34. The coffeehouse was, of course, very popular in Taisho, Japan, and "among the symbols of Taisho high life." As Edward Seidensticker describes, the cafe was "the forerunner of the expensive Ginza bar. Elegant and alluring female company came with the price of one's coffee, or whatever. The Plantain was the first of them, founded in 1911." See his *Low City, High City: Tokyo from Edo to the Earthquake* (Cambridge, Mass.: Harvard University Press, 1991), 104, 201.

resses trained in literature will make the customer enjoy the pleasure of good books and good conversation over drinks." All this occidental "exotica" naturally converged on a Bohemian self-image. Visiting the painter and poet Ni Yide in his small attic room, Zhang Ruogu jokingly remarked: "This room has the atmosphere of the painter Rodolfo's room, but regrettably you don't have a Mimi to be your companion."[35] Tian Han went so far as to incorporate the characters of La Bohème into the first part of a film he scripted, Fengyun ernü [Valiant heroes and heroines], which ends with a call to war accompanied by the film's theme song, "The March of the Volunteers," which eventually became the national anthem of the People's Republic.

Another public institution, somewhat lower in cultural prestige than the coffeehouse, is the ballroom/cabaret and dance hall (wuting or wuchang): The ballroom/cabaret had a more deluxe decor and often featured cabaret performances, patronized mostly by foreigners, whereas the dance hall had only a small band and "taxi dancers" or dance hostesses. By 1936, there were over three hundred cabarets and casinos in Shanghai.[36] The foreigners and the wealthy Chinese patronized the leading high-class ballrooms and cabarets (with shows and performances) — the Tower atop of the Cathay Hotel, the Sky Terrace at the Park Hotel, the Paramount Theater and Ballroom, Del Monte's, Ciro's, Roxy's, the Venus Cafe, the Vienna Garden Ballroom, and the Little Club. The very foreignness of these names seems to evoke an alienating effect similar to that of high-class Western hotels and serves as a pronounced reminder of their colonial-metropolitan origins: New York, London, Vienna. Still, the Chinese clientele managed to domesticate them to some extent by translating the exotic names into Chinese equivalents with native allure: Thus Ciro's became Xianluosi (Fairy land of pleasures), and Paramount became Bailuomen (Gate of a hundred pleasures); the legendary fame of the latter, in particular, has left an enduring mark on the Chinese literary imagination.[37] Although social dancing, like horse racing, was decidedly a Western custom which was first introduced by Shanghai's for-

35. Zhang, Kafei zuotan, 8, 24.

36. Frederic Wakeman, Policing Shanghai, 1927–1937 (Berkeley: University of California Press, 1995), 108.

37. See Pai Hsien-yung, Wandering in the Garden, Waking from a Dream: Tales of Taipei Characters, trans. Pai Hsien-yung and Patia Yasin, ed. George Kao (Bloomington: Indiana University Press, 1982), 51.

eigners in the mid-nineteenth century, it did not stop the Chinese from embracing it as a vogue. Shanghai natives reportedly flocked to the first dance halls in droves as soon as they were opened in the early 1920s.[38]

By the 1930s, dance halls had become another famous—or infamous—hallmark of Shanghai's urban milieu. The popular women's magazine *Ling Long* [Petite], in addition to showcasing movies and movie stars in every issue, also introduced social dancing through a three-part series of articles. One article described dancing as a social activity and as a serious subject of study, pointing to the large number of schools and teachers devoted to dancing in Shanghai, as well as abroad. A short description of the various popular dances was also included, ranging from the quick step, the slow fox-trot, the waltz, and the tango to the new Charleston and the rhumba. But the article also describes dance as a "natural act" that "enlivens the forces within the body," as well as a "civic" activity that may also be "an effective way to attract a mate."[39] However, as Frederic Wakeman has observed, "the line between attached couples learning how to dance together and solitary males seeking part-time companions via the dance hall was not altogether distinct, but the latter pursuit proved to be overwhelming—no doubt because of the disproportionate ratio of the genders in Shanghai in 1930: 135 men for every 100 women in the Chinese municipality, 156:100 in the International Settlement, and 164:100 in the French Concession."[40]

In terms of the number of customers, the popularity of dance halls in Shanghai definitely surpassed that of the coffeehouses. Whereas coffeehouses remained a place for upper-class Chinese and foreigners and for writers and artists, the dance hall reached out to people of all classes and became a fixture in the popular imagination. This is evidenced in the numerous reports, articles, cartoons, drawings, and photographs in the daily newspapers (especially the mosquito presses) and popular magazines. In fact, some of the leading Shanghai artists—Ye Qianyu, Zhang

38. Tu Shimin, *Shanghai shi daguan* [Panorama of Shanghai], 56–57. This source also indicates that in 1946 when dance hostesses were required to register with the city police thirty-three hundred of them did.

39. Quoted in Andrew D. Field, "Selling Souls in Sin City: Shanghai Singing and Dancing Girls in Print, Film, and Politics, 1920–1949" (unpublished manuscript), 14. I am most grateful to Andrew Field, a Ph.D. candidate at Columbia University, for permission to use this article and for other forms of research assistance.

40. Wakeman, "Licensing Leisure," 27.

Yingchao, and Zhang Loping—used the dance hall and dance waitresses as subjects of their cartoons. Their typical portrait consists of variations of a man and a woman dancing (except for one with two women dancing): The man can be young or old, wearing a Chinese long gown or a Western suit, but the woman is invariably dressed in a *qipao*. The portrait unwittingly conveys a gendered differentiation of the woman as a fixed object for the desires of men of various classes, her *qipao* revealing the contours of her body. In other words, these variations of the dancing couple are all drawn from the model of the dance hostess and her different clients. These visual portraits are reinforced by the accompanying articles in which the authors describe and comment on the dance hostess and the allure of female flesh as a commodity. Most articles focus on the small, lower-class dance halls that outnumbered the large, renowned cabaret-clubs.

If we compare the descriptions by modern Chinese writers, it would seem that while the coffeehouse waitress was celebrated by the Francophile writers as a romantic figure within an idealized vision of a Bohemian life, the dance hall hostess was denigrated as a miserable, though still alluring, creature. There was no attempt to construct a literary pedigree for hostesses in small dance halls (whereas the Western cabaret hostesses came to be romanticized in films—for example, Marlene Dietrich in *The Blue Angel*). In this regard, some of the fictional portraits of dance hostess do serve more than a purely literary purpose. The dance hostesses in Mu Shiying's and Liu Na'ou's stories are often portrayed as larger than life, and they take a more active, even dominant, role over men; as objects of male desire they also defiantly return the erotic gaze at men. Such portraiture of the emerging femme fatale in the world of the cafe/ballroom/racecourse may be interpreted as a fictional projection of the author's male fantasy or as an embodiment of urban material glamour, hence further reinforcing the inevitable process of commodification.

I would like to argue a slightly different thesis, however: The popularity of the dance halls in Shanghai's urban life serves ironically as the necessary, albeit still negative, backdrop for the emergence of a new public persona for women. Combining the descriptions of dance hostesses with earlier portraits of courtesans and movie stars and reading them symbolically as marking different facets in a cultural genealogy, we see them within a long tradition of literary tropes that, in varying ways, center on women figures in the public arena. Before leftist critics in the 1930s began to imagine all women as oppressed and downtrodden, some Shanghai writers—particularly those of the neo-Sensualist school (Xin ganjue pai)—had chosen to "modernize" such a long-standing trope in traditional Chinese popular literature by making these women figures, even as embodiments of urban material culture, more dynamic and ironically more confident in their own subjectivity as women—to the extent that they can play with men and make fools of them in such public places of leisure as the dance hall, the coffeehouse, and the racecourse.[41] In a hilarious fantasy story by Mu Shiying titled "Camel, Nietzscheist, and Woman," the male protagonist—himself a satirical characterization of the urban *flaneur qua* philosopher—takes his nocturnal strolls through a jai alai court, a dance hall, a gambling joint, a bar with a bewitching air of "beauté exotique," and a coffeehouse, all the while puffing his favorite Lucky brand cigarettes and quoting Nietzsche's *Thus Spoke Zarathustra*. Finally, at a place called Cafe Napoli, he encounters a mysterious woman with painted "Garbo-like eyebrows, dark eyes as soft as velvet, and red, ripe lips" who drinks coffee with five helpings of sugar and smokes a Camel cigarette.[42] In the ensuing match of wits over dinner, she proceeds to "enlighten" him about 373 brands of cigarettes, 28 kinds of coffee, and 5,000 kinds of drinks together with their mixing formulas!

Parks and Race Club   It only remains for me to discuss briefly the two public sites that are clearly derived from the British colonial legacy: public parks and the Shanghai Race Club (Paomating).

A most humiliating reminder of Western imperialist presence was, of course, the notorious sign of exclusion that was reportedly hung at the gate of the Public Gardens in the International Settlement: "No Chinese or Dogs Allowed." The real sign did not exactly read this way, though it was no less humiliating to the Chinese: It was a bulletin that listed the five regulations first decreed in 1916. The second regulation stipulated

41. For an illuminating discussion of this trope, see Shumei Shih, "Gender, Race, and Semicolonialism: Liu Na'ou's Urban Shanghai Landscape," *Journal of Asian Studies* 55 (1996): 934–58.

42. Mu Shiying, "Luoto, Nicaizhuyizhe yu nuren" [Camel, Nietzscheist, and woman], included in *Xin ganjue pai xiaoshuo xuan* [Selected stories from the Neo-Sensualist school], ed. Li Ou-fan (Taipei: Yunchen Wenhua, 1988), 191–97.

that "dogs and bicycles are not admitted," which was followed by the third: "Chinese are not admitted" except "in the case of native servants accompanying their white employers." The fourth and fifth regulations, respectively, excluded Indians (except for those in dignified attire) and Japanese (except for those wearing Western clothing).[43] These posted regulations finally came down as the Nationalist forces under Chiang Kai-shek assumed control of Shanghai in 1927. Although there was still an admission charge, "the people of Shanghai responded to this opening of facilities with great enthusiasm. Admittance figures kept by municipal authorities show an impressive number of visitors to the public parks" — from 1,625,511 in June–December 1928 to 2,092,432 in 1930.[44] Aside from the half dozen parks in the International Settlement, of course, there were parks and gardens in the French Concession and in the Old City. A guidebook of the period listed nearly forty public and private parks and gardens.[45] Of these, a particular favorite for writers was the new amusement park, Rio Rita's, which became a literary legend with the publication of Mao Dun's novel *Midnight*. Thus for the Chinese, parks and gardens served the purpose not only of relaxation — taking a leisurely stroll on Sundays or holidays (when a British band would play in one of the parks), as the foreigners would do — but also of pleasure-seeking "recreation" and rendezvous for romantic trysts. In the films of the 1930s, such as *Crossroads* [*Shizu jietou*], romantic rendezvous or chance encounters in the park almost became a plot convention.

The history of horse racing has been fully documented in a recent book by Austin Coates, *China Races* (1983), which was commissioned, appropriately enough, by the Royal Hong Kong Jockey Club to mark its centenary in 1984. Hong Kong held its first race-meeting in 1845, possibly a year or so earlier than any in Shanghai. In 1862, the Shanghai Race Club was established, overtaking Hong Kong as the leader in East Asia. The Shanghai racecourse was rebuilt at least three times. This British sport became immediately popular with the Chinese, who participated

---

43. Pan Ling, *In Search of Old Shanghai* (Hong Kong: Joint Publishing, 1982), 36; Wu Guifang, *Songgu mantan* [Random talks on old legends about Shanghai] (Shanghai: Shanghai Renmin Chubanshe, 1991), 193. See also Bickers and Wasserstrom, "Shanghai's 'Dogs and Chinese Not Admitted' Sign," 446.
44. Betty Pehi-t'i Wei, *Old Shanghai* (Hong Kong: Oxford University Press, 1993), 232.
45. *Shanghai zhinan* [Shanghai guide] (Shanghai: Guoguang Shudian, n.d.), 10–16.

eagerly from the very beginning and even began to form their own race clubs. In Coates's succinct words, "Chinese always claimed they went to the races for the sheer enjoyment of it, which means they were betting." Even in the late nineteenth century, "Chinese, in fact, were infiltrating the proceedings. Respectable Chinese, as they were called, had always been allowed into the enclosure on payment . . . and there were two incredible Stands, known as the 'Grand' and the 'Little Grand,' the perilous edifices crammed with Chinese — crazy-looking erections which somehow never fell down."[46] Despite sharing the stands as spectators during race days, however, the Chinese were not allowed into the club grounds or to become formal members of the Shanghai Race Club.[47] The club building itself, constructed in 1933, was a "massive six-story building with an imposing clock tower twice as high" that became "one of the landmarks of downtown Shanghai."[48] The club grounds "covered sixty-six acres of the choicest property in the city" and "constituted an extravagant spatial intervention of Western culture in the Chinese city space."[49] While it brought an English-style countryside idyll into the modern metropolis, one would also find that "the city encroached on this countryside idyll" and that "the vast lawn could not conceal the proximity of the city" with its crowded streets and the high-rise buildings of the British concession. This jarring cityscape, "suspended between countryside scenery and urban construction," provided a fantastic setting, a visual spectacle, for Liu Na'ou's story, "Two People Impervious to Time" ["Liangge shijian de buganzheng zhe"], in which the heroine plays an elaborate game of seducing the hero right from the grandstand. Gambling — betting on the horses — becomes a fitting incentive in the "economy" of "exchanging one currency of desire for another."[50]

46. Austin Coates, *China Races* (Hong Kong: Oxford University Press, 1983), 26, 34, 121.

47. Ma Xuexin et al., *Shanghai wenhua yuanliu cidian* [Dictionary of Shanghai's cultural sources] (Shanghai: Shenghai Shehuikexueyuan Chubanshe, 1992), 50. See also Wakeman, *Policing Shanghai*, 99.

48. Yomi Braester, "Shanghai's Economy of the Spectacle: The Shanghai Race Club in Liu Na'ou's and Mu Shiying's Stories," *Modern Chinese Literature* 9 (1995): 41–42. According to another Chinese source, it was four stories high, but the tower was ten stories high. See Ma, *Shanghai wenhua yuanliu cidian*, 639.

49. See Wakeman, *Policing Shanghai*, 98; Braester, "Shanghai's Economy," 41.

50. Braester, "Shanghai's Economy," 42, 49.

As the Shanghai racecourse illustrates, the contrast between East and West in Shanghai's urban space cannot be greater. It is a contrast in both space and style: The Western buildings flanking the Bund and along the major thoroughfares in the concessions clearly dominate Shanghai's landscape and visibly mark the hegemonic presence of the foreign powers. We can see a clear colonial imprint in the concession areas, on which are inscribed elements of Paris, London, and New York. Thus the mixture of architectural styles, while lending a cosmopolitan flavor to the city, also betrays the ignoble origins of Western intrusion into China. How did the Chinese residents cope with such an urban environment? Does it mean that the hegemonic Western presence effectively turned Shanghai into a Western colony?

With materials presented in the previous section I have suggested that the public spaces in the foreign concessions were appropriated and reappropriated by Chinese writers through their actual or imaginary acts of "transgression," to the extent that they, in turn, became the background for constructing a cultural imaginary of Chinese modernity. The Shanghai writers seem to have taken full advantage of the foreign concessions together with Western material culture. While they shunned the more expensive restaurants and cabarets in the big hotels, the relatively inexpensive cafes run by exiled Russians became their favorite gathering places. Cinemas showing first-run Hollywood movies were another popular site, as were dance halls. Even Shanghai's racecourse and jai alai courts were not beyond their reach: Liu Na'ou, Mu Shiying, and Hei Ying used them as settings to introduce the most outlandish and adventurous of their fictional heroines.

This process of appropriation is not one of material possession, but it nevertheless extends the "imaginary" boundaries of Chinese residents' lives. Not only did the Chinese feel they had every right to share such an urban space with Shanghai's foreign residents, but their imaginary occupation of it, in turn, formed a link with an even larger world. As Zeng Pu walked along Rue Massenet or Rue de Corneille in the French Concession, he was "literarily" transported to the world of French culture. Other writers, such as Zhang Ruogu, had similar experiences at Shanghai's coffeehouses. Both Shi Zhecun and Xu Chi told me during interviews that their most exciting experience while cruising Shanghai's foreign quarters was to buy books, new or used, in a number of Western bookstores. In his reminiscences, Ye Lingfeng recounted his elation at spotting a copy of Joyce's *Ulysses* published by the Shakespeare Bookstore in Paris (retailing at U.S. $10) for the unbelievable price of seventy cents.[51] Clearly, the treaty-port concessions made it possible for writers like Ye and others to partake of the goods—and to participate in an imagined community—of world literature. It is through such imaginary acts that they felt they were connected to the city and to the world at large.

Of course, writers and artists do not belong in either the wealthy upper class or the great mass of the urban poor. They may seem as Westernized as the Chinese "compradors" who work in Western firms, but perhaps more so in their intellectual predilections than in their lifestyle (although, as mentioned earlier, they adopted certain public sites as their favorites). They bought and read foreign books and journals, from which they extracted materials for translation. In their works they were obviously engaged constantly in an imaginary dialogue with their favorite Western authors. Even their writings were "dialogically" engaged in a kind of intertextual transaction in which the Western textual sources were conspicuously foregrounded in their own texts. Thus in discussing the writer's creative relationship with the city, it may be relevant to turn to another "model."

The City and the Flaneur Walter Benjamin's unfinished but incomparable cultural commentary, *Charles Baudelaire: A Lyric Poet in the Era of High Capitalism,* has been a source of inspiration for many scholars. Benjamin's genius lies in defining a critical role and an allegorical space for the writer in the city. "With Baudelaire, Paris for the first time became the subject of lyrical poetry. This poetry is no local folklore; the allegorist's gaze which falls upon the city is rather the gaze of alienated man. It is the gaze of the *flaneur*." A man of leisure, the flaneur moved along the Parisian streets and arcades and interacted with the city crowd in an unending and curiously ambivalent relationship. "The *flaneur* still stood at the margin, of the great city as of the bourgeois class. Neither of them had yet overwhelmed him. In neither of them was he at home.

51. Ye Lingfeng, *Dushu suibi* [Random notes on reading] vol. 1 (Beijing: Sanlian, 1988), 115.

He sought his asylum in the crowd. The crowd was the veil from behind which the familiar city as phantasmagoria beckoned to the *flaneur*." [52]

It was with Benjamin's text in mind that I first tried to "remap" Shanghai from a literary angle. However, in the attempt to conceptualize Shanghai along a Benjaminian trail, several problems immediately arose as I tried to cross the cultural boundaries between Paris and Shanghai. The discrepancies between the two cities are obvious: Although Shanghai was often called the "Paris of the Orient," due in part to its French Concession, there was no Chinese concession in Paris. Thus in a sense, the Paris of Baudelaire's time was less diversified and less cosmopolitan than Shanghai, and far more monolithic and imperial in its architectural style—in fact, this French metropolitan capital had itself become the model for French colonial cities.[53] By contrast, with its mixture of Western and Chinese urban spaces Shanghai presented a more "vernacular" landscape. Paris also had a much longer history than Shanghai, and by Baudelaire's time it had reached a high point of capitalist development—such that French writers and artists began to take on a critical attitude toward the city's increasingly philistine bourgeois crowd. By comparison, Shanghai developed into a modern metropolis in only a few decades in the early twentieth century, and its material splendor seems to have so dazzled its writers that they had yet to develop a highly reflective and ambivalent mentality characteristic of the Parisian flaneur.

In Benjamin's study, the most significant urban space that defines the ambivalent relationship between the flaneur and the city is the arcade—and by extension, the department store. Benjamin's celebrated views on the Parisian "arcades" are now well known.[54] The arcades, a new invention of "industrial luxury" in nineteenth-century Paris, "are glass-covered, marble-paneled passageways," and "both sides of these passageways, which are lighted from above, are lined with the most elegant shops, so that such an arcade is a city, even a world, in minia-

52. Walter Benjamin, *Charles Baudelaire: A Lyric Poet in the Era of High Capitalism*, trans. Harry Zohn (London: Verso, 1983), 170.

53. See Paul Rabinow, *French Modern: Norms and Forms of the Social Environment* (Cambridge, Mass.: MIT Press, 1989).

54. See Susan Buck-Morss, *The Dialectic of Seeing: Walter Benjamin and the Arcades Project* (Cambridge, Mass.: MIT Press, 1991).

ture." [55] It is in this world that the flaneur is at home. But there were no such arcades in Shanghai. The traditional amusement halls like the "Great World" (Da shijie) or the modern department stores were certainly no substitutes for the arcades for leisurely loitering. They may be fitting spaces for the Shanghai middle class, but not necessarily the world where a Chinese flaneur would feel at home.

As the Baudelairean prototype implies, the flaneur's relationship to the city is both engaged and detached: He cannot live without the city, as he surrenders himself to the intoxication of its commodity world; at the same time, he is marginalized by the city to which he is condemned to live. Thus he keeps himself at a distance from the crowd, and it is from his distanced gaze that the city is allegorized. His *leisurely* walk is both a posture and a protest "against the division of labor which makes people into specialists. It is also a protest against their industriousness. Around 1840 it was briefly fashionable to take turtles for a walk in the arcades. The *flaneurs* liked to have the turtles set the pace for them." [56] Thus it has been pointed out that the flaneur embodied a paradox, a modern artist who rebels against the very circumstances which has made his existence possible—in other words, an embellishment of Baudelaire's famous characterization in "A Painter of Modern Life." [57] Such a paradoxical reaction against modernity is not shared by the avowedly modeng writers of Shanghai who were much too enamored with the light, heat, and power of the new metropolis to have any detached reflection.

Benjamin has barely mentioned the more degrading female counterpart of the male flaneur—the woman who walked the streets, the prostitute. In fact, this familiar sight was equally characteristic of nineteenth-century Paris as of early-twentieth-century Shanghai, where streetwalkers were called, derogatorily, *yeji* or "wild chicks." [58] The phenomenon is an ironic reminder of another exalted posture of the male flaneur—the freedom and flair of his *walking* on the streets. In fact, this "street-walking" tradition has been further theorized by Michel de Cer-

55. Benjamin, *Charles Baudelaire*, 36–37.

56. Benjamin, *Charles Baudelaire*, 54.

57. See Bruce Mazlich, "The *Flaneur:* From Spectator to Representation," in *The Flaneur*, ed. Keith Tester (London: Routledge, 1994), 49.

58. Wakeman described *yeji* as "streetwalkers who wore gaudy clothes and were thought to go here and there like wild birds" in Wakeman, *Policing Shanghai*, 112.

teau as a specific form of spatial practice in the modern city—a social and "enunciative" process of appropriating the urban space.[59] It can be said that Shanghai writers and residents certainly traversed the various urban spaces in the practice of their everyday lives. But this does not mean that they had made an art of urban walking.

To be sure, there is no shortage of literary references to walking (*sanbu*) itself in Chinese poetry and fiction, both traditional and modern. But such literary walks often take place against or amidst a pastoral landscape. The modern writer Yu Dafu was much influenced by Rousseau's *Reveries du promeneur solitaire* and cast several of his stories in a similar vein of a solitary traveler.[60] But his fictional alter egos, though sufficiently sensitive and pensive, are not *urban* strollers in the flaneur mode. Other Shanghai writers, especially the Francophiles, consciously flaunted a habit of frequenting coffeehouses—but only so that they could meet and chat with friends instead of sitting alone and gazing at the crowd. A seemingly aimless stroll is reserved only for a romantic rendezvous in the public parks which, as mentioned earlier, by this time were mostly open to the Chinese. In these situations, the act of walking is seldom done alone and does not necessarily contribute to the lofty image of *flanerie*. Perhaps only in some of the tree-lined streets in the French Concession, such as Rue Massenet, do we find an occasional stroller like Zeng Pu (who also lived there) who could "conjure up the images of an aesthetically saturated French life." [61] Surprisingly, even for this most enthusiastic member of Chinese Francophiles there is no mention of either Baudelaire or the flaneur.

In his recent study of *The City in Modern Chinese Literature and Film*, Yingjin Zhang has demonstrated that indeed the flaneur figure can be sighted in several creative works, both fiction and poetry. Zhang seems to have given this flaneur figure an erotic charge by emphasizing his voyeuristic gaze and his "acting out" of the roles of dandy and reluctant detective. In another article Zhang has cited a story by He Ying to show that the protagonist, by walking on Shanghai's streets, "acquires his knowledge of the city" and is able to "select for his aesthetic ap-

59. Michel de Certeau, *The Practice of Everyday Life*, trans. Steven Rendall (Berkeley: University of California Press, 1988), 97–98.
60. For a brief discussion, see Leo Ou-fan Lee, *The Romantic Generation of Modern Chinese Writers* (Cambridge, Mass.: Harvard University Press, 1973), 280–81.
61. Fruehauf, "Urban Exoticism," 144.

preciation a number of urban images and icons that provide new ways of perceiving the urban metropolis." However, unlike Benjamin's flaneur, he is not a loner in the urban crowd; rather, he "prefers to be known" and enjoys the various spots of the urban spectacle in the company of a city girl called Suzie who is most likely a prostitute.[62] Obviously, He Ying's narrator-hero, like that in the fiction of Liu Na'ou and Mu Shiying, is too enamored of the city and too immersed in the excitements it provides to obtain an attitude of ambivalence and ironic detachment.

Is it possible for Chinese writers to accomplish a similar feat of aesthetic reflection in a different urban cultural context? In Benjamin's view of Baudelaire, the "allegorist's gaze" that turns the city into "the subject of lyrical poetry" is an aesthetic act that, by "taking stock" of all the sights and sounds and commodities that the city can offer, transforms them into art. In this sense the flaneur can only be a modern artist who cannot exist without the city and whose object of inquiry, as Susan Buck-Morss reminds us, "is modernity itself."[63] In what ways, then, can we expect Shanghai writers to fulfill a comparable mission when Chinese modernity itself was being constructed as a cultural imaginary? What did modernity mean to modern Chinese writers and intellectuals?

Modernity and Nationhood   Modernity in China, as I have argued elsewhere, was closely associated with a new linear consciousness of time and history which was itself derived from the Chinese reception of a Social Darwinian concept of evolution made popular by the translations of Yen Fu and Liang Qichao at the turn of the century. In this new temporal scheme, present (*jin*) and past (*gu*) were polarized as contrasting values, and a new emphasis was placed on the present moment "as the pivotal point marking a rupture with the past and forming a progressive continuum toward a glorious future."[64] This new mode of time consciousness was, of course, a "derivative" discourse stemming from

62. Yingjin Zhang, "The Texture of the Metropolis: Modernist Inscriptions of Shanghai in the 1930s," *Modern Chinese Literature* 9 (1995): 19–20.
63. Buck-Morss, *Dialectic of Seeing*, 304.
64. Leo Ou-fan Lee, "In Search of Modernity: Reflections on a New Mode of Consciousness in Modern Chinese Literature and Thought," in *Ideas across Cultures: Essays in Honor of Benjamin Schwartz*, ed. Paul A. Cohen and Merle Goldman (Cambridge, Mass.: Harvard East Asian Monographs, 1990), 110–11.

the Western post-Enlightenment tradition of modernity—the intellectual package now criticized by postmodern theorists for the positivistic and inherently "monological" tendencies embedded in its faith in human reason and progress. One could further argue that the very same post-Enlightenment legacy has infused the expansionist projects of the colonial empires, particularly England, and that one of its political by-products was the modern nation-state. However, once transplanted into China, such a legacy served to add a new dimension to Chinese semantics: In fact, the very word "new" (*xin*) became the crucial component of a cluster of new word compounds denoting a qualitative change in all spheres of life: from the late Qing reform movement (*weixin yundong*) with its institutional designations like "new policies" (*xinzheng*) and "new schools" (*xinxue*) to Liang Qichao's celebrated notion of "new people" (*xinmin*) and May Fourth slogans like "new culture" (*xin wenhua*) and "new literature" (*xin wenxue*). Two terms that gained wide popularity in the 1920s were *shidai* (time or epoch) and *xin shidai* (new epoch), based on the Japanese word *jidai.* This sense of living in a new epoch, as advocated by the May Fourth leaders such as Chen Duxiu, was what defined the ethos of modernity. By the 1900s, another Japanese term was adopted: *wenming* (*bunmei*), or "civilization," [65] which came to be used with words like *dongfang* (east) and *xifang* (west) to form the common May Fourth dichotomy of "Eastern" and "Western" civilizations as contrasting categories. The underlying assumption was that Western civilization was marked by dynamic progress made possible by the manifestation of what Benjamin Schwartz has called the "Faustian-Promethean" strain that resulted in the achievement of wealth and power by the Western countries. [66]

Schwartz's pioneering study of Yan Fu has not covered the rapid spread of these new categories of value and thought in the Chinese popular press. In newspapers like *Shenbao* [Shanghai news] and magazines like *Dongfang zazhi* [Eastern miscellany] published by the Commercial Press, such new vocabularies became a regular feature of most

65. This term is inluded in appendix D, "Return Graphic Loans: Kanji Terms Derived from Classical Chinese," in Lydia Liu's recent book, *Translingual Practice: Literature, National Culture, and Translated Modernity—China, 1900–1937* (Stanford, Calif.: Stanford University Press, 1996), 308.

66. Benjamin Schwartz, *In Search of Wealth and Power* (Cambridge, Mass.: Harvard University Press, 1964), 238–39.

articles. Thus by the 1920s, it came to be generally acknowledged that "modernity" was equated with the new "Western civilization" in all its spiritual and material manifestations. Whereas conservative or moderate commentators in the *Dongfang zazhi* and other journals voiced concerns over the possible bankruptcy of Western civilization signaled by the First World War, all intellectuals of a radical persuasion continued to be firm believers in this idea of modernity. The center of cultural production of such ideas of modernity was indisputably Shanghai, where most newspapers and publishing houses were located, congregated in one small area around Fuzhou Road. It is also worth noting that the earliest use of the Western calendar was found in *Shenbao,* a newspaper started by a Westerner, Ernest Major, and which began to place both Chinese and Western calendar dates side by side on its front page in 1872. But it was not until Liang Qichao proclaimed his own use of the Western calendar in an 1899 diary of his voyage to America that a pradigmatic change in "time-consciousness" was effected.[67] By the 1920s, if not earlier, the commercial calendar poster had become a popular advertisement item for Shanghai's tobacco companies and a fixture in urban daily life.

It was against such a "timely" background that a Chinese nationhood came to be "imagined." Benedict Anderson's widely cited book suggests that before it becomes a political reality a "nation" is first an "imagined community." This "community" is itself based on a conception of simultaneity "marked by temporal coincidence and measured by clock and calendar." The technical means for representing this "imagined community," according to Anderson, were the two forms of print culture—newspapers and the novel—that first flowered in the eighteenth and nineteenth centuries in Europe.[68] However, Anderson does not fully flesh out the complicated process by which these two forms were used to imagine the nation. Another theorist, Jürgen Habermas, has likewise pointed to the close connection between periodicals and salons that contributed to the rise of the "public sphere" in England and France.[69] But neither Anderson nor Habermas has seen fit to connect

67. Rengong (Liang Qichao), "Hanman lu," *Qingyi bao* 35 (1899), 2275–78.
68. Benedict Anderson, *Imagined Communities: Reflections on the Origin and Spread of Nationalism* (New York: Verso, 1991).
69. Jürgen Habermas, *The Structural Transformation of the Public Sphere* (Cambridge, Mass.: MIT Press, 1989), 40–41, 50–51.

the two phenomena of nationhood and the public sphere. In my view, this was precisely what constituted the intellectual "problematique" for China at the turn of the century, when intellectuals and writers sought to imagine a new "community" (*chun*) of the nation (*minzu* or *guojia* but not yet *minzuguojia*) as they endeavored to define a new reading public. They attempted to draw the broad contours of a new vision of China and disseminate such a vision to their audience, the newly emergent public of largely newspaper and periodical readers and students in the new schools and colleges. But such a vision remained a "vision"—an imagined, often visually based, evocation of a "new world" of China—not a cogent intellectual discourse or political system. In other words, this visionary imagination preceded the efforts of nation-building and institutionalization. In China, modernity, for all its amorphousness, became the guiding ethos of such a vision, yet without the critical awareness of what the workings of "instrumental rationality" would inevitably entail.

The nation as an imagined community in China was made possible not only by elite intellectuals like Liang Qichao, who proclaimed new concepts and values, but also and more importantly by the popular press. It is interesting to note that the rise of commercial publishing—particularly the large companies such as the Commercial Press (Shangwu yinshu guan, literally, "the shop that printed books for commercial purposes") and China Bookstore (Zhonghua shuju)—also predated the establishment of the Republican nation-state in 1912. They made fortunes principally by compiling and printing new textbooks whenever the political wind blew. The Commercial Press even published a volume of photos and accounts of the 1911 Revolution simultaneously for sale! After the founding of the Republic in 1912, it continued with publications of translations of Western literature, history, thought, and institutions, which were organized into gigantic repositories. In this regard we might give Homi Bhabha's terminological coinage about nationalism another twist in meaning: "dissemiNation" indicated, thus more literally and less ironically, that the knowledge about the new nation must first be *disseminated*.[70]

70. Homi K. Bhabha, "DissemiNation: Time, Narrative, and the Margins of the Modern Nation," in *Nation and Narration,* ed. Homi K. Bhabha (London: Routledge, 1990).

These commercial ventures in publishing were all in the name of introducing new knowledge (*xinzhi*), the textual sources of modernity, of which the general journals like the *Dongfang zazhi* [Eastern miscellany] and the *Xiaoshuo yuebao* [Short story monthly] served as showcases. In a way, they are comparable to the eighteenth-century French "business of Enlightenment" as described by Robert Darnton, in which the ideas of the "philosophes" were popularized and vigorously disseminated by a network of printers and booksellers.[71] However, in the name of promoting new culture and education, the books in China were sold quite cheaply as study aids for students in new-style schools and other readers who were deprived of schooling. In short, from its beginning Chinese modernity was envisioned and produced as a cultural enterprise of "enlightenment" — "*qimeng*," a term taken from the traditional educational practice in which a child received his first lesson from a teacher or tutor. That the term took on the new meaning of being "enlightened" with new knowledge in the national project of modernity should come as no surprise.

By the time the Nationalist government was formally established in 1928 in Nanjing, following more than a decade of warlord rule that made a mockery of the nominal Republic in Beijing, Shanghai had become *the* center of the cultural production and consumption of Chinese modernity. Despite its failures in other areas, the new Nationalist (Guomindang) government in the early 1930s took key steps in a nation-building project, from the actual design and construction of buildings in the new capital to diplomatic negotiations that gradually reestablished China's sovereignty in the "family of nations" and led to the abolishment of the treaty-port concessions in the 1940s. By the early 1930s a strong sense of modern Chinese nationhood was already in place, and despite the existence of the concessions both the central government and Shanghai residents considered the city a *Chinese* metropolis. If colonialism remained a historical and legal factor, this legacy did not necessarily turn Shanghai into a colony.

The Colonial Condition   The configurations of colonialism, modernity, and nationalism are surely the larger intellectual background

71. Robert Darnton, *The Business of Enlightenment: A Publishing History of the Encyclopedia* (Cambridge, Mass.: Harvard University Press, 1968).

against which all the literary figures and texts discussed here must be reexamined. These larger issues involve, first of all, a reexamination of postcolonial discourse itself in this particular historical context.

All postcolonial discourse, it seems to me, assumes a colonial structure of power in which the colonizers have the ultimate authority over the colonized, including its representation. It is a theoretical construct based on the situation of former British and French colonies in Africa and India. In such a discourse, the colonized "subjects" can only serve as the "object" or "other" to the real "subjects"—the colonial masters. In Shanghai, this "subject" situation was more complicated than in British-governed India. Western "colonial" authority was indeed legally recognized in the concession treaties, but it was also conveniently ignored by the Chinese residents in their daily lives—unless, of course, they got arrested in the concessions. But it is also well known that the concessions also provided a protective haven for both criminals and political dissidents, including writers. The Chinese Communist Party was founded in Shanghai in 1921, and its first congress was held in the French Concession.

Whether or not they lived in the foreign concessions, the writers I have discussed were well adjusted to living in this bifurcated world of China's largest treaty-port. Though they had little personal contact with Westerners, they were also among the most "Westernized" in their lifestyle and intellectual predilection. Yet they never conceived of their role as colonized subjects or as the native other to a real or imagined Western colonial master. In fact, with few exceptions, Western "colonial masters" did not even appear as central characters in their fiction. Rather, it was the Chinese writers' fervent espousal of a Western or occidental exoticism that had turned Western culture itself into an other in the process of constructing their own modern imaginary. This process of appropriation was crucial to their own quest for modernity—a quest conducted with full confidence in their own identity as Chinese nationalists; in fact, in their minds, modernity itself was in the service of nationalism.

This is evidently not the same situation as in colonial India, where nationalism was a direct product of colonial history. It should be obvious to all historians that, despite a series of defeats since the Opium War, China was victimized but never fully colonized by a Western power. The treaty-port system may be considered a "semi-colony"—not necessarily in the Maoist sense of double negativity (it is worse, as it is com-bined with "semi-feudalism"), but in the sense of a mixture of colonial and Chinese elements. One could argue, in a kind of postcolonial twist to Mao, that the situation in Shanghai was even worse than in a strict colony as the discrepancies between the privileged "colonial" status of the concessions and the rest of city could have levied a heavier psycho-logical toll on all Chinese. The issue of "internal colonialization" may well be relevant here, but on the basis of my research I am not fully prepared to share this view.

In a country in which Western colonialism was not a total sys-tem governing the entire nation, the situation might be different, even more complicated. Perhaps one might find Bhabha's theory of colonial "mimicry"[72] at work in the "compradorial" and commercial elite who had close personal and business relations with Westerners. Because of their jobs and their desire for total Westernization, they could be willing colonial "subjects" even if they still carried Chinese citizenship papers. Still, I would argue that the theory of mimicry does not necessarily apply to Shanghai natives in the field of literary and cultural produc-tion. When Chinese writers used compradors or bank clerks in their fiction, their attitude was often one of condescension — not by assuming the superior authority of their Western masters but from their assumed position of a new Chinese nationalism.

This new sense of Chinese nationalism was itself composed of diverse elements. However, unlike British India (at least in more Westernized Bombay), the colonizer's language did *not* assume a dominant status. Despite their knowledge of English or French, most Chinese writers

72. Bhabha has defined "mimicry" both subtly and opaquely. According to him, "colonial mimicry is the desire for a reformed, recognizable Other, as a subject of a difference that is almost the same, but not quite . . . a desire that, through the repe-tition of partial presence . . . articulates those disturbances of cultural, racial, and historical difference that menace the narcissistic demand of colonial authority." Thus Bhabha's theory suggests that even the "partial representation" of the colonial object can be both submissive and subversive. Although the "mimic man" is created by a colonial education — "almost the same but not white" — his very "partial presence" and his "gaze of otherness" give the lie to the post-Enlightenment beliefs of British colonial policy-makers. Obviously, such a phenomenon is a product of a long history of *total* colonization. See Homi Bhabha, "Of Mimicry and Man: The Ambivalence of Colonial Discourse," in his *Location of Culture* (London: Routledge, 1994), 86–90.

continued to use Chinese as the *only* language in their writing. This obvious point nevertheless harks back to a long and deeply entrenched tradition of written Chinese unchallenged by any foreign language throughout Chinese history. Unlike some African writers who were forced by their colonial education to write in the language of their colonial masters, the Chinese never faced such a threat. Their works of poetry and fiction continued to be written in Chinese so that the syntactical structures of the modern vernacular are preserved and, in some cases, enriched (some would say adulterated) by translated terms and phrases. No one wrote fiction in English or French or experimented with the possibilities of bilingual writing. In the rare case of a story or novel involving a Western character, Chinese diction remains unchanged, and in no way are we led to believe that English is somehow implicated in the dialogue.

Thus I argue that for all their flaunted Westernism the Shanghai writers I have discussed never imagined themselves, nor were they regarded, to be so "foreignized" (*yanghua*) as to become slaves to foreigners (*yangnu*), because their sense of Chinese identity was never in question. In my view it was precisely their unquestioned confidence in their "Chineseness" that enabled these writers to openly embrace Western modernity without fear of colonization.

A Chinese Cosmopolitanism   This conjunction of Westernism and nationalism—or more precisely, the intellectual interest in appropriating elements from foreign cultures in order to enrich a new national culture—gives the Shanghai case a somewhat different "take" from what can be summarized under the rubric of colonialism and postcolonialism. It seems to me that in this historical context Shanghai's modern culture in the 1930s can be understood as a manifestation of cosmopolitanism.

The term *cosmopolitanism* is being resurrected by current theorists in cultural studies as perhaps another conceptualization of postmodern globalism in this era of late capitalism—of the circulation of commodities and migration of peoples that constantly cut across national boundaries. But the cosmopolitanism of Shanghai stemmed from an earlier and much different historical context in which the Chinese nation-state was still in the making. In this early stage of national formation, cosmopolitanism became a desirable attitude characterized by an abiding curiosity about other countries and an absorbing zeal toward other cultures. It grew out of a need on the part of the more "modern" segment of the population to look out—to seek new knowledge and inspiration from the outside. The task was made easier by Shanghai's international position as the treaty-port par excellence and the largest metropolis in Asia, replacing Tokyo, which had not recovered from the damages wreaked by the earthquake in 1923.

Aside from being the world's fifth largest city, Shanghai in the 1930s was also the center of a network of cities linked together by ship routes for purposes of marketing, transportation, and tourism. This can be seen in the thriving book trade: Kelly and Walsh, Shanghai's largest foreign bookstore, had branch stores in seven Asian cities—Shanghai, Hong Kong, Tientsin, Yokohama, Singapore, New Delhi, and Bombay. While a British colonial imprint is clearly discernible in its distribution network, this chain of cities nevertheless formed a cosmopolitan cultural space in which Shanghai stood at the intersection between China and other parts of the world. In trying to find out how Chinese writers and translators were able to locate their Western sources, I was told again and again during interviews that foreign books and journals were easily available, some at secondhand bookstores at affordable prices, which in turn received their goods from Western tourists as they dumped their shipboard reading matters after landing in Shanghai. In books as in other commercial goods, Shanghai was at the center of traffic; its cosmopolitanism was a product of this culture of circulation. In this connection, Japan, more than England or France, was the crucial intermediary that both facilitated and complicated the picture of Shanghai cosmopolitanism.

Since around 1900, the North China Sea was traversed constantly by Chinese and Japanese intellectuals, writers, students, businessmen, and tourists. The de facto Japanese "concession" (though not legalized in the treaties) in the northern part of Shanghai was another enclave in which Chinese writers like Lu Xun lived together with a population of Japanese expatriates who outnumbered both the British and the French. As is well known, this "Japanese connection" provided a key to Chinese leftist literature, as most Chinese leftists, including Lu Xun, had been educated in Japan. But the Japanese impact was not limited to leftist literature and thought. Most of the seminal terms and concepts from Western literature came from Japanese translations which were adopted or retranslated into Chinese.[73] During the early 1930s, as the Japanese invasion of China became imminent, Chinese leftist writers denounced Japanese militarism in the name of nationalism as they continued to learn from Japanese leftists, translating their treatises and slogans and trying to figure out what had really transpired in Soviet Russia through Japanese sources, until the entire proletarian scene in Japanese literature came to an end with the massive "conversion" to Japanese imperial nationalism. By 1937, when war finally broke out, the nature of nationalism itself had changed in both China and Japan.

Thus, from a leftist point of view, cosmopolitanism prevailed in Shanghai almost by default, because the more conservative nationalism in both Japan and China had in fact facilitated the growth of a loose alliance of left-wing intellectuals against Japanese imperialism in Asia and fascism in Europe, which the urban wing of the underground Chinese Communist Party (CCP) exploited to its great advantage. Several international bodies, including the Comintern, sent their delegates to Shanghai to meet with Chinese followers and sympathizers in the concessions. Thus a kind of informal international brotherhood was forged. The French writer Henri Barbusse took a leading role in this movement. Unable to visit China himself, Barbusse sent his former classmate Paul Vailliant-Couturier, an editor of the French leftist newspaper *l'Humanité,* and published an article written especially for Chinese readers, "To the Chinese Intelligentsia," in the journal edited by Shi Zhecun, *Xiandai* or *Les contemporains* (vol. 4, no. 1, Nov. 1933). Vailliant-Couturier also attended an "antiwar congress" under the secret sponsorship of the CCP, "that was publicly announced and conspiratorially held right in the heart of the city." Fifty Chinese delegates from all parts of the country, including those from the "Red Army districts" attended. Other foreign delegates included Lord Marley of the British Labor Party; a Belgian communist named Marteau; a French socialist named Poupy; and an American journalist, Harold Isaacs, editor of the English-language journal in Shanghai, *China Forum,* which duly reported the proceed-

73. See appendix D on Japanese terms incorporated in Chinese in Liu, *Translingual Practice.*

ings.[74] This brand of leftism seemed to fit the general ideological temper of the literary scene at the time—a leftism reinforced by the patriotic sentiment against Japanese aggression among writers in China combined with a vague feeling of internationalist alliance against fascism in Europe. Even after war was declared in 1937, clandestine anti-Japanese activities could still be conducted in Shanghai under the legal protection of the Western concessions.

Thus despite—or because of—all these special circumstances, Shanghai reached the pinnacle of its urban glory in the early 1930s. It continued during the "insulated island" period of 1937–41, when Shanghai was only partially occupied by Japan while the concessions still maintained legal autonomy, and even after the Japanese occupied the entire city in 1942. Shanghai under Japanese occupation was already on the wane, but it was not until the Sino-Japanese War was over in 1945, when the chaos caused by inflation and the civil war brought the city's economy to shambles, that Shanghai's urban glory came to an end. The triumph of the rural-based Communist Revolution further reduced the city to insignificance. For the next three decades in the new People's Republic, Shanghai was dominated and dwarfed by the new national capital of Beijing, to which it had also to contribute more than 80 percent of its annual revenue. Moreover, despite its growing population, Shanghai was never allowed to transform its physical surroundings: The city remained largely the same as in the 1940s, and its buildings and streets inevitably decayed as a result of neglect and disrepair.

Under the stern gaze of an authoritarian government, the city had lost all its glitz and glamour, its dynamism and decadence. Mao Dun's "midnight" world of "light, heat, and power" seemed to have vanished. Recently, however, as a result of Deng Xiaoping's economic reforms, the city has experienced spectacular rebirth. Ironically, in the midst of the current craze for new constructions, a nostalgia for Old Shanghai is becoming widespread in Shanghai's commercial and popular culture. A new cosmopolitan spirit seems to be ascendant as it is widely reported, first by the Shanghainese themselves, that in the process of renovation at the old building of the Shanghai and Hong Kong Banking Corpora-

74. Harold Isaacs, *Re-Encounters in China: Notes from a Journey in a Time Capsule* (Armonk, N.Y.: M. E. Sharpe, 1985), 21.

tion, a series of old wall murals have been discovered in which Shanghai was clearly placed as one of the eight international metropolises.[75]

This is a much condensed version of two chapters of my book, *Shanghai Modern: The Flowering of New Urban Culture in China, 1930–1945* (Cambridge, Mass.: Harvard University Press, 1999). A longer version was presented to the conference on Alternative Modernities in Delhi, 16–20 December 1997.

75. See a long feature article, "Shanghairen weishenmo milian 30 niandai" [Why do Shanghai people become obsessed with the 1930s?], *Xin zhoukan* [New weekly] 22/23 (15 December 1997): 13–25.

Adda, Calcutta: Dwelling in Modernity

Dipesh Chakrabarty

And it is a good sign that I still enjoy adda, *for* adda *and youth are inseparable.*
—Manashi Das Gupta (1957)

Now that it is clear at the end of this millennium that there is no es-
caping capitalist modernization anywhere in the world, a question that
Marshall Berman asked a while ago becomes even more insistent in the
lives of many. In his justly celebrated book, *All That Is Solid Melts into
Air,* Berman was interested in exploring how "modern men and women
may become subjects as well as objects of modernization," how they
might "get a grip on the modern world and make themselves at home
in it."[1] I am not confident that this can be achieved by or for all in a
programmatic manner, for the control that different groups can exercise on capitalism is at best uneven and subject to global distribution
of institutional power. But the struggle to make a capitalist modernity
comfortable for oneself, to find a sense of community in it, to be—as

I acknowledge with pleasure a double debt of gratitude to my friend and fellow historian Gautam Bhadra, a "boon companion" of many an adda of our shared youth. He
most generously shared with me both his rich thoughts on the subject and "sources"
from his personal collection. This essay has gained immensely from criticisms made
by Ranajit Guha, Anne Hardgrove, Manashi and Arun Das Gupta, Dhruba Gupta,
Asok Sen, Arjun Appadurai, Fiona Nicoll, Barbara Metcalf, Tom Metcalf, Sanjay Seth,
Lawrence Cohen, Tom Laqueur, Keya Ganguly, Crystal Bartolovich, and audiences at
seminars at Carnegie-Mellon University, Australian National University, and at the
Universities of Melbourne, Chicago, Cambridge, Calcutta, Washington, Michigan,
Illinois (Urbana-Champaign) and Wisconsin (Madison). It was Meaghan Morris's
superb essay on "Things to Do with Shopping Centres" that inspired me to think
about adda. I dedicate this essay to her in humility and friendship.
1. Marshall Berman, *All That Is Solid Melts into Air: The Experience of Modernity* (New
York: Penguin Books, 1988), 5.

Berman puts it — at home in modernity, is an ongoing, ceaseless process for all. We do not have a choice in the matter even when the problem does not admit of any permanent resolutions. Whatever our philosophical critiques of metaphysics today, the process of producing metaphysical identities for oneself — both collectively and individually — is what marks this struggle. The history I present here of a social practice, *adda,* from the city of Calcutta in the first half of the twentieth century is a specific historical study of that struggle.

The word *adda* (pronounced "uddah") is translated by the Bengali linguist Sunitikumar Chattopadhyay as "a place" for "careless talk with boon companions" or "the chats of intimate friends" (I will have more to say later on this interchangeability of "talk" and "place").[2] Roughly speaking, it is the practice of friends getting together for long, informal, and unrigorous conversations. Bengali intellectuals have produced a lot of unintended metaphysics in their discussions of adda. Adda is often seen as something quinessentially Bengali, as an indispensable part of the Bengali character or as an integral part of such metaphysical notions as "life" and "vitality" for the Bengalis. Benoy Sarkar, a sociologist of the 1940s, many of whose writings were published in dialogue forms as though they were fragments of coversations from an adda, spoke in 1942 of the "vitality" of adda that had helped Bengalis "sustain and enrich" their natural instincts as a people. "What we need is *adda,*" he declaimed in one of his conversations.[3] Calcutta's tricentenary celebrations in 1990 saw the publication of a whole book devoted to the topic — *Kolkatar adda* or "The Addas of Calcutta." In his preface to this book, the historian Nisithranjan Ray describes Bengalis as "an *adda*-loving people."[4] The Bengali writer Nripendrakrishna Chattopadhyay wrote thus in the 1970s in praise of the institution: "Bengalis enjoy a tremendous reputation in the world as the people best at practicing *adda.* No other race has been able to build up such an institution as *adda* which stands above all ideas of need or utility. To enjoy *adda* is a primordial and perennial principle of life — no other people have succeeded in acknowledging this

2. Sunitikumar Chattopadhyay, "Hostel Life in Calcutta" [in Bengali, 1913], in *Jiban katha* (Calcutta: Jijnasha, 1979), 210.
3. Benoy Sarkar, "Addar darshan," in *Binay sarkarer baithake,* ed. Haridas Mukhopadhyay (Calcutta, 1942), 273.
4. Nishithranjan Ray, "Preface" to *Kolkatar adda,* ed. Samarendra Das (Calcutta: Mahajati prakashan, 1990), 10.

in life as Bengalis have." And a page later he adds: "So deep is the spiritual connection between *adda* and the water and atmosphere of Bengal that *adda* . . . has now spread to the [Calcutta] Corporation, offices, state-meetings, *rawk* [veranda, the raised terrace of a building], tea-shops, sports-pavilions, to the district organizations of political parties, to schools and colleges—to everywhere. Everywhere, in the pores of all activity, it is *adda* that exists in many different guises."[5] In the reckoning of Saiyad Mujtaba Ali, a distinguished Bengali writer of humor, the men of Calcutta—in the matter of their devotion to adda—come second only to the men of Cairo. The latter, according to a humorous essay by Ali, are to be found at home only for a reluctant six hours every day (midnight to six in the morning), preferring instead to spend the rest of their time at work and cafeterias enjoying conversations with their male friends.[6]

By many standards of judgments in modernity, adda is a flawed social practice: It is predominantly male in its modern form in public life; it is oblivious of the materiality of labor in capitalism; and, in its middle-class form, it is usually forgetful of the working classes. Some even see it as a practice promoting sheer laziness in the Bengalis. Yet its perceived gradual disappearance from the urban life of Calcutta over the last three decades—something related no doubt to changes in the political economy of the city—has now produced an impressive amount of mourning and nostalgia on the part of Bengali writers for the practice of adda. It is as if they fear that with the slow death of adda, the identity of being a Bengali will also die.

Because adda is now perceived to be a dying practice, Calcutta has seen a series of self-conscious efforts in recent times to collect and preserve memories and descriptions of Bengali addas of the last hundred years or so. A veritable market has now developed for adda nostalgia. The Internet carries several "chat" networks for Bengalis of both West Bengal and Bangladesh which are designated addas.[7] The book of essays,

5. Nripendrakrishna Chattopadhyay, "Adda," in *Nana katha* (Calcutta: Deb Sahitya Kutir, 1978), 2–3.

6. Saiyad Mujtaba Ali, "Adda Passport" [in Bengali], in *Saiyad mujtaba ali rachana-bali,* vol. 3 (Calcutta: Mitra o ghosh, 1975), 404–11.

7. Try, for instance, "Calcutta Online," where it is possible to subscribe to "Bengali adda." The legendary nature of addas at the College Street Coffee House may also be seen in the fact that a news digest published from New York for immigrant and dias-

Kolkatar adda, mentioned above, is a response to this market. It begins by pointing to the "horrendous possibility" that Bengalis might soon forget to enjoy adda and that a busy and all-consuming ethic of work might overtake their lives.[8] Saiyad Mujtaba Ali touched a note of mourning over the alleged disappearance of adda as early as the 1970s: "It is incontrovertible that genuinely distinguished *addas* are now as good as dead even if they seem alive. How many of the five-story, ten-story buildings going up in Calcutta today have [spaces] for *adda*?"[9] Even a catalog of Bengali books in print brought out by the Publishers' Guild in Calcutta on the occasion of the Calcutta Book Fair in 1997 began by mourning the loss of the spirit of adda from the trade itself. The introductory essay surveying the history of the last fifty years of book publishing in Calcutta ended on a nostalgic and melancholy note: "The cover designs of [Bengali] books have changed, as has changed the artistry of publication. There is a larger variety of topics now. Along with new writers will come new publishers. . . . But will we ever get back that which has now disappeared for ever from the world of Bengali literature—literary addas? Perhaps some will be struck by pain at this. But what other path is there to follow except to press forward even as our hearts' ache?"[10]

---

poric Bengalis in the United States carried news of the retirement of an "upcountry" working-class man, Ramuchacha, who for forty-five years served *addabaj* Bengali patrons of the Coffee House. See *Udayan,* 3 December 1997, 8: "The man who was inseparable from all the joys and sorrows, hope and despair, poetry and adda of Coffee House over the last four decades, formally accepted farewell on last Saturday. . . . Ramuda alias Ramuchacha has now left behind forty-five of his seventy years of life in the main hall and in the balconies of Coffee House. . . . His white moustache moist with tears, Ramuchacha said in his slightly upcountry style: 'I am an ignorant man. I do not know the names of any of those whom I have seen here over the last forty years. But I can still recognize their faces. Students come, sip coffee, chat, write poetry—I only see them. Now I will return to my village and spend time in the company of my grandchildren.'" Had it not been for the association Ramuchacha had with a space treated in Bengali middle-class memory as a sacred site in the history of Bengali literary modernism, the retirement of an "unknown" working-class person, who was not even a Bengali himself, would have scarcely made news in the American-Bengali diaspora.

8. Ray, "Preface."

9. Saiyad Mujtaba Ali, "Adda," in *Saiyad mujtaba ali racanabali,* vol. 3 (Calcutta: Mitra o ghosh, 1975), 396.

10. Sabitendranath Ray and Rabin Bal, "Bangla prakashanar panchash bochhor,

I am not interested in reading this nostalgia as an error of some kind (for as a migrant, I have no easy critique of nostalgia). Nor is it my aim to defend the Bengali metaphysical claim that the practice of adda is anything peculiarly Bengali. The tradition of men and women gathering in social spaces to enjoy company and conviviality is surely no monopoly of any particular region. Nor is the word only a Bengali word; it exists in Hindi and Urdu and means a "place of gathering" (bus terminals in north India are called "bus-addas"). What is peculiar, if anything, in twentieth-century Bengali discussions of the practice of adda is the *claim* that the practice is peculiarly Bengali and that it marks a primary national characteristic of the Bengali people to such a degree that the "Bengali character" could not be thought without it. It is this claim and its history that I study here in terms of Berman's question. For it seems to me that the apparent nostalgia for adda today occupies the place of another — and unarticulated — anxiety: How does one sing to the ever-changing tunes of capitalist modernization and at the same time retain a comfortable sense of being at home in it?

A few qualifying words are in order. My use of the expression *Bengali* has some serious limitations. Bengalis now are a people divided in their loyalties to the nation-states of India and Bangladesh; most of the material used here, however, comes from the histories of the Hindu-Bengalis and from what is now the Indian state of West Bengal, in particular from the city of Calcutta. Also, my concern with the history of the practice of adda is restricted to the world and culture of twentieth-century Bengali literary modernism. After all, it was within that world, as we shall see, that the practice was given a self-consciously nationalist home. This is one reason I focus on developments in the city of Calcutta. Calcutta was the leading center of Bengali literary production.

THE BENGALI DEBATE ON ADDA

The widespread acceptance of the status of adda as a marker of Bengali character did not mean, however, that Bengali intellectuals were all of the same opinion as to the value of this practice. Let me begin, therefore, with some sense of the kind of debates in which the practice is

---

1947–97," in *Books in Print from West Bengal and Fair Directory 1997* (Calcutta: Publisher's Guild, 1997), xxxii.

embroiled. A good starting point is provided by the contradictory opinions of two very well-known cultural commentators in modern Bengali history, the critic Nirad Chaudhuri and the writer Buddhadev Bose, who also founded the discipline of comparative literature in India.

Chaudhuri, in his famous book, *The Autobiography of an Unknown Indian,* sees adda as something symptomatic of a deep and continuing malaise in the Bengali character. He uses the word "gregariousness" in both describing the institution of adda and explaining what, in his view, is wrong with Calcutta's men. He begins by noticing how old and ubiquitous the Bengali cultural practice of adda is. Bhabanicharan Bandyopadhyay's *Kalikata kamalalaya*—a text published in 1823 containing vignettes of Bengali social life in the early history of the colonial city of Calcutta—provides him with convincing evidence that the common Bengali practices of "the morning gossip, the midday spell of business or siesta, the afternoon relaxation, and the evening court, had all come down unmodified" from the 1820s to the Calcutta of the 1930s.[11] Chaudhuri's description of this Bengali penchant for company is evocative, though its caricaturing tone betrays the moral disapproval with which he regarded this cultivation of "gregariousness":

> What the native of the city lacked in sociability he made up in gregariousness. No better connoisseur of company was to be found anywhere in the world, and no one else was more dependent on the contiguity of his fellows with the same incomprehension of his obligation towards them. The man of Calcutta found the company he needed so badly and continuously readily assembled, without any effort on his part, in his office, or in his bar-library, or in his college, which were no less places for endless gossip than for work.
>
> ... Perhaps gregariousness was the only disinterested thing in Calcutta society. Outside working hours the true native would always be roving in search of company, and his very striving for it often defeated its purpose. Every able-bodied person after his return from office and a hurried wash and tea rushed out of his house with the intention of meeting his friends, and these friends being on the same errand it occasionally happened that everybody missed everybody

11. Nirad Chaudhuri, *The Autobiography of an Unknown Indian* (1951; reprint, New York: Macmillan, 1989), 382.

else. The more usual practice, however, was to avoid these misadventures by having fixed rendezvous or, as they were called in Bengali, *addas*. Each *adda* had its fixed adherents. . . . These gathering places were most often in the outer parlour of one of the wealthier members of the group, but at times also an office after office hours, and more rarely, a tea-shop. . . . As a general rule, these meeting places were located in the quarter in which the greater majority of the frequenters lived. But it was not at all unusual to find a man travelling five or six miles by tram in order to join his company. . . . A man was far less ready to join a new *adda* than he was to shift to a new house in a new quarter.

The colonial-Victorian prejudices lurking behind Chaudhuri's disapproval of adda are not hard to discern. In Chaudhuri's description, adda is, first, idleness itself; it denotes a lethargy of spirit. "In sharp contrast to the demoniac energy shown in rushing to the rendezvous," he writes, "the languor of the actual proceedings was startling." Second, the practice of adda revealed to him a lack of individuality, the presence of a "herd instinct." He writes:

> I did not understand this behaviour until in 1922 I read for the first time McDougall's *Social Psychology,* in which I found the distinction between the social and the gregarious instinct clearly drawn and properly emphasised. Reinforcing my critical armoury from the book, I began to call the gregarious natives of Calcutta Galton's Oxen, that is to say, the oxen of Damaraland in Africa. Individually these animals hardly appear even to be conscious of one another, but if separated from the herd they display extreme signs of distress.

Third, adda signified for Chaudhuri the absence of a controlled sociality which, according to him, only individuals with a developed sense of individuality were capable of achieving. The people of Calcutta had addas because "there was very little" of what Chaudhuri understood by "social life": "No afternoon or evening parties, no dinners, no at-homes, and, of course, no dances, enlivened their existence." Finally, for Chaudhuri, adda was inimical to bourgeois domesticity. As he puts it: "The strong herd-instinct of the natives of Calcutta has virtually killed family life. There is no custom among them of a man sitting with his wife and children in the evening. It is hardly possible even to find them at home at any hour of the day suitable for calls, because their days are divided into three major outings—the morning wandering in search of casual gossip, the midday stay in office, and the systematised cultivation of company in the evenings."[12]

Clearly, what Chaudhuri's critique both values and finds missing from the lives of his contemporaries in Calcutta is the familiar trichotomous bourgeois grid of home-work-leisure by which many textbooks in the discipline of sociology attempt to explain modernity. Chaudhuri's writings remind us that the grid is clearly there, at least as an object of desire if not as a practice in the lives of modern Bengalis. Chaudhuri's was not an exogenous critique.

In the 1950s, at the same time as Chaudhuri published his denunciation of adda, Buddhadev Bose wrote an essay on the same subject, but his mood could not be more opposed to that of Chaudhuri's reflections. The opening two paragraphs of Bose are worth quoting at length, if only to document the elaborate nature of the affection that many Bengali intellectuals have felt for the institution of adda:

> I am not a pundit, I do not know the etymology of the word [adda]. It sounds non-Sanskritik [and] Muslim. If we Hindu-ize it and call it *sabha,* it loses everything. If we Anglicize it and call it "party," we kill its spirit. The [appropriate] dress for meetings is khaki or *khadi* [coarse hand-spun cotton], while the clothes one wears at a party are light but firmly pressed, and the *sabha* is white, decorous [and yet] uncomfortable. I don't know if the French salon still exists, but their descriptions suggest a degree of elaborateness which may not be good. Does adda have an exact synonym in any other language of the world? Even without being a linguist, I can say, no. Because in no other country would there be the spirit of adda or the right environment. People of other countries make speeches, crack jokes, offer arguments, have fun all night, but they do not do [the Bengali verb is "give"] adda. . . . What will they do with the club, those who have the *adda*?

Bose was quite clear that the "they" of his description could only be the Bengalis. Not only that—much like Nripendrakrishna Chatto-

12. All quotations from Chaudhuri are from *Autobiography,* 383–86.

padhyay whom I have already quoted, he literally naturalized this practice, seeing in adda a reflection of the soft, alluvial soil of Bengal:

> Adda is an all-India thing but it is only in the moist, tender soil of Bengal that it can achieve its fullest expression. Just as our seasons give rise to poetry, in the same way do they help make addas intense. Our *chaitra* [mid-March to mid-April, the last month of the Bengali year] evenings, the rain-patter-filled afternoons of *sravan* [the rainy fourth month of the Bengali calendar], the moon-washed nights of autumn, the sweet and bright mornings of winter — they all go ringing the silent bell of adda, some hear it and some don't. It is inevitable that [the spirit of] adda will wither in countries of extreme heat and cold. . . . My heart trembles if I have to go to a *sabha,* I run away at the mention of a party, but adda? I cannot live without it. . . . That is why I cannot be satisfied simply being its worshipper; I also have to be its [high] priest and preach its glory.[13]

Formed at the opposite pole of Chaudhuri's sensibility, such self-consciously lyrical panegyric to the spirit of adda is relatively rare. There are, after all, Bengali words like *gultani* and *gyajano* that generally refer to "useless talk" and suggest the existence of a critical attitude to adda which is not necessarily indebted to the modern capitalist-colonial theme of "the lazy native." It is possible that the middle-class emphasis on discipline prevalent since the colonial times built not only on Victorian conceptions of laziness but also on preexisting understandings of what constituted "work" and "idleness." In any case, even confirmed votaries of adda such as Chattopadhyay and Bose mention how the word *adda* was never popular with "guardians and parents," who presumably associated it at least with neglect of duties when they did not see it as a complete waste of time.[14] At the same time, there is enough evidence to suggest that in Bengali modernity, adda provided for many a site for self-presentation, of cultivating a certain style of being in the eyes of others. To be good at adda was also a cultural value. Two very well-known examples from recent Bengali history may suffice to show this. The famous Bengali physicist Satyen Bose (of the Bose-Einstein

13. Buddhadev Bose, "Adda," in *Kolkatar adda,* ed. Samarendra Das (Calcutta, 1990), 13.
14. Chattopadhyay, "Hostel Life," 210; Bose, "Adda," 13.

statistics fame) was often fondly described by many others of his time as "addar raja," the king of adda, while the writer Saiyad Mujtaba Ali, whose speech and writing both displayed the raconteur style popular in addas, was decorated by his admirers with the mock royal title "adda chakrabarti" (Emperor of Adda).[15]

The many different tensions that constitute the modern Bengali understanding of adda is encapsulated in the semantic range that a contemporary Bengali-to-English dictionary ascribes to the word. Here is a dictionary entry from 1968:

> Adda—n. a dwelling-place; a haunt; a (fixed or permanent) meeting-place, a rendezvous; a place or institution for practising anything (*ganer adda:* [*adda* for musicians]); a club; a company of idle talkers, their meeting-place or talk; a place for assemblage, a station or stand (*garir adda* [*adda* for vehicles]). *adda gara*—v. to take up abode (usu[ally]. permanently), to settle. *adda deoya, adda mara*—v. to join in an assembly of idle talkers; to indulge in idle talk with others. *addadhari*—n. the keeper or the chief person of a club; a regular club-goer. *addabaj*—a. fond of indulging in idle talk with others or of haunting clubs where such talk is indulged in.[16]

The reader will note that something of Chaudhuri's sensibility survives in this extract in the moralistic description of adda as "idle talk." The aspiration to "modernity," in contrast, survives in the comparison suggested to the English "club": The Sanskritized word *addadhari* and the Persianized expression *addabaj(z)* point to the ways of being, a certain temperament or character, that the word connotes, while the word also carries the older sense of "dwelling," a "gathering place," a settlement, suggesting perhaps a dialectic of settlement and nomadology whose full sense is now beyond our grasp.

The very different meanings of the word obviously bear witness to the heterogeneous pasts that are invoked by the practice of adda, a simultaneously celebrated and condemned—but in any case ubiquitous—institution of Calcutta's urban life. I want to trace some of these heterogeneities in order to highlight the tensions that have historically

15. See Hirankumar Sanyal, *Porichoyer kuribochhor o onnanno smritichitra* (Calcutta: Papyrus, 1978), 145. See also Gaurkishor Ghosh, "Preface" to *Saiyad mujtaba ali granthabali* (Calcutta: Mitra o ghosh, 1978), vol. 4.

16. "Adda," in *Samsad Bengali-English Dictionary* (Calcutta: Sahitya samsad, 1968).

constituted the Bengali modern. It would be simplistic to see adda simply as a hangover of an older feudal lifestyle, as a vestige of rural, pre-urban past surviving as an obstacle to Bengali modernity, or to read Bose as defending a precapitalist sense of time and sociality while we hear the ghosts of Martin Luther and Max Weber speak through the prose of Chaudhuri. The institution of adda resists being seen within such a stark feudal-capitalist binary for the simple reason that it was embraced as a practice precisely by those who helped form a modern Bengali literary public in Calcutta and who contributed to a distinctly modern sense of nationality.

ADDA AND THE BIRTH OF DEMOCRATIC SPEECH: A GENEALOGY

In contemporary Bengali language, *adda, majlish* (from the Arabic *majlis,* meaning a gathering, meeting, or party), and *baithak* (an assembly; *baithakkhana:* drawing room) are used as practical synonyms, just as one could now use both *majlishi* and *addabaj* to refer to a person who truly enjoys being part of an adda or majlish. I want to suggest that this equivalence — at least in Bengali usage of these words — is of recent origin. The word *adda* has gained in respectability in the twentieth century due to developments one associates with modernity.

Of course, it is true that the custom of men gathering together — and women, too, gathering in separate social spaces — to talk informally about all kinds of things that affect their lives is an old tradition in rural Bengal. The word *chandimandap* — meaning a permanent place for the worship of the goddess Chandi but used by village elders at other times to mean any meeting place — attests to that, and it is interesting that self-conscious discussions of the institution of adda often remind Bengali authors of this older feature of Bengali village life.[17] One of the spaces in Calcutta most associated with adda was that of the *rawk* or *rowak* — elevated verandas attached to older Calcutta houses — where young men of the neighborhood often assembled to have their noisy addas, much to the annoyance of middle-class householders who saw these raucous addas of the rawk as a threat to their respectability, especially if there were young women resident in the house. The external veranda or rawk,

17. See Ray, "Preface," 9.

an architectural feature of Bengali houses until rising land prices made it obsolete, may indeed have been a structural remnant of the *daoa* (veranda) that went around a traditional mud hut in the villages of Bengal. Similarly, the practice of men collecting in such a space may have had something to do with earlier practices. But the addas of the rawk in the city mainly involved young men, and were not usually associated with modern literary production. In the nineteenth century, some of these were dominated by men who were the social leaders in a neighborhood.[18] The Bengali writer Premankur Atarthi has left us word pictures of addas of young men gathering on the rawks of Calcutta neighborhoods around the middle of the twentieth century:

> One house in the neighbourhood had a wide *rowak*. The boys would have their adda there on every Sunday and on other holidays. . . . Conversation ran across all different kinds of topics: patriotism, wrestling, sports, England, Germany, Switzerland. . . .
>
> Often arguments that began in a friendly way in these addas would turn so acrimonious and abusive that the people living inside the house would get worried fearing an outbreak of physical violence. But people those days were so devoted to adda that they would dutifully turn up at their addas in spite of all their fights.[19]

What made the word *adda* respectable in the twentieth century was its association with the spaces for the production of a modern Bengali reading public. I have not come across any use of the word in the nineteenth century that confers respectability on the practice. In nineteenth-century writings, the word *adda* does not appear to replace the word *majlish* as frequently as it does now. In Lal Behari Day's *Recollections of My School-Days*—written for the *Bengal Magazine* in the 1870s but reminiscing about the 1830s—the word *adda* is used to mean a resting place and features in the following way in his discussion of his first trip to Calcutta from his native village of Talpur (Sonapalashi): "We travelled only eight miles. We put up in an *adda,* or inn, bathed, cooked our food, ate and drank (Adam's Ale only), lounged about, again cooked and ate at night, washed our feet in hot water, and laid ourselves on

18. Pyarimohan Mukhopadhyay, *Amar dekha kolkata* (Calcutta, 1981). Pages 207–11 and 222–24 describe such *addas* at the turn of the century.

19. Premankur Atarthi, *Mahasthabirer galpashamagra* (Calcutta, 1988), 231, 364–65.

the ground — a thin piece of date-matting being interposed between our flesh and the mud floor." [20]

In the famous satirical social sketches of *Hutom pyanchar naksha* [hereafter *Hutom*] — written by Kaliprasanna Sinha and first published 1861 and later in 1862 with the English title "Sketches by Hootom [Night-owl] Illustrative of Every Day Life and Every Day" — the word *adda* is kept distinctly different from the word *majlish*. *Adda* in *Hutom* refers to a place of gathering, but its use is at least as irreverent as when he used it to make fun of the congregational form of worship, modeled on Christian practices and introduced into Calcutta by the Hindu reformist sect of the Brahmo samaj: "It is almost impossible to understand the ways of Brahmo dharma [religion] these days. . . . Is the Almighty an upcountry immigrant or a Maharashtrian brahman that He wouldn't be able to hear unless addressed [in the collective voice of] an *adda*?" [21]

The other uses of *adda* in *Hutom* associate the word with "lowly lives" and "dens" where opium or ganja were consumed: *charaser adda, ganjar adda*. Pyarimohan Mukhopadhyay's reminiscences of Calcutta in the early part of the twentieth century confirm this: He refers to places near the "burning ghats" (where the Hindu dead were cremated, the word *ghat* literally referring to steps on the banks of river leading to the water) and underneath the Howrah Bridge on the northern side of the city as harboring addas for those addicted to opium and marijuana.[22] This use is consonant with the way older Bengali dictionaries suggest a connection between adda and marginalized existence: a gathering place of "bad" people or people of bad occupations (*kulok, durbritta*).[23]

20. Lal Behari Dey, *Recollections of My School-Days* (along with *Bengal Peasant Life* and *Folk Tales of Bengal*), ed. Mahadevprasad Saha (Calcutta, 1969), 464. Unfortunately, Saha does not give the original date of publication of *Recollections*.

21. Kaliprasanna Sinha, *Hutom pyanchar naksha,* ed. and annotated by Arun Nag (Calcutta: Subanarekha, 1992), 52

22. Mukhopadhyay, *Amar dekha,* 207–11.

23. For evidence of the older association of the word with life-forms of the subaltern classes, see the entries for *adda* in the following Bengali dictionaries: Gyanendramohan Das, *Bangla bhashar abhidhan,* vol. 1 (Calcutta: Sahitya samsad, 1988; first pub. 1916–17), Haricharan Bandyopadhyay, *Bangiyo shabdakosh* (Calcutta: Sahitya akademi, 1988; first pub. 1924–25), and Subal Chandra Mitra, *Saral bangala abhidhan* (Calcutta: New Age Publishers, 1984; first pub. 1906). Similar associations of the word are to be found in *Hutom,* 63, 105, and Sivanath Shastri, *Ramtanu lahiri o tatkalin bangasamaj* (Calcutta, 1957; first pub. 1903).

Majlish, by contrast—whether in *Hutom* or elsewhere—suggests forms of social gathering that invariably involve wealth and patronage, often conjuring up the picture of men gathered in a rich man's parlor (*baithak* or *baithakkhana*). In *Hutom,* for instance, majlish goes with wine, dancing girls, chandeliers, expensive apparel, and drunken brawls among the rich, involving the new rich of early-nineteenth-century Calcutta and their "spoiled" descendants.[24] Many of these associations weaken in the twentieth century, but, structurally, majlish as a place retains the idea of a patron, the wealthier person without whose parlor or baithakkhana the gathering cannot take place. And, usually, the word is also associated with a place where some kind of performance takes place—singing, dancing, recitation of poetry, and so on. Conversation here, even when it was not directly sycophantic, could never be totally democratic, for the very presence of a patron would influence the speech pattern of such a group in all kinds of ways. It is not surprising that Subal Mitra's dictionary, first published in 1906, explains *majlish* as *kartabhaja daler sabha* or literally "a meeting of those who worship their master" (the *kartabhaja,* incidentally, were also a religious sect in Bengal).[25]

In contrast, whatever the later overlaps between the semantic fields of the two words *adda* and *majlish,* the adda that Buddhadev Bose celebrates in the 1950s has an unmistakably middle-class, "democratic" ring to it. "Everybody must enjoy equal status in an adda," Bose writes, and adds:

> It is inevitable that there will be distinctions made between human beings in that part of life which is concerned with the earning of one's livelihood. But those who cannot shed that sense of division just as one sheds one's office clothes will never know the taste of adda. If there happens to be somebody around whose status is so exalted that we can never forget his glory, then we will sit at his feet as devotees but he will have no invitation to [share in] our pleasure, for the very spring of adda will freeze to ice the moment his eyes fall over it. But similarly, if there are people whose mental level [*maner star*] is

24. *Hutom,* 21, 23, 78–97, 87, 94, 102–3.
25. Mitra, *Saral bangala abhidhan,* entry for *majlish.* It is not entirely clear whether Mitra is simply referring to the religious sect here.

much below that of others, they need to be kept out too, and that is comfortable for them as well.[26]

Of course, no adda was ever just this, a pure practice of democracy. Many addas were dominated by important people who often acted as patrons by providing the venue for the gathering. Addas met in the living rooms of the houses of such people. Adda in the twentieth century remained a hybrid form combining elements of the majlish with that of coffeehouse conversation. Yet the emergence of a democratic sensibility is what separates the speech pattern of an adda in someone's baithak-khana (parlor/living room) from that of an adda in a public place.

Parashuram's [Rajshekhar Bosu] humorous and witty short stories "Lambakarna" and "Dakshinray"—the first published around 1915/16 and the second around 1928/29, both written during the period of the anti-British nationalist movement—give us interesting examples of conversations in a fictional adda that meets regularly in somebody's bai-thakkhana (parlor). The patron in these two stories is a well-to-do Bengali landlord introduced in the story as "Roy Bangshalochan Banerjee Bahadur, Zamindar and Honorary Magistrate, Beleghata Bench." The first story, "Lambakarna," introduces the regular cast of characters of the adda that meets at Bangshalochan's place:

> The evening adda that gathers at the baithakkhana of Bangshalo-chanbabu hears many tall claims every night. The Governor, Suren [dranath] Banrujje [a leading nationalist politician], Mohunbagan [a soccer club], spiritual truths, the funeral ceremony of the old man Adhar in the neighbourhood, the new crocodile at the Alipore [zoo] —no subject is left undiscussed. Recently, for the last seven days, the subject of discussion has been the tiger. Nagen, Bangshalochan's brother-in-law, and Uday, a distantly related "nephew" of his, almost came to blows last night over this [topic]. With great difficulty, the other members persuaded them to desist.[27]

This description captures the spirit of a Bengali adda. "A pure *adda,*" writes Radhaprasad Gupta, who was a member of a well-known adda

26. Bose, "Adda," 14.
27. Parashuram [Rajshekhar Bosu], "Lambakarna," in *Gaddalika* (Calcutta: M. C. Sarkar and Sons, 1974), 79.

in the 1940s, "has no . . . hard and fast *agenda* . . . There is no certainty as to what topic an adda will start with one day, what will cause argumentation and fights, and where it will all end. Suppose this moment the conversation is about [a] *supernova* beyond the solar system; the next moment the discussion could be about Plekhanov's *The Role of the Individual in History*."[28]

By the very catholicity of their interests—subjects ranging from the nationalist movement to the Royal Bengal tiger—the members of Bagshalochanbabu's parlor establish the fact that the nature of their gathering is indeed that of an adda. Yet the second story, set in the same living room with the same characters but now placed somewhere in the 1920s, illustrates how the patron of a majlish-cum-adda could intervene at critical points to direct the conversation, making it fall significantly short of the democratic speech Bose idealized in his praise of the modern adda. Here is the beginning of the second story, "Dakshinray," the subject being once again that of the tiger. Notice how Bangshalochan's participation is minimal yet critical:

> Mr. Chatterjee said, "Talking about tigers, those at Rudraprayag [a pilgrimage spot] are [the best]. Huge, gigantic things. . . . But such is the [sacred] power/glory of the place that they do not attack anybody. After all, [the people there] are all pilgrims. They only catch and eat *sahibs* [Europeans, white people]." . . . Binod, the lawyer, said, "What wonderful tigers! Couldn't a few be imported here? *Swaraj* [self-rule, independence, a word associated with Gandhi] would come quickly. *Swadeshi* [economic nationalism], bombs, the spinning wheel, splitting the legislative councils [each a particular nationalist tactic]— none of these would be needed."
>
> The conversation was being conducted one evening in the *baithakkhana* of Bangshalochanbabu. He was engrossed in reading an English book, *How to Be Happy though Married*. His brother-in-law, Nagen, and his nephew, Uday, were also present.
>
> Chatterjee sucked on the pipe of the hookah for one long minute and said, "Why do you presume that that [method] has not been tried?"

28. Radhaprasad Gupta, "Amader jubakaler adda: jhankidarshan," in *Kolkatar adda*, ed. Samarenda Das (Calcutta, 1990), 27. The italicized English words are used in the original.

"Really? But the Rowlatt Report [on sedition] doesn't mention it."

"So what if you have read the report? Look, does the government know everything? There are more things — or however the saying goes."

"Why don't you tell us about it?"

Chatterjee remained silent for a while and then said, "Hmm."

Nagen pleaded, "Why don't you, Mr. Chatterjee?"

Chatterjee got up and looked out through the door and the window, and resuming his seat, repeated, "Hmm."

Vinod: "What were you looking for?"

Chatterjee: "Just making sure that Haren Ghosal didn't turn up all of a sudden. He is a spy of the police, it is better to be careful from the beginning."

Bangshalochan put the book aside and said, "You'd better not discuss these matters here. It is better that these stories are not told in a magistrate's house."

Eventually, Chatterjee proceeds to narrate the story only after agreeing to Bangshalochan's condition that he would leave out the "overly seditious" elements.[29]

There are two aspects of the narrative that I want to highlight here. First is the editorial-censorial role of the patron — this becomes clear only at the end of the sequence when the patron of the gathering, Bangshalochan, speaks minimally, and yet his speech has the effect of deciding the rules of speaking at this adda. This marks the space of this gathering as more of a majlish than that of a democratic, modern adda. Second is the subtle way — through the title of an English book that Bangshalochanbabu is reading — the author of the story draws our attention to the gendered nature of this space, a theme I will return to later.

If the patron's hospitality gave him the subtle (or sometimes not-so-subtle) power to edit the conversations of a majlish, at the other extreme was the coffeehouse or teashop adda where the absence of a patron was signaled by the acceptance of the ritual of "going Dutch" (with Bengali apologies to the Dutch!).[30] There is, however, an interesting twist to this

29. Parashuram [Rajshekhar Bosu], "Dakshinray," in *Kajjali* (Calcutta: M. C. Sarkar and Sons, 1969), 65–66. The italicized English words are used in the original.
30. My friend Peter van der Veer tells me that what is known in English or Australian as "going Dutch" or in American as "Dutch treat" is known to the Dutch themselves

Bengali adaptation of democracy and individualism to the culture of adda. The Bengali expression for "going Dutch" is actually a string of English words that, of course, do not make any sense in English: "His his, whose whose." It is a literal and (reversed) translation of "jar jar tar tar" (whose whose, his his). The expression was already in use in the 1960s. I do not know when it originated, but Sagarmay Ghosh, the editor of the well-known Bengali literary magazine *Desh,* mentions this expression in his reminiscences of an adda that seems to have met in the 1950s and 1960s.[31]

Why was "going Dutch" given a funny, English-sounding name? A deep analysis of this phenomenon would no doubt have to engage with the question of language use and the production of linguistically based humor by Bengalis. But I also think that the humorous use of English words here is meant to cover up a sense of embarrassment felt precisely over the absence of hospitality that "going Dutch" signifies. The Bengali expression "jar jar tar tar" is a disapproving description of what is in effect seen as an attitude of selfishness. The deep association between food and munificence in Bengali culture meant a certain unease in middle-class consciousness over acknowledging the individualism entailed in everybody paying separately for their own food. The deliberately absurd grammar of the expression "his his whose whose" probably helped a teashop adda overcome its sense of embarrassment when faced precisely with the moment that spoke of the death of the patron. It was as though the democratic adda carried within its structure a nostalgia for the majlish. No wonder then that the aesthetics of the twentieth-century adda should always relate to a hybrid form that would never be able to tear itself away completely from the form that was the majlish.

ADDA AND THE PRODUCTION OF URBAN SPACE

Between the majlish and the adda, then, there is the history of modernity, the process of emergence of a Bengali middle class whose public

---

as "American party"! Obviously, no people want to assume responsibility for the death of the patron and the subsequent death of hospitality that democracy brings in its trail.

31. Sagarmoy Ghosh, "Hirer nakchhabi," in *Kolkatar adda,* ed. Samarenda Das (Calcutta, 1990), 52.

life was marked by its literary and political endeavors. The word *adda,* as I have said, attained respectability by its associations with the literary and political groups that flourished in the city in the 1920s, 1930s, and later. But this respectability, in turn, was mediated by the development of certain institutions and spaces, characteristics perhaps of modernity anywhere.

The first of these was the (high) school and the space it made for literary intimacy among young men, a space surely homosocial and sometimes bordering on the homoerotic. An early instance of such friendship may be seen in the letters the young Michael Madhusudan Dutt, eighteen in 1842, wrote to his schoolfriend Gourdas Bysack (Basak), both students of the Hindu College in that year. They were written in English and the emphases are Dutt's own, and the influence of English Romantic literature is clear:

> My heart beats when the thought that *you* are my friend, comes into my mind! You say you will honour my place . . . with your "Royal presence." Your presence, Gour Dass, is something more than Royal. Oh! it is *angelic!* oh! no! it is something *more exquisite* still!
>
> Wednesday last I did go to the Mechanics — not to learn Drawing, Oh! no! "twas for something more exquisite still!" that is to see you . . . Shall I see you at the Mechanics tomorrow? O! come for my sake![32]

Later in the century Bipinchandra Pal would form a similarly intense friendship with Sundarimohan Das, and Dineschandra Sen with somebody called Ramdayal.[33] For the twentieth century, a similar friendship is recorded between Achintyakumar Sengupta and Premendra Mitra in their youth, a sense of attachment in which one experienced feelings not altogether dissimilar from those of romantic love.[34] (Similar friendships have blossomed between young women, too, with the establishment of girls' schools, but their histories, for understandable reasons, are per-

---

32. Jogindranath Bosu, *Michael madhusudan datter jibancharit* (Calcutta: Ashok pustakalaya, 1990), 48–49, 51.

33. Bipinchandra Pal, *Sattarbatshar: atmajibani* (Calcutta: Jugajatri, 1957), 202–3; Dineshchandra Sen, *Gharer katha o juga sahitya* (Calcutta: Jijnasha, 1969), 95–98.

34. See the letters exchanged between Mitra and Sengupta in their adolescence — they have been reproduced in Achintyakumar Sengupta, *Kallol jug* (Calcutta: M. C. Sarkar and Sons, 1960), 6–16.

haps harder to recover.) My point is that the history of the modern Bengali adda has some roots in the way literature came into the space of friendship and fashioned new sentiments of intimacy.

The Tagores were pioneers and patrons of many forms of literary gatherings which combined more formal set-ups — usually given Sanskritized names like *ashar* and *sammilani* — with some of the more spontaneous elements of adda.[35] The pleasures of kinship were garnished in this family with those of literature. Sarala Devi, a niece of the poet Rabindranath Tagore, wrote later about the period 1887–88 when, on a holiday with the family at Darjeeling, the poet would read out English literature to his family at a gathering (*ashar*) that met every evening. Sarala Devi writes: "My literary tastes were formed by Rabimama [*mama* = maternal uncle]. He was the person who opened my heart to the aesthetic treasure in Matthew Arnold, Browning, Keats, Shelley and others. I remember how when we were at the Castleton House in Darjeeling for a month or so . . . every evening [he] would read aloud from and explain [to us] Browning's 'Blot in the Schuteon.' That was my first introduction to Browning."[36]

Anecdotes from the life of the nationalist writer Bankimchandra Chattopadhyay also provide evidence of this process of percolation of literature into the space of intimacy and sociality. The Bengali essayist Akshoychandra Sarkar mentions once spending a few hours in a waiting room at a railway station in the company of Bankimchandra discussing the literary genre of "mysteries": "Out of that sharing of aesthetic pleasure [*rasa*] [in 1870] was born a feeling of mutual appreciation between us. Over time that grew into . . . a special friendship. He was my superior in age, caste, education, and accomplishment, but this never interfered with our friendship."[37] Bankimchandra's nephew and biographer Sachishchandra Chattopadhyay relates the story of a stormy argument one day between Bankimchandra and a literary friend of his that continued uninterrupted from nine in the evening to after midnight, and comments: "The mention of Hugo, Balzac, Goethe, Dante, Chaucer and others still reminds me of that night." Sachishchandra also men-

35. See Prasantakumar Pal, *Rabijibani,* vol. 3 (Calcutta, 1988), 39, 60, 237, 268, 270.
36. Sarala Devi Chaudhurani, *Jibaner jharapata* (Calcutta: Rupa, 1982), 34. See also Pal, *Rabijibani,* 74 where this statement is set in the context of Tagore's life.
37. Quoted in Amitrasudan Bhattacharya, *Bankimchandrajibani* (Calcutta: Ananda Publishers, 1991), 109.

Figure 1. baithak *by Charu Ray*

tions how Bankimchandra's baithakkhana was sometimes transformed into a space for literary adda (he in fact uses both of these words writing in 1911–12) where writers met.[38]

Two other institutions helped move the discussion of a baithak toward cosmopolitan concerns. One of these was the newspaper. *Hutom* mentions how the "anglicized" of the 1860s were always excited about the "best news of the day," but in those years the newspaper was something that distinguished the anglicized.[39] The sketch (circa 1920s) by the Bengali artist Charu Ray that depicts a typical scene of a baithak suggests the newspaper and books as permanent, defining, everyday features of the new, twentieth-century baithakkhana (fig. 1).[40] Compare this, however, with the drawing of Suniti Chattopadhyay that illustrates an adda in a students' hostel in Calcutta in 1913 (fig. 2) and with Chattopadhyay's description of the usual proceedings of a typical adda. The process of democratization and indigenization of literary tastes in the lives of the young of the middle classes will become clear.[41]

Unlike in the sedate and aristocratic baithak, the atmosphere here is animated and the furnishing more sparse and much less comfortable than in the picture of the baithak. The scene gathers most of its energy from the extended arms, pointed fingers, and focused eyes in the fore-

38. Sachishchandra Chattopadhyay, *Bankim-jibani* (Calcutta: Pustak bipani, 1989), 283, 311.

39. *Hutom,* 41.

40. This sketch is entitled "Betaler baithake" [In the parlor of Betal] and was used as a masthead for a regular column by "Betal" (a pen name with obvious reference to the Sanskrit text *Vetalapanchavimsati*) in the literary magazine *Prabashi,* first published in 1901 and then resumed in the 1920s. I have reproduced it from an essay by Hirendranath Datta, "Sahityer adda" [Literary *addas*] in *Desh,* Special Issue on Literature, 1975, 49.

41. The sketch is reproduced from Chattopadhyay, "Hostel Life," 199.

Figure 2. adda *by*
Suniti Chattopadhyay

ground, suggesting intense argumentation. As Chattopadhyay explains, the arguments themselves showed an emergent new association between literature and the production of Bengali selves:

> The evening is one of the liveliest hours of the day in the hostel. . . . There is no end to talk and discussion on all manners of topics, and joking and singing. . . . Some of the favorite literary topics are Mr. Rabindra Nath Tagore and the late Mr. D. L. Roy as poets, the places of Hem Chandra Banerji and Michael Madhusudan Datta in Bengali poetry, the dramatic genius of the late Girish Chandra Ghosh. . . . The first subject is by far the most popular one: and there are "Rabi-ites" and "Dijoo-ites" in every hostel, as hostile to each other's opinions as were the Whigs and Tories of the past.[42]

It is important to note that the literary references here are all Bengali, marking a further step in the popularization of literature into Bengali lives, a development that was soon to be aided by the fact that Bengali literature was recognized as a formal subject of study by the Calcutta University early in the twentieth century. Debates in addas among young men were critical to this propagation of literature into middle-class lives. And this, in turn, brought respectability to adda as a form of social activity. As Chattopadhyay wrote of his student days: "The student has a large stock of hybrid words [mixing Bengali with English],

42. Chattopadhyay, "Hostel Life," 198–99.

which he can invent whenever he likes. *Addify* and *addification* have got nothing to do with mathematical addition; they simply mean *to enjoy a chat* . . . and come from the Bengali word *adda*."[43]

One begins to see in the early part of the twentieth century the tendency on the part of literate Bengali men to form something like "clubs" where the arts and literature (and, later, politics) could be discussed. One such club that has recently had a certain amount of writing devoted to it was the Monday Club, so called because it was to meet on Mondays, involving such future luminaries as the famous writer Sukumar Ray (the father of film director Satyajit Ray), the statistician Prasantachandra Mahalanobis, the linguist Sunitikumar Chattopadhyay, and others. In Hirankumar Sanyal's description, "this was a regular club" with formal membership and a four-anna rate of subscription every month."[44] Their activities included discussing "everything beginning from Plato–Nietzsche to Bankim–Vivekananda–Vaisnava poetry, Rabindra[nath's] poetry" as well as music, feasts, and picnicking.[45]

Rabindranath Tagore won the Nobel Prize for literature in 1913. One can only imagine how this would have helped embed literature in "ordinary" Bengali lives. If the nineteenth-century cultivation of the literary self was mainly the province of the relatively well-to-do, the young nationalist, radical, and socialist writers of the 1920s and 1930s were no longer the rich. They were, sociologically speaking, small people who often lived in financial difficulty yet whose love for their own literature and that in other parts of the world had an unmistakable touch of idealism about it. Tagore was a great believer in the Goetheian idea of "world-literature," and his winning the Nobel Prize seems to have democratized the ideal of literature as a vocation. To be a literary person now—even if one were unemployed—was to be someone respectable, as literary activity was now by definition a thing of cosmopolitan and global relevance. Or so, at least, could the argument go for some.

Adda could thus become a space for the practice of literary cosmopolitanism by members of the middle and lower-middle classes. In 1921, two young men, Dineshranjan Das and Gokulchandra Nag, started a new organization called the Four Arts Club with the express intention

43. Chattopadhyay, "Hostel Life," 201.
44. Sanyal, *Porichoyer*, 145.
45. Satyajit Ray, Preface to Sukumar Ray, *Shamagra shishusahitya* (Calcutta: Ananda Publishers, 1977).

of involving women. The "four arts" referred to literature, music, crafts, and painting. Neither Das nor Nag came from any aristocratic background. Das worked initially for a sporting goods shop in the Chowringhee part of the city and later for a pharmacist's shop; Nag worked in a florist's shop in the New Market. The democratization, as well as a certain social radicalism, of this particular form of the adda may be seen in the fact that nobody's parlor was available to them. As Jibendra Singha Ray, who has studied the history of this club in detail, writes: "The chief problem after the establishment of the club was the venue. Many were reluctant to rent a room out for the purpose of meetings that would involve both men and women. Faced with this situation, Dineshranjan's sister and her husband Sukumar Dasgupta . . . let out their lounge room for a small rent." [46]

Also remarkable was the idealism of the founders of this club, colored as it was with a heavy dose of a post-Tagore Bengali faith in the redemptive role of arts and literature in middle-class lives. Dineshranjan was later to describe the origin of the club in terms that bespoke an idealism seeking to embrace nothing short of the whole world itself. He may have been an unknown Bengali writer, but what he did, he assumed, was for the benefit of humanity at large. He saw himself as a citizen of the global literary cosmopolis. Das's description is a testimony to the way literature, male friendships, and a certain humanism came together to make literary addas of Calcutta of the 1920s spaces where a democratic and cosmopolitan vision of the world could be nurtured and sustained:

> The ideal and an imaginary [shape] of this club had been unfolding in my mind for many years. Witnessing the sign of a silent pain on the faces of many men and women of [this] idealistic country [would make my] heart wish that I could bring to light [my own] imagination from the dark caverns of my mind. . . . My pathos must have cast a shadow over my face. Gokul asked me one day, "What's going on in your mind? I feel as though I am also thinking the same thought as you are but cannot quite tell what the thought is." I said, "I imagine a [kind of] resting-house [an inn] — where people tired by the burden of their lives can come and rest, where *nationality, sex, and position will not be any barriers,* [where] men will make their own work joyful and by freely mixing with others will find themselves fulfilled in

46. Jibendra Singha Ray, *Kolloler kal* (Calcutta: Deys, 1973), 5

the easy working out of their own desires." Gokul put his hand over mine, clapped, and cried out in joy, "That is the dream of my life too but I could not figure out its exact shape until now!" [47]

The growing book trade in the city—the market in global literature, that is—was itself organized around the culture and institution of adda. Conversation and orality remained important factors in the creation and dissemination of literary taste in a city where the production and consumption of books were all based on relations that remained fundamentally personal. Every bookshop, every little office of a literary magazine hosted an adda at which writers, critics, editors, and readers gathered.[48] Nripendrakrishna Chattopadhyay gives us a lively sketch of this small but significant subculture:

> Right behind College Square was a big bookshop called The Book Company. A few new bookshops like this were established toward the beginning of this century around College Square. These shops played a very helpful role in spreading the *culture* of the period. They began to import freshly produced books from Europe and America on various literary, poetic, and scientific subjects; it was through their efforts that the young and the writers of those times got an opportunity to know the trends in world literature and thinking.

Chattopadhyay reconstructs what might typically happen at this bookshop. His story, whether apocryphal or not, underlines the close connection that existed between adda and literary cosmopolitanism in Calcutta of the mid-twentieth century. In Chattopadhyay's somewhat dramatic narrative, the owner of this new shop, Girinbabu, suddenly calls out to a familiar customer he spots on the pavement outside. The customer happens to be none other than the reputed Bengali sociologist, professor at the University of Lucknow, and a well-known correspondent of Tagore, Dhurjatiprasad Mukherjee. Girinbabu invites Mukherjee to go into the warehouse at the back of the shop where an adda of a select group of book-crazy readers of Calcutta gathers regularly: "Go inside, Nadu was looking for you." Nadu, an employee of the shop, is in charge of opening the newly arrived shipping crates containing the fresh imports of literature from overseas. He knows the readers

47. Ray, *Kolloler kal*, 2–3; emphasis mine.
48. See *Desh*, Special Issue on Literature, 1975.

by their personal reading tastes. Here is the scene, in Chattopadhyay's reconstruction, that Mukherjee witnesses on stepping inside the warehouse:

> Nadubabu is engaged in opening a crate that has just arrived. Around him are two *addadharis* [the central characters of an adda; see below] staring at the wooden box, their eyes thirsty like those of an alcohol-lover eyeing a bottle of champagne. The younger of the two is very young. . . . The older person is middle-aged. An aristocrat from top to bottom, the latter is dressed in perfect Bengali attire white as the feathers of a crane, holding — through sheer habit it seems — an empty, golden cigarette holder between his two fingers. A closer look would reveal his fingers to be trembling a little — [this is] Pramatha Chaudhuri [a famous writer and critic of the 1920s and the editor of the avant-garde magazine *Sabujpatra*]. Addressing the young man, he says, "You see, this new poetry now being written in England and France contains a very big tragedy behind all that seeming disorder of metre and rhyme. The Great War [1914] came and destroyed all the old-world beliefs in the minds of their young; their restless minds are seeking a new refuge. I will show you [an example] if the book has arrived by this mail . . . oh, here you are, Dhurjati, welcome!" [49]

Thus the market and taste in the consumption of literature are all mediated, as in this anecdote, by the conversation of the adda.

The practice of adda seems to have been critical in the creation and dissemination of taste in the areas of films and arts as well. In remembering an adda that used to gather at "3-B, Kalighat Park South" in the 1950s and which revolved around the personality of Bimal Ghosh, "Kanuda" to his younger friends, the historian Arun Das Gupta says: "For as long as he lived amongst us, Kanuda was our expert, adviser, and guide in matters relating to films." [50] The communist artist Debabrata Mukhopadhyay reminds us in his memoirs of the College Street Coffee House that it was from an adda at the Central Avenue Coffee House (of which Satyajit Ray and the future film critic Chidananda Das Gupta were regular members) that "the renewal of Bengali filmmaking began."

49. Chattopadhyay, "Adda," 4–6.
50. Arun Das Gupta, "Three-B kalighat park southe kanuda," in *Kicchu chintakana, kichhu smriti: bimal ghosh smaranik patra*, ed. Manashi Das Gupta (Calcutta, 1987), 62.

And speaking of the education of his own taste, Mukhopadhyay is even more forthright in his insistence on the modernity of adda: "I have no academic training," he says. "My education, whether in art or culture generally, is largely a contribution of *adda*."[51]

These changes would have acted in tandem with some other transformations in the nature of public space in the city. Two in particular deserve our attention. We need a history of parks in the city. The nineteenth-century material mostly does not mention "parks," at least not under that designation. *Hutom,* which is very good and detailed on streets, verandas, baithakkhanas, and opium-addas, has nothing on parks. Yet the park that Calcuttans usually call Hedo or Hedua (on Cornwallis Street) figures prominently in quite a few literary reminiscences of the twentieth century. Bipinbehari Gupta's *Puratan prasanga,* for example—an indispensable sourcebook on nineteenth-century history—is really a series of conversations between him and Krishnakamal Bhattacharya (a contemporary and an acquaintance of Bankim and the Tagores) which takes place at this park (Beadon Gardens/Hedua) around 1910–11.[52] When he was an undergraduate student, that is, in the 1910s, the physicist Satyendranath Bose was part of a literary adda that used to meet on the rooftop—yet another unresearched urban site in Calcutta—of the house of Girijapati Bhattacharya, both Bose and Bhattacharya becoming later prominent members of another famous literary adda that formed around the magazine *Parichoy.* Sometimes, we are told, this adda would shift to the park at Hedua. Discussing Tagore's stories, reciting his poems, and singing songs written by him were the staple of this adda.[53] The journal *Prabashi,* in its later incarnation under the editorship of Ashok Chattopadhyay, was conceived at an adda at this same park in 1924. We need to find out more about rooftops and parks and the roles they play in the cultural life of the city in the twentieth century.[54]

51. Debabrata Mukhopadhyay, *Kofir kaape shomoyer chhobi* (Calcutta, 1989), Preface and 10.

52. Bipinbehari Gupta, *Puratan prasanga* (Calcutta: Bidyabharati, 1977; first pub. ca. 1913–14).

53. Amiyabhusan Majumdar, "Rabindranath o bigyanacharya satyendranath," *Desh,* Special Issue on Literature, 1975, 131.

54. Parimal Goswami, "Prabashir adda," in *Desh,* Special Issue, 59–64. Ranajit Guha tells me that in the Calcutta of his youth (1930s) parks were indeed the place for adda,

The other important question is, When do teashops, coffeehouses, and restaurants proliferate in Calcutta and from when do they begin to act as major sites for literary addas?[55] There have been, of course, places like "Puntiram's Shop" near College Street in north Calcutta which has now run for more than a hundred years, though its specific history needs research. In his reminiscences of the poet Kazi Nazrul Islam, the communist author and leader Muzaffar Ahmad mentions teashops where he and others could drop in to sit down for a chat in the early 1920s.[56] But the reader will recall Nirad Chaudhuri's comments, which suggested that addas in teashops were relatively rare in the 1920s compared to those in someone's parlor. In his introduction to Hirankumar Sanyal's reminiscences of the literary magazine *Parichoy* (started around 1932), the historian Susobhan Sakar writes: "In our college life, the streets and lanes of central Calcutta provided the chief meeting places. Eating out at restaurants was not yet a popular practice."[57] These statements receive support from a remark of Radhaprasad Gupta's. Gupta remembers how, in the late 1930s, many teashops "from Shyambazar to Kalighat" (i.e., from the north to the south of the city) used to advertise on red banners their desperately cheap rates: "Only two annas for a cup of tea, two pieces of toast, and an omelette made of two eggs."[58] While it seems that there were indeed shops—Gupta mentions Gyanbabu's Teashop, Favourite Cabin on Mirzapur Street, Basanta Cabin opposite Calcutta University, and the College Street YMCA restaurant—that fostered a culture of adda among university students in the mid- to late 1930s, the

---

removed as they were from parental surveillance. Premankur Atarthi's writings explore these urban spaces in fictional and autobiographical forms and remain to be mined by a future historian of the city. For a captivating description of the social use made of terraced roofs in Calcutta in the early and middle parts of the twentieth century, see, for example, Atarthi's short story "Chhate," in *Mahasthabirer granthabali,* 354–63.

55. Unfortunately, nothing like Frank Conlon's "Dining out in Bombay," in *Consuming Modernity: Public Culture in a South Asian World,* ed. Carol Breckenridge (Minneapolis: University of Minnesota Press, 1995), 90–127, exists for Calcutta.

56. Muzaffar Ahmad, *Kazi nazrul islam smritikatha* (Calcutta: National Book Agency, 1965), 277–78.

57. Susobhan Sarkar, "Bhumikar bodole," in Hirankumar Sanyal, *Porichoyer Kuribochhor o onnanno smiritichitra* (Calcutta, 1978), 9.

58. Radhaprasad Gupta, "Amader jubakkaler adda," in *Kolkatar adda,* ed. Samarenda Das (Calcutta, 1990), 24.

chain of Coffee Houses and Sangu Valley Restaurants that were to dominate the city's adda scene soon after independence did not appear until the late 1930s or during the war.[59] The big Coffee Houses were started by the Indian Coffee Expansion Board as a way of marketing coffee to a city that belonged—and still does—predominantly to tea drinkers. However, the practice of drinking coffee, says Gupta, was introduced into the Bengali culture of Calcutta in the 1930s by immigrant "southerners" (the Bengali word *dakshini* refers to people from the south—for example, Tamilnad, Kerala, Andhra) who set up small eating places around Ballygunge. The drama of his first introduction to a "coffeehouse" is best captured in Gupta's own words:

> One evening in 1941–42, I went to . . . Waterloo Street to see my childhood friend the dentist Gopal Banerjee. The young man Gopal, though bred in . . . Konnagar, would in those days turn himself out sometimes as a full fledged *sahib* and sometimes as a pure Calcutta-bred Bengali dandy. That day, when I showed up, he was *ready* to go out . . . dressed in a fine *dhoti* and *kurta*. On seeing me, he said, "Come, let me take you to a new place." When I asked him about this new place, he said, "Oh no, on that matter I should remain *speakti not* [a jocular Bengali expression which makes use of English to say "I am not speaking"]. It's close, why don't you just come along? You will soon see for yourself." So saying, he took me past . . . Bentinck Street to the just-opened India Coffee House at the crossing of Meredith Street and Central Avenue. Young people these days, even the children, do not seem to be taken by surprise by anything. But my jaw dropped even in my "older" years at the sight of this coffeehouse with its huge size, liveried bearers ["boys"] wearing badges, its clean appearance, polished tables and chairs, and nicely dressed customers at every table. . . . The College Street Coffee House started soon after this.[60]

Indeed, evidence from fiction would suggest that while adda may have been a general and plebeian practice among the residents of Calcutta, its more respectable form—self-consciously imitating the European coffeehouse—made only tentative beginnings in the 1930s. Para-

59. Gupta, "Amader jubakkaler adda," 24.
60. Gupta, "Amader jubakkaler adda," 27–28. The English words in italics are used in the original.

shuram's celebrated story "Ratarati" (Overnight), written around 1931, creates a funny situation at a fictitious restaurant called the Anglo-Mughlai Cafe located somewhere in Dharmatola, the central business district of the city, its location itself signifying a degree of cultural distance from the everyday lives of the middle classes. The joke of the situation turns on many things. On the one hand, the Anglo-Mughalai Cafe is about the aspiration to Europeanize the adda form, to turn it into something like the conversation at a European cafe. At the same time, the Bengali lack of familiarity with European forms is suggested through the manager's ignorance as it reveals itself during an altercation with a customer, Bantlo, who prides himself on his superior knowledge of these things:

> The Manager: Do you realize that this is Anglo-Moglai kef?
>
> Bantlo cannot tolerate wrong pronunciation. He said, "It's not Kef—Kaafe."
>
> The Manager: It is all the same. Do you realize that this is not an ordinary place, that this is a respectable res-tau-rant [says it phonetically]?
>
> Bantlo: Restora [tries the French version].
>
> Manager: It is all the same. Do you realise that this is a ren-des-vos for the educated people?
>
> Bantlo: [using French] Rendezvous.[61]

ORALITY AND COMMUNITY IN ADDA

That there should be tension between the ideals of the adda and those of the modern civil society is understandable. They are mutually antithetical organizations of time and place. The civil society, in its ideal construction, builds into the very idea of human activity the telos of a result—a product and a purpose—and structures its use of time and place on that developmentalist and utilitarian logic (even when that logic is not simply linear). Conversations in an adda, on the other hand, are by definition opposed to the idea of achieving any definite outcome. To enjoy an adda is to enjoy a sense of time and space that is not subject to the gravitational pull of any explicit purpose. The introduction

61. Parashuram [Rajshekhar Bosu], "Ratarati," in *Hanumaner shapna ityadi galpo* (Calcutta: M. C. Sarkar and Sons, 1962), 79.

of a purpose that could make the conversation "instrumental" to the achievement of some object other than the social life of an adda itself, kills, it is claimed, the very spirit and the principle of adda. Buddhadev Bose says as much in his essay on adda: "Suppose we decide that we will convene a literary meeting once a week or twice a month, so that knowledgeable and talented people can come and discuss good things. . . . Good idea no doubt, and it is possible that the first few sessions will be so successful that we will ourselves be surprised. But we will observe after a while that the whole thing has fallen from the heaven of adda and has turned into the barren land of 'duty.' "[62]

The center of gravity of the adda lay in a direction away from the telos of productivity or development (in this case that of purposeful discussion). Hirankumar Sanyal recalls how food (and I might add, a gendered division of labor) were once used in a meeting of the Monday Club to defeat Prasantachandra Mahalanobis's plans to inject into the proceedings a sense of purpose. Sanyal writes:

> Every . . . [meeting] included a feast. But one day, Prasantachandra turned obstinate [and said], "Eating makes discussion impossible. Why do you waste so much time just eating? I will serve you only tea and cheap biscuits." The meeting was at his place that day. There were some tiny little biscuits available those days called "gem" biscuits — usually offered to pet cats and dogs. Everybody raised a hue and cry. Tatada [Sukumar Ray] realised protesting would not achieve anything, for Prasanta would not listen. He whispered to me, "Go inside [the house] and tell Prasanta's sister that Prasanta has invited a group of people for tea but has not arranged for any food. Just say this and come back." After about fifteen or twenty minutes a variety of food appeared. . . . Prasanta said, "What is this? Who got all this?" Tatada replied, "How does that concern you? The food is here, and we will eat it."[63]

Even without the aid of food, conversation in an adda could itself ensure that arguments never reached a terminal point. Take this entry for 24 January 1936 from Shyamal Ghosh's (published) diary in which he used to keep records of the conversations at the highbrow adda of people

62. Bose, "Adda," 14.
63. Sanyal, *Porichoyer*, 163–64.

associated with the magazine *Parichoy.* The discussion here broaches large questions but not with a view to solving them:

> Ayyub asked: "Putting aside the matter of physical reactions, are there any qualitative differences between emotions such as anger, fear, love, etc.?"
>
> Mallikda asked a counterquestion: "Can you isolate emotions if you leave the body out [of consideration]?"
>
> It was not possible to reach a conclusion even after about an hour's argumentation. I heard Ayyub say once, "Let us assume that no feeling is possible without the mediation of the body, still I want to know why, if all emotions are of the same type, someone will be beside themselves when called a 'pig' at one time, and just brush it off at another. . . . Why does this happen?"

Ghosh closes his entry with a matter-of-fact remark that suggests how used he was to such discussions: "There cannot be conclusions to such debates."[64]

Focused on the oral, Bengali addas represented a certain capacity on the part of their members to take pleasure in the pure art of conversation.[65] By its very nature, the pleasure was communal. The writer Hemendrakumar Ray's memoirs distinguish between the speaking style of a meeting and that of a baithak. Pramatha Chaudhuri, the editor of *Sabujpatra,* was famous for his baithaki style of speech: "It was in small rooms that his baithaki style of conversation would become so captivating."[66] The life of the adda was always a person with some specialty to their speech — someone who could tell a good story, coin a new word, turn a phrase interestingly, or produce smart quips that made an impression on others. They were the people who could, as the Bengali expression goes, make an adda "congeal" or "thicken" (in the same way that a plot does). Hirankumar Sanyal says of Sukumar Ray in the context of the Monday Club: "[He] . . . had a remarkable capacity to help the *ashar* come into its own. On days on which the Monday Club had no

64. Shyamalkrishna Ghosh, *Porichoyer adda* (Calcutta: K. P. Bagchi, 1990), 11.

65. The compound word used by Susobhan Sarkar to describe the nature of conversation at an adda is *galpagujob* (lit. tales and rumors). See Sarkar's preface to Sanyal, *Porichoyer,* 3.

66. Hemendrakumar Ray, *Jader dekhechhi,* vol. 1 (Calcutta, 1948–49), 112.

specific subject to discuss, he kept us enthralled by telling us all kinds of stories."[67] The adda, in this way, must have drawn on older styles of speech such as those of *kathakata* (traditional practices of telling devotional stories). The pleasure of conversation is also suggested by another story about Ray told by Sanyal. The austere Brahmo teacher Herambachandra Maitra once asked Ray, "Sukumar, can you tell me what life's ideal is [should be]?" Sukumar is said to have replied [in English]: "Serious interest in life." Maitra was so pleased at this answer that he immediately ordered sweets for everybody present.[68] The communal nature of the pleasure exchanged by this verbal transaction is signified by the fact that everybody present celebrated the answer by making it an occasion for eating *sandesh* (a popular variety of Bengali sweet made out of ricotta cheese) — yet another exercise in public practices of orality.

The connection between orality and a certain kind of aesthetic-communal pleasure was thus already given in the form of the adda. The entry of English literature (or literature available in English) into the lives of the lower-middle classes made possible certain distinct variations on this orality in the adda of the educated. Adda became an arena where one could present oneself as a character — from Wilde or Shaw or Joyce or Faulkner — through the development of certain mannerisms (meant for the enjoyment of others), habits of speech, and gestures. Adda was a place where one could develop techniques of presenting oneself as a "character." This becomes very obvious when I think of adda as a form of memory (for this is indeed what I have been working from). In the reminiscences of addas, people are typically remembered not in a way "history" or "biography" as genres would remember them (in the round, as it were) but rather as relatively one-dimensional characters who are remembered for how they presented themselves to the adda. A

---

67. Sanyal, *Porichoyer,* 167.

68. Sanyal, *Porichoyer,* 166–67. I find this piece of conversation quite illuminating in thinking about our modernity. The tradition of testing someone by putting to them big questions in the form of puzzles is as old as the Indian epic the *Mahabharata.* There is a sequence there in which the mythical demigod Yaksha tests the eldest of the Pandavas, Yudhisthira, with a series of such unconnected questions. In our nineteenth-century history, similar encounters are reported between the young (and future) Vivekananda and the different people in whom he searched for a suitable guru, and between Ramakrishna (eventually Vivekananda's guru) and the many Calcutta personalities he met and tested.

case in point would be Radhaprasad Gupta's memories of a member of their adda called Amitabha Sen:

> His command over mathematics, science, literature and arts used to leave us dazzled. All the developments in the [different] fields of knowledge-science [I have translated the Bengali expression literally] were at his fingertips, thanks to good books and foreign journals. It was through him that we first saw today's ubiquitous ball[-point] pen. That perhaps was the first ball[-point] pen in the world, called Reynolds. We were rendered speechless by it. Everyone took his turn at writing with it. You could write any way you wanted. Amitabhababu's face wore his familiar gentle smile. Watching us, he only made one remark [in English]: "Mankind at last has been freed from the tyranny of the pen-angle."[69]

WOMEN, ADDA, AND PUBLIC CULTURE

Was the space of the modern adda—the one that was opened up by the coming of universities, student dormitories, modern literary production, restaurants, teashops, coffeehouses, and parks—was this a male space?

Manashi Das Gupta made the point to me in the course of a discussion of a draft of this paper that the very public acts of orality—speaking, eating—through which an adda created its sense of community tended to form "traditional" barriers to women's participation in a male adda. Women, if they were to adhere to nineteenth-century middle-class ideas about respectability in public (that is, when exposed to the gaze of men from beyond the confines of kinship), were barred from these practices of orality. Yet this does not mean that women did not enjoy or practice adda. First, one has to remember that the separation of spheres for men and women both before and after British rule in India meant that women could have their own addas, and that in part is still the practice. The sites of such addas would have been different, being organized around spaces where women could meet. The topics discussed may have also reflected the separation of social domains. The 1990 collection *Kolkatar* adda has both female contributors on the subject and an essay on "women's *adda.*" Women working in Calcutta and

69. Gupta, "Amader," 29.

commuting to the city by train every day in their specially designated "women's compartments" develop their own sense of adda.[70]

Male addas of the mid-twentieth century were predicated, practically, on a separation of male and female spaces. As Nripendrakrishna Chattopadhyay bluntly asserted: "The biggest natural enemy of adda are women!" The statement is not as misogynist as it may seem at first sight. He actually also refers to the gender problem as a "defect" and takes a more sympathetic view of the position to which women are relegated by the structure of adda:

> A big natural defect of adda is that it is an intimate world for men. And yet this weakness is the amulet that also protects it. An adda breaks up if a woman comes within ten cubits of it. . . . Every married woman looks on adda with poisoned eyes. It is, after all, for the *addadhari* husband of hers that she has to sit up and wait into the silence of the night. Every husband who returns home from an adda, comes back prepared to be asked this single [sarcastic] question: "So the adda finally ended, did it?"[71]

This (imagined) wifely hostility to adda drew on a culturally conceived opposition between the world and the word, between "worldly responsibilities"—the world of chores, dominated by needs—and the noninstrumental pleasure of company and conversation that an adda was. In speaking of the role of the *addadhari*—literally one who holds an adda together—Nripendrakrishna pictured him as a man who artfully and devotedly evaded everything to do with domestic and social duties. In words that in Bengali brim over with both humor and irony, Nripendrakrishna thus described the ideal addadhari:

> Every adda has a central personality, someone who could be called an *addadhari*. . . .
>
> He is the sun of the solar system of an adda, it is around him that the adda revolves. The addadhari is like a stable center in a world that is otherwise restless. He has no office to go to, no wedding invitations to attend, no speeches to deliver at any meeting, no obsessions about going to the movies, no obligations to do with the marriage of his sister-in-law, no first-rice ceremonies of a son of his wife's brother; he

70. See the essay "Meyeder adda" in *Kolkatar adda.*
71. Chattopadhyay, "Adda," 9, 16.

has no Darjeeling, no Puri; his only job is to sit there like the immobile image of a deity lighting up the adda. The streets of Calcutta may be under water, the asphalt on them may have been molten by the sun, the Japanese may have dropped a few bombs, but every *addabaj* [adda-addicted person] has the assurance of knowing that there will be at least one person present at the adda. And that person is the addadhari.[72]

This could not be the whole story, however. Women's education and their entry into public life — a historical process that started in the 1850s — made a difference. The tension between the old separation of male and female domains of life and the new ideals of companionate marriage is the subject of the Parashuram's (Rajshekhar Bosu) humorous story "Dvandik kobita" [Dialectical poetry] written in 1957. "Dialectical poetry" — the name itself mocking some of the chantlike aspects of Bengali Marxism — is a tale told in an adda and concerns a character called Dhurjati and his wife, Shankari. Dhurjati lectures in mathematics but has devoted his life to writing love poems addressed, in the fashion of Bengali romanticism started by Tagore, to unknown, unseen, and completely imaginary women from imaginary foreign lands. Needless to say, this practice of addressing male romantic sentiments to fictional women consciously described as "unknown" (*ajana, achena*) itself reflected the distance between these sentiments and everyday, routine rounds of domesticity. After his marriage, the protagonist of Bose's story, Dhurjati, tried to make a dent in this tradition. For a while he deliberately made his wife the addressee of his expression of romantic and poetic love, but he gave up the effort in frustration when he found that Shankari was more interested in the baby that they had had soon after their marriage than in his poetic exuberance:

> Dhurjati gradually realized that the "ladylove" of his marriage had nothing in common with the beloved of his [poetic] fancy. Shankari does not understand the pleasure of poetry, there is no romance in her heart. She had received a lot of cheap presents . . . at the time of the wedding, she treated the poems that Dhurjati had written ad-

---

72. Chattopadhyay, "Adda," 4, 10. Darjeeling and Puri were among the favorite locations for holidays for Bengali middle-class families from Calcutta.

dressing her as though they were the same as these ordinary presents. She is just absorbed in domestic chores and in [their] newborn son.

Dhurjati goes back to addressing his poems to his imaginary sweetheart while Shankari devotes herself to domesticity.

If Bose's story had ended here, it would have depicted a nineteenth-century resolution of the tension between domesticity and the modern, expressivist male self: A man reserves his literary cosmopolitanism for his male friends and sustains a practical, mundane companionship with his wife. But Bose wrote in a period when literature was part of women's lives as well. So, Bisakha, a friend of Shankari's from her university days, steps in and plants doubt into Shankari's mind. She says one day:

> "Your husband is, after all, a famous poet. . . . Can you tell me whom his poems of love are written for? Surely not for you, for he wouldn't have written things like 'my unknown sweetheart [whom] I have met in dreams' in that case."
>
> Shankari said, "He writes for nobody. Poets are fanciful people, they erect somebody in their imagination and address her."
>
> ". . . Don't you feel angry?"
>
> "I don't care much for it."
>
> "You will have to regret later. . . . Take some *steps* now."
>
> "What do you suggest?"
>
> "[That] you also start writing poems addressed to some imaginary man."

Shankari has never written poetry, so Bisakha offers to write for her. Soon poems appear in literary magazines in Shankari's name. They are addressed to such characters as the "belligerent young man of Red China" — "I want to take shelter in your hairless chest" — or to "the young man of Pakhtunistan":

> Take me into your jungle-haired chest
> Hold me tight with those crankshaftlike arms of yours
> Let the bones of my ribcage break and crumble
> Crush me, crush me.

And a male friend of Dhurjati says to him one day: "I say Dhurjati, isn't this Shankari Devi your wife? What extraordinary poetry she is writing, regular *hot stuff.* . . . Professor Bhar, the psychologist, said [the other day], this is *libido* gone wild." The subsequent conversation between Dhurjati and Shankari is not one that could have taken place in the nineteenth century. Dhurjati said:

"What is this rubbish you are writing? People are talking."

Shankari said, "Let them talk. It is selling very well, I have given another book to the press."

Dhurjati shook his head and said, "I am telling you this cannot go on."

"That's funny. There's no harm if you write [this] but it's bad if I do! . . . Why do you write such rubbish?"

"You compare yourself to me? It's all right if a man writes about imaginary women [lovers], but it's very bad for women to do so."

"All right, you stop writing poetry and burn all your books, and I will do the same."

Unable to resolve the conflict exclusively on his own terms, Dhurjati gives up writing poetry and takes to writing books on algebra, while Shankari decides to write only recipes for magazine sections of Sunday newspapers.[73]

Bose's resolution to this problem is not one that completely destroys the division between male and female spaces even in modern public life. It is one that would have made an adda laugh, however, and that laughter itself would have been a resource with which Bengalis would have dealt with the changes and tensions created by women's entry into public life.

The point is that the question of friendship in public life between modern literary men and women is part of a complicated history of modern heterosexual practices in Bengal. In his magisterial survey of the history of the Bengali novel, the literary critic Sreekumar Bandyopadhyay made the perceptive suggestion that it was within male—rather than male-female—friendship that European romantic and cosmopolitan sentiments made their initial home in our history and thus expanded

---

73. Parashuram [Rajshekhar Bosu], "Dvandik kobita," in his *Neel tara ityadi galpa* (Calcutta: M. C. Sarkar and Sons, 1962), 121–26. The English words in italics are used in the original.

and intensified the space of that friendship. Surveying the novels written at the turn of the century, Bandyopadhyay remarked:

> Given the closed-door nature of our social arrangements, friendship [between men, as opposed to romantic, heterosexual love] is the only opening through which external revolutions can enter the Bengali family. Only the claim of friendship or being a classmate of some-body allows us to overcome the barriers of . . . [women's space] of a different family and become intimate with them. The narrower the opportunities for free mixing between men and women, the greater the expanse of and the possibilities for male friendship. That is why Bengali novels see an excess of friendship [between men]. In the majority of cases, complexity arises from the force and counterforce of the affection, the sense of comfort, and yet, at the same time, the intense spirit of competition that such friendship generates.[74]

This is true not only of the nineteenth century. As recently as the 1960s, the sight of a woman engaged in adda with her male peers at the College Street Coffee House was rare enough to elicit this comment and sketch (fig. 3) from the communist artist Debabrata Mukhopadhyay: "Girls had just begun to come to the midday adda [at the coffeehouse]. But they were extremely few in number. It was about this time a certain group of boys set up a regular adda around a particular girl. We, who had always been addadharis sans the company of women, felt a little jealous. We named the girl 'the queen-bee.' One day, I captured her in a sketch."[75]

Bengali modernity, for complicated reasons, never quite transcended the structure of opposition between domestic space and that of adda. If I could take out of context an expression of Henry Lefebvre's and give it a stronger sense of irony than Lefebvre intended, I might say that literary modernity and its attendant spaces of the school, university, coffeehouse, bookshops, and magazines did indeed help to expand, deepen, and modernize the homosocial space of adda and even allowed for women's participation in it. But its male character was never erased,

74. Sreekumar Bandyopadhyay, *Bangasahitye upanashyer dhara* (Calcutta: Modern Book Agency, 1988), 148.

75. Mukhopadhyay, *Kofir Kaape,* 16.

মক্ষিরানী

Figure 3. "the queen bee" by Debabrata Mukhopadhyay. Communication and Media People, Calcutta.

and it often left the heterosexual men involved in literary endeavor with a sense of—this is where I register my debt to Lefebvre's coinage—"phallic solitude."[76] The "human" on whose behalf Gokul Nag and Dinesh Das dreamed their cosmopolitan dreams barely included Bengali women.

76. See Henri Lefebvre, *The Production of Space*, trans. Donald Nicholson-Smith (Oxford: Blackwell, 1992), 304–6.

The modern and hybrid space of Bengali adda thus does not in any way resolve the tensions brought about by the discourses of modernity and capitalism. The adda, thematically, is a site where several of the classic and endless debates of modernity are played out — discipline versus laziness, women's confinement in the domestic sphere versus their participation in the public sphere, separation of male and female domains versus a shared public life for both groups, leisure classes versus the laboring classes, an openness to the world versus the responsibilities of domestic life, and other related issues. Yet, as I said in the very beginning of this essay, the idea of adda now evokes in Bengali writings sentiments of mourning and nostalgia at the passing away of a familiar world. It is possible that the world mourned today was never real. The cultural location of adda perhaps has more to do with a history in which the institution came to symbolize — in problematic and contested ways — a particular way of dwelling in modernity, almost a zone of comfort in capitalism. For all the claims made by the celebrants of adda, we know that it did not work equally well for everybody, that there were aspects of exclusion and domination in the very structure of adda itself. In spite of these problems, however, the institution played enough of a role in Bengali modernity for it to be tagged "Bengali." And Bengalis continue seemingly to invest adda with certain metaphysical talk: about life, vitality, essence, and youth. It could not be insignificant, after all, that the epigraph to this essay was penned by a woman, the Bengali cultural and literary critic Manashi Das Gupta. Das Gupta, herself a trained academician and an active participant in many literary and political addas from the late 1940s to now, is no stranger to the ways male addas tended to dominate if not exclude women. One would not expect her to "romanticize" adda. Yet the lines I quote from her — "And it is a good sign that I still enjoy *adda*, / for *adda* and youth are inseparable" — were part of a poem she wrote back home in 1957 describing her life at Cornell University, from where she earned her Ph.D.[77] Why is it that even a cultural and feminist critic who is otherwise acutely aware of the male nature of the space of adda, still associates that space with something as vital and metaphysical as youth, the sign of life? Why does

77. Personal communication from Manashi Das Gupta.

the mention of adda generate such affection in most Bengali writing about the distinctiveness of their modernity?

The history sketched in this essay attempts to answer this question. What remains buried in the current Bengali nostalgia for adda, I suggest, is an unresolved question of the Bengali present: How to be at home in a globalized capitalism now. An idealized image of adda points to the insistent pressures of that anxious question.

Miniaturizing Modernity: Shahzia Sikander in Conversation with Homi K. Bhabha

edited by Robert McCarthy

On 8 March 1998 a public discussion inaugurated a Renaissance Society exhibition of Shahzia Sikander's work at the University of Chicago. Portions of that talk are abridged here, beside a selection of Sikander's work engaging the Indo-Persian classical form of miniature painting.

HOMI BHABHA: I was reminded while walking through your show of David Sylvester's interview with Francis Bacon where Bacon said that he never wanted to invent a new technique, that people who wanted to invent new techniques in fact were limiting their scopes. What Bacon wanted to do was to *re*invent an earlier technique, one that had been handed down to him. Somehow the distinction between the traditional and the avant garde is profoundly problematized and confused in your work. The terms don't seem to operate in opposition to each other. Do you think that reinvention describes what you have done? Does your work fit into this tradition/modernity sort of binarism?

SHAHZIA SIKANDER: I think that the boundaries are blurred, and that that blurring comes out of the act of making art in particular circumstances of time and place. The appeal of miniature painting was that it embodied both the past and the present. It was vulnerable to the kinds of practices that happened in the National College of Art in Lahore and to the incorporation of the personal and the cultural, but, although I always intended to go beyond miniature painting, I did not set out to reinvent it.

Public Culture is grateful to Lori Bartman, Susanne Ghez, Pat Scott, and Hamza Walker of the Renaissance Society at the University of Chicago for their generous assistance and permission to reproduce this interview.

Reinventing the Dislocation, 1997. Vegetable color, watercolor, dry pigment, tea wash on "wasli" paper 13" × 9½". Deitch Projects

HB: It is interesting that the game-playing that happens in institutions of instruction also actually produces particular practices. Usually, when people look at work that comes from other cultural or historical contexts, or work by diasporic or migrant artists, there is an attempt to see cultural differences in the image, in a style, at some mimetic level of the work. What I find interesting is something else, which is that cultural difference is not merely for the eye; it is in the way one is trained—it is what art school means "there" as opposed to "here." What distinguishes culturally different kinds of work seems not merely to be the making of one image different from another but the whole training that happens before paint touches paper.

SS: My decision to study miniature painting was questioned by some of my colleagues and other faculty. They said it would retard my creativity, that miniaturism was just rigorous copying. I was attracted to understanding *why* the form existed. Being in that position forced the issue of establishing a relationship to craft or technique, in this case a highly stylized, even fated, genre. And the instructor did play kinds of mind games. To gauge his student's seriousness and resilience, one of the first assignments was to catch baby squirrels for the making of brushes. He did teach us how to make brushes by hand, but what fascinated me more was the way our training was conducted—the play, the subtle provocation—I was interested in seeing what could be learned in this process of submission, of subjection to the technique as it was lodged in this patriarchal arrangement. At the same time, it was not that he was teaching what would have been taught during the Moghul period, either. All of this was happening in a place of experimentation. The distinctions do get confused. The illustrations we studied were printed in catalogs published by Western scholars.

Separate Working Things, *1995. Vegetable color, watercolor, dry pigment, tea wash on "wasli" paper 8″ × 11″. Deitch Projects*

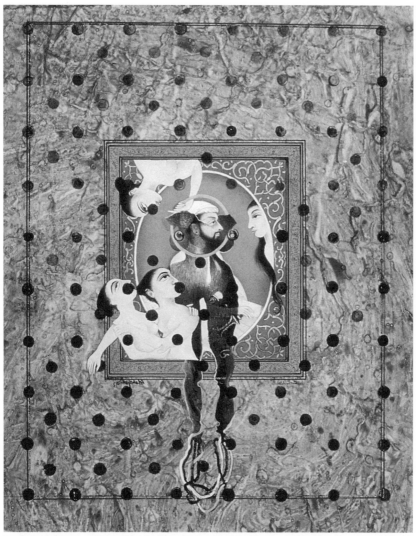

Perilous Order, *1997. Vegetable color, dry pigment, watercolor, tea wash on hand-prepared "wasli" paper 10½" × 8". Deitch Projects*

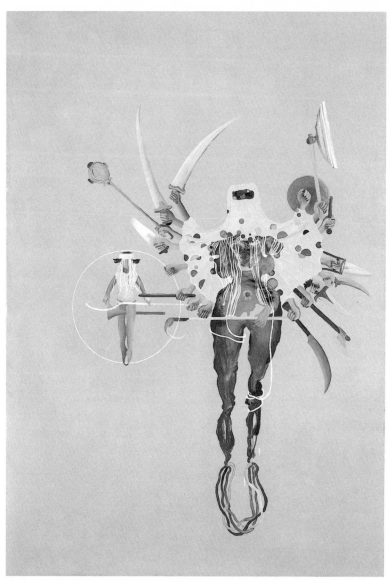

Fleshy Weapons, *1997. Acrylic, dry pigment, watercolor, tea wash on linen. 96" × 70"*

HB: You have developed a Durga figure, a Kali figure, from the Hindu pantheon, and then uncannily doubled it, overlaid it with the enigmatic veiled woman. It seems to me that sometimes you don't so much bring the East and the West together but, more interestingly, the East and the East, and that in doing so you are bringing out the nearness of difference, the intimacy of difference that can exist within any culture.

SS: In my experience, in Pakistan, representations of Hindu mythology were unacceptable. I was interested in how history simplified the visual in terms of Hindu and Muslim or, in my experience, Indian and Pakistani—a visual that I felt did not lend itself to simplistic dissection and separation. Maybe this refusal is where I've entered the work myself: the central, footless figure in *Fleshy Weapons* is rooted to herself.

Two Theories of Modernity

Charles Taylor

There seem to be at large in our culture two ways of understanding the rise of modernity. They are in effect two different takes on what makes our contemporary society different from its forebears. In one take, we can look at the difference between present-day Western society and, say, that of medieval Europe as analogous to the difference between medieval Europe and medieval China or India. In other words, we can think of the difference as one between civilizations, each with their own culture. Alternatively, we can see the change from earlier centuries to today as involving something like "development"—as the demise of a traditional society and the rise of the modern. From this perspective, which seems to be the dominant one, things look rather different.

I want to call the first kind of understanding a cultural one, and the second acultural. In using these terms, I am leaning on a use of the word *culture,* which is analogous to the sense it often has in anthropology. I am evoking the picture of a plurality of human cultures, each of which has a language and a set of practices that define specific understandings of personhood, social relations, states of mind/soul, goods and bads, virtues and vices, and the like. These languages are often mutually untranslatable.

With this model in mind, a *cultural* theory of modernity characterizes the transformations that have issued in the modern West mainly in terms of the rise of a new culture. The contemporary Atlantic world is seen as a culture (or a group of closely related cultures) with its own specific understandings of, for example, person, nature, and the good. This culture can be contrasted to all others, including its own predecessor civilization (with which it obviously also has a lot in common).

By contrast, an *acultural* theory describes these transformations in terms of some culture-neutral operation. By this I mean an operation that is not defined in terms of the specific cultures it carries us from and to, but is rather seen as of a type that any traditional culture could undergo. An example of an acultural type of theory, indeed a paradigm case, would be one that conceives of modernity as the growth of reason, defined in various ways: for example, as the growth of scientific consciousness, or the development of a secular outlook, or the rise of instrumental rationality, or an ever-clearer distinction between fact-finding and evaluation. Or else modernity might be accounted for in terms of social, as well as intellectual changes: Transformations, including intellectual ones, are seen as coming about as a result of increased mobility, concentration of populations, industrialization, or the like. In all these cases, modernity is conceived as a set of transformations which any and every culture can go through — and which all will probably be forced to undergo.

These changes are not defined by their position in a specific constellation of understandings of, say, person, society, or good; rather, they are described as a type of transformation to which any culture could in principle serve as "input." For instance, any culture could suffer the impact of growing scientific consciousness, any religion could undergo secularization, any set of ultimate ends could be challenged by a growth of instrumental thinking, any metaphysic could be dislocated by the split between fact and value.

Modernity in this kind of theory is understood as issuing from a rational or social operation which is culture-neutral. This is not to say that the theory cannot acknowledge good historical reasons why this transformation first arose in one civilization rather than another, or why some may undergo it more easily than others. Rather, the point is that the operation is defined not in terms of its specific point of arrival but as a general function that can take any specific culture as its input.

To grasp the difference from another angle, this operation is not seen as supposing or reflecting an option for one specific set of human values or understandings among others. In the case of social explanations, causal weight is given to historical developments, like industrialization, that have an impact on values but are often not seen as reflecting specific options in this domain. When it comes to explanations in terms of rationality, this is seen as the exercise of a general capacity, which was only awaiting its proper conditions to unfold. Under certain conditions human beings will come to see that scientific thinking is valid, that instrumental rationality pays off, that religious beliefs involve unwarranted leaps, that facts and values are separate. These transformations may be facilitated by our having certain values and understandings, just as they are hampered by the dominance of others. They are not *defined* as the espousal of some such constellation; rather, they are defined by something we come to see concerning the whole context in which values and understandings are promulgated.

It should be evident that the dominant theories of modernity over the last two centuries have been of the acultural sort. Many have explained the development of modernity at least partly by our "coming to see" something like the range of supposed truths mentioned here. Or else the changes have been explained partly by culture-neutral social developments, such as Emile Durkheim's move from mechanical to differentiated, organic forms of social cohesion or Alexis de Tocqueville's assumption of creeping democracy (by which he meant a push toward equality). In Max Weber's interpretation, rationalization was a steady process, occurring within all cultures over time.

But above all, explanations of modernity in terms of *reason* seem to be the most popular. Even social explanations tend to invoke reason: Social transformations, like mobility and industrialization, are thought to bring about intellectual and spiritual changes because they shake people loose from old habits and beliefs — religion or traditional morality — which then become unsustainable because they lack the kind of independent rational grounding that the beliefs of modernity — such as individualism or instrumental reason — are assumed to have.

But, one might object, what about the widespread and popular *negative* theories of modernity, those that see it not as gain but as loss or decline? Curiously enough, they too have been acultural in their own way. To see this, we have to enlarge somewhat the preceding description. Instead of seeing the transformations as the unfolding of capacities, negative theories have often interpreted modernity as a falling prey to dangers. But these have often been just as aculturally conceived. Modernity is characterized by the loss of the horizon; by a loss of roots; by the hubris that denies human limits, our dependence on history or God, that places unlimited confidence in the powers of frail human reason; by a trivializing self-indulgence that has no stomach for the heroic dimension of life; and so on.

The overwhelming weight of interpretation in our culture, positive and negative, tends to the acultural. The voices on the cultural side are fewer if powerful. Friedrich Nietzsche, for instance, offers a reading of modern scientific culture that describes it as actuated by a specific constellation of values. Weber, besides offering a theory of rationalization as a steady, culture-independent force, gave a reading of the Protestant ethic as a particular set of religio-moral concerns that in turn helped to bring about modern capitalism.

So acultural theories predominate. Is this bad? I think it is. To see why, we have to bring out a bit more clearly what these theories foreground and what they tend to screen out.

Acultural theories tend to describe the transition of modernity in terms of a loss of traditional beliefs and allegiances. This loss may be seen as coming about as a result of institutional changes: For example, mobility and urbanization are understood to erode the beliefs and reference points of static rural society. Or the loss may be supposed to arise from the increasing operation of modern scientific reason. The change may be positively valued, or it may be judged a disaster by those for whom the traditional reference points were valuable and for whom scientific reason is too narrow. But all these theories concur in some respects: old views and loyalties are eroded; old horizons are washed away, in Nietzsche's image; the sea of faith recedes, following Arnold. This stanza from Arnold's *Dover Beach* captures this perspective:

> The Sea of Faith
> Was once, too, at the full, and round earth's shore
> Lay like the folds of a bright girdle furled.
> But now I only hear
> Its melancholy, long, withdrawing roar,
> Retreating, to the breath
> Of the night-wind, down the vast edges drear
> And naked shingles of the world.[1]

The tone here is one of regret and nostalgia. But the underlying image of eroded faith could serve just as well for an upbeat story of the progress of triumphant scientific reason. From one point of view, humanity has shed a lot of false and harmful myths. From another, it has lost touch

1. Matthew Arnold, *Dover Beach,* ed. Jonathan Middlebrook (Columbus, Ohio: Merrill, 1970), 21–28.

with crucial spiritual realities. But in either case, the change is seen as a loss of belief.

What emerges comes about through this loss. The upbeat story cherishes the dominance of an empirical-scientific approach to knowledge claims of individualism, negative freedom, and instrumental rationality. But these come to the fore because they are what we humans "normally" value, once we are no longer impeded or blinded by false or superstitious beliefs and the stultifying modes of life that accompany them. Once myth and error are dissipated, these are the only games in town. The empirical approach is the only valid way of acquiring knowledge, and this becomes evident as soon as we free ourselves from the thraldom of a false metaphysics. Increasing recourse to instrumental rationality allows us to get more and more of what we want, and we were only ever deterred from this by unfounded injunctions to limit ourselves. Individualism is the normal fruit of human self-regard absent the illusory claims of God, the Chain of Being, or the sacred order of society.

In other words, we moderns behave as we do because we have "come to see" that certain claims were false — or, on the negative reading, because we have lost sight of certain perennial truths. What this view omits from the picture is the possibility that Western modernity might be powered by its own positive visions of the good — that is, by one constellation of such visions among available others — rather than by the only viable set left after the old myths and legends have been exploded. It screens out whatever there might be of a specific moral direction to Western modernity, beyond what is dictated by the general form of human life itself, once old error is shown up (or old truth forgotten): People behave as individuals because that's what they naturally do when no longer constrained by the old religions, metaphysics, and customs, though this may be seen as a glorious liberation or a purblind enmiring in egoism, depending on our perspective. What it cannot be seen as is a novel form of moral self-understanding, not definable simply by the negation of what preceded it.

Otherwise put, what gets screened out is the possibility that Western modernity might be sustained by its own original spiritual vision — that is, not one generated simply and inescapably by transition.

Before trying to say how bad or good this is, I want to speculate about the motives for this predominance of the acultural. Such a scenario is understandable when we reflect that Westerners have for centuries been living the transition to modernity out of the civilization we used to call Christendom. It is hard to live through a change of this moment without being partisan, and in this spirit we quite naturally reach for explanations which are immediately evaluative, on one side or the other. Now nothing stamps the change as more unproblematically right than the account that we have "come to see" through certain falsehoods, just as the explanation that we have come to forget important truths brands it as unquestionably wrong. To make such confident judgments on the basis of a cultural account would presuppose our having carried through a complex comparative assessment of modernity's original vision, over against that of the Christendom which preceded it, to a clear unambiguous conclusion — hardly an easy task, if realizable at all.

Indeed, since a cultural theory supposes the point of view in which we see our own culture as one among others, and this at best is a recent acquisition in our civilization, it is not surprising that the first accounts of revolutionary change were acultural. For the most part our ancestors looked on other civilizations as made up of barbarians, infidels, or savages. It would have been absurd to expect the contemporaries of the French Revolution, on either side of the political divide, to have seen the cultural shift within this political upheaval, when the very idea of cultural pluralism was just dawning in the writings of, for example, Johann Gottfried von Herder.

But even when this standpoint becomes more easily available, we are drawn by our partisan attachments to neglect it. This is partly because an immediately evaluative explanation (on the right side) is more satisfying — we tend to want to glorify modernity, or to vilify it. And it is partly because we fear that a cultural theory might make value judgments impossible. The latter notion is, I believe, a mistake; but mistake or not, it plays a role here.

Another factor driving acultural theories has been the vogue for materialistic explanations in social science and history. By this I mean, in this context, explanations that shy away from invoking moral or spiritual factors in favor of (what are thought to be) harder and more down-to-earth causes. And so the developments I adverted to above — the growth of science, individualism, negative freedom, instrumental reason, and the other striking features of the culture of modernity — have often been accounted for as by-products of social change, spinoffs from industrialization, greater mobility, or urbanization. There are certainly important causal relations to be traced here, but the accounts that invoke them frequently skirt altogether the issue of whether these changes in culture and outlook owe anything to their own inherent power as moral ideals. The implicit answer is often in the negative.[2]

Of course, the social changes that are supposed to spawn the new outlook must themselves be explained, and this will involve some recourse to human motivations unless we suppose that industrialization or the growth of cities occurred entirely in a fit of absence of mind. We need some notion of what moved people to push steadily in one direction — for example, toward the greater application of technology to production or toward greater concentrations of population. But what is invoked here are often nonmoral motivations. By that I mean motivations that can actuate people quite without connection to any moral ideal, as I defined this earlier. As a consequence, we very often find these social changes explained in terms of the desire for greater wealth or power, or the means of survival or control over others. Of course, all these things can be woven into moral ideals, but they need not be. And so explanation in terms of them is considered sufficiently hard and scientific.

Even where individual freedom and the enlargement of instrumental reason are seen as ideas whose intrinsic attractions can help explain their rise, this attraction is frequently understood in nonmoral terms. That is, the power of these ideas is often understood not in terms of their moral force, but as accruing from the advantages they seem to bestow on people regardless of their moral outlook, regardless even of whether they have a moral outlook. Freedom allows you to do what you want, and the greater application of instrumental reason gets you more of what you want, whatever that is.[3]

2. Of course, for a certain vulgar Marxism, the negative answer is quite explicit. Ideas are the product of economic changes. But much non-Marxist social science operates implicitly on similar premises, and this in spite of the orientation of some of the great founders of social science, like Weber, who recognized the crucial role of moral and religious ideas in history.

3. Individualism has in fact been used in two quite different senses. In one it is a moral ideal, one facet of which I have been discussing. In another, it is an amoral phenomenon, something like what we mean by egoism. The rise of individualism in this sense is usually a phenomenon of breakdown, where the loss of a traditional horizon leaves mere anomie in its wake, and people fend for themselves. It is, of course,

*

It is obvious that wherever this kind of explanation becomes culturally dominant, the motivation to explore the original spiritual vision of
modernity is very weak; indeed, the capacity even to recognize some
such thing nears zero. And this effectively takes cultural theories off the
agenda.

So what, if anything, is bad about this? Three things: two massive
errors in judgment, which ought to be on reflection fairly obvious to us,
and a third more subtle mistake, about the whole framework in which
human history unfolds.

THE FIRST MASSIVE ERROR

I think Western modernity *is* in part based on an original moral outlook. This is not to say that our account of it in terms of our "coming to
see" certain things is wholly wrong. On the contrary: Post-seventeenth-
century natural science has a validity, and the accompanying technology
an efficacy, that we have established. And, sooner or later, all societies
are forced to acquire this efficacy or be dominated by others (and, hence,
have it imposed on them anyway).

But it would be quite wrong to think that we can make do with an
acultural theory alone. It is not just that other facets of what we identify as modern, such as the tendency to try to split fact from value or
the decline of religious practice, are far from reposing on incontestable
truths which have finally been discovered—as one can claim for modern physics, for example. In the West science itself has grown in close
symbiosis with a certain culture, in the sense in which I am using that
term here—that is, a constellation of understandings of person, nature,
society, and the good.

To rely on an acultural theory is to miss all this. One gets a distorted
understanding of Western modernity in one of two ways: On one side,
we misclassify changes that reflect the culture peculiar to the modern
West as the product of unproblematic discovery, or the ineluctable con-

---

catastrophic to confuse these two kinds of individualism, which have utterly different causes and consequences. Which is why de Tocqueville carefully distinguishes
individualism from egoism.

sequence of some social change, like the introduction of technology. The decline in religious practice has frequently been seen in this light. This is the error of seeing everything modern as belonging to one Enlightenment package. On the other side, we fail altogether to examine certain facets of the modern constellation, closely interwoven with our understandings of science and religion, that don't strike us as being part of the transformation to modernity. We don't identify them as among the spectacular changes that have produced contemporary civilization, and we often fail to see even that there have been changes, reading these facets falsely as perennial. Such is the usual fate of those, largely implicit, understandings of human agency that I have grouped under the portmanteau term, the "modern identity,"[4] such as the various forms of modern inwardness or the affirmation of ordinary life. We all too easily imagine that people have always seen themselves as Westerners do, as in respect of dichotomies like inward/outward. And we thus utterly miss the role these new understandings have played in the rise of Western modernity. I want to make a claim of this kind in the following discussion in relation to the rise of the modern public sphere.

And so a purely acultural theory distorts and impoverishes our understanding of the West, both through misclassification (the Enlightenment package error) and through too narrow a focus. But such a theory's effects on our understanding of other cultures is even more devastating. The belief that modernity comes from a single, universally applicable operation imposes a falsely uniform pattern on the multiple encounters of non-Western cultures with the exigencies of science, technology, and industrialization. As long as we are bemused by the Enlightenment package, we will believe that all cultures *have* to undergo a range of cultural changes, drawn from our experience — for example, secularization or the growth of atomistic forms of self-identification. As long as we leave Western notions of identity unexamined, we will fail to see how other cultures differ and how this difference crucially conditions the way in which they integrate the truly universal features of modernity.

---

4. See Charles Taylor, *Sources of the Self: The Making of the Modern Identity* (Cambridge, Mass.: Harvard University Press, 1989).

The view that modernity arises through the dissipation of certain unsupported religious and metaphysical beliefs seems to imply that the paths of different civilizations are bound to converge. As they lose their traditional illusions, they will come together on the "rationally grounded" outlook which has resisted the challenge. The march of modernity will end up making all cultures look the same. This means, of course, that we expect they will end up looking Western.

This idea of modernity (in the singular) as a point of convergence is very much imbued with the logic of the acultural theory. "Development" occurs in "traditional" societies through modernization. For this concept of the traditional, what matters is not the specific features of earlier societies, which are very different from each other. What is crucial is just that by holding people within a sacred horizon, a fixed community, and unchallengeable custom, traditions impede development. Over against the blazing light of modern reason, all traditional societies look alike in their immobile night.

What they hold us back from is "development," conceived as the unfolding of our potentiality to grasp our real predicament and apply instrumental reason to it. The instrumental individual of secular outlook is always already there, ready to emerge when the traditional impediments fall away. Development occurs through modernization, which designates the ensemble of those culture-neutral processes, both in outlook (individuation, rise of instrumental reason) and in institutions and practices (industrialization, urbanization, mass literacy, the introduction of markets and bureaucratic states) which carry us through the transition. This outlook projects a future in which we all emerge together into a single, homogeneous world culture. In our traditional societies, we were very different from each other. But once these earlier horizons have been lost, we shall all be the same.

A cultural theory opens up a rather different gamut of prospects. If the transition to modernity is like the rise of a new culture, analogous to the conversion of the Roman Empire to Christianity in the early centuries, or of Indonesia to Islam after the fourteenth century, then, as in all such cases, the starting point will leave its impress on the end product. So Christianity was deeply marked by Greek philosophy, and Indonesian Islam is rather unlike the rest of the Islamic world. In a parallel fashion, transitions to what we might recognize as modernity, taking place in different civilizations, will produce different results that reflect their divergent starting points. Different cultures' understandings of the person, social relations, states of mind, goods and bads, virtues and vices, and the sacred and the profane are likely to be distinct. The future of our world will be one in which all societies will undergo change, in institutions and outlook, and some of these changes may be parallel, but they will not converge, because new differences will emerge from the old.

Thus, instead of speaking of modernity in the singular, we should better speak of "alternative modernities."

The belief in modernity as convergence is not just the fruit of an acultural theory. Just as the account of the transition to modernity as our "coming to see" certain things contains a partial truth, so here there is undoubtedly *some* convergence involved in the triumphal march of modernity. A viable theory of alternative modernities has to be able to relate both the pull to sameness and the forces making for difference.

From one point of view, modernity is like a wave, flowing over and engulfing one traditional culture after another. If we understand by modernity, inter alia, the changes discussed here which carry the transition—the emergence of a market-industrial economy, of a bureaucratically organized state, of modes of popular rule—then its progress is, indeed, wavelike. The first two changes, if not the third, are in a sense irresistible. Whoever fails to take them, or some good functional equivalent, on will fall so far behind in the power stakes as to be taken over and forced to undergo these changes anyway. It was a stark appreciation of these power relations that impelled Japanese elites in the Meiji era, for instance, to undertake preemptive modernization. The fate of other Asian societies that had not managed to modernize was an eloquent plea for this policy. There are good reasons in the relations of force for the onward march of modernity so defined.

But modernity as lived from the inside, as it were, is something different. The institutional changes just described always shake up and alter traditional culture. They did this in the original development in the West, and they have done this elsewhere. But outside of those cases where the original culture is quite destroyed, and the people either die or are forcibly assimilated—and European colonialism has a number of such cases to its discredit—a successful transition involves a people finding resources in their traditional culture which, modified and transposed, will enable them to take on the new practices. In this sense, modernity is not a single wave. It would be better, as I have just suggested, to speak of alternative modernities, as the cultures that emerge in the world to carry the institutional changes turn out to differ in important ways from each other. Thus a Japanese modernity, an Indian modernity, and various modulations of Islamic modernity will probably enter alongside the gamut of Western societies, which are also far from being uniform.

Seen in this perspective, we can see that modernity—the wave—can be felt as a threat to a traditional culture. It will remain an external threat to those deeply committed against change. But there is another reaction, among those who want to take on some version of the institutional changes. Unlike the conservatives, they don't want to refuse these innovations; they want, of course, to avoid the fate of those aboriginal people who have been engulfed and made over by the external power. What they are looking for is a creative adaptation, drawing on the cultural resources of their tradition, that would enable them to take on the new practices successfully. In short, they want to do what has already been done in the West. But they see, or sense, that this cannot consist of just copying the West's adaptations. By definition, the creative adaptation using traditional resources has to be different from culture to culture. Simply taking over Western modernity couldn't be the answer. Or, otherwise put, this answer comes too close to engulfment. They have to invent their own.

There is thus a call to difference felt by modernizing elites that corresponds to something objective in their situation. This is of course part of the background to nationalism. But merely wanting a creative adaptation doesn't ensure that one brings it off. And some of the formulae that have been proposed appear with hindsight pretty much nonstarters; as for instance the idea put forward by the government of Ching China after the Opium War, which can be roughly rendered "We'll take their technology and keep our culture." There are moments where the modernizers begin to look indistinguishable from the conservative enemies of change.

This kind of resistance results in what Rajeev Bhargava has called "patchwork" solutions,[5] which attempt to tack the new power-conferring practices onto an unchanged way of life. But these institutions and practices almost always require new disciplines, new understandings of agency, or new forms of sociability. We have only to think of what is required to participate as an entrepreneur in a modern market economy, or the kind of rationalized coordination required by a modern bureaucracy, to see that this is so. The really creative adaptation can modify an existing culture to make, for example, successful entrepreneurship and bureaucratic organization henceforth part of its repertory. This generally cannot be brought about without profound changes in earlier ways of life.

The point of the alternative modernities thesis is that these adaptations don't have to and generally won't be identical across civilizations. Indeed, something is converging here, while other things diverge. It might be tempting to say that the institutions and practices converge, while the cultures find new forms of differentiation. But that can only be a first approximation. Because, in fact, the institutional forms will also frequently be different.

Take the example just mentioned of entrepreneurship. It is a condition of successful participation in a market economy, itself a condition of economic growth and hence welfare and/or power. But it is clear that the entrepreneurial cultures of Japan, Chinese societies, and the Indian merchant castes and groups differ from each other and from those of the West. Indeed, business cultures differ even between the societies of the Atlantic region, as Francis Fukuyama has persuasively argued.[6] But with the cultures also go differences in form: in size of firm, basis of trust within it, and its modes of procedure. These forms and cultures will be more or less successful in different circumstances, and they may thus keep tabs on each other and even try to borrow, but this doesn't mean that they can or will converge.

We have to remember that what is required by the wave of modernity is that one come up not with identical institutions but with functionally equivalent ones. The "bottom line" is, for example, competing success-

5. Oral communication to the seminar on alternative modernities held by the Center for Transcultural Studies, Delhi, December 1997.
6. See Francis Fukuyama, *Trust: The Social Virtues and the Creation of Prosperity* (New York: Free Press, 1995).

fully in the international market. More than one kind of firm and business culture can enable this. A given society will, indeed must, adopt the mode for which it has the cultural resources. That is the essence of creative adaptation.[7]

If this perspective of divergence in convergence is right, then we can see how exclusive reliance on an acultural theory unfits us for what is perhaps the most important task of social sciences in our day: understanding the full gamut of alternative modernities which are in the making in different parts of the world. It locks us into an ethnocentric prison, condemned to project our own forms onto everyone else and blissfully unaware of what we are doing.

THE THIRD MAJOR PREMISE

The view from Dover Beach foreshortens our understanding of Western modernity and blinds us to the diversity in our world. But it also gives us a false and distorted perspective on the transition. It makes us read the rise of modernity in terms of the dissipation of certain beliefs, either as its major cause (rational explanations), or as inevitable concomitant (social explanations). What is beyond the horizon on Dover Beach is the possibility that what mainly differentiates us from our fore-

---

7. I have been defining successful adaptation here in terms of a functional challenge — how to meet the demands of economic growth and military power. But we can also look at these solutions in another perspective. For many of us, modernity may also carry normative force, centering around such goods as freedom, equality, and the respect of human rights. From this point of view, functionally successful adaptations may be bad. Pinochet's Chile was a stunning economic success, for a while anyway. There is some evidence that the most horrendous regimes — Nazism, Bolshevism — end up being maladaptive or even self-destructing. But it is hard to believe that this will always be the case. Even the best regimes on earth incorporate injustices and modes of exclusion.

One can envisage another kind of search for an alternative modernity, one that would realize its normative promise more fully. This is an important issue — indeed, one of the great issues — of our time. But the two questions are distinct: Can we create a normatively superior alternative modernity? Can there be a plurality of culturally different alternative modernities? We should add that the attempt to realize new positive answers to the second question should be subject to the normative conditions that the first raises. Not every mode of cultural distinctness is thereby justified and good.

bears is not so much our explicit beliefs as what I want to call the background understanding against which our beliefs are formulated.

Here I am picking up on an idea from the work of Martin Heidegger, Maurice Merleau-Ponty, Ludwig Wittgenstein, and Michael Polanyi and further elaborated recently by John Searle and Hubert Dreyfus.[8] The notion is that our explicit beliefs about our world and ourselves are held against a background of unformulated (and perhaps in part unformulable) understandings, in relation to which these beliefs make the sense they do. These understandings take a variety of forms and range over a number of matters. In one dimension, the background incorporates matters that *could* be formulated as beliefs but aren't functioning as such in our world (and couldn't *all* function as such because of their unlimited extent). To take Wittgenstein's example from *On Certainty:* I don't normally have a *belief* that the world didn't start only five minutes ago, but the whole way I inquire into things treats the world as being there since time out of mind.[9] Similarly, I don't usually have the belief that a huge pit hasn't been dug in front of my door, but I treat the world that way as I emerge in the morning to go to work. In my ways of dealing with things is incorporated the background understanding that the world is stable and has been there a long time.

In other dimensions, I have this kind of understanding of myself as an agent with certain powers, of myself as an agent among other agents, on certain, only partly explicit footings with them. And I want to add: an agent moving in certain kinds of social spaces, with a sense of how both I and these spaces inhabit time, a sense of how both I and they relate to the cosmos and to God or whatever I recognize as the source(s) of good.

In my addition here, I have entered controversial territory. While perhaps everyone can be got easily to agree on the kinds of background understandings I cited from Wittgenstein, and it is arguably obvious

8. Martin Heidegger, *Sein und Zeit* (Tübingen: Niemeyer, 1927); Maurice Merleau-Ponty, *Phénoménologie de la perception* (Paris: Gallimard, 1945); Ludwig Wittgenstein, *Philosophical Investigations* (Oxford: Basil Blackwell, 1953); Michael Polanyi, *Personal Knowledge* (New York: Harper, 1958); John Searle, *Intentionality* (Cambridge: Cambridge University Press, 1983); and Hubert Dreyfus, *What Computers Can't Do* (New York: Harper, 1979).

9. Ludwig Wittgenstein, *On Certainty* (Oxford: Basil Blackwell, 1977), par. 260 and forward.

that I have some sense of myself as agent, the notion that different modes of social belonging, different understandings of time, and even more, of God, the good, or the cosmos, should be part of the background may arouse resistance. That is because we easily can believe that we have background understanding in the inescapable dimensions of our lives as agents, functioning in a physical and social world. But when we come to our supposed relations to God, the good, or the cosmos, surely these things only enter our world through our being inducted into our society's culture, and they must enter in the form of beliefs that have been handed down to us.

But this is in fact not how it works. Of course, in any theistic culture there will be *some* beliefs about God, but our sense of a god and our relation to one will also be formed by, for example, modes of ritual, the kinds of prayer we have been taught, what we pick up from the attitudes of pious and impious people, and the like. A similar point can be made about the different kinds of social space. There may be some doctrines formulated about the nature of society and the hierarchical rankings that constitute it which are explicitly proffered for our adherence, but we also come to understand whole "volumes" in the ways we are taught—for example, to show deference to certain people or at certain times and places. A social understanding is built in to what Pierre Bourdieu calls our "habitus," the ways we are taught to behave, which become unreflecting, second nature to us.[10]

We know our way around society somewhat the way we know our way around our physical environment, not primarily and principally because we have some map of either in our heads, but because we know how to treat different people and situations appropriately. In this know-

---

10. See Pierre Bourdieu, *Outline of a Theory of Practice* (Cambridge: Cambridge University Press, 1977), and Bourdieu, *Le sens pratique* (Paris: Minuit, 1980). "On pourrait, déformant le mot de Proust, dire que les jambes, les bras sont pleins d'impératifs engourdis. Et l'on n'en finirait pas d'énumérer les valeurs faites corps, par la transsubstantiation qu'opère la persuasion clandestibe d'une pédagogie implicite, capable d'inculquer toute une cosmologie, une éthique, une métaphysique, une politique, à travers des injonctions aussi insignifiantes que 'tiens-toi droit' ou 'ne tiens pas ton couteau de la main gauche' et d'inscrire dans les détails en apparence les plus insignifiants de la *tenue,* du *maintien* ou des *manières* corporelles et verbales les principes fondamentaux de l'arbitraire culturel, ainsi placés hors des prises de la conscience et de l'explicitation" (Bourdieu, *Le sens pratique,* 117).

how there is, for example, a stance toward the elders which treats them as having a certain dignity. What it is about them that is felt to command this stance may not yet be spelled out: There may be no word for *dignity* in the vocabulary of the tribe. But whatever it is which we will later want to articulate with this word is already in the world of the youngsters who bow in that particular way and address their elders in low tones and with the proper language. *Dignity* is in their world in the sense that they deal with it, respond to it, perhaps revere it or resent it. It is just not formulated in a description and hence does not figure in an explicit belief. Its being in their world is part of their background understanding.

It is in similar ways that God or the good can figure in our world. Surrounding express doctrines will be a richer penumbra of embodied understanding. We can imaginatively extend the example of the previous paragraph. Suppose that one of the things that makes the elders worthy of respect is just that they are closer to the gods. Then the divine, too, which we revere through these old people, will be in our world in part through our knowing how to treat them. It will be in our world through the appropriate habitus.

In fact, we might distinguish three levels of understanding from the preceding discussion. There is the level of explicit doctrine—about society, the divine, and the cosmos. There is the level of what I called, following Bourdieu, the habitus, or embodied understanding. Somewhat between the two is a level which we might call (with some trepidation, because this is a semantically overloaded term) the symbolic. I mean by this whatever understanding is expressed in ritual, in symbols (in the everyday sense), and in works of art. What exists on this level is more explicit than mere gesture or appropriate action, because ritual or work can have a mimetic or an evocative dimension and hence point to something they imitate or call forth. But it is not explicit in the self-conscious way of doctrinal formulations, which can be submitted to the demands of logic, permit of a metadiscourse in which they are examined in turn, and the like.

We can see why it might be a big mistake to think that what distinguishes us from our premodern forebears is mainly a lot of beliefs of theirs which we have shed. Even if we want, following *Dover Beach*, to see their age as one of a faith which we have lost, it might be very misleading to think of this difference in terms simply of doctrines to which they subscribe and we do not. Because below the doctrinal level are at least two others: that of embodied background understanding and that which while nourished in embodied habitus is given expression on the symbolic level. As well as the doctrinal understanding of society, there is the one incorporated in habitus, and a level of images as yet unformulated in doctrine, for which we might borrow a term frequently used by contemporary French writers: *l'imaginaire social*—what we can call the social imaginary.

Why does it matter to see the changeover as more than doctrinal? Because otherwise we might have a very distorted picture of it. When people undergo a change in belief, they shift their views between already formulated possibilities. Formerly, they thought that God exists. But in formulating this belief they were quite aware that there was another option; indeed, usually they are aware that others have already taken the atheist option, that there are arguments for and against it, and so on. Now, when they switch to atheism, they move within positions already in their repertory, between points already within their horizons.

But some of the major changes in embodied understanding and social imaginary alter the very repertory and introduce new possibilities that were not before on the horizon. I will sketch presently what this might involve in connection with the rise of the public sphere. Modernity involves the coming to be of new kinds of public space, which cannot be accounted for in terms of changes in explicit views, either of factual belief or normative principle. Rather, the transition involves to some extent the definition of new possible spaces hitherto outside the repertory of our forebears and beyond the limits of their social imaginary. The consequence of seeing these changes as alterations of (factual or normative) belief is that we unwittingly make our ancestors too much like us. To the extent that we see ourselves as differing from them in *belief,* we see them as having the same doctrinal repertory as ours, merely opting differently within it. To give them the same repertory, we have to align their embodied understanding and social imaginary with ours. We falsely make them in this sense our contemporaries and grievously underestimate the nature and scope of the change that brought our world about.

So an acultural theory tends to make us both miss the original vision of the good implicit in Western modernity and underestimate the nature of the transformation that brought about this modernity. These two drawbacks appear to be linked. Some of the important shifts in culture, in our understandings of personhood, the good, and the like, which have brought about the original vision of Western modernity, can only be seen if we bring into focus the major changes in embodied understanding and social imaginary which the last centuries have engendered. They tend to disappear if we flatten these changes, read our own background and imaginary into our forebears, and concentrate on their beliefs which we no longer share.

*

These connections will, of course, have to be made in detail, and there is not space here to do that. Just to give a taste of what is involved, I could invoke the modern understanding and reality (the two are linked) of a public sphere of open debate and exchange through media. This is thought to be an essential feature of any mature and legitimate society — so much so that dictatorial and totalitarian regimes tend to try to fake it, offering supposedly objective news broadcasts, editorials in party newspapers that purport to be the communication of someone's opinion, "spontaneous" demonstrations, and the like.

Now the modern public sphere is a strange kind of reality in an important respect. It is supposed to be a space of discussion linking in principle or potentially everyone, even though its many participants never meet all together in one place. This space has to be sustained by a particular kind of social imaginary, one that is in many respects rather different from premodern modes of imaginary and that has a lot to do with specifically modern understandings of secular time and simultaneity.[11] Or so, anyway, I want to claim that closer study would demonstrate. Such a study would reveal, I believe, just how our understanding of our relations to society, time, the cosmos, the good, and God have been transformed with the coming of our era.

If this transformation is true, then we can see how inadequate and misleading acultural accounts can be. In my sense of this term, these are explanations of Western modernity that see it not as one culture among others but, rather, as what emerges when any "traditional" culture is put through certain (rational or social) changes. On this view, modernity is

11. There is an interesting discussion of this in Benedict Anderson, *Imagined Communities*, rev. ed. (London: Verso, 1991), 28–31.

not specifically Western, even though it may have started in the West. Instead, it is that form of life toward which all cultures converge, as they go through, one after another, substantially the same changes. These may be seen primarily in intellectual terms as the growth of rationality and science; or primarily in social terms as the development of certain institutions and practices: a market economy or rationalized forms of administration. But in either case, the changes are partly understood in terms of the loss of traditional beliefs, either because they are undermined by the growth of reason or because they are marginalized by institutional change.

Even the social explanations assume that these beliefs suffer from a lack of rational justification, since the solvent effect of social change is held to lie in the fact that it disturbs old patterns that made it possible to hold on to these earlier beliefs in spite of their lack of rational grounding. For instance, the continuance of a static, agricultural way of life, largely at the mercy of the vagaries of climate, supposedly makes certain religious beliefs look plausible, which lose their hold once humans see what it is to take their fate in their own hands through industrial development. Or a largely immobile society leads individuals to see their fate as bound up closely with that of their neighbors and inhibits the growth of an individualism which naturally flourishes once these constricting limits are lifted.

The acultural theory tends to see the process of modernity as involving among other things the shucking off of beliefs and ways which don't have much rational justification, leaving us with an outlook many of whose elements can be seen more as hard, residual facts: that we are individuals — that is, beings whose behavior is ultimately to be explained as individuals — living in a profane time, who have to extract what we need to live from nature and whom it behooves therefore to be maximally instrumentally rational, without allowing ourselves to be diverted from this goal by the metaphysical and religious beliefs that held our ancestors back.[12] Instrumental rationality commands a scientific attitude to nature and human life.

12. This development of instrumental rationality is what is frequently described as secularization. See, for instance, Gabriel Almond and G. Bingham Powell, *Comparative Politics: A Developmental Approach* (Boston: Little, Brown, 1966). "A village chief in a tribal society operates largely with a given set of goals and a given set of means

At the heart of the acultural approach is the view that modernity involves our "coming to see" certain kernel truths about the human condition, those I have just adverted to. There is some justification for talking of our "coming to see" the truth when we consider the revolution of natural science which began in the seventeenth century. But the mistake of the acultural approach is to lump all the supposed kernel truths about human life into the same package, as though they were all endorsed equally by science, on a par, say, with particle physics.[13]

I have been arguing that this is a crucial mistake. It misrepresents our forebears, and it distorts the process of transition from them to us. In particular, seeing the change as the decline of certain *beliefs* covers up the great differences in background understanding and in the social imaginary of different ages. More, it involves a sort of ethnocentrism of the present. Since human beings always do hold their explicit beliefs against a background and in the context of an imaginary, failure to notice the difference amounts to the unwitting attribution to them of our own. This is the classic ethnocentric projection, matched by and indeed connected with the inability to perceive the differences in our contemporary world.

This projection gives support to the implicit Whiggism of the acultural theory, whereby moderns have "come to see" the kernel truths. If you think of premoderns as operating with the same background

---

of attaining these goals which have grown up and been hallowed by custom. The secularization of culture is the processes whereby traditional orientations and attitudes give way to more dynamic decision-making processes involving the gathering of information, the evaluation of information, the laying out of alternative courses of action, the selection of a given action from among those possible courses, and the means whereby one tests whether or not a given course of action is producing the consequences which were intended" (24–25). And later: "The emergence of a pragmatic, empirical orientation is one component of the secularization process" (58).

13. Even Ernest Gellner, who is light years of sophistication away from the crudities of Almond and Powell, puts himself in the acultural camp, for all his interesting insights into modernity as a new constellation. He does this by linking what I am calling the supposed kernel truths with what he calls cognitive advance in a single package. The modern constellation unchained science, and that in his view seems to confer the same epistemic status on the entire package. "Specialization, atomization, instrumental rationality, independence of fact and value, growth and provisionality of knowledge are all linked with each other." See *Plough, Sword and Book* (Chicago: University of Chicago Press, 1989), 122.

understanding of human beings as moderns—that is, as instrumental individuals—and you code their understandings of God, cosmos, and multidimensional time as beliefs held against this background, then these beliefs do, indeed, appear as arbitrary and lacking in justification, and it is not surprising that the social changes dislodged them. But an examination of the rise of the public sphere would show, I believe, that this is not what happened. It is not that we sloughed off a whole lot of unjustified beliefs, leaving an implicit self-understanding which had always been there to operate at last untrammeled. Rather, one constellation of implicit understandings of our relation to God, the cosmos, other humans, and time was replaced by another in a multifaceted mutation. Seeing things this way not only gives us a better handle on what happened but also allows us to understand ourselves better. As long as we think that our implicit self-understanding is the universal human one, as long as we fail to note its contrast with others, we will have an incomplete and distorted understanding of it. This is always a price of ethnocentrism.

From a standpoint immured within any culture other cultures look weird. No doubt we would look strange—as well as blasphemous and licentious—to our medieval ancestors. But there is a particularly high cost in self-misunderstanding which attaches to the ethnocentrism of the modern. The kernel truths of the acultural theory incorporate an often unreflective methodological individualism, along with a belief in the omnicompetence of natural science. Impelled by the latter, its protagonists are frequently tempted to cast our "coming to see" the kernel truths as a sort of discovery in science. But the discoveries of natural science are of neutral facts—truths that are "value-free," on which value may be subsequently placed by human beings but which themselves are devoid of moral significance. It belongs to the range of such "natural" facts as that we are individuals, impelled to operate by instrumental reason, maximizing our advantage when we are not deterred from doing so by unfounded belief.[14]

Now this hides from view two important connections. First, the way in which our implicit understanding of ourselves as agents always places us in certain relations to others. Because of the very nature of the human

14. Thus Gellner includes "independence of fact and value" in his package, along with "growth and provisionality of knowledge" (*Plough, Sword and Book*, 122).

condition—that we can only define ourselves in exchange with others, those who bring us up and those whose society we come to see as constitutive of our identity—our self-understanding always places us among others. The placements differ greatly, and understanding these differences and their change is the stuff of history.

We can see a good example of what this involves in the speculative sketch I offered of the rise of the public sphere. This, and other similar modes of social imagining, is closely tied up with the rise of modern individualism. The account I would like to offer would have us see the rise of this new individual identity as inextricably linked to the new understandings of time and society. Individualism is one side of a coin, of which the flip side is new modes of social imaginary.

By contrast, a widespread alternative view sees individualism as involving a completely self-referential identity; one in which agents are first of all aware of and focused on themselves and only subsequently discover a need for and determine their relations to others. The human of the "state of nature" was, indeed, an important constituent of the early modern imaginary, but we must not make the mistake of understanding the people who imagined it in its light. Modern individualism is coterminous with—indeed, is defined by—a new understanding of our placement among others, one which gives an important place to common action in profane time and hence to the idea of consensually founded unions, which receives influential formulation in the myth of an original state of nature and a social contract. Individualism is not just a withdrawal from society but a reconception of what human society can be. To think of it as pure withdrawal is to confuse individualism, which is always a moral ideal, with the anomie of breakdown.

Similarly, our understanding of ourselves always incorporates some understanding of the good and our relation to it. Here, too, there are radical differences. The good may be conceived theistically, or as in the cosmos (as with Plato's Idea of the Good). But it may also be understood as residing in us, in the inherent dignity of the human person as a reasoning being, for instance, as we find with Immanuel Kant. However understood, the notion of a human identity without such a sense brings us close to the unimaginable limit of total breakdown.[15]

15. I have tried to argue this point at greater length in *Sources of the Self,* chaps. 1–4.

All this is occluded, indeed doubly. Seeing the evolution of instrumental individualism as the discovery of a natural fact does not just involve projecting our background onto our ancestors. In addition, the naturalist, scientistic outlook which generates this error has been heavily intricated with the representational, foundationalist epistemology that descends from Descartes and Locke. This epistemology has suppressed all recognition of the background. It conceives our knowledge of the world as consisting of particulate, explicit representations. This means that we not only project our own background backward but also render this error invisible by repressing all awareness of backgrounds as such.[16] The ethnocentric colonization of the past cannot be brought to light, because the very terms in which it might appear have been abolished.

The very idea of an individual who might become aware of himself and then only subsequently, or at least independently, determine what importance others have for him and what he will accept as good, belongs to post-Cartesian, foundationalist fantasy. Once we recognize that our explicit thoughts only can be entertained against a background sense of who and where we are in the world and among others and in moral space, we can see that we can never be without some relation to the crucial reference points I already enumerated: world, others, time, the good. This relation can, indeed, be transformed as we move from one culture or age to another, but it cannot just fall away. We cannot be without *some* sense of our moral situation, *some* sense of our connectedness to others.

The naturalistic account of the discovery of the kernel truths, implicit in the acultural theory, misses all these connections. When the old metaphysical and religious beliefs crumble, we find as a matter of neutral fact that we are instrumental individuals, and we need to draw from elsewhere our values and acceptable grounds for association with others. In contrast, I want to describe the change as moving us from one dense constellation of background understanding and imaginary

16. I have discussed the nature of this modern epistemology and its suppression of the background at greater length in "Overcoming Epistemology" in *After Philosophy: End or Transformation?* ed. Kenneth Baynes, James Bohman, and Thomas McCarthy (Cambridge, Mass.: MIT Press, 1987) and "Lichtung oder Lebensform," *Der Löwe spricht . . . und wir können ihn nicht verstehen* (Frankfurt: Suhrkamp, 1991).

to another, both of which place us in relation to others and the good. There is never atomistic and neutral self-understanding; there is only a constellation (ours) which tends to throw up the myth of this self-understanding as part of its imaginary. This is of the essence of a cultural theory of modernity.

On Reconciling Cosmopolitan Unity
and National Diversity

Thomas McCarthy

There are few ideas as important to the history of modern democracy as that of the nation as a political community. And yet, by comparison to its companion idea of political community as based on the agreement of free and equal individuals, it remained until recently a marginal concern of post–World War II liberal theory. The aftermath of decolonization and the breakup of the Soviet empire, among other things, has changed that and brought it again to the center of theoretical attention. And once there, the deep-seated tensions in theory between nationalism and liberalism have proved to be as hard to overlook as their all too familiar tensions in practice. Thus many liberal political theorists have taken to framing their inquiries into nationalism by asking whether there is a conception of nationhood that is compatible with basic liberal principles. Can the values of nation and culture be combined with those of freedom and equality within the basic structure of the democratic constitutional nation-state? One fault line that has attracted its share of attention divides liberal universalism from nationalist particularism. That division becomes all the more salient when the topic of cosmopolitanism comes up, as it does more and more frequently, partly in reaction to horrors perpetrated under the banner of ethnonationalism. The framing question then is whether there is a conception of nationhood that is compatible with cosmopolitanism when the latter is understood as the establishment of a basic structure of cosmopolitical justice under a global rule of law.

Immanuel Kant was among the first to understand cosmopolitanism in these terms, and his attempt to reconcile it with nationalism, most famously in his essay on "Perpetual Peace," has remained among the most influential. Kant was writing during the birth of the modern nation-state from the American and French Revolutions. Political theorists addressing these issues today can look back on a two-hundred-year history of the nation-state and ahead to the anticipated consequences of the accelerated globalization processes now under way. The work of Jürgen Habermas is particularly interesting in this regard, for he explicitly takes up Kant's reading of history "with a cosmopolitan intent," complicates it with lessons drawn from the intervening two centuries of experience with the nation-state, and projects it into a hoped-for cosmopolitan future. In this essay, after framing the problem of reconciling nationalism and cosmopolitanism in a certain way, I want to take a new look at how Kant tried and failed to resolve it and then to examine Habermas's recent efforts to update the Kantian project. In the final section, I will consider some doubts about that project raised by Charles Taylor in his defense of "alternative modernities."

NATIONALISM

From the time of the French Revolution to the present, through successive waves of nation-state formation in the nineteenth and twentieth centuries, a distinctively modern form of political community has gradually prevailed over all competitors.[1] Within the boundaries of preexisting territorial states and through the formation of new states, amidst the disintegration of empires and the dismantling of colonialism, it has become the characteristic modern expression of shared political identity. The idea of the nation as political community was present not only at the birth of modern democracy, when "we the people" became the bearers of sovereignty, but also through the wars of national liberation and the struggles for national self-determination that shaped this

1. Among the works I have found helpful on the points raised in this section are the following: Benedict Anderson, *Imagined Communities: Reflections on the Origin and Spread of Nationalism* (New York: Verso, 1983); Ernest Gellner, *Nations and Nationalism* (Ithaca, N.Y.: Cornell University Press, 1983); Liah Greenfeld, *Nationalism: Five Roads to Modernity* (Cambridge, Mass.: Harvard University Press, 1992); Jürgen Habermas, *Die Einbeziehung des Anderen* (Frankfurt: Suhrkamp Verlag, 1996); E. J. Hobsbawm, *Nations and Nationalism since 1780* (Cambridge: Cambridge University Press, 1990); J. Hutchinson and A. D. Smith, eds., *Nationalism* (New York: Oxford University Press, 1994); R. McKim and J. McMahon, eds., *The Morality of Nationalism* (New York: Oxford University Press, 1997); David Miller, *On Nationality* (New York: Oxford University Press, 1995); and Yael Tamir, *Liberal Nationalism* (Princeton, N.J.: Princeton University Press, 1993).

century. The development of the nation-state system that now covers the globe is, of course, a complex and variegated story, whose proper telling requires extensive historical and comparative analysis. But here I am interested only in the core idea of linking political communities to communities of origin. In this sense, the basic principle of nationalism, in its strictest form, demands that every nation have its own state; and the basic right of nationalism, in its strictest form, is the right of every people to political self-determination.

Taken in this strict sense, nationalism as a normative doctrine today raises specters of ethnic cleansing, forced resettlement, massive repression, and the like. Nation-states require territories within whose boundaries they have a monopoly on force. But the earth is entirely covered by already existing states, which are less than 200 in number, while the identifiable ethnic groups that might conceivably invoke the nationalist principle and the nationalist right number some 5,000.[2] Moreover, the globe is not divided into ethnically homogeneous regions that might become independent states; ethnic intermingling is almost everywhere the rule. So taking ethnonationalism as the basic principle of state formation is, in the world we actually inhabit, a recipe for bloody disaster. This should be kept in mind when considering nationalism's claimed superiority as regards sensitivity to and accommodation of difference. A global mosaic of politically organized, ethnically homogeneous enclaves is about as unaccommodating, not to mention unrealistic, a scheme as could be imagined. So we have to turn to less extreme conceptions of nationalism if we want to get at the unresolved theoretical issues.

It is now generally recognized that national identities are neither natural nor prepolitical. They are socioculturally constructed—"imagined communities" as Benedict Anderson has it, or "imagined commonalities" as Max Weber had it; and they typically serve political purposes—as vehicles of emancipation or aggression, for instance, or of political unification and economic modernization. To be sure, they are usually constructed *as* quasi-natural, precisely as the prepolitical basis of and justification for the national political communities embracing them. Thus national consciousness typically includes a belief by mem-

2. I take these estimates from Will Kymlicka, *Multicultural Citizenship* (New York: Oxford University Press, 1995), 1. He notes his own sources for them on page 196, note 1.

bers of the national community that they share some distinct subset of such "objective" features as common descent, language, culture, homeland, customs, traditions, religion, history, destiny, or the like. But these commonalities are as often fictive as real. The classical nation-states were never as homogeneous in these respects as members characteristically took them to be, and contemporary nation-states are even less so. As historians have documented, the process of *nation-building* typically involved the work of intellectuals and writers, scholars and publicists, historians and artists using media of mass communication to forge a national consciousness and generate a common allegiance, first among the professional classes and through them among the masses. Correspondingly, standard languages were typically not a ground but a goal of nation-building processes. In short, nations were not found but created (not ex nihilo, of course); and they were created in response to historical contingencies and for political purposes. This is especially clear in the case of states that emerged from former colonies within territorial boundaries that cut across traditional ethnicities and homelands. But it is true, in varying degrees, of the classical nation-states as well.

The constructed character of national identity makes it notoriously susceptible to being instrumentalized for political purposes, good and bad. Raising national consciousness in the liberation struggles of oppressed groups usually counts as the former, fanning nationalist xenophobia for aggressive or expansive purposes as the latter. Historical sociologists and sociological historians often maintain that nation-building fulfilled essential functions in processes of modern state-formation — functions of cultural and linguistic unification, for instance, or of economic and political modernization — and in particular that nation-building was an important catalyst in the spread of republican government. Some argue, even, that for many purposes there were no functional alternatives to nationalism, and thus that it was an indispensable element in social, cultural, political, and economic modernization processes. In the same vein, theorists of contemporary politics sometimes claim that political integration in complex societies is not possible in the absence of strong national identification, that a purely "constitutional" or "civic" patriotism is no adequate substitute for loyalties rooted in culture, history, religion, or the like. This is said to be true even, or rather especially, of liberal democratic societies. The arguments here are familiar from the recent liberal-communitarian debates in political theory.

One basic issue is whether a citizenship of individual liberties and a politics of interest aggregation are a functionally and normatively adequate basis for democratic societies, or whether citizenship has rather to be tied to community and politics to common values if we are to have the solidarity and stability that democratic societies require.

Another important line of argument for the indispensability of nationalism intersects the main line of normative political theory in the modern period. There is, the argument goes, a huge gap in classical social contract theories: These theories provide no convincing normative delimitation of the "multitude of men" (Hobbes) or "number of men" (Locke) who are to be parties to the contract—that is, no normative account of just who must consent to the terms of association and why just them, though it seems generally to be assumed that the parties share a language and culture.[3] Nationalism claims to fill this normative-theoretical gap rather than leaving the matter, as liberal theorists in effect have, to the contingencies of history, which means, in practice, to shifting constellations of power. On this view, the boundaries of the nation should be the boundaries of the state.

Against these functional and normative arguments, a growing number of theorists have been arguing that the traditional nation-state system of national and international organization has outlived its usefulness, that it has become, in a word, dysfunctional and thus must be superseded. The path to a postnational system is variously conceived, but in all the different scenarios the inexorable thrust of globalization plays a significant role. Globalization of capital and labor markets, of production and consumption, of communication and information, of technological and cultural flows is already posing problems that cannot be resolved within the borders of individual states or with the traditional means of interstate treaties. Just as the problems that accompanied the rise of capitalism in modern Europe created a need for delocalizing law and politics, which led eventually to the formation of the nation-state, the globalization of capitalism and of everthing that goes with it

3. This theoretical gap is the subject of Vernon Van Dyke's "The Individual, the State, and Ethnic Communities," in *The Rights of Minority Cultures,* ed. W. Kymlicka (New York: Oxford University Press, 1995), 31–56. As Van Dyke notes, there are exceptions within the tradition of liberal political theory, for instance John Stuart Mill, who held that the boundaries of the state and of the nation should in general coincide (35). For a somewhat different take, see Kymlicka, *Multicultural Citizenship,* ch. 4.

is creating a growing need for denationalizing—in the sense of supra-nationalizing—law and politics. Many fear that if legal and political institutions do not expand to global proportions so as to keep up with the economy, we will be left with a more or less self-regulating capitalism that simply "creates a world in its own image" as national governments become less and less able to sustain the regulatory, steering, and social-welfare mechanisms with which they have heretofore sought to "domesticate" capitalism within their borders.[4] In this conjuncture, the task of a political theory committed to principles of freedom and equality under the rule of law is to think beyond the present, to elaborate normative models—or even utopian projections—of a world order that could measure up to such principles, that is, in which they would no longer be institutionalized, however imperfectly, only at the national level and below. To borrow a term from John Rawls, political theorists should attempt to sketch the "basic structure" of a system of cosmopolitical justice that could serve as a point of normative orientation and guide to political practice. They should strive to overcome the deep-seated inclination to think largely within the taken-for-granted confines of the nation-state and seek to conceptualize transnational structures for guaranteeing individual rights, securing democratic accountability, and ensuring fair distribution on a global scale.

The local "inside" is now increasingly linked with the global "outside," but it is not only this aspect of globalization that sets the idea of the ethnocultural nation-state at odds with reality. The vast movements and minglings of populations around the world have a parallel effect: The "inside" is also increasingly diverse. And there seems to be no halting this diversification short of violence, coercion, and repression. The growing heterogeneity of most populations makes any model of political community based on ethnocultural homogeneity or on forced assimilation to a hegemonic culture increasingly unsuitable as a normative model. The political-theoretical challenge it raises is, rather, to think unity in diversity, to conceptualize forms of political integration that are sensitive to, compatible with, and accommodating of varieties of difference. Reconciling national diversity with cosmopolitan unity is one component of a response.

4. This is, for instance, a chief concern of Eric Hobsbawm in his history of the "short twentieth century," *The Age of Extremes* (New York: Vintage, 1996), and of Habermas in *Die Einbeziehung des Anderen.*

And this brings us back to the tensions between liberalism and nationalism, between voluntary membership and ascriptive membership, between citizens with legally defined basic rights and conationals with culturally defined shared features. It is clear that any attempt at reconciliation will have to involve transformation. In particular, if we are trying to conceptualize a *liberal* nationalism, in the broadest sense, then it will have to be compatible with the universalist content of the basic rights of citizens under the rule of law. To be sure, these basic or "human" rights are given particular and various expressions in different constitutional traditions. But it belongs to their very meaning that they claim a universal validity transcending any particular legal system — a surplus of meaning characteristic of basic normative or "regulative" (Kant) ideas. Liberal theorists have always known this and thus have felt obliged to explain, again and again, why it was that women, slaves, the unpropertied and uneducated, and virtually the entire non-Western world could not in practice be granted the fundamental rights that in theory belonged to "all men."[5]

If nationalism has to be transformed to be compatible with liberal universalism, what of liberal universalism? What changes must it undergo to be compatible even with a transformed nationalism? That will become clearer as we proceed. But even at the start, it is evident that it will have to accommodate somehow the cultural differences that nationalism stresses and liberalism has, until quite recently, largely ignored. For it is clear that a theory of justice which respects individuals' rights to define and pursue happiness in their own ways should, in particular, take into consideration their desires to continue living with others their distinct forms of life — to go on speaking the languages, adhering to the customs, passing on the traditions, practicing the religions, and so forth, which inform who they are and who they want to be as individuals and as communities. Of course, the formation of an independent state is by no means the only way of safeguarding the integrity of a valued form of life. In addition to antidiscrimination legal protections and voluntary cultural associations, there is a wide range of political-organizational possibilities for securing some measure of autonomy short of sovereign statehood: consociation, federal union, loose

5. See the interesting discussion of this in Charles W. Mills, *The Racial Contract* (Ithaca, N.Y.: Cornell University Press, 1997).

confederation, functional decentralization, devolution, special representation or veto rights, special language or land rights, and so on and so forth. Given the demographics of the planet, it seems evident that a vast array of such arrangements would be necessary even to begin to accommodate existing diversity in any cosmopolitical legal and political order. The one arrangement that would have to go is precisely the absolutely sovereign nation-state—which does not mean that the nation-state must simply disappear. For the present, it seems, any viable scheme of cosmopolitan unity will have to preserve while transforming it. To borrow a term from Hegel, the nation-state must be *aufgehoben.*

On the other hand, a liberal cosmopolitanism could not countenance granting communal rights for the sake of protecting cultures that deny individual rights. More specifically, if culturally diverse nations are the rule, then cultural pluralism has to be integral to national self-understanding. And this suggests that ethnic nationalism will have to give way increasingly to civic nationalism. To be sure, the latter is a more abstract form of integration, but allegiance to a national community was itself already more abstract than the local ties it transcended. And, as we saw, the nation, however powerful the "we" consciousness it generated, is not a natural but a constructed object of group loyalty. There seems to be no reason in principle, then, why it cannot itself be transformed to be compatible with a liberal cosmopolitanism. A look at Kant and Habermas will help us get clearer on the conceptual issues involved.

KANT

Kant has long been a favorite target of those opposed to abstract universalism in political theory generally and to undifferentiated cosmopolitanism in international affairs particularly.[6] Indeed, his moral ideal

6. For this account of Kant's views on cosmopolitanism and nationalism I will be drawing on the following works (bracketed abbreviations are used for citations in the text): (1784) "Idea for a Universal History with a Cosmopolitan Purpose" [UH], in *Kant: Political Writings,* ed. H. Reiss, trans. H. B. Nisbet (Cambridge: Cambridge University Press, 1991), 41–53; (1793) "On the Common Saying: 'This May Be True in Theory, but It Does Not Apply in Practice'" [TP], in Reiss, *Kant,* 61–92; (1795) "Perpetual Peace: A Philosophical Sketch" [PP], in Reiss, *Kant,* 93–130; (1797) *The Metaphysics of Morals* [MM], ed. and trans. M. Gregor (Cambridge: Cambridge University Press, 1966); (1797) *Anthropology from a Pragmatic Point of View* [AP], trans.

of a kingdom of ends, as a systematic union of rational beings under laws they give to themselves, seems to warrant that characterization and that critique. But Kant's moral theory is not his political theory.[7] And a closer look at his specifically political writings, especially at his essay on "Perpetual Peace"—perhaps the single most influential discussion of cosmopolitanism by a major philosopher—shows that first and very widespread impression to be mistaken. Kant was indeed a cosmopolitan thinker; but he was also concerned to reconcile his universalistic aspirations with the diversity of national cultures, of which he had a wider knowledge than most of his contemporaries. Kant did, after all, lecture on anthropology and geography at Königsberg University for more than thirty years; he was, in fact, the first to do so. Thus it was quite in keeping with his interests when in 1785, one year after his "Idea for a Universal History with a Cosmopolitan Purpose" had appeared, he published a two-part review of Johann Gottfried von Herder's "Ideas on the Philosophy of History of Mankind," that early harbinger of nationalist thinking.[8]

In his *Anthropology from a Pragmatic Point of View*, Kant defined "people" and "nation" as follows: "By the word 'people' [*Volk*] we mean a multitude of men assembled within a tract of land insofar as they comprise a whole. That multitude, or part thereof, which recognizes itself as united into a civil whole by its common descent [*Abstammung*] is called a nation [*Nation*]" (AP, 174). This mix of subjective ("recognizes itself"), objective ("common descent"), and political ("united into a civil whole") elements is not unlike that involved in the contemporary conception of the nation-state just discussed. Certainly, in *The Metaphysics of Morals* Kant tells us that the term *Völkerrecht* actually refers to a kind of *Staatenrecht*—to the right of peoples organized as states, or to the right of nation-states.[9] But there are other elements,

---

M. Gregor (The Hague: Martinus Nijhoff, 1974). I will alter the translations, usually without making special note of the fact, when that is required for consistency or transparency.

7. Their distinctness is, of course, his rationale for separating the *Rechtslehre* from the *Tugendlehre* in MM.

8. "Reviews of Herder's *Ideas on the Philosophy of History of Mankind*," in Reiss, *Kant*, 201–20.

9. MM, 114. See also PP, 102, where the discussion of *Völkerrecht* in the Second Definitive Article is said to apply to *Völker als Staaten*.

having to do with race and ethnicity, that clearly mark his views as belonging to another time. Thus in the *Anthropology* he goes on to characterize peoples in terms of a mix of biological and cultural factors. The inborn [*angeboren*] character of a people is a function of its racial makeup; it is "in the blood."[10] Its acquired [*erworben*] character develops out of the former through culture, especially language and religion.[11] Human biological-cultural diversity thus belongs to the natural history of the human species, which in Kant's philosophy of history means that "nature wills" it, which for him is also to say that it is part of the providential ordering of things. More specifically, on Kant's reading of history, the separation, competition, and conflict among peoples are central ingredients in the dynamics of cultural progress. But they bring hostility and war as well, or rather as the other side of the very same developmental process. And it is here that Kant locates his reconciling project: As moral beings we must hope that "as culture grows and men gradually move towards greater agreement over their principles, [this diversity] will lead to mutual understanding and peace. And unlike that universal despotism which saps all men's energies and ends in the graveyard of freedom, this peace is created and guaranteed by an equilibrium of forces and a most vigorous rivalry"(PP, 114). To understand Kant's cosmopolitanism we have to understand this conception of unity in difference.

The main elements can be read off the lines just cited: belief in political-cultural progress and convergence; rejection of a centralized global state, and retention of national difference and even national "rivalry" amidst global unity. These same elements can already be found in the conception of cosmopolitan unity advanced in "Idea for a Universal His-

10. AP, 174, 184. For a critical account of Kant's unfortunate views on race, see Emmanuel Chukwudi Eze, "The Color of Reason: The Idea of 'Race' in Kant's Anthropology," in *Postcolonial African Philosophy*, ed. Chukwudi Eze (London: Basil Blackwell, 1997), 103–40. Eze makes a convincing case for the significance of race in Kant's thinking about human nature, culture, and history, as well as for the claim that Kant constructed one of the more elaborate theories of race and philosophical justifications of racial hierarchy of his time. His argument for the claim that Kant's racial theories are transcendentally grounded and thus are inseparable from his transcendental philosophy and his humanist project more generally is, in my view, less conclusive.

11. AP, 174 and PP, 113. The relative influence of biology, i.e., race, and of culture is different for different peoples; see AP, 176.

tory with a Cosmopolitan Purpose" in 1784, some ten years before "Perpetual Peace." They remained more or less constant thereafter, but their relative weights and precise configuration underwent subtle changes. In a word, while a federal union of distinct peoples under a global rule of law remained the rational ideal, its distance from the real was increasingly emphasized and the more practicable goal of a loose confederation of sovereign states took center stage.

For Kant, the ideal form of systematic union among rational beings with diverse, often conflicting interests is civil union under a rule of law that permits the greatest individual freedom compatible with a like freedom for all under general laws. Accordingly, "the highest task which nature has set mankind," as he puts it in "Idea for a Universal History," is that of "establishing a perfectly just civil constitution," which, by placing enforceable limits on the "continual antagonism" among men, makes it possible for the freedom of one to coexist with a like freedom for all others.[12] By the same logic, the coexistence of the freedom of one independent state with a like freedom for all others is possible only under a rule of public coercive law governing relations between them. Thus, practical reason requires not only that individuals abandon the lawless state of nature and enter into a law-governed commonwealth but also that individual nations, in their external relations, "abandon a lawless state of savagery and enter into a federation of peoples in which every state, even the smallest, could expect to derive its security and right . . . from a united power and the law-governed decisions of a united will" (UH, 47). At the global level, too, natural rivalries and antagonisms are to be constrained by a rule of law that derives from a united will and is backed by a united power. Kant is well aware of the ridicule to which earlier cosmopolitical schemes, notably those of the Abbé St. Pierre and Rousseau, were subjected, but he contends that constant war and its accompanying evils irresistibly push us in that direction. "They compel our species to discover a law of equilibrium to regulate the—in itself salutary—opposition of many states to one another, which springs from their freedom. Men are compelled to reinforce this law by introducing a system of united power, hence a cosmopolitan condition of general

12. UH, 45. Kant immediately concedes that "a perfect solution is impossible," for, as he famously puts it, "Nothing straight can be constructed from such crooked timber as that which man is made of." But we can and must continually strive to "approximate to this idea" (UH, 46).

political security [*einen weltbürgerlichen Zustand der öffentlichen Staats-sicherheit*]."[13] This cosmopolitan condition or "perfect civil union of mankind" is the "highest purpose of nature" and the most encompassing idea of political-practical reason, for the approximate realization of which we may hope and must strive.[14]

If we move now from the "Idea for a Universal History" of 1784 to Kant's 1793 essay "On the Common Saying: 'This May Be True in Theory, but It Does Not Apply in Practice,' " the central elements of his cosmopolitan conception remain essentially the same, though his upholding of the ideal in the face of a recalcitrant reality already evinces a note, if not of desperation, at least of reservation. He repeats the claim that war and its attendant distress will eventually force people to do for reasons of self-interest what practical reason anyway prescribes, that is, "to enter into a cosmopolitan constitution" [*weltbürgerliche Verfassung*] (TP, 90). But he immediately adds that "if such a condition of universal peace is in turn even more dangerous to freedom, for, as has occurred more than once with states that have grown too large, it may lead to a most fearful despotism, distress must force men into a condition that is not a cosmopolitan commonwealth under a single ruler, but a lawful condition of federation under a commonly agreed upon international law [*Völkerrecht*]" (TP, 90). The threat of despotism attaches, it seems, to the form of cosmopolitan unity marked by a single global state, under a single ruler, of whom all human beings are subjects. As we shall see, such a fusing or melting together [*zusammenschmelzen*] of distinct peoples is the very source of danger that Kant will later cite in "Perpetual Peace" against the idea of a universal monarchy. But whereas there it will provide grounds for espousing the very weak "substitute" of a voluntary league of nations, in this essay the alternative espoused is the still very strong idea of a federation of nation-states under a rule

13. UH, 49. The term rendered as "cosmopolitan," *weltbürgerlichen*, will later be used to designate a specific type of transnational law. In this 1784 essay, the institutional form of the "cosmopolitan condition" is characterized as a "federation of peoples" [*Völkerbund*], which clearly refers here to a federal union with a "united power." As we shall see, in the 1790s the corresponding institutional form is designated as a *Völkerstaat* or "state of nations," while *Völkerbund* is reserved for the more practicable arrangement of a voluntary and revocable "league of nations."

14. UH, 51. Note that the cosmopolitan—*weltbürgerliche*—condition is the civil—*bürgerliche*—union of the *Welt*, or of humanity.

of international law, which, he elaborates, is "backed by power" and "to which every state must submit" (TP, 92). Against the latter, Kant concedes, political realists may still object that independent states will never freely submit to such coercive laws [*Zwangsgesetzen*], and thus that the proposal for a "universal state of nations" [*allgemeinen Völker-staat*], however fine it sounds in theory, does not apply in practice. It is just another "childish," "academic" idea.[15] Nevertheless, it is here that Kant takes his stand: "For my own part, I put my trust in the theory of what the relationship between men and states ought to be according to the principle of right." In his view, individuals and states should act in such a way "that a universal state of nations may thereby be ushered in"; accordingly, "we should thus assume that it is possible (*in praxi*), that there can be such a thing" (TP, 92).

Over the next two years, perhaps partly in reaction to the course and consequences of the French Revolution, which he followed very closely,[16] Kant shifted his emphasis in the direction of the realities of practice, endorsing in "Perpetual Peace" the more "practicable" or "achievable" [*ausführbar*] goal of a voluntary federation or league of sovereign nation-states [*Völkerbund*] under an international law [*Völkerrecht*] that was *not* public coercive law backed by the united power of a universal state of nations, though he still maintained that the latter was what was called for by reason:

> There is only one rational way in which states coexisting with other states can emerge from the lawless condition of pure warfare. Just like individuals, they must renounce their savage and lawless freedom, adapt themselves to public coercive laws, and thus form a state of nations (*civitas gentium*) which would necessarily continue to grow until it embraced all the peoples of the earth. But since this is not the will of nations, according to their conception of international law (so that they reject *in hypothesi* what is true *in thesi*), the positive idea of

15. TP, 92. Kant's use of the term *Zwangsgesetzen* shows that the federation he has in mind is not the loose, voluntary federation he later proposes in "Perpetual Peace." The same thing is indicated by his use of *Völkerstaat* to characterize it: The federation of peoples envisaged here is a state of nations under international laws backed by the state.

16. The Treaty of Basel was concluded between France and Prussia early in 1795; PP appeared later that year.

a world republic cannot be realized. If all is not to be lost, this can at best find a negative substitute in the shape of an enduring and gradually expanding federation to prevent war. The latter may check the current of man's inclination to defy the law and antagonize his fellows, although there will always be the risk of it bursting forth anew. (PP, 105)

Thus, the "positive idea" of establishing a universal and lasting peace is the idea of a "world republic," the member states of which are themselves republics: a world republic of national republics. The "public coercive" law of this world republic would regulate external relations among states, among individuals who are citizens of different states, and among individuals and states of which they are not citizens.[17] This type of law is variously referred to by Kant as *Völkerstaatsrecht,* the right of a state of nations, and *Weltbürgerrecht,* the right of world citizens.[18] Whatever its precise form, for Kant only this type of global public law completes our emergence from the state of nature in which rights and possessions are merely "provisional" rather than "peremptory" or "conclusive" [*peremtorisch*]. Prior to its establishment, "any rights of nations and any external possessions states acquire or retain by war are merely provisional. Only in a universal union of states, analogous to that by which a people become a state, can rights come to hold conclusively and a true condition of peace come about."[19] Nevertheless, as indicated in a passage cited here, Kant concedes that in the given circumstances global public coercive law is unachievable. Not only are individual states unwilling to give up their unlimited sovereignty, but also there are intrinsic difficulties in administering global justice owing to the vastness of the earth's surface and the variety of its inhabitants.

At this point in Kant's argument, many commentators head in the

17. Compare MM, 114.

18. Thus in PP (98–99) he characterizes a global civil constitution as one "based on *Weltbürgerrecht,* insofar as individuals and states, coexisting in an external relationship of mutual influences, may be regarded as citizens of a universal state of humankind (*ius cosmopoliticum*)." And in MM, 114, he refers to this type of law as "*Völkerstaatsrecht* or *Weltbürgerrecht*"—note the "or."

19. MM, 119. See the discussion of provisional and conclusive acquisition in relation to the "civil condition" at MM, 51–53, which ends with the thought that until this condition "extends to the entire human race," acquisition will remain provisional.

wrong direction by taking his admonitions against a world state in the form of a universal monarchy for a rejection of world government in any form.[20] Kant's language is occasionally less clear on this than it could be.[21] But there is overwhelming textual evidence for distinguishing his conception of a "world republic," which he consistently upholds as the most encompassing idea of political-practical reason, from the conception of a "universal monarchy" or any other form of world state that might result from one power subjugating all the others. It is the latter which he characterizes as a "soulless despotism" that would inevitably give rise to widespread resistance and ultimately lapse into anarchy (PP, 113). For our purposes here, it is interesting to note that one basic complaint he voices against it is the *Zusammenschmelzung* of diverse peoples.[22] Any viable conception of global unity has to be compatible with national diversity, for "nature wills" this diversity and "uses two means to separate peoples and prevent their intermingling [*Vermischung*], the variety of languages and of religions" (PP, 113). At the same time, however, nature (or providence) also wills that the

20. Sharon Byrd has a good discussion of this point in "The State as a 'Moral Person,'" in *Proceedings of the Eighth International Kant Congress*, vol. 1, part 1, sections 1–2, ed. H. Robinson (Milwaukee, Wisc.: Marquette University Press, 1995), 171–89. She lists some of those who have gotten it wrong in n. 57 (186). To that list can be added the names of John Rawls, "The Law of Peoples," in *On Human Rights*, ed. S. Shute and S. Hurley (New York: Basic Books, 1993), 41–82, at 54, and Jürgen Habermas, "Kant's Idea of Perpetual Peace, with the Benefit of Two Hundred Years' Hindsight," in *Perpetual Peace: Essays on Kant's Cosmopolitan Ideal*, ed. J. Bohman and M. Lutz-Bachmann (Cambridge, Mass.: MIT Press, 1997), 113–54, at 119 and 128.
21. See especially the oft-cited passage in PP (102,) which is not only ambiguous in the original German but too freely translated by H. B. Nisbet in the Reiss edition of Kant's *Political Writings*. Kant did not write that the federation which he espouses "would not be" the same thing as an international state, but that it "need not be" such. Nor did he write "the idea of a *Völkerstaat* is contradictory." The German phrase *darin aber wäre ein Widerspruch* could refer to the very idea of a civil condition among independent nation-states, which he is discussing in this paragraph. In any case, this is one of the very few passages in which there is any ambiguity on the point. As I shall now argue, his principled opposition is to a universal monarchy that ignores the ethnocultural differences among peoples and not to a state of nations that builds them into its institutional arrangements.
22. This is rendered by Nisbet as "welded together" and "amalgamation" at PP, 102, and PP, 113, respectively.

war and violence resulting from this separation be overcome by global peace. For one thing, cultural development leads to a growing agreement on basic principles and an expansion of mutual understanding (PP, 114). For another, nature unites peoples by means of their mutual self-interest, especially in the economic sphere. "For the spirit of commerce [*Handelsgeist*] sooner or later takes hold of every people and it cannot exist side by side with war. Of all the powers (or means) at the disposal of the state, the power of money is probably the most reliable; so states find themselves compelled to promote the noble cause of peace, though not from motives of morality" (PP, 114).

Kant concedes that the idea of global civil unity amidst national cultural diversity is unachievable or unworkable [*unausführbar*] in the circumstances of the time; it can at most be approximated or approached [*annähern*]. And he judges the degree of approximation possible under the given conditions to be the rather limited one of a voluntary, revocable league or federation of nations [*Völkerbund*] with the sole purpose of preserving the peace.[23] The correspondingly weak conception of international law or the law of peoples [*Völkerrecht*] he joins to it remained in central respects the predominant one well into the twentieth century, a century of global slaughter without equal. Conceding unlimited sovereignty to independent states and presenting no effective barrier to their use of arms in pursuing what they take to be their vital interests, that arrangement has proved incapable of checking the resort to violence and to the threat of violence in international affairs, incapable, that is, of fulfilling the purpose Kant intended for it. It is, in short, no longer—if it ever was—a practically adequate approximation to the idea of legal pacifism.

By contrast, there are features even of Kant's weaker version of a peaceful world order that strike us still today as rather strong requirements, particularly the First Definitive Article, which requires that "the civil constitution of every state shall be republican" (PP, 99). On his understanding of the term, a "republican" constitution is founded on the freedom of members as human beings, their equality as subjects, and their independence as citizens.[24] It encompasses the rule of law, repre-

23. See the Second Definitive Article, PP, 102.
24. See, for instance, TP, 74–79.

sentative government, and the separation of powers. It expressly does not include either substantive equality[25] or universal suffrage.[26]

Thus, Kant's "practicable" scheme for global peace combines international law [*Völkerrecht: ius gentium*] that is based on a voluntary league of nations with state law [*Staats(bürger)recht: ius civitatis*] that is republican without being democratic or egalitarian. There is also a third principal component, namely, cosmopolitan law [*Weltbürgerrecht: ius cosmopoliticum*], which, in the context of this more practicable scheme, is reduced to "the conditions of universal hospitality"—that is, "the right of a stranger not to be treated with hostility when he arrives on someone else's territory."[27] This last, Kant maintains, is the minimum required to enable inhabitants of one society to attempt to enter into relations with those of another and thus to foster the sorts of mutual relations among peoples that may "bring the human race nearer and nearer to a cosmopolitan constitution," that is, to a "public human right in general."[28] This conception of cosmopolitan law is said in *The Metaphysics of Morals* to be rooted in the finitude of the earth that is our common home:

> Nature has enclosed all [nations] together within determinate limits by the spherical shape of the place they live in. . . . They stand in a community of possible physical interaction (*commercium*), that is, in a thoroughgoing relation of each to all the others of offering to engage in interaction [*Verkehr*] with any other, and each has right to make this attempt . . . [which,] since it concerns the possible union of all nations with a view to certain universal laws for their

25. See, for instance, TP, 75: "This uniform equality of human beings as subjects of a state is however perfectly consistent with the utmost inequality of the mass in the degree of its possessions," where "possessions" is meant in the broadest sense.

26. See, for instance, TP, 77: "In the question of actual legislation, all who are free and equal under existing public laws may be considered equal, but not as regards the right to make these laws," which is, roughly speaking, reserved to male property owners. Acccordingly, at PP, 100, as elsewhere, he warns against confusing the republican constitution with the democratic one.

27. PP, 105, Third Definitive Article. For the three types of law involved, see the note at PP, 98.

28. PP, 106. Pauline Kleingeld, "Kant's Cosmopolitan Law: World Citizenship for a Global Order," *Kantian Review* 2 (1998): 72–90.

possible interaction, can be called cosmopolitan right (*ius cosmopoliticum*).[29]

Some of the most serious violations of the conditions of hospitality in his time, Kant repeatedly inveighs, are the conquest and colonization that mark the relations of "the civilized states of our continent" to the rest of the world.[30] Thus, while himself proposing a racial theory of ethnic difference and cultural hierarchy, Kant vigorously condemns the colonizing efforts that often appeal to such theories for justification!

The view of global peace advanced two years later in Kant's most systematic work of *Rechtslehre,* Part I of *The Metaphysics of Morals,* is substantially the same as that elaborated in "Perpetual Peace." Thus his tripartite division of public right in section 43 mirrors that noted in the earlier essay—*Staatsrecht, Völkerrecht, Weltbürgerrecht*—only this last is now characterized as "ineluctably" resulting from the first two, being in essence a kind of *Völkerstaatsrecht.*[31] And the internal relation among them is characterized in the strongest terms: "So if the principle of outer freedom limited by law is lacking in any one of these three possible forms of rightful condition, the framework of all the others is unavoidably undermined and must finally collapse" (MM, 89). In a word, there is no final exit from the condition of nature to the condition of right until a state of nations under the rule of cosmopolitan law is established. This last, then, is "the entire final end of the doctrine of right within the limits of reason alone" (MM, 123). Without it, the law of peoples remains merely provisional (MM, 119). But here, too, Kant concedes the impracticability under present conditions of instituting a *Völkerstaatsrecht* based on a world republic and proposes to substitute a *Völkerrecht* based on a league of nations, once again restricting *Weltbürgerrecht* to the right of hospitality: "A federation of nations in accordance with the

29. MM, 121. The Gregor translation renders *Verkehr* as "commerce," adding a note on its broad range of meanings from social interaction to economic exchange. In this passage, it is clear that Kant intends the broadest sense of *commercium;* thus to foreclose misleading identifications with our previous use of "commerce" to render *Handel,* I have here rendered *Verkehr* as "interaction."

30. PP, 106. See also MM, 53 and MM, 121.

31. MM, 89. The Gregor translation doesn't capture the idea of the third resulting from the combination of the first and second which is conveyed by the German *beides zusammen.*

idea of an original social contract is necessary, not in order to meddle in one another's internal disagreements, but to protect against attacks from without. This alliance must, however, involve no sovereign authority (as in a civil constitution), but only an association (federation); it must be an alliance that can be renounced at any time." [32] Since a "universal union of states" in which alone "right [can] come to hold conclusively and a true condition of peace come about" is an "unachievable idea," the basic principles of right require only that we strive to fashion alliances among states which more and more closely approximate it. [33] In the circumstances of late-eighteenth-century Europe, the closest practicable approximation is, in Kant's view, the league of nations he described. However, he hastens to add, this concession does not absolve moral-political agents from persistently "working toward the kind of constitution that seems to us most conducive to perpetual peace, say, a republicanism of all states together and separately. . . . Even if the complete realization of this objective always remains a pious wish, still we are certainly not deceiving ourselves in adopting the maxim of working incessantly towards it" (MM, 123).

If Kantian cosmopolitanism is to be of service to the project of conceptual reconciliation proposed here, it will have to be altered in important respects. To mention only the most obvious:

1. Kant's quasi-naturalistic account of "peoples" as the prepolitical bases of political communities has to be revised in line with our heightened awareness of the historically contingent, politically motivated, and socioculturally constructed character of representations of race, ethnicity, and nationality. [34]

32. Jules Vuillemin surmises that Kant was influenced by contemporary discussions of federalism in the United States and France: "On Perpetual Peace, and On Hope as a Duty," in Robinson, *Proceedings,* 19–32, at 22 and 31, n. 24.

33. MM, 119. Kant variously designates such arrangements as congresses, leagues, federations, associations, and coalitions, among other things. But the essential point remains the same: The more feasible kind of arrangement is "a coalition of different states that can be dissolved at any time, and not a union like that of the American states which is based on a constitution and therefore cannot be dissolved" (MM, 120). The latter, stronger kind of federal union among nations would call for just the sort of constitutional *Völkerstaat* that he has conceded to be unachievable.

34. Kant seems to have had some doubts of his own about the naturalness of nation-

2. Correspondingly, Kant's understanding of nations as, at least to a considerable degree, racially, ethnically, and culturally homogeneous has to be revised to allow for the internal heterogeneity of political communities. This means dropping his claim that through racial and cultural differences "nature" prevents the "intermingling" [*Vermischung*] of peoples[35] and making conceptual room in his constitutional republicanism for the pluralism that has become a hallmark of democratic politics.

3. Kant's eighteenth-century understanding of republican government has to be revised to incorporate the basic democratic and social reforms achieved through political struggle in the nineteenth and twentieth centuries.

4. The Enlightenment universalism underlying Kant's construction of the cosmopolitan ideal has to be replaced by a multicultural universalism more sensitive to the dialectic of the general and the particular.

The unprecedented slaughter of the twentieth century has made a mockery even of Kant's wavering faith in the capacity of traditional international law and interstate treaties to preserve global peace. The principal theoretical alternative to these failed measures remains some form of legal pacificism — that is, of the global rule of law. Kant's own account of *Völkerstaatsrecht* and *Weltbürgerrecht* is far too sketchy to serve as anything more than a starting point for developing that alternative. In this respect, as in the others mentioned, Habermas's "discourse theory of law and democracy," which he presents as a reworking of Kant's basic approach "with the benefit of two hundred years' hindsight," can take us a few steps further in the task of conceptual reconciliation.

---

hood — nurtured, perhaps, by observing the formation of the first modern nation-state. Thus, writing of the state, he notes: "Because the union of the members is (presumed to be) [*anmasslich*] one they inherited, a state is also called a nation [*Stammvolk*] (*gens*)" (MM, 89). That this parenthetical reservation was no mere slip of the pen is suggested by a remark later in the same work: "As natives of a country, those who constitute a nation [*Volk*] can be represented analogously to descendents of the same ancestors (*congeniti*) even though they are not" (MM, 114).

35. PP, 113. See also AP, 182: "This much we can judge with probability: that a mixture of races (by extensive conquests), which gradually extinguishes their characters, is not beneficial to the human race."

Critics typically also situate Habermas's approach to law and politics at one extreme of the universalism-particularism spectrum: It is taken to be the very archetype of abstract, difference-leveling universalism. This assessment too is usually arrived at in one short stroke, by extrapolating from his moral universalism. But that is no less an oversimplification than was the corresponding extrapolation from Kant's moral ideal of a kingdom of ends, which, as we saw, ignored the principled differentiation between law and morality he had elaborated in *The Metaphysics of Morals*. For the past decade at least, Habermas has been similarly concerned to spell out the differences between these two domains of "practical reason." [36] From his discourse-theoretical perspective, one of the major differences that emerges is the variety of types of reasons relevant to the legitimation of positive law. Moral arguments figure in legal and political discourse, along with a balancing of interests and a weighing of pragmatic and of what he calls "ethical political" considerations as well. It is this last type of consideration that is most interesting for our purposes, as Habermas uses the term "ethical" here in somewhat the way Hegel used *sittlich* and *Sittlichkeit* to represent cultures and forms of life from a normative and evaluative perspective. Thus Habermas's discussion of "ethical-political" justifications in law and politics is, roughly speaking, a discussion of the ways in which the values, goods, and identities embedded in different cultural contexts figure into legal and political discourse. Here are two characteristic passages:

> In contrast to morality, law does not regulate interaction contexts in general but serves as a medium for the self-organization of legal communities that maintain themselves in their social environments under particular historical conditions. As a result . . . laws also give expression to the particular wills of members of a particular community. (FN, 151)

36. These efforts culminated in *Between Facts and Norms: Contributions to a Discourse Theory of Law and Democracy*, trans. W. Rehg (Cambridge, Mass.: MIT Press, 1996); cited in the text as FN. See also his 1986 Tanner Lecture, "Law and Morality," in *The Tanner Lectures on Human Values, VIII* (Salt Lake City: University of Utah Press, 1988), 217–79, and *Die Einbeziehung des Anderen*, available in English translation by C. Cronin and P. De Greiff as *The Inclusion of the Other* (Cambridge, Mass.: MIT Press, 1998).

In justifying legal norms we must use the entire breadth of practical reason. However, these further [i.e., other than moral] reasons have a relative validity, one that depends on the context. . . . The corresponding reasons count as valid relative to the historical, culturally molded identity of the legal community, and hence relative to the value orientations, goals, and interest positions of its members. . . . The facticity of the existing context cannot be eliminated. (FN, 156)

It is not only statutory law that is pervaded with particularity in these respects: constitutional undertakings to spell out the basic principles of government and the basic rights of citizens ineluctably also express the particular cultural backgrounds and historical circumstances of founding generations. Though Habermas expressly regards "the system of basic rights" as a normative (or "regulative") idea that should guide every legitimate constitution-framing process (FN, chap. 3), he is equally clear that any actually existing system of rights is, and can only be, a situated interpretation of that idea: "The system of rights is not given to the framers of a constitution in advance as a natural law. These rights first enter into consciousness in a particular constitutional interpretation. . . . No one can credit herself with access to the system of rights in the singular, independent of the interpretations she already has historically available. 'The' system of rights does not exist in transcendental purity"(FN, 128–29). Surveying the history of democratic constitutional law over the past two centuries, the theorist can at most attempt a critical, systematic reconstruction of the basic intuitions underlying it. Of course, to accommodate even the existing range of legitimate variation, any such reconstruction will of necessity be highly abstract, as is indeed the case with Habermas's own.

Getting clear about the content of basic constitutional norms is only the beginning of the story, for "every constitution is a living project that can endure only as an ongoing interpretation continually carried forth at all levels of the production of law" (FN, 129). Thus, historically and culturally situated interpretation should not be seen as an unfortunate but unavoidable fall from transcendental grace but as the very medium for developing "constitutional projects," which are by their very nature always unfinished and ongoing: "The constitutional state does not represent a finished structure but a delicate and sensitive — above all fallible and revisable — enterprise, whose purpose is to realize the system of rights anew in changing circumstances, that is, to interpret the system of rights better, to institutionalize it more appropriately, and to draw out its contents more radically" (FN, 384).

Even these few sketchy remarks on Habermas's legal and political theory should make clear that for him the rule of law in the democratic constitutional state is not a fixed essence but an idea that has to be actualized in and through being variously interpreted and embodied in historically and culturally distinct constitutional projects. This suggests that there should be space in his conception of cosmopolitical justice for distinct political cultures, and indeed there is. His version of civic patriotism, which he calls "constitutional patriotism," is construed broadly as allegiance to a particular constitutional tradition—that is, to a particular, ongoing, historical project of creating and renewing an association of free and equal citizens under the rule of laws they make for themselves. Each democratically constituted nation of citizens will understand and carry out that project from perspectives opened by its own traditions and circumstances. If that self-understanding is itself to include space for a pluralism of worldviews and forms of life, as Habermas insists it must, then constitutional patriotism may not be wedded to monocultural or hegemonic-cultural interpretations of basic rights and principles to the exclusion, repression, or marginalization of minority-cultural perspectives.[37] In a move reminiscent of Rawls's introduction of the idea of an "overlapping consensus" on basic political values amidst a persistent pluralism of "comprehensive doctrines" about the meaning and value of human life, Habermas, employing sociological terminology, proposes "decoupling" political integration from the various forms of subgroup and subcultural integration among the population of a democratic constitutional state: "In multicultural societies . . . coexistence with equal rights for these forms of life requires the mutual recognition of the different cultural memberships; all persons must also be recognized as members of ethical communities integrated around different conceptions of the good. Hence the ethical integration of groups and subcultures with their own collective identities must be decoupled

37. See especially the papers collected in *The Inclusion of the Other.* I shall be citing an earlier publication of one of these papers, J. Habermas, "Struggles for Recognition in the Democratic Constitutional State," trans. S. Weber Nicholsen, in *Multiculturalism,* ed. Amy Gutmann (Princeton, N.J.: Princeton University Press, 1994), 107–48; cited in the text as SR.

from the abstract political integration that includes all citizens equally"
(SR, 133).

Rawls's proposal has given rise to vociferous debate, as have other
proposals for conceptualizing legal-political neutrality in our increasingly multicultural societies. Habermas can hardly hope to avoid such
controversies. If his approach is to have a chance of surviving them, he
will, to start with, have to understand "decoupling" in process terms —
as an ongoing accomplishment of something that is never fully realized.
As Charles Taylor, Will Kymlicka, and others have convincingly argued,
there can be no culturally neutral system of law and politics, no privatization of culture analogous to the privatization of religion, and thus
no strict separation of culture and state. Official languages, school cur-
ricula, national holidays, and the like are only the most obvious expressions of a public culture that is never perfectly neutral with respect to
the diverse cultural backgrounds of members. And as we saw, Habermas
himself maintains that political goals, policies, and programs are inevitably permeated by cultural values and goods, and that putting them
into effect just as inevitably has cultural consequences. This suggests
that "decoupling" may be the wrong notion for what we want here. If we
understand the core of a constitutional tradition dynamically and dialogically — as an ongoing, legally institutionalized conversation about
basic rights and principles, procedures and practices, values and institutions — then we can allow for a conflict of interpretations concerning
them and for a multiplicity of situated perspectives upon them. Insofar
as these interpretations purport to be of the same constitutional tradition, and insofar as their proponents are and want to remain members of
the same political community, the ongoing accomplishment of a working consensus on fundamental legal and political norms seems to be a
basic requirement of public discourse in official and unofficial public
spheres. A central element of such a working consensus would be sufficiently widespread agreement about the institutions and procedures
through which persistent reasonable disagreements may be legitimately
settled, at least for the time being.

This is, in fact, close to the conception that Habermas actually defends:

> The political integration of citizens ensures loyalty to the common
> political culture. The latter is rooted in an interpretation of consti-

tutional principles from the perspective of the nation's historical experience. To this extent, that interpretation cannot be ethically neutral. Perhaps one would do better to speak of a common horizon of interpretation within which current issues give rise to public debates about the citizens' self-understanding. . . . But the debates are always about the best interpretation of the same constitutional rights and principles, which form the fixed point of reference for any constitutional patriotism. (SR, 134)

Even this common horizon of interpretation is in flux, however, as it too reflects participants' situated understandings, which are themselves continually shifting. Habermas remarks on this in connection with immigration. In his view, while it is not legitimate for a democratic constitutional state to require "ethical-cultural integration" of immigrants (that is, assimilation to the dominant culture in the broad sense), it is, he maintains, legitimate to require political integration—that is, assent to the principles of the constitution within the scope of interpretation set by the political culture of the country (SR, 138). But he immediately adds that the latter is itself subject to contestation and alteration from the new perspectives brought to the political public sphere through immigration:

The legitimately asserted identity of the political community will by no means be preserved from alteration in the long run in the wake of waves of immigration. Because immigrants may not be compelled to surrender their own traditions, as other forms of life become established the horizons within which citizens henceforth interpret their common constitutional principles may also expand. . . . A change in the composition of the active citizenry changes the context to which the ethical-political self-understanding of the nation as a whole refers. (SR, 139–40)

Despite this recognition of the "ethical permeation" of law and politics at every level, Habermas continues to speak of the "neutrality" of the law vis-à-vis internal ethical differentiations. Like "decoupling," "neutrality" is, in my view, not the best choice of terminology for what is at issue, which is rather impartiality or fairness in the sense of equality of respect, treatment, and opportunity to participate in the political process. What Habermas is concerned to preclude, above all, is that a majority culture "usurp state prerogatives at the expense of the equal rights of other cultural forms of life" (SR, 134–35). And that case would, I think, better be made by extending to cultural membership the types of arguments historically advanced to address systematic inequalities of social position.

In any case, it is evident that Habermas's conception of a multiplicity of political-cultural realizations of the "same" system of rights is already sketched from a cosmopolitan point of view akin to Kant's. For Kant, the cosmopolitan civil condition, as a regulative idea, was characterized by a multiplicity of republics under a rule of law regulating relations among them and guaranteeing the rights of individuals as world citizens. Habermas's version of cosmopolitanism may be read as updating this idea, first, to take account of the internal relation between the rule of law and democracy—so that Kant's republics become democratic constitutional states—and, second, as we saw, to make room for an irreducible plurality of forms of life. But he also wants, third, to build into his version a strong egalitarian component—so that the democratic constitutional project is understood as that of realizing an association of free and *equal* citizens under the rule of laws they can all reasonably consent to. There is, as we know, an unavoidable dialectic of de jure and de facto, formal and substantive equality that has played itself through successive waves of critical social and political theory. Class, gender, race, ethnicity, sexuality, and the like mark respects in which existing forms of equality under law have been revealed to sanction gross inequalities in life circumstances and positions of power.

Habermas's contribution to this ongoing discussion turns on his account of the internal relation between "private and public autonomy," or, to put it another way, on his attempt to connect internally the basic values of liberal individualism and civic republicanism. Against a purely liberal-individualist conception of equal rights, he argues that "in the final analysis, private legal persons cannot attain the enjoyment of equal individual liberties unless they themselves, by jointly exercising their autonomy as citizens, arrive at a clear understanding about what interests and criteria are justified, and in what respects equals will be treated equally and unequals unequally in any particular case" (SR, 113). Understood in this way, the ongoing project of realizing a system of equal rights must be sensitive to any systematic causes of substantive inequality. And that, according to Habermas, requires a democratic politics, for there is no other nonpaternalistic way of deciding what the prerequisites are for the equal opportunity actually to exercise legally granted rights. In other words, the basic liberal ideas of equal respect, equal consideration, equal treatment, and the like cannot be specified in the abstract, once and for all, but only concretely, in the ongoing discourses of democratic public life:

> It must therefore be decided from case to case whether and in which respects factual (or material) equality is required for the legal equality of citizens who are both privately and publicly autonomous. The proceduralist paradigm gives normative emphasis precisely to the double reference that the relation between legal and factual equality has to private and public autonomy. And it privileges all the arenas where disputes over the essentially contestable criteria of equal treatment must be discursively carried out. (FN, 415)

In shifting from the national to the cosmopolitan perspective, it is impossible to overlook the relative paucity of transnational arenas of this type. Insisting, as Habermas does, on the internal connection between individual rights and democratic politics implies that there could be no adequate institutionalization of human rights on a global scale without a corresponding institutionalization of transnational forms of democratic participation and accountability. Inasmuch as individual liberties, democratic procedures, and redistributive mechanisms are interdependent aspects of cosmopolitical justice, as he understands it, no one can be adequately realized without the others. This, of course, renders his cosmopolitan ideal more ambitious in theory and more difficult in practice than Kant's. And it makes all the more palpable the existing gap between a political integration that is largely restricted to the national level and an economic integration that is increasingly global. If that gap is not closed, there is a danger that the structure of mass-democratic, welfare-state integration that has predominated at the national level since World War II will itself disintegrate; for the constellation of individual freedom, democratic government, and social security that generally sustains it is being increasingly undermined by processes and problems to which the individual nation-state can no longer adequately respond. In Habermas's phrase, "Under the conditions of a globalized economy, 'Keynesianism in one country' no longer functions."[38]

In addition to the daunting practical problems that attend the establishment of a basic structure of cosmopolitical justice as Habermas conceives it, there are a number of important theoretical issues his approach raises, of which I shall mention only the following.

1. Habermas's conception of civil union amidst cultural diversity takes "constitutional patriotism" to be the political-cultural glue holding multicultural polities together. This obviously raises feasibility questions as to whether allegiance to legal-political institutions, practices, ideas, values, traditions, and the like can function as the core of social integration in modern societies, whether it can provide sufficient "glue" to keep together the socially differentiated, culturally heterogeneous, and ideologically fragmented populations that characterize them. But it also raises conceptual questions concerning the very idea of "decoupling" a shared civic culture from culture(s) more broadly. I have already touched on some of them above and will here add only the following consideration. Habermas's discussion of political-cultural neutrality (or impartiality) vis-à-vis a multiplicity of subcultures tends to focus on the contrast of civic with ethnic culture, for one of his chief aims is to disentangle state from nation. Other aspects of the politics-culture nexus tend to be neglected, at least in the context of this discussion. In *The Structural Transformation of the Public Sphere* and *The Theory of Communicative Action*, however, some of these other aspects figured prominently.[39] There, the interpenetration of public-political and public-cultural spheres was an important theme: The analytic distinctions between them did not occlude their real interconnections. In particular, the powerful connections of political culture to popular culture, which increasingly means mass-mediated culture, was identified as a key issue for contemporary democratic theory and practice. Supposing that

---

38. J. Habermas, "Learning by Disaster? A Diagnostic Look Back on the Short 20th Century," in *Constellations*, vol. 5, no. 3 (September 1988): 307–320.

39. J. Habermas, *The Structural Transformation of the Public Sphere*, trans. T. Burger with the assistance of F. Lawrence (Cambridge, Mass.: MIT Press, 1989); Habermas, *The Theory of Communicative Action*, vols. 1 and 2, trans. T. McCarthy (Boston, Mass.: Beacon Press, 1984, 1987).

mass-mediated popular culture is a permanent feature of modern society, what implications does that have for shaping and sustaining a sense of national belonging? How is this likely to be affected by the transnationalization of the culture industry? To what extent and in what ways is political culture transmitted and political integration achieved in and through mass-mediated popular culture? And if the answers are "considerably" and "many," what are the consequences for Habermas's distinction between assimilating to a particular political culture and assimilating to a hegemonic national culture?

2. Similar questions can be posed at the global level, as can questions peculiar to it. Habermas's cosmopolitan scheme turns on the idea of realizing the "same" system of rights in a diversity of political-cultural settings, and that immediately raises issues concerning the transcultural notion of rights invoked here, the nature of their transcultural justification, the sense in which the "same" rights can be said to animate the rather different political-cultural traditions that embody them, and so on. In brief, how could a transnational legal-political consensus regarding the basic structure of cosmopolitical justice be achieved across the wide range of political-cultural diversity?

3. To deal with this issue, Rawls introduces the idea of an "overlapping consensus" on a law of peoples among political societies marked by widely different political cultures — liberal and nonliberal, democratic and nondemocratic, egalitarian and hierarchical, secular and religious.[40] Habermas's cosmopolitan ideal does not allow for the same broad scope of variation among political cultures. He defends a more "comprehensive" version of a rights-based theory of justice. This has the advantage of reducing the need for citizens to develop the starkly split political/nonpolitical mentalities that Rawls's scheme requires. But it makes cosmopolitan justice turn on institutionalizing at a global level a version of the same system of rights that is variously institutionalized in national constitutional tradi-

40. Rawls, "Law of Peoples." See my discussion of his approach in T. McCarthy, "On the Idea of a Reasonable Law of Peoples," in *Perpetual Peace: Essays on Kant's Cosmopolitan Ideal,* ed. J. Bohman and M. Lutz-Bachman (Cambridge, Mass.: MIT Press, 1997), 201–17.

tions. Thus it requires a far greater degree of convergence among political cultures than does Rawls's scheme: For cosmopolitan constitutionalism to be fully realized, subglobal political systems would themselves have to become rights-based. Nationally, as well as sub-, supra-, and transnationally, what Kant called "civil union" would comprise a diversity of historically and culturally situated projects of realizing the same system of basic human rights. Kant's world republic of national republics is thus reenvisioned as a global constitutional union of constitutional democracies. What warrants this stress on human rights in connection with cosmopolitanism?

4. Habermas, like Kant, is committed to some form of at least legal- and political-cultural convergence, such that "as culture grows and men generally move toward greater agreement over their principles, they lead to mutual understanding and peace."[41] In *Communication and the Evolution of Society* and *The Theory of Communicative Action* Habermas propounds the broader account of cultural and societal development as "rationalization" that underlies this political-theoretical commitment.[42] But in the present context, he argues simply that the conditions of modernity leave individual states with no other practicable option but to modernize their relations both internally and externally. This is, of course, a disputable claim, even if we restrict its ambit to the legal-political domain. Couldn't we conceive of "alternative modernities"? Charles Taylor thinks so; and in the final section of this essay I want to air some of the issues raised here by examining his instructive differences with Habermas on that question.

41. PP, 114. In fact, like Kant, Habermas sees cultural convergence as extending beyond the legal and political spheres to include science and technology, as well as aspects of morality and even of art. The resulting disagreement with Rawls on the "reasonability" of "comprehensive doctrines" generally, and on the relation of law to morality particularly, comes through clearly in Habermas's discussion of human rights in "Kant's Idea of Perpetual Peace," 134–40, where he argues that though they are properly legal and not moral rights, part of their distinctness derives from the fact that the principal arguments for them are themselves moral in nature. See also Habermas's exchange with Rawls in the *Journal of Philosophy* 92 (1995): 109–80.

42. J. Habermas, *Communication and the Evolution of Society*, trans. T. McCarthy (Boston, Mass.: Beacon Press, 1979).

As Habermas is well aware, "the general validity, content, and ranking of human rights are as contested as ever. Indeed, the human rights discourse that has been argued in normative terms is plagued by a fundamental doubt about whether the form of legitimation that has arisen in the West can also hold up as plausible within the frameworks of other cultures."[43] The liberation struggles of the past 150 years, particularly of the last few decades, have again and again revealed the ideological functions that established understandings of human rights have served. That much is clear. But is the meaning of human rights exhausted by such ideological functions? Or is there a normative surplus of meaning that can be rescued by critically rethinking them and offering alternative accounts of their practical implications in given circumstances? One argument that speaks for the latter option is that many of the most telling critiques of established rights regimes have themselves been mounted precisely as critical rights discourses of various sorts. In the contemporary world, social, political, and cultural criticism would be severely incapacitated if such discourses were unavailable.

In any case, rethinking human rights is the route Habermas chooses, not only for normative but also for historical and sociological reasons:

> My working hypothesis is that [human rights] standards stem less from the particular cultural background of Western civilization than from the attempt to answer specific challenges posed by a social modernity that has in the meantime covered the globe. Whether we evaluate this modern starting point one way or another, it confronts us today with a fact that leaves us no choice and thus neither requires, nor is capable of, a retrospective justification. The contest over the adequate interpretation of human rights has to do not with the desirability of the "modern condition" but with an interpretation of human rights that does justice to the modern world from the viewpoints of other cultures as well as our own. (HR, 13)

To the obvious question of whether there could be such an interpretation, one can, I think, presently respond only that that remains to be seen. Writing expressly as "a Western participant in a cross-cultural dis-

43. J. Habermas, "Remarks on Legitimation through Human Rights," in *The Modern Schoolman* 75 (1998): 89–100.

cussion of human rights," Habermas has tried to rethink some of the aspects of the Western rights tradition that have proved most objectionable to non-Western participants. In that spirit, he has drawn upon his theory of communicative action to denaturalize and deindividualize the notion of rights and to disentangle it from the matrix of possessive individualism in which it has been ensnarled since Locke.[44] Further, through accentuating elements of the republican tradition of democratic thought, he has sought to restore the balance between individual and community and to resist the liberal displacement of the search for the common good by the aggregation of individual interests.

Together with his attention to the inequities produced by uncontrolled market processes and his concern to accommodate cultural diversity, these changes certainly present a version of human rights less starkly at odds with traditionally "communitarian" styles of thought. But of course the differences that remain are considerable. Though human rights are viewed as socially constituted, they are still borne by individual legal persons; and though rights-bearing subjects are seen as socioculturally embedded, personal and political autonomy retain their normative status; moreover, the "decoupling" of political integration from overarching views of the meaning and value of human life remains a basic requirement. For many, such differences would be sufficient to make a conception of human rights incorporating them unacceptable.

This consideration serves as the starting point of Charles Taylor's recent reflections on the possibility of "a world consensus on human rights."[45] His line of reasoning is particularly interesting in our present context, because he agrees with Habermas about having to start from the fact of global modernity and about the need this creates for agreement on norms of coexistence across different cultural traditions; but he disagrees with him on the type of agreement we should expect. Ex-

---

44. See *Between Facts and Norms,* especially sections 1.3, 2.3, and 3.2, and *The Inclusion of the Other.*

45. C. Taylor, "A World Consensus on Human Rights?" in *Dissent* (Summer 1996): 15–21; cited in the text as WC. This is an abbreviated version of an unpublished ms. on the "Conditions of an Unforced Consensus on Human Rights." I will also be drawing on his discussion of "Nationalism and Modernity" [NM], in McKim and McMahon, *The Morality of Nationalism,* 66–73, and his talk "Two Theories of Modernity," delivered in December 1997 at a conference on "Alternative Modernities" at the India International Center in Delhi, a revised version of which is included in this volume.

amining their differences will allow us to bring the issue of transcultural human rights into somewhat sharper focus and to connect it with another question, namely, the extent to which there can be functional equivalents for modern law and thus alternative modernities in respect to legal and political culture.

Like Habermas, Taylor regards at least some aspects of modernity as irresistible:

> From one point of view, modernity is like a wave, flowing over and engulfing one traditional culture after another. If we understand by modernity, inter alia, the developments discussed above—the emergence of a market-industrial economy, of a bureaucratically organized state, of modes of popular rule—then its progress is, indeed, wavelike. The first two changes, if not the third, are in a sense irresistible. Whoever fails to take them or some good functional equivalent on will fall so far behind in the power stakes as to be taken over and forced to undergo these changes anyway. . . . [They] confer tremendous power on the societies adopting them. (NM, 43–44)

But while these sorts of institutional changes are unavoidable, their cultural accompaniments in the West are not. Some alterations or others of traditional cultures will be necessary, but there is a good deal more latitude here than with economic and administrative structures:

> A successful transition involves a people finding resources in their traditional culture to take on the new practices. In this sense modernity is not a single wave. It would be better to speak of alternative modernities, as the cultures that emerge in the world to carry the institutional changes turn out to differ in important ways from each other. . . . What they are looking for is a creative adaptation, drawing on the cultural resources of their tradition . . . [which] by definition has to be different from culture to culture. (NM, 44)

A crucial question for our purposes is where modern law, with its conception of basic human rights, belongs. Taylor assigns it an ambivalent position, partly institutional, partly cultural, by distinguishing between norms of action and their justifications. It is only with regard to the former that we can reasonably expect convergence; the latter may and should vary with alternative modernities. This move enables him to adopt a position on human rights that, while appealing to Rawls's notion of overlapping consensus, is in some respects more universalistic than the one Rawls himself adopts in "The Law of Peoples." Taylor writes:

> What would it mean to come to a genuine, unforced international consensus on human rights? I suppose it would be something like what John Rawls describes in his *Political Liberalism* as an "overlapping consensus." That is, different groups, countries, religious communities, civilizations, while holding incompatible fundamental views on theology, metaphysics, human nature, and so on, would come to agreement on certain norms that ought to govern human behavior. Each would have its own way of justifying this from out of its profound background conception. We would agree on the norms, while disagreeing on why they were the right norms. And we would be content to live in this consensus, undisturbed by the differences of profound underlying belief. (WC, 15)

Taylor then goes on to draw a further distinction between norms of action and the "legal forms" in which they are inscribed, and assigns the latter to the variable part of modernity as well. What this means in connection with human rights is that neither "rights talk" nor "rights forms" are necessary accompaniments of a modern economy and state.

As to the talk, Taylor notes that the language of rights has its roots in Western culture; although the norms expressed in it do turn up in other cultures, they are not expressed in rights language; nor are the justifications offered for them based in views of humans and societies that privilege individual liberty and legitimation by consent. As to the forms, the Western rights tradition ensures immunities and liberties in the peculiar form of "subjective rights," which not only reverses the traditional ethical priority of duties over rights but also understands the latter as somehow possessed by individuals. This understanding is itself embedded in the philosophical justifications mentioned here. So Western legal philosophy and Western legal forms are tightly interconnected; but according to Taylor, neither is inextricably tied to the basic norms that are expressed and inscribed in them. Hence, while some of the norms are integral to modernity, their philosophical justifications and institutional forms may vary from culture to culture. And so, the inquiry into the possibility of a world consensus on human rights can now be pointed in a specific direction: "What variations can we imagine in philosophical justifications or in legal forms that would still be compatible with meaningful universal consensus on what really matters to us, the enforceable norms?" (WC, 18). What Taylor hopes to encounter along this route is "a convergence on certain norms of action, however they may be entrenched in law," together with "a profound sense of difference, of unfamiliarity, in the ideals, the notions of human excellence, the rhetorical tropes and reference points by which these norms have become objects of deep agreement for us" (WC, 20). Further along the same path he sees "a process of mutual learning," leading to a "fusion of horizons" through which "the moral universe of the other becomes less strange" (WC, 20).

This adaptation of Rawls's idea of an overlapping consensus stands or falls with the independent variability of legal norms, forms, and justifications. If it turned out that what is required by modern economies and modern states is not only the norms but the forms, that is, certain ways of entrenching the norms in law, the range of alternative modernities would be more constrained than Taylor takes it to be. That is precisely what Habermas maintains to be the case. One of the central sociological lines of argument in *Between Facts and Norms* is that modern law must have most of the formal properties it has in order to fulfill the functions it fulfills: There are no functional alternatives to its formality, positivity, reflexivity, individuality, actionability, and the like.

The fact that modern law is based on individual rights and liberties releases legal persons from moral obligations in certain spheres of action and gives them latitude, within legally defined limits, to act on their own choices free from interference by the state or by third parties—as is required in decentralized market societies. If these rights and liberties are to have the protection of the law, they must be connected with actionable claims, such that subjects who consider their rights to have been violated may have recourse to legal remedies.

At the same time, as membership in the legal communities of diverse modern societies can less and less be defined in terms of gender, race, religion, ethnicity, and the like, it comes to be more and more abstractly defined in terms of the equal rights and responsibilities of citizens as legal subjects. The fact that positive law issues from the changeable decisions of a legislator loosens its ties with traditional morality and makes it suitable as a means of organizing and steering complex modern societies. This requires that the enactment, administration, and application of the law themselves be legally institutionalized; law becomes reflexive. And since modern law, as a positive, reflexive, and therefore fungible "steering medium," can no longer be legitimated solely by appeal to inherited beliefs and practices, there is a need for new forms of legitimation. That need is compounded by the facts that cultural pluralism limits the authority of any one tradition and that rights-based conceptions of citizenship increase the pressure for political participation. In the long run, it is not clear that there are functional alternatives to democratic forms of securing legitimacy in modern societies. One could go on in this vein. The general line of argument is that the functions and forms of modern law are tailored to one another. Because no contemporary society, whatever its cultural traditions, can do without the former, none can do without some version of the latter.

As Habermas notes: "The decisive alternatives lie not at the cultural but at the socioeconomic level. . . . The question is not whether human rights, as part of an individualistic legal order, are compatible with the transmission of one's own culture. Rather, the question is whether traditional forms of political and societal integration can be reasserted against, or must instead be adapted to, global economic modernization" (HR, 15). If the latter proves to be the case, then we would expect the transition to modernity to involve cultural changes more extensive than those Taylor envisages, for, as he himself remarks, legal form and legal culture are closely intertwined. To the extent that individuals are guaranteed spheres of choice free from collectively binding beliefs and values, that citizenship qualifications are made independent of religious profession or cultural membership, that legislation is legitimated by its democratic provenance, and so forth, to that extent legal and political culture is being differentiated from traditional worldviews and forms of life. What further cultural changes are likely to be associated with that differentiation and its consequences is a disputed question.

Taylor is right, I think, to pose the question of alternative modernities in the way he does: Assuming that some degree of convergence in economic, governmental, and legal institutions and practices is an unavoidable feature of a globalized modernity, what kinds and degrees of divergence remain possible and desirable? In particular, how much room do such modernizing tendencies leave for deep cultural differences? Taylor is also right, in my view, to emphasize that different starting points for the transition to modernity are likely to lead to different outcomes, and thus that new forms of modern society are likely to evince new forms of difference. This is, of course, already true of European modernity: Swedish society is not the same as French or Italian society, let alone U.S. society. And yet they are too much the same to satisfy Taylor's interest in alternative modernities, for he envisions much broader and deeper differences in ideas and beliefs, outlooks and attitudes, values and identities, institutions and practices. Above all, he is interested in the differences among largely implicit, embodied, cultural understandings of self, society, nature, and the good. Thus, what he is most concerned to refute is the claim that there is only one viable modern constellation of such background understandings, the one that came to dominate in the West, which he understands as the claim that modern cultures can be expected sooner or later to share atomistic-individualistic understandings of self, instrumentalist conceptions of agency, contractualist understandings of society, the fact-value split, naturalism, scientism, secularism, and so on.[46] And what he is most concerned to defend is the possibility and desirability of alternative spiritual and moral ideals, visions of the good, and forms of self-identification. What moves him, then, is resistance to the idea that modernity will force all cultures to become like ours.

To the question of how much and what kinds of difference we have good empirical and theoretical reasons to expect, there is clearly no generally accepted answer. But one might well conjecture that it is more than most modernization theorists have predicted, although less than Taylor hopes for. Taylor concedes that market economies and bureaucratic states are inescapable features of modern societies and that with them come certain legal norms and spheres of instrumental action, as well as increased industrialization, mobility, and urbanization. He also mentions science and technology as something all modern societies have to assume, as well as general education and mass literacy. We might add to these the concomitant legal forms I mentioned earlier, together with the legal cultures that support them. We might further add a host of changes that Taylor presumably would also regard as highly likely in modern societies: the decline of the agricultural mode of life that has defined most of humanity for most of our recorded history; the functional

46. See "Two Theories of Modernity." This is, of course, a highly tendentious rendering of both the claim and the culture.

differentiation and specialization of occupational and professional life; a diversity of lifestyles, outlooks, and attitudes; a pluralism of belief systems, value commitments, and forms of personal and group identity; a steady growth of knowledge understood as fallible and susceptible to criticism and revision; challenges to patriarchal, racist, and ethnocentric stereotypes and role demands, as to all other "natural," "God-given," or time-honored hierarchies of that sort; the inclusion, as equals, of all inhabitants of a territory in its legal and political community; the spread of mass media and of mass-mediated popular culture; the existence of public political spheres that allow for open exchange and debate; and, of course, an ever-deeper immersion in transnational flows of capital, commodities, technology, information, communication, and culture. One could go on, but these few remarks are enough to suggest that the scope of deep divergence is somewhat more constricted than Taylor lets on, especially if we take into account the very dense internal relations and causal connections between the aforementioned changes and the cultural elements, particularly the background understandings, that Taylor sometimes seems to treat as swinging free of them.

These considerations are not meant to detract from the legitimacy or significance of Taylor's concern with identifying possibilities of divergence within convergence. Nor are they intended to contravert his claim that the extent of divergence can and likely will be greater than that countenanced in most classical and contemporary theories of modernization. And they do not profess to provide a theoretical argument for the superficiality or marginality of the differences, as compared to the similarities, among possible alternative modernities. In a word, their main purpose is not the negative one of placing a priori limits on societal and cultural variation but the positive one of showing that the idea of a global rule of law is not as hopelessly impracticable as it might seem if we attended only to cultural differences. The respects in which there is a credible case for different modern societies coming together seem to me to be sufficient to ground a "rational hope," as Kant would say, for the degree of legal- and political-cultural convergence required for some form of transnational agreement on what Habermas calls "the basic system of human rights."

How much or how little cultural convergence of other sorts will accompany it is, it seems to me, an open question. I do think, however, that Taylor tends to overestimate the extent to which cultural differences are likely to survive societal change. To mention just one basic dimension of change: The implicit, embodied, background understandings of gender identity, difference, roles, relations, and hierarchy characteristic of traditional (and, of course, modern) patriarchal cultures are, in the long run, incompatible with the changes in legal and political culture mentioned in this essay. Moreover, as any anthropologist or sociologist can attest, significant changes in this dimension of cultural self-understanding inevitably bring with it significant changes in any number of others. And though the new forms of gender relations that develop are not likely to be the same from culture to culture, insofar as they are tied to legal and political equality they will likely become more similar than they have been.[47]

Spiritual descendants of Herder might see these sorts of cultural convergences as tragic loss. Spiritual descendants of Kant will see some of them at least as signaling the "move toward greater agreement on principles . . . [that] leads to mutual understanding and peace," of which he wrote at the birth of the modern era.

47. See the interesting discussion between Susan Moller Okin and her critics, "Is Multiculturalism Bad for Women?" in *Boston Review* 22 (1997): 25–40.

Camera Zanzibar

William Cunningham Bissell

In 1994, a sign advertising a new resort, the Mbweni Ruins Hotel, materialized along the airport road to Zanzibar city. If tourists on arrival expected to be sipping tea on a balcony overlooking the picturesque remnants of a twelfth-century mosque—something distinctly Arabesque and Zanzibari—they were in for something of a surprise. With origins much closer to home and less distant in time, the Mbweni ruins are in fact the forlorn remains of a church station established by the Universities' Mission to Central Africa in the late nineteenth century.

The billboard is a sign of the times in Zanzibar—marking a moment in which past and present have congealed in complicated ways in the discourse and practice of conservation. Over the last fifteen years a series of preservation campaigns has sought to save old structures and sites, to restore the "cultural heritage" of the islands. From the development of museums in colonial landmark buildings, to tourist promotions brandishing an Oriental exoticism drawn straight from the nineteenth-century era of slaves, spices, and ivory caravans, Zanzibar's past is being zealously carved up and dished out as the new monoculture (replacing cloves) of the island's economy. Consistent with typical scenarios of Third World tourism, the engines of investment are largely external and expatriate; the results, inequitable.

The preservationist effort to classify

Zanzibar's architectural heritage inevitably raises the question of origins. According to a logic borrowed from diffusionist anthropology, buildings are routinely identified by tracing them back to their "source," typically construed in racial or ethnic terms. Hence conservation reports break the city down into "Arab," "Indian," "Swahili," or "European-colonial" types. It remains unclear how we are to make sense of the Beit el Amani (House of Peace) — the Peace Memorial Museum (see following pages) constructed to commemorate the end of World War I. The structure, in the "Indo-Saracenic" style — a British version of what Muslim monumental architecture should be — was intended "to instruct the people of Zanzibar not to desert what is good in their own traditional art for what is bad or mediocre from Europe." The building has, however, little to do with Zanzibar, traditional or otherwise.

*Right: Shopfront
Building, Central Market
Below: Beit el Amani*

"There are few places of the same size where one can study the races of mankind with greater facility and ease. One will see none of the ordered pomp of India; no bejeweled rajah will pass by; and no bespectacled B.A. of Calcutta University will obtrude the view; but the spectator will be able to rub shoulders with some of the wilder and less-known people of Africa and of Asia; and the lack of display is compensated for by the genuineness of the whole scene. Zanzibar is an epitome of the ancient Bagdad [*sic*] of Haroun-el-Raschid, rather than of the Europeanised India of today. It must be confessed that Zanzibar possesses no building of interest." — Major F. B. Pearce, British Resident, 1920

Designed by the British Resident

J. H. Sinclair, the Beit el Amani was inspired by
Orientalist notions of a generic "Eastern" tradition.
The logic of its construction was explained in the
following way: The Ottomans, being a "nomad race,"
had no "building tradition of their own." Thus they
adopted the Christian designs of Byzantium,
especially the Hagia Sophia, to make their mosques
and secular buildings, and these forms spread from
Constantinople throughout the Ottoman world.
When the "charming old buildings" of Zanzibar were
"fast disappearing," the British copied what they saw
as Ottoman copies of Byzantine forms, to restore
what was best and brightest in Zanzibari "traditional"
architecture. No matter that the islands had no
historical or cultural links whatsoever with the
Ottoman empire.

To locals, the Beit el Amani was known as the
"house of ghosts" or simply "Sinclair's mosque."

Old Dispensary

On Zanzibar, the historic fabric of

the colonial city was not obliterated by capitalist "redevelopment." Instead, it was overthrown by the revolution of 1964, which occupied and reworked the old city under the sign of Africanization and socialism. When former elites (Arabs, Indians, and Europeans) fled abroad, the stately dwellings they abandoned in Stone Town were confiscated and transformed into public housing. All the old names were rewritten to fit a new script: The Mnazi Mmoja Hospital was christened V. I. Lenin; the English Club became Africa House Hotel; St. Joseph's school was reborn as the triumphal "Tumekuja" ("We Have Come," or "Arrived"). Stone Town was left then to its own devices, allowed to languish as an outmoded relic. The revolutionary government sought to construct a new city around it, channeling spending into the largely African quarters of Ng'ambo, where ambitious programs to construct modernist blocks of flats were implemented by East Germans.

Today expatriates and Zanzibaris

involved in conservation cite the revolution as the
cause of Stone Town's decline. By the early 1980s the
city core had become dilapidated, with an average of
fifteen structures collapsing each year. The reasons
behind the decay are complex; but, beyond question,
the "revolution" is the conservationists' preferred
scapegoat. Of course, it could as easily be argued
that the revolution saved Stone Town by removing
it forcibly from international circuits of capital,
preventing the most destructive forms of "urban
renewal" in the 1960s and 1970s. Spatial isolation took
the city off the market, so to speak, holding it "in
reserve." Over time, colonial buildings, those former
"objects of utility," could acquire the patina of
history, being seen, from a distance established by
the revolution, "as rare and precious objects." If
structures were run down, they could suddenly
acquire the status of "ruins," being burnished by a
spurious antiquity.

Conservationists have succeeded in restoring a handful of Zanzibar's colonial monuments. In practice, they have echoed colonial precedent by privileging Stone Town and ignoring Ng'ambo—designating only the former as "historic"—despite the fact that both parts of the city were formed in reciprocal relation and at approximately the same time. It is by no means the past of abandoned cars and cubist vernacular architecture that conservation seeks to rehabilitate; nor is there any concern to bring back the lively bars and brothels of Vuga, or the fishermen's shanties of Malindi. Conservation's history is monumental.

Michenzani, the spectacularly willful blocks of low-income flats imposed on the periphery of Stone Town under East German inspiration, do not merit renewal. The structures are neither spatially distinct (where are we: Chicago? Berlin? London?) nor properly "historic": they cannot be coded as "Arab" or "Indian" and assimilated within an exotic past.

Socialist modernism, it would seem, cannot yet be reshaped as the commodity of a marketable nostalgia.

"Left to the Imagination": Indian Nationalisms and Female Sexuality in Trinidad

Tejaswini Niranjana

This business about the women is the weakest and the irredemiable part of the evil. . . . These women are not necessarily wives. Men and women are huddled together during the voyage. The marriage is a farce. A mere declaration by man or woman made upon landing before the Protector of Immigrants that they are husband and wife constitutes a valid marriage. Naturally enough, divorce is common. The rest must be left to the imagination of the reader. — M. K. Gandhi, Speech on Indentured Labor, 1916

Contrary to appearances, this essay is not about Trinidad or the West Indies; it is primarily an attempt to alter the lens through which we have been accustomed to viewing or framing the emergence of that discursive subject, the modern Indian woman. In analyzing the formation of *woman* in India, we often use, almost as though by default, the implicit comparisons with Western or metropolitan situations. I want to ask whether our frameworks might look different when the points of reference include other nonmetropolitan contexts. Also, what happens

An earlier version of this article appeared in *small axe* no. 2 (1997). The research was made possible in part by grants from the Homi Bhabha Fellowships Council, India, and the Sephis Programme for South-South Research, the Netherlands. I am indebted to the work of West Indian scholars such as Bridget Brereton, Kusha Haraksingh, Patricia Mohammed, Kenneth Parmasad, Kenneth Ramchand, Marianne Ramesar, Rhoda Reddock, Brinsley Samaroo, Verene Shepherd, and many others who have helped me begin to understand what it might mean to claim India in the Caribbean. Special thanks to Kirk Meighoo and Sheila Rampersad for our many thought-provoking conversations. Versions of this article have been presented in Ann Arbor, Cape Town, Chennai, Chicago, Durban, Palo Alto, and Santa Cruz, with useful critical comments being offered in particular by Ajit Menon and Uma Mesthrie. Thanks also to Vivek Dhareshwar, Mary John, Janaki Nair, and David Scott for their suggestions. For not always acting on them I have only myself to blame.

to our terms of comparison when the history of the context being compared with ours is entangled with our own, in ways that have been made invisible in the postcolonial present?

INDIA IN THE CARIBBEAN

One cannot talk about Trinidad without talking about India, close to 45 percent of the island's population being of subcontinental origin, the descendants of indentured laborers taken there between 1845 and 1917. The obverse, however, is clearly not true; one can talk endlessly about India without the Caribbean, or most other Third World regions, figuring in the conversation. What difference might it make to how we in India think about our past—and perhaps how we think about our present as well—to reflect on that which binds India to a west that is not the West?

One motivation for writing this article is my general interest in comparative cultural analyses, especially those which involve non–First World locations. I have suggested elsewhere that the commonsensical basis for comparative study, in India in particular, has been the implicit contrast between India and Europe (and now North America) and that to alter the primary reference point might yield new insights into and fresh perspectives on our contemporary questions.[1] Searching for relevant and viable frameworks of comparison, I began to think about the possibility of contrasting the formation of the "Indian" in the subaltern diaspora with the hegemonic construction of "Indians" in India.[2] Investigating the latter formation has been for the past few years an urgent task for those of us in India engaged in the critique of what one might call the national-modern.

To sketch quickly the immediate historical-political context of the contemporary critique of *nation* in the case of India, one might recall that for radical politics in the 1970s and 1980s (especially those of

1. See my "Alternative Circuits? Third World Scholars in Third World Spaces," unpublished manuscript, University of Hyderabad, Hyderabad (1995).
2. I use the term *subaltern* to distinguish between people of Indian origin in metropolitan countries such as the United States and the United Kingdom (by and large a product of postcolonial migration) and those in nonmetropolitan countries, such as the former British colonies in the Caribbean, as well as Surinam, Fiji, Mauritius, and South Africa.

the Marxist-Leninist [M-L] groups and the women's movement), the nation-state was a significant addressee. While the critique of the nation was central to radical politics, this critique was in many ways still part of the political and cultural logic of the national-modern. The secularism and modernity of the politics depended, as we can now see, on the disavowal of caste, community, and ethnic, regional, and linguistic differences. Indeed, the energy and reach of feminism and the M-L movement seemed to issue from these very disavowals. In the 1990s, however, political events such as the anti-Mandal agitation, the rise of the Bharatiya Janata Party, and the formation of successful "regional" parties, in conjunction with the drive to privatize and liberalize the Indian economy, have disrupted the narratives of the national-modern, a disruption within which the work of many of us today is situated. For someone like myself, affiliated with the critique of the languages of dominance in her society, a study of the subaltern diaspora (in Trinidad, for example) may suggest yet another entry point into the problematization of the universal modern.

My interest in Trinidad comes out of my longtime involvement in the teaching of West Indian literature and dates back to my first serendipitous visit to the island in 1994. I was spending three months in Jamaica, doing research in cultural politics in the Anglophone Caribbean. Having come to understand the West Indies through the reggae of Bob Marley, the poetry of Derek Walcott and Kamau Brathwaite, the cricket writings of C. L. R. James, and Garveyism and Black Power, like many other researchers I saw the Caribbean as profoundly "African," its otherness from the Indian context framed primarily in those terms. Of course, the demographic fact that Jamaica, the largest West Indian island, has an overwhelmingly Afro-Caribbean population only confirmed my conviction regarding the culture of the Caribbean at large. Having heard a great deal about Carnival in Trinidad in the Eastern Caribbean, a five-hour air journey away, I decided to make a short trip there to witness the festival. Before I left Jamaica, I was told by friends of the stark differences between that island and Trinidad, the Protestant seriousness of the one contrasted with the Catholic exuberance of the other. But nothing had prepared me for the visual shock of seeing a Caribbean population of which nearly half looked like me. In Jamaica, I was — safely — a foreigner, my Third Worldist solidarities with the Jamaicans undisturbed by conflicts of race or ethnicity. In Trinidad,

I felt claimed by the East Indians as an "Indian," and inserted sometimes into oppositional formations which asserted themselves *against* the dominant "African" culture.

Deeply disturbed at being implicated in this manner, my first impulse was to disavow all the tacit claims made on me, to dismiss the East Indians as a marginal and reactionary group which could only undermine the possibility of conducting dialogue across the south. Much later, however, as I became more familiar with the details of Caribbean history and with contemporary Caribbean politics, I began somewhat unwillingly to recognize the salience of the "Indian" in that part of the world, and to perceive how the dominant narratives of West Indianness excluded a large proportion of the population of at least two major countries, Guyana, and Trinidad and Tobago. As I see it now, one of the main causes of my discomfort in Trinidad was the encounter with "modern Indians" whose modernity did not seem to have been formed by the narratives of nation and citizenship which were part of my own interpretive and existential horizon in India. What I did not seem to understand in particular was the kind of negotiation with the "West" that Trinidadian Indians had undertaken in producing their modernity. Most disconcerting of all was my interaction with East Indian women, the semiotics of whose bodies and lives I could not read.

The aim of this essay, then, is to investigate a conjuncture of modernity, "Indianness," and woman that is radically different from that which operates in India, in the hope that it will defamiliarize the Indian formation, as well as throw new light on the elements that led to its consolidation.

I plan to approach the investigation through an analysis of two "moments": the early-twentieth-century campaign against indenture by nationalists in India, and a contemporary controversy around East Indian women and popular music in Trinidad. I have chosen these moments for their foregrounding of the question of female sexuality, an issue which is increasingly being seen as central to the formation of gendered citizenship and dominant narratives of nationhood. Historically, the moments are also those of "Indian" political assertion, as well as of the availability of new possibilities for "Indian" women. I use the quote marks for the term Indian to signal its double use: marking in my first "moment" a (future) nationality in South Asia, and in my second an "ethnic" category in the Caribbean. Much of the current literature, both scholarly and popular, tends to blur the difference between the two usages.

I also argue that indentureship enabled a different sort of accession to the modern for the subaltern diaspora than that which was being consolidated in India in the late nineteenth and early twentieth centuries. I draw here on the West Indian thinker C. L. R. James's notion that Caribbean society, with its plantation system based on the carefully regulated labor of slaves, in place as early as three centuries ago, is in terms of organization of industrial production and ways of living the first "modern" society in the history of the world.[3]

INDENTURED INDIANS

The following provides a brief historical background to the presence of "Indians" in the Caribbean. When slavery was abolished in 1838, the British colonies expressed a need for sugarcane plantation labor to replace the freed slaves, who for the most part chose to work elsewhere than on the scene of their former labors. A more crucial factor leading to indentureship, some historians have suggested, was the need to depress the wages of free labor in a context where former slaves had begun to agitate for better wages.[4] About 8,000 African immigrants were brought over to increase the labor pool and resolve the problem, but many more would have been required for wages to come down. Neither increasing African immigration nor initiating immigration from China proved feasible. Eventually, a system was devised for recruiting laborers from the Indian subcontinent, from areas where long spells of drought and famine had pauperized agriculturists and driven peasants away from their villages in search of work. Between 1845 and 1917, about 143,900 Indians were brought to Trinidad (with a total of over 500,000 to the Caribbean). While about 22 percent of emigrants returned to India at the end of their period of indenture, some of them reindentured and came back to the plantations.

3. Discussed in James's appendix to *The Black Jacobins* (1938; reprint, London: Allison and Busby, 1980), 392.
4. See Walter Rodney, *A History of the Guyanese Working People, 1881–1905* (Baltimore: Johns Hopkins University Press, 1981) and K. O. Laurence, *A Question of Labour: Indentured Immigration into Trinidad and British Guiana, 1875–1917* (Kingston: Ian Randle, 1994).

Throughout the years of recruitment of indentured laborers, there was a tremendous disparity between the number of men and the number of women; this was mainly due to the planters' reluctance to permit the growth of a permanent community of migrants, a proposition seen as both uneconomic and dangerous. When recruiters attempted to induce more women to migrate, for diverse reasons including pressure from the government of India, they were usually not able to find "the right kind of women," or the docile laborers the planters wanted. So among the people who indentured themselves, not more than an average of 25 percent were women.[5] Migration to the Caribbean took place mainly from northern India: 90 percent of the migrants were from the "Ganges plain," that is, from the United Provinces, Central Provinces, Oudh, Orissa, and Bihar; a few were from Bengal, the North West Provinces, and the south (primarily Tamil and Telugu speakers). At first there were two ports of embarkation, Calcutta and Madras, but the West Indian plantation owners soon declared that "the Madrasis were inferior both in health and as labourers," and the agency at Madras was closed down.[6]

The caste-class and religious composition of the migrants reflected, to some extent, the composition in the regions of migration. Historians give us varying figures, but we can estimate that roughly 15 percent were Muslim; there was a small number of Christians, mainly from the south; among the Hindus 40 percent were from the artisanal and agricultural castes like the Kurmi and Ahir, more than 40 percent from the "chamar" or what were then called the Untouchable castes, and about 18 percent from the upper castes like Brahmin and Kshatriya.[7] We must

5. Rhoda Reddock argues that the question of the number of "Indian women" was "a major point of contention and policy" from the very beginning of indenture. See her *Women, Labour and Politics in Trinidad and Tobago* (London: Zed Books, 1994), 27 (henceforth *WLP*). As she points out, between 1857 and 1879 the prescribed ratio of women to men changed about six times, "ranging from one woman to every three men in 1857 to one to two in 1868 and one to four in 1878–79. These changes reflected the difficulties and contradictions in recruiting *more* women at the same time as recruiting 'the right kind of women'" (27–29). See also Laurence, *Question of Labour,* esp. chap. 4.

6. Laurence elaborates that during years of labor shortage there were a few attempts to recruit workers from southern India and even, in 1884 and once again in 1905, to reopen the Madras agency. These attempts, however, were soon abandoned as unsuccessful (*Question of Labour,* 104).

7. Figures are from Bridget Brereton, "The Experience of Indentureship, 1845–1917,"

also remember that subsequent to migration there was a complex process of recomposition of castes in Trinidad, as in other colonies. Many people "changed" their caste, often within one generation, and caste endogamy was not strictly practiced because of the scarcity of women.[8] What is clear, however, is that most of the migrants were either poor or destitute, having lost their land or never having owned any.

The system of indenture took several years to formalize. Continual problems of illness, desertion, and destitution of laborers even led to a temporary halt in immigration between 1848 and 1851. However, it was not until 1854 that an Immigration Ordinance was passed, which regularized the pattern of a three-year contract with free return passage after ten years of residence in the colony. The contract actually ended up being for a period of five years, two years being treated as mandatory "industrial residence." For a short period between 1869 and 1880, free lots of Crown land were given to laborers in lieu of return passage, but after 1895 full passage even for those otherwise eligible was not paid.

On the estate, there was a sexual division of labor in the sense that certain jobs were only done by men; women did weeding, manuring, supplying, and cane cutting, and children also did small tasks. According to Rhoda Reddock, however, this division was not constant;[9] truck loading, for example, was a heavy male task, but many women preferred to do it, too. Men earned approximately 50 to 70 cents per day and women 25 cents no matter what work they did. Only about 25 percent of the female immigrants were married; the rest had come to Trinidad as single women.[10] But the wages they earned did not allow them to remain single for long, and most women had to take more than one male protector in order to survive. Prabhu Mohapatra suggests that there came

---

in *Calcutta to Caroni,* ed. John La Guerre (Trinidad and Tobago: University of West Indies, Extramural Studies Unit, 1985), 22. Brereton cautions us against possible errors in these figures due to confusions in recordkeeping.

8. See the articles in Barton Schwartz, ed., *Caste in Overseas Indian Communities* (San Francisco: Chandler, 1967).

9. Reddock, *WLP,* 36.

10. Reddock draws our attention to the fact that even as late as 1915, when Commissioners McNeill and Chimman Lal came out to the Caribbean to prepare their report on indenture, they found that only about a third of the women came from India as married women; the rest were either widows or runaway wives, and a small number had been prostitutes (*WLP,* 30). See also Laurence, *Question of Labour.*

into being a variety of households because of the scarcity of women, including those with a single woman with or without children and a visiting male partner or partners. Mohapatra has also studied the phenomenon of "wife murders" common in Trinidad and British Guiana, where there was a high rate of killing of "reputed wives" by "reputed husbands."[11]

Working conditions on the plantations were so poor that hundreds of "coolies" took ill and died, especially in the first years of emigration. Those who survived did so in constant ill health, often physically punished when the planters decided they were feigning sickness. Many could not earn enough even to pay for their rations and accumulated large debts to the estate. Laborers were not allowed to leave the estate except for strictly limited purposes. Their living spaces were cramped and unhygienic, having no piped water or arrangements for latrines. Several historians have argued that indenture was just another form of slavery.[12] As Walter Rodney points out, it was "the regimented social and industrial control which caused indenture to approximate so closely to slavery."[13] Antislavery societies in England were in fact among the early opponents of indentureship, but it was only after Indian nationalists in India began a campaign against the system that it was finally abolished.

NATIONALISM AND INDENTURE

Indenture did not figure in early nationalism as a significant anti-colonial issue. On the contrary, as B. R. Nanda points out, in 1893 the

11. Prabhu P. Mohapatra, " 'Restoring the Family': Wife Murders and the Making of a Sexual Contract for Indian Immigrant Labour in the British Caribbean Colonies, 1860–1920," unpublished manuscript, International Institute for Asian Studies, Leiden. Mohapatra argues that the planters' need to create a permanent labor force at the end of the nineteenth century led to an attempt to reconstitute the Indian family, so that laboring women withdrew from estate work but did unpaid work, both on the land and at home, in addition to reproducing the labor force. It is through the colonial effort to prevent "wife murders" (by passing a series of legislations regarding marriage, for instance), according to Mohapatra, that the Indian family in British Guiana is formed.

12. Among others, see Hugh Tinker, *A New System of Slavery: The Export of Indian Labour Overseas 1830–1920* (London: Hansib Publishers, 1993) (henceforth *NSS*).

13. Although Rodney writes about British Guiana, his analysis is applicable to Trinidad as well (*History of the Guyanese*, 39).

leading nationalist M. G. Ranade actually wrote an article on "Indian Foreign Emigration" in which he argued that emigration afforded some "relief" to the growing population of India and that the expansion of the British Empire could be seen as a "direct gain" to the masses of this country.[14] Eventually, however, due in significant measure to the efforts of a diasporic Indian, M. K. Gandhi, indentured emigration became an important issue for Indian nationalism. In 1896, Gandhi, who was still living in South Africa at the time, had a meeting with nationalist leader Gopal Krishna Gokhale to try and interest him in the cause of overseas Indians. In 1902, Gandhi again spent some time with Gokhale, who was to become one of his earliest admirers and supporters in India. At Gandhi's urging, in February 1910 Gokhale piloted a resolution through the Imperial Legislative Council, of which he was a member, calling for a complete ban on the recruitment of indentured labor. In 1911, a ban was imposed on recruitment for Natal, and finally in 1917 it was extended to all overseas colonies, but not before a large-scale campaign had been mounted against indenture by Gandhi and a host of other nationalists.

As historian Hugh Tinker points out, the campaign was, in fact, Gandhi's first big political intervention in India—he gave anti-indenture speeches all over the country, wrote about the topic at length in newspapers, and was able to have an Anti-Indenture Resolution passed at the Lucknow Congress in December 1916. By 1915, "the indenture issue became the central question of Indian politics." Even as emigration itself declined for a variety of reasons, there was widespread nationalist protest, with meetings organized in Hyderabad, Sind and Karachi, Allahabad, Madras, and in parts of Punjab and Bengal. The agitators called for an end to a system that they said was a "moral stigma" for India.[15]

The historical significance of the anti-indenture campaign, suggests Tinker, lies in the fact that "this was the first major Indo-British political and social issue to be decided in dependent India, and not in metropolitan Britain."[16] An examination of the nationalist discourse on indenture would reveal the crucial place the question of women's sexuality

14. Published in the *Sarvajanik Sabha Quarterly Journal,* October 1893, edited by Gokhale. See B. R. Nanda, *Gokhale* (Delhi: Oxford University Press, 1977), bk. 4, chap. 37.
15. Tinker, *NSS,* 341, 334, 347.
16. Tinker, *NSS,* 288.

occupied in it, helping us understand why it was believed to be some-thing unspeakable, and why—paradoxically—it needed to be spoken about so interminably.[17] Given this campaign's centrality to nationalist thought, it would be interesting to see how women were represented in the criticism of indentureship. I will take as my point of departure some aspects of Partha Chatterjee's well-known argument about the nationalist resolution of the women's question. Chatterjee has tried to account for the relative insignificance of the "women's question" in the late nineteenth century by suggesting that nationalism was able to "re-solve" the question by this time in accordance with its attempt to make "modernity consistent with the nationalist project." In constructing a new woman, the middle-class, upper-caste *bhadramahila*, nationalism in India was able to produce and enforce distinctions between the ma-terial might of the colonizer and the spiritual superiority of the colo-nized. The new woman was "modern," but not heedlessly Westernized. Neither was she like the uneducated, vulgar, and coarse lower-caste and lower-class working woman.[18]

The period when indentured emigration to the other colonies began, the 1830s, was also the period of the initial formation, via the social re-form movements, of nationalist discourse in India. Since, for the nation-alists, official modernity came to be produced through the project of the future nation, there was no room for formations of modernity other than those which involved as its subjects middle-class, upper-caste Indi-ans. The problem with indentured laborers, both men and women, was that their geographical displacement and the new context they came to inhabit was enabling them also to become "modern." The transforma-tions caused in the lives of the indentured by displacement, the planta-tion system, the disparate sex ratio, and racial politics had to be made

17. In conceptualizing this essay, I have found useful the insights provided by the work of Michel Foucault: "The central issue, then . . . is not to determine whether one says yes or no to sex, whether one formulates prohibitions or permissions, whether one asserts its importance or denies it; but to account for the fact that it is spoken about, to discover who does the speaking, the positions and viewpoints from which they speak, the institutions which prompt people to speak about it and which store and distribute the things that are said." Michel Foucault, *The History of Sexuality*, vol. 1, trans. Robert Hurley (New York: Vintage, 1980), 11.

18. Partha Chatterjee, *The Nation and Its Fragments* (Princeton, N.J.: Princeton Uni-versity Press, 1993), 121, 127.

invisible by nationalist discourse. This was accomplished, I suggest, by erasing the difference between the agricultural laborer in Bihar and the one in Trinidad ("Chinitat," as the indentured called it) and imaging the latter in particular as victimized, pathetic, lost, and helpless. Even when the changes in the emigrant were acknowledged, they were criticized as "artificial" and "superficial," loss rather than gain. Gandhi writes that the laborer came back to India "a broken vessel," robbed of "national self-respect." Any "economic gain" he might have obtained could not be set off "against the moral degradation it involves."[19]

The indentured woman in particular could not be accommodated in the nationalist discourse, again except as a victim of colonialism. By 1910 or so when the campaign against indenture was gathering momentum, nationalism had already produced the models of domesticity, motherhood, and companionate marriage which would make the Indian woman a citizen of the new India. The question of what constituted the modernity of the Indian woman had been put forward as an *Indian* question, to be resolved *in India.* What, then, of the Indian women who were "becoming modern," but elsewhere? For nationalism, theirs would have to be considered an illegitimate modernity because it had not passed through, been formed by, the story of the nation-in-the-making. The route to modernity—and emancipation—for the Indian woman in India was well established: education, cultivation of household arts, refinement of skills, and regulation of one's emotions. The class-caste provenance of this project, and of the new woman, needs no reiteration here.

What sort of ideological project, then, did nationalism envisage for the indentured woman laborer who was shaping her own relationship with the "West" in a distant land? Reform was not practical. Disavowal of this figure would not have been possible while the system of indenture still existed. The only solution, therefore, was to strive for the abolition of indenture. The manifest immorality and depravity of the indentured woman would not only bring down the system but also serve to reveal more clearly the contrasting image of the virtuous and chaste Indian woman at home. As Gandhi asserted, "Women, who in India

19. Gandhi's speech on Indentured Indian Labour, Bombay, District Congress Committee. In M. K. Gandhi, *Collected Works,* Vol. 13 (Delhi: Publications Div., Govt. of India, 1964), 133, 249.

would never touch wine, are sometimes found lying dead-drunk on the roads."[20] The point is not that women never drank in India and started doing so in Trinidad or British Guiana, but that for Gandhi and others this functioned as a mark of degraded Westernization and "artificial modernity." The nationalist reconstitution of Indian tradition, I suggest, was not a project that was complete when the new phase of the nationalist struggle, marked by the anti-indenture campaign, was inaugurated.

Although according to Chatterjee the nationalists had "resolved" the women's question without making it a matter for political agitation, with the anti-indenture campaign there seems to have been a refocusing on women. At the end of the first decade of the twentieth century a *political* campaign was undertaken—mobilizing "a wider public than any previous protest"[21] against the colonial rulers—to dismantle a system that was said to be turning Indian women into prostitutes. As Gandhi wrote, "The system brings India's womanhood to utter ruin, destroys all sense of modesty. That in defence of which millions in this country have laid down their lives in the past is lost under it."[22] The nationalist discourse on indentured female sexuality, however, veered time and again from denouncing the women as reprobate and immoral to seeing them as having been brought to this state by colonialism.[23] The Indian nationalists were joined by the European critics of indenture, led by C. F. Andrews, Gandhi's associate, who had worked with him in South Africa and had been mobilized by him to prepare a report on Indians in Fiji. As anthropologist John Kelly puts it, Andrews and others "portrayed indenture . . . as a degenerating force and blamed it for the moral condition of the 'helots of Empire.' But they accepted the claim that the 'coolies' were degraded, and they agreed especially about what we might call the 'harlots of Empire.'"[24]

20. Gandhi, "Indenture or Slavery?" in Gujarati, published in *Samalochak*, December 1915. Reprinted in English translation in *Collected Works*, Vol. 13, 1467.

21. John D. Kelly, *A Politics of Virtue: Hinduism, Sexuality, and Countercolonial Discourse in Fiji* (Chicago: University of Chicago Press, 1991), 48.

22. Gandhi, *Collected Works*, Vol. 22, 349.

23. Kelly, for instance, points out that in the case of Fiji the critics of indenture stressed the sexual abuse of Indian women. Kelly, *Politics of Virtue*, 30.

24. Kelly, *Politics of Virtue*, 33. C. F. Andrews, Gandhi's emissary on the indenture issue, wrote in 1915: "Vice has become so ingrained that they have not been able to

As the campaign against indenture gained momentum, among the delegations which met Viceroy Hardinge to press for action were several organized by Indian women's associations.[25] At the meeting between Colonial Office and India Office representatives on 9 May 1917, James Meston, representing India in the war cabinet, spoke of how "the women of India" felt "deeply on the question [of indenture]." Satyendra Sinha, the other India representative, declared that "there was an intensely strong feeling of concern . . . [which included] ladies who lived in purdah, but read the news." In spite of Englishmen such as Alfred Lyall, governor of the North Western Provinces, and G. A. Grierson, who reported on emigration from Bengal and recommended it for its benefits to women, representing emigration as giving a chance for a new life to "abandoned and unfaithful wives," Viceroy Hardinge was not willing to continue supporting a system when "its discussion arouses more bitterness than any other outstanding question." Hardinge was convinced that Indian politicians firmly believed that it "brands their whole race . . . with the stigma of helotry" and condemns Indian women to prostitution.[26]

By mid-1917, the end of indenture was certain. Historians tend to see it as an issue that brought a new focus to nationalist politics in India and gave it a wider base. I would argue that it was not simply that. We need to reframe the indenture question so that it can be seen as marking for us the consolidation of the early national-modern, a setting in place of new (nationalist) moralities, new ways of relating between women and men, appropriate "Indian" modes of sociosexual behavior, the parameters for the state's regulation of reproduction and sexuality, as well as the delineation of the virtues that would ensure for Indian women citizenship in the future nation. It should be obvious that the historical formation of these virtues, for example, and the contemporaneity of their description, was obscured by the nationalist presentation of them as the essential, and "traditional" qualities of Indian women.

---

recover their self-respect. . . . The women of India are very chaste; but these women, well, you know how they are, and how can it be different, situated as they are, living the lives they do, brought up in this atmosphere of vice and degradation?" (33–34).
25. Tinker, *NSS*, 350.
26. Tinker, *NSS*, 352, 267–68, 340–41.

While it is evident that the immigrant female was an important figure invoked by Indian nationalism in India, the centrality of this figure to "East Indian nationalism" in Trinidad has not yet been systematically elaborated.[27] An overview of the cultural history of East Indians, however, suggests that since the emergence of Indians in the Trinidadian public sphere in the 1920s, at no time has the issue of female sexuality been a matter of such heated debate as in the 1990s. One of the reasons for this could be the emergence of new narratives of "Indianness" leading up to and coinciding with the 150th anniversary celebrations of the arrival of Indians in Trinidad. The assertion of an "Indian" ethnic identity has sometimes been seen as the manifestation of "Indian nationalism." Before we go into the validity of this concept, however, it would be worth looking briefly at the significations of nationalism in the West Indies. Here it is a somewhat different entity than that found in South Asia, where it is more common to see nationalism as a form of relationship to a nation-state, either one in the making or one that has already come into existence. While Caribbean (particularly elite) nationalism may well take the form of a specifically Jamaican or Trinidadian anti-colonial nationalism, all classes of people often represent themselves as West Indian, too. Political movements such as Garveyism in the early twentieth century or midcentury Pan-Africanism, built on perceptions of a shared past of slavery, extended far beyond the Caribbean islands. The short-lived Federation (1958 to 1962) was another attempt to bring together the political units of the region even before the achievement of full independence.[28] The Black Power movement in the 1970s had African American origins, but it resonated powerfully with Caribbean critiques of elite nationalism, such as Rastafarianism.

In spite of the ambiguous nature of the relationship between nation and nationalism in the West Indies, what is evident is the Afrocentric basis of the claim to being West Indian. It is this basis which "Indian

27. Recent unpublished work by Rhoda Reddock, Patricia Mohammed, and Prabhu Mohapatra makes interesting beginnings in this direction.
28. In spite of the absence of common structures of governance, however, two major Caribbean institutions, the cricket team and the university, are shared by all the West Indian countries.

nationalism" appears to address, its project not being the creation of an Indian nation-state but one of claiming equal cultural rights *in Trinidad*.

To me, the most salient factor in the East Indian narratives of Indianness in the Caribbean is not the question of producing and maintaining a "colonial" difference — that is, difference from the colonizing European is not the issue, as it would have been with elite Indian nationalism in India; rather, the difference at stake is difference from the "African" ("the other race," as East Indians say today). "Indians" have a slight demographic edge over "Africans" in Trinidad, being a little over 42 percent of the population, while the latter comprise 40 to 41 percent, and those of Chinese, Lebanese, and West European origin make up the rest.[29]

It may be worth emphasizing that the maintenance of distinctions between the "Christianized African Creole" and the "Asiatic coolie" was a matter of some concern for the colonial authorities as well.[30] After the establishment of the republic of Haiti in 1803, the specter of successful nonwhite revolt haunted every European in the Caribbean. Any hint of solidarity between laborers, especially of different races, was speedily crushed. As the planters faced the prospect of the end of indenture, and the imminent formation of a purely domestic labor force, images of the shiftless, lazy African and the industrious coolie circulated with increasing frequency. The colonial construction of "Indian" and "African" continues to inform the contemporary formations of the two groups' identities.[31]

With regard to the indentured woman, too, the immediate contrasting image for the colonialist was the African woman, the ex-slave, the urban *jamette* of Carnival whose sexuality was othered, and sought

29. There is also a "mixed" population that is said to be as high as 8 to 10 percent of the total.

30. See Rodney, *History of the Guyanese,* and also Malcolm Cross, "East Indian–Creole Relations in Trinidad and Guiana in the Late Nineteenth Century," in *Across the Dark Waters: Ethnicity and Indian Identity in the Caribbean,* ed. David Dabydeen and Brinsley Samaroo (London: Macmillan Caribbean, 1996).

31. For illuminating discussions of the formation of such stereotypes, see, among others, Ramabai Espinet, "Representation and the Indo-Caribbean Woman in Trinidad and Tobago," in *Indo-Caribbean Resistance,* ed. Frank Birbalsingh (Toronto: Tsar, 1993), and Gordon Rohlehr, *Calypso and Society in Pre-Independence Trinidad* (Port of Spain: G. Rohlehr, 1990).

to be regulated, by the European ruling class.[32] The *jamette* was seen as vulgar, promiscuous, loud, and disruptive, and her removal from Carnival and related activities became part of the project of creating a new urban middle class in Trinidad in the early twentieth century. Much of the elite's anxiety around the *jamette,* or even the rural Creole woman, seemed to hinge on the fact of her being seen as independent, in both sexual and economic terms. The East Indian woman in postslavery society, then, brought in to compensate colonial planters for the loss of captive labor, had to be imaged as completely different from the African woman. For this, "Indian tradition" was invoked by different groups, and the lack of conformity of indentured women to the virtuous ideal of Indian culture was deplored. For example, the Canadian Presbyterian missionaries who targeted the "Indians" exclusively attempted to account for the position of Indian women in Trinidad.[33] Sarah Morton, wife of missionary John Morton, narrated her experiences with Indian women:

> The loose actions and prevailing practices in respect of marriage here are quite shocking to the newcomer. I said to an East Indian woman whom I knew to be the widow of a Brahmin, "You have no relations in Trinidad, I believe?" "No, madame," she replied, myself and two children; when the last immigrant ship came I took a 'papa.' I will keep him as long as he treats me well. If he does not treat me well I shall send him off at once; that's the right way, is it not?"[34]

32. Rohlehr, *Calypso and Society,* esp. chap. 1.

33. The Canadian Presbyterian Mission was founded in Trinidad in 1868.

34. Cited in Reddock, *WLP,* 42–43. Sarah Morton's comment implies a wilfulness on the part of the Indian woman, while East Indian men seemed more inclined to stress her susceptibility to "enticement," as did the colonial authorities who framed the marriage laws intended to reduce the numbers of "wife murders" in Guyana and Trinidad among the East Indians. All of these, however, concurred in the implicit argument that the indentured woman's "immorality" was due to the disparity in the sex ratio. Reddock quotes a petitioner called Mohammed Orfy who, on behalf of the "destitute Indian men of Trinidad," wrote several letters to the Secretary of State for the Colonies, to the Indian government, and to others. Orfy described as "a perforating plague" "the high percentage of immoral lives led by the female section of our community." In order "to satisfy the greed and lust of the male section of quite a different race to theirs" (he indicts elsewhere the "Europeans, Africans, Americans, and Chinese"), Indian women "are enticed, seduced and frightened into becoming

The stories about these immoral Indian women lead, in Reddock's analysis, to the construction of a new patriarchy and to the closure of the question of women's agency, or "freedom denied." The implicit argument here concerns East Indian women in the present, and Reddock's perception that—like women in India—they do not live lives that are "free." While not wanting to question this rather problematic perception or its underlying conceptual assumptions here, I would merely stress the irreversibility of the indenture experience for women and suggest that it opened up different possibilities, even of self-representation, for succeeding generations of East Indian women in the Caribbean.

Today one cannot speak of how the sexuality of the East Indian woman in Trinidad is constituted except through the grid provided by discourses of racial difference (the question of "the opposite race"), cultural/ethnic difference (the supposed cultural attributes of the "Indian" woman as opposed to the "African"), and caste-class or "nation" (*low nation* and *high nation* are terms I have heard used by older Trinidadians to refer to caste).[35] These discourses intersect in various ways with that of "East Indian nationalism," which is often seen as being at odds with "Trinidadian" or "West Indian" nationalism. Unlike in the nationalist discourse in India, where East and West were thematized by the race and culture of the colonized and the colonizer, respectively, in Trinidad the presence of the "Afro-Saxon" (the term used by some Trinidadian scholars like Lloyd Best to refer critically to the culture of the ex-slave, part Anglo-Saxon and part African) indicates that in many ways the "African," who had been in contact with the West a couple of centuries before the Indians who migrated to the Caribbean, came to stand in for

---

concubines, and paramours." These women, according to Orfy, "have absolutely no knowledge whatever of the value of being in virginhood." This makes them, says the petitioner, "most shameless and a perfect menace to the Indian gentry." Cited in Reddock, *WLP,* 44.

35. To understand the material coordinates of the construction of East Indian femininity, we would need to build on the work, among others, of Mangru and Reddock. The work of Basdeo Mangru on British Guiana and of Rhoda Reddock on Trinidad indicates that sometimes as few as ten out of a hundred migrants were female. Basdeo Mangru, "The Sex Ratio Disparity and Its Consequences under the Indenture in British Guiana," in *India in the Caribbean,* ed. David Dabydeen and Brinsley Samaroo (London: Hansib/University of Warwick Centre for Caribbean Studies, 1987); Reddock, *WLP.*

the West as far as the Indians were concerned.[36] We may speculate that contact with the European in India did not affect labor to a great extent, partly because the Western master belonged to a different social class and his ways of life were not part of the milieu of the Indian laborer. In Trinidad, however, the African (already part of the "West" in the New World) was of *the same class* as the Indian. The transformations among Indians, therefore, had to do with finding ways of inhabiting, and changing, their new home through a series of complex negotiations with other racial groups, the most significant of which was the African. Exposure to "Western" ways, therefore, came to the Indian through interaction with the Afro-Caribbean rather than through contact with the European. Even today when Trinidadian Indians speak of Westernization, they often treat it as synonymous with "creolization," the common term for the Afro-Trinidadian still being "creole."[37]

It is not surprising, then, that the recent controversy in the East Indian community over the phenomenon of chutney-soca is structured in terms of creolization and the degradation of "Indian culture." Popular music is one of the most central of West Indian cultural forms, and calypso—which emerged in the late nineteenth century as a mode of social-political commentary—is one of the most popular of the musical genres. Calypso, which has been sung with a few rare exceptions solely by Afro-Trinidadian men, engages in explicit discussion of current politics. However, there has always been a strand in calypso that comments on relations between women and men.[38] In the 1980s, a new form called soul-calypso, or soca, emerged, claimed by its inventor Lord Shorty as being inspired by East Indian music. Soca is different from calypso in that it is meant more as music to dance to and does not usually talk

36. I owe this insight to Kirk Meighoo, with whom I have had many useful discussions on the topic of Afrocentrism in the Caribbean. The term *Indo-Saxon* is employed to refer to "Westernized" Indians, but it does not seem to be as frequently used as "Afro-Saxon."

37. Just as the African in the Caribbean was seen as "Western" or Westernized, one can say that the West too was Africanized, and then Indianized, in Trinidad.

38. Several "African" calypsonians have sung about East Indian women, who appear in the songs as exotic objects of desire. Rohlehr has pointed out that the women frequently appear against a background of the "Indian feast" that the "African" is trying to gatecrash (*Calypso and Society,* 251–57).

about the political situation.[39] At the end of that decade, several East Indian women, including the versatile Drupatee Ramgoonai, began to perform their own blend of Indian folk music and soca—Drupatee's 1989 song was called "Indian Soca": "The music of the steeldrums from Laventille / Cannot help but mix with rhythm from Caroni. . . . Indian soca, sounding sweeter / Hotter than a chula / Rhythm from Africa and India / Blend together in a perfect mixture" — which came to be known as chutney-soca.[40]

Although "chutney" is also a generic name given to East Indian folk songs, which used to be sung primarily in Bhojpuri or Hindi, of late the term has also been applied to "Indian" songs sung predominantly in English. The word refers also to the "spicy" themes of the songs. Chutney-soca draws from the folk forms brought to Trinidad by the indentured laborers from rural North India. It is related especially to the *maticore* and *laawa* ceremonies performed on the night before a wedding. The participants in the ceremonies were all women, except for the young boys who played the drums, and the songs and "performances" were known to be full of humor and sexual explicitness. Chutney also derives from the songs sung by women after the birth of a child.[41] In the late 1980s, chutney came to be performed in public, sometimes with five or ten thousand people present, both men and women.[42] The lyrics are now as often sung in Trinidadian English as in Bhojpuri or

39. As with many musical terms in the Caribbean, however, there is some controversy as to the exact distinction between calypso and soca, although there are separate annual competitions for National Soca Monarch and National Calypso Monarch during the Carnival season.

40. There are also several popular male chutney singers such as Sundar Popo and Anand Yankarran.

41. Ramaya writes: "About half a century ago, after the birth of a child the women celebrated at the *chhatti* and sang *sohar,* songs which were like lullabies, delivered in a slow tempo with measured beats and rhythms. After the *sohars,* the women diverted into songs that were spicy with faster beats. They were called chutney because of the hot, spicy tempo." Narsaloo Ramaya, "Evolution of Indian Music: From Field to Studio," *Trinidad and Tobago Review* 14 (1992): 22–23.

42. Much of this information comes from personal conversations with Patricia Mohammed and Hubert Devonish in Jamaica and Rhoda Reddock in Trinidad, February–March 1994. For access to newspaper accounts of the chutney controversy, I am indebted to Rawwida Baksh-Soodeen and the CAFRA archives in Trinidad. See also Baksh-Soodeen, "Power, Gender and Chutney," *Trinidad and Tobago Review* 13 (1991): 7.

Hindi, which accounts for their greater accessibility to people outside the East Indian community and, indeed, to young East Indians, most of whom do not speak any "Indian" languages. However, the surprise hit of Carnival 1996 was a Bhojpuri chutney song about a man seducing his sister-in-law, "Lotay La," whose singer—Sonny Mann—reached the National Soca Monarch finals. There were several Afro-Trinidadian calypsonians who did "remixes" of Sonny Mann's song, which was also used in the 1995 general election campaign of the People's National Movement (PNM), the African-dominated party. This election, incidentally, brought to power for the first time an Indian-dominated party, the United National Congress, and its leader, Basdeo Panday, who became prime minister of the country in late 1995.[43]

As West Indian cultural critic Gordon Rohlehr points out, to be "visible" in the Caribbean is literally to be on stage, to perform.[44] And when East Indian *women* take to the stage as singers or dancers, or as politicians, the protracted struggle over "culture" and "authenticity" takes a new turn, not only in the national arena between different ethnic groups but also within the East Indian community itself.[45] The chutney-soca controversy of the early 1990s has provoked some rethinking of what the claim to Indianness involves in Trinidad. The singers, and the (specifically female) participants in the chutney dances, have been denounced by many in the East Indian community for what is termed their "vulgarity" and "obscenity." [46] Leaders of the commmunity have indicated that their objection has to do with the display in a public space of a cultural form that used to be confined to the home. The public sphere is

43. It is a measure of post-Independence racial polarization in Trinidadian political life that the two major parties, the PNM and the UNC, have come to be identified as the "African" and "Indian" parties, respectively.

44. Rohlehr, personal communication, St. Augustine, Trinidad, February 1994.

45. A 1993–94 controversy surrounded East Indian MP Hulsie Bhaggan, who became the target of political satire in the calypsos of the 1994 Carnival in Trinidad. In 1996, former Speaker of the Parliament Occah Seapaul, an East Indian woman, was the subject of some calypsos. Given the space constraints of this essay, I will not go into the details of these controversies.

46. Female East Indian singers and dancers, however, are not necessarily a new phenomenon. There appears to be a tradition of women who took part in public performances, such as Alice Jan in the early part of the twentieth century and Champa Devi in the 1940s. But their performances clearly did not evoke the kind of response that chutney-soca has obtained in the 1990s.

here considered to be an "African" realm, so the making public of chutney (and its Englishing) necessarily involves making it available to the gaze of Afro-Trinidadians. The disapproval of "vulgarity" can be read also as an anxiety regarding miscegenation, the new form of chutney becoming a metonym for the supposed increase in relationships between Indian women and African men.

The responses of East Indians to the public appearance of chutney have been diverse. "Chutney is breaking up homes and bringing disgrace," proclaimed a letter writer in the *Sunday Express*.[47] "Culture means refinement, and this is not culture," declared a participant in a seminar on the chutney phenomenon.[48] The Hindu Women's Organisation (HWO), a small but vocal urban group, demanded that the police intervene at chutney performances and enforce the law against vulgarity and obscenity. The "Indian secularist" position, however, was that chutney was "functional," that it represented "Indian cultural continuity and persistence." Social interaction between boys and girls in an "exclusively Indian environment" was only to be encouraged, argued the secularist. Not only was chutney an East Indian alternative to Carnival, but also it was a way of establishing "cultural unity with India."[49] Others accused the "Muslim producers" of some chutney festivals for using tunes from Hindu *bhajans,* an act they considered sacrilegious.[50] A few East Indian men expressed alarm at what they called the "creolization" or "douglarization" of "Indian culture," and alleged that African men were writing the songs for the chutney performers in such a way as to "denigrate" East Indian cultural values.[51] One letter writer who had attended the opening ceremony of the World Hindu Conference protested against "the lewd and suggestive behaviour of the female dancer" during the chutney part of the cultural program; "this standard of behaviour," he

47. Michael Ramkissoon, letter to the editor, *Sunday Express,* 16 December 1990, 46.
48. Musician Narsaloo Ramaya, quoted in news item, "Critics Rage over Chutney Wine," *Sunday Express,* 9 December 1990, 17.
49. Kamal Persad of the Indian Review Committee, Viewpoint Column, *Sunday Express,* 16 December 1990, 43. See also L. Siddhartha Orie, letter to the editor, *Trinidad Guardian,* 8 January 1991, 8.
50. Jagdeo Maharaj, letter to the editor, *Trinidad Guardian,* 30 July 1990, 9.
51. "Dougla" is the East Indian term for a person of mixed East Indian and African descent. It is derived from the Hindi word for bastard.

felt, could not be sanctioned by Hinduism, which he claimed had "high moral and spiritual values."[52]

While one writer contended that chutney represented a unique new *Trinidadian* cultural form,[53] yet another argued that it was self-deluding to think of chutney as creative or unique: "No creation whatsoever has taken place in chutney. The form and content have simply moved from the private domain to the public and from a female environment to a mixed one."[54] "Indianness" is seen in many of these responses to be inextricable from cultural purity, which in turn is seen to hinge on questions of female propriety and morality. In the global context of the reconfiguration of a "Hindu" identity, the chutney phenomenon is inserted by elite Trinidadian Indians into the process that disaggregates Hindus from other "Indians" while at the same time redescribing their space as inclusive of all that is Indian, as being identical with Indianness. Curiously enough, this formation of elite Trinidadian Indian identity today is facilitated not only by organizations such as the Vishwa Hindu Parishad but also by the "secular" Indian state, which intervenes in Trinidad in both the academic and cultural spheres.[55]

A news item in the *Trinidad Guardian* of 22 April 1991 reports the speech of Pundit Ramesh Tiwari, president of the Edinburgh Hindu Temple, who says that "the concept of the liberated woman" had created a "crisis in womanhood" threatening to the Hindu religion, which was "taking steps to reintroduce values to the Hindu woman." Indrani Rampersad, a leading figure in the HWO, writes that it is "Hindus" (and not

52. Kelvin Ramkissoon, "A Brand of Dancing not Associated with Hinduism," *Express*, 14 July 1992.

53. Baksh-Soodeen, "Power, Gender and Chutney," 70.

54. Indrani Rampersad of the Hindu Women's Organisation, "The Hindu Voice in Chutney," *Trinidad Guardian*, 25 December 1990, 10. Here I draw mainly on textual sources for East Indian views on chutney. These probably represent a range from lower- to upper-middle class. Most of my conversations with women and men from this class background indicate that these views are representative. My recent fieldwork (1997), however, suggests radically different attitudes toward chutney on the part of working-class women.

55. The government of India funds two professorships at the University of the West Indies, one in sociology and the other in Hindi. The Indian High Commission also has a Hindi professor to conduct language classes for Trinidadians. In addition, the High Commission helps bring exponents of classical "Indian culture" to Trinidad.

"Indians") who form the largest ethnic group in Trinidad. The HWO condemned chutney performances for their "vulgarity," claiming that "as a Hindu group the HWO is best placed to analyse the chutney phenomenon from such a [namely, Hindu] perspective, and as a women's group they are doubly so equipped." [56] The HWO, however, was not supported by some who otherwise shared their position on chutney-soca. East Indian academic and senator Ramesh Deosaran questioned, in another context, one of the objectives of the HWO, which was to "advance" the status of women. Deosaran took objection to the use of this word in a context of "increasing sexual freedom." [57] This freedom, Deosaran argued, had resulted in such things as the "intense gyrations" of chutney dancing, "a serious cause for concern by members of the Hindu and Indian community." Taking issue with this kind of position are some East Indian feminists who see chutney-soca as a positive development, symbolic of the attempts of women to overcome inequality in many spheres.[58]

The resemblance between the vocabulary of the anti-indenture campaign and that of the critics of chutney-soca may allow us to conclude rather misleadingly that what is asserting itself in both is "Indian patriarchy." This conclusion is misleading because elite nationalism in India in the early twentieth century and elite assertions of "Indian" ethnicity in late-twentieth-century Trinidad are phenomena somewhat different from each other. I have tried to demonstrate that although there is a historical connection between Indian nationalism and indentured labor in the British colonies, the analysis of contemporary Trinidadian discourses of East Indian women's sexuality has to be placed in the framework of the predominantly biracial society of the island. Indian tradition (and Indian women) in Trinidad come to be defined as that which is not, cannot be allowed to become, African. While the assertion of a separate and unchanging "Hindu" or "Indian" identity in Trinidad is enabled in part by the colonial and Indian nationalist reconstructions of ethnic and racial identities, reconstructions in which definitions of women and what is "proper" to them occupy a crucial position, it is today part of a Trinidadian reconstruction of such identities, a process

56. Rampersad, "The Hindu Voice in Chutney," 10.

57. The wording is that of reporter Deborah John of the *Express*, "Controversy Reigns," 23 October 1991.

58. See Baksh-Soodeen, "Power, Gender and Chutney," 7.

whose participants include both "Indians" and "Africans." And while the chutney-soca controversy could be read as marking an attempt to reconstitute East Indian patriarchy, perhaps it could also be read as a sign of patriarchy in crisis. The East Indian attempt to "resolve" the question of women can be seen as aligned with the effort to consolidate the meanings of cultural and racial identity at a time when the new political visibility of "Indians" is providing newer spaces for assertion for women as well as men. Both of these, however, are impossible projects, rendered impossible precisely because of the need to continually refigure the distinctions between the two groups, signified as "Indian" and "African," which share the postcolonial space of Trinidad.

This essay set out to look at the Trinidadian conjuncture of woman, modernity, and Indianness, attempting thereby to examine the formation of our own national-modern in India from an unfamiliar angle. This exercise may also yield, I hope, unexpected benefits for those intervening in issues of modernity and gender in Trinidad. The larger project for which this essay is an initial attempt to establish a conceptual framework and modes of investigation is likely to address, among others, these questions: what might be the implication of Indian women from India in Trinidadian debates, such as the one over chutney-soca? What supposed excesses are sought to be contained by this invocation? What would be the consequences of measuring Indo-Trinidadian women against the Indian national-modern? What specific histories are mobilized in the performance of female desire in chutney-soca singing and dancing? What does the singer's public display or acting out of desire make available for the female audience? How might analyzing the chutney-soca phenomenon help us look afresh at women's involvement in popular culture in India? How, indeed, may our contemporary critiques of the Indian national-modern benefit from its illegitimate and disavowed double, "Indian" modernity in the Caribbean?

Afro-Modernity: Temporality, Politics, and the African Diaspora

Michael Hanchard

People of African descent have often been depicted as the antithesis of Western modernity and modern subjectivity. There is an ample, if sometimes frustrating, literature written by both Western and non-Western scholars that attests, purposely or not, to this depiction. I am not interested, however, in adding to this vast heap of documentation in an effort to prove or disprove the absolute villainy of the West; nor am I preoccupied with displaying the unqualified humanity of people of African descent. This article seeks to respond to the following question: How and in what ways have African-descended peoples been modern subjects?

My interest in the relationship between the discourses, institutions, norms, and practices of modernity and people of African descent has been motivated by the belief that virtually all discussions and literatures pertaining to people of African descent, ranging from black nationalism to Pan-Africanism, to anticolonialism and civil rights, are undergirded by premises of and reactions to some notion or practice of modernity. Whether in the form of the nation-state or universal ideas about human rights, black nationalism, and racial as well as other modes of collective identity have invariably reacted against or innovated on discourses of modernity. Virtually all transnational black movements of the nineteenth and twentieth centuries have utilized ideas about racial selfhood and collective identity, capitalism and socialism, justice and democracy that emerged as the economic, political, normative, religious, and cultural consequences of the epoch in which they lived. Unlike the Middle Ages, wherein neither peasants nor serfs could use the language of Calvinist predetermination, divine right, natural law, or monarchy to upend conditions of inequality, the era of the Industrial,

French, and American Revolutions provided the conditions for the critique of their subordinated condition. Marx recognized a key paradox of the modern age in the formation of an industrial proletariat. The socio-economic and political conditions which would lead to its formation would also nurture the preconditions for its dissatisfaction with the very mode of production that brought it into being. Similarly, only under conditions of modernity could people defined as African utilize the very mechanisms of their subordination for their liberation.

African diaspora scholarship is dominated by two tendencies: the Herskovitzean model, which focuses on African residuals in culture and language, bodily and figurative arts;[1] and what I call the mobilizational model—studies that have focused on resistance, overt as well as veiled (song, dance, slave revolts, postemancipation rebellions, or civil rights movements). As John Thornton, Basil Davidson, and others have demonstrated, there has been a popular and academic tendency to diminish, deny, or neglect the impact that African peoples, practices, and civilizations have had on the West's development, as well as to forget the extent to which these populations have sought paths that have veered away from Western modernities even while being interlocked with them.[2] Both models invariably encompass the forces of technology and the Industrial Revolution, the Middle Passage, racial slavery, and colonial plunder as irrefutable evidence of Africa's contributions to the West.

These facets of Africa's and the African diaspora's history are certainly indispensable. Yet these are not the only categories of engagement that involve people of African descent and the West after the fifteenth century. Equally if not more important have been the means by which various African-descended populations and political actors consulted one another to devise political responses to their collective subordination. Thus, their reactions to slavery, racism, capitalism, and cultural imperialism should be seen as responding not to isolated institutions and practices but to a broader array of forces.

1. See Melville J. Herskovitz, *The New World Negro: Selected Papers in Afroamerican Studies,* ed. Frances Herskovitz (Bloomington: Indiana University Press, 1966).
2. See John K. Thornton, *Africa and Africans in the Making of the Atlantic World, 1400–1800* (Cambridge: Cambridge University Press, 1994) and Basil Davidson, *The Black Man's Burden: Africa and the Curse of the Nation-State* (New York: Times Books, 1992).

In his work on the political culture of the African diaspora, Paul Gilroy has argued that Afro-Modernism and the black Atlantic represents a counterculture of modernity.[3] Perhaps more than any other contemporary theorist, Gilroy has attempted to problematize the African diaspora's relationship to the West. Gilroy's theorizing begs even more fundamental questions about the nexus of the African diaspora and the West; if Afro-Modernism is a counterculture of modernity, as Gilroy suggests, is it merely an appendage of Western modernity and European modernism? Is its existence to be defined solely in terms of its critique of the West, or does its presence hint at one of several divergent paths of modernity?

What I shall call Afro-Modernity represents a particular understanding of modernity and modern subjectivity among people of African descent. At its broadest parameters, it consists of the selective incorporation of technologies, discourses, and institutions of the modern West within the cultural and political practices of African-derived peoples to create a form of relatively autonomous modernity distinct from its counterparts of Western Europe and North America. It is no mere mimicry of Western modernity but an innovation on its precepts, forces, and features. Its contours have arisen from the encounters between people of African descent and Western colonialism not only on the African continent but also in the New World, Asia, and ultimately Europe itself.

Marshall Berman has suggested that the world historical processes of modernism and modernization "have nourished an amazing variety of visions and ideas that aim to make men and women the subjects as well as the objects of modernization, to give them the power to change the world that is changing them, to make their way through the maelstrom and make it their own."[4] Dialectically, Afro-Modernity can be seen as the negation of the idea of African and African-derived peoples as the antithesis of modernity. Gilroy has suggested that "the cultures of diaspora blacks can be profitably interpreted as expressions of and com-

---

3. See Paul Gilroy, *The Black Atlantic: Modernity and Double Consciousness* (Cambridge: Harvard University Press, 1994).
4. Marshall Berman, *All That Is Solid Melts into Air: The Experience of Modernity* (New York: Penguin, 1982), 16.

mentaries upon ambivalences generated by modernity and their locations in it."[5]

Such expressions and commentary are more than responses to the Middle Passage and racial slavery. They are responses to the age and the technological, normative, and societal conditions that made the Middle Passage and racial slavery possible. Consequently, the responses of Afro-Modern subjects to their enslavement, servitude, and derogation helped constitute politics among people of African descent and their desire to render possible conditions that were qualitatively superior to those they found themselves in. As a self-conscious political and cultural project, Afro-Modernity is evidenced in the *normative convergence* of two or more African and African-descended peoples and social movements in response to perceived commonalities of oppression. Afro-Modern politics are characterized by (a) a supranational formulation of people of African descent as an "imagined community" that is not territorially demarcated but based on the shared belief in the commonalities of Western oppression experienced by African and African-derived peoples; (b) the development of alternative political and cultural networks across national-state boundaries; and (c) an explicit critique of the uneven application of the discourses of the Enlightenment and processes of modernization by the West, along with those discourses' attendant notions of sovereignty and citizenship.

Events and movements that exemplify the normative convergences of Afro-Modern politics include (but are not restricted to) Afro–New World activists involved in the abolitionist movement, the Universal Negro Improvement Association, the Friends of Abyssinia Movement (a response to the Italian invasion of Ethiopia), Caribbean independence movements, the antiapartheid movement, and, most recently, continental and diaspora critiques of the sustained authoritarian regimes of Kenya and Nigeria. In the absence of nation-state power and territorial sovereignty, Afro-Modern political actors have often utilized a combination of domestic and international institutions to redress situations of inequality for specific African-descended populations, much in the way that Jewish transnational political actors have operated on behalf of Jewish populations throughout the world.

5. Gilroy, *Black Atlantic*, 117.

As Gilroy has noted, Afro-diasporic consciousness grew out of the nation-state's neglects and exclusions, since "the African diaspora's consciousness of itself has been defined in and against constricting national boundaries."[6] The derogation of blackness, though varied from nation-state to nation-state, has been and remains global and transnational, making Afro-diasporic peoples' relation to the nation-state "contingent and partial."[7]

Partha Chatterjee claims that nationalist movements in Asia and Africa have been "posited not on an identity but rather on a *difference* with the 'modular' forms of the national society propagated by the modern West."[8] I would like to take up Gilroy's and Chatterjee's claims here, by noting that many forms of nationalism expressed by African-descended populations—be they the literal nationalisms of the African continent after World War II or the figurative nationalisms of black power movements in the United States or South Africa—contained within them a recognition of the nonterritorial character of their nationalist claims. The nonterritorial character of these nationalisms stemmed from the recognition that people of African descent in various parts of the world were stateless subjects. Thus, Ghanaian independence was not merely the instantiation of political sovereignty for Ghanaian nationalists—who desired an independent state—and would-be citizens, but a "political kingdom" for people of African descent the world over. Conversely, the Black Power movement in the United States was not solely preoccupied with the conditions of U.S. African Americans but people of African descent in Africa and the Caribbean. African and African-descended nationalisms have always had a transnational, interactive character.

The transnational linkages between African, Caribbean, and North American political actors bear great similarities with other transnational, nongovernmental and noncapitalist linkages of the first half of the twentieth century—anarchosyndicalism, communism, unionism, and other secular global movements. Afro-Modernity helps to under-

6. Paul Gilroy, *"There Ain't No Black in the Union Jack": The Cultural Politics of Race and Nation* (London: Hutchinson, 1987), 155.
7. Gilroy, *"There Ain't No Black in the Union Jack."*
8. Partha Chatterjee, *The Nation and Its Fragments: Colonial and Postcolonial Histories* (Princeton, N.J.: Princeton University Press), 5.

score what Jorge Castañeda refers to as "longitudinal nationalism"—the development of horizontal, non–state-based relationships between political actors in various nation-states for the purpose of challenging or overturning policies in one or more nation-states.[9] In its various incarnations, from national liberation and civil rights movements to artistic trends, Afro-Modernity has pushed egalitarian discourses of Western modernity to their limits by critiquing the selective access that people of African descent have had to cultural, political, and economic sovereignty.

I will highlight three features of Afro-Modern politics and consciousness, articulated across various African diaspora and African communities: first, the distinctive role of history in Afro-Modernity; second, that inequalities visited on African and African-descended populations have often been understood temporally, as impositions on human time; and third, that this temporal understanding of racial and colonial orders in turn affected ideas about freedom, progress, and racial solidarity, evidenced in various communities in the distinct epochs of racial slavery, freedom, and emancipation, and in the post–World War II period of civil rights, black nationalist, and anticolonial movements.

TEMPORALITY: BONDAGE AND BONDING

Intrinsic to Afro-Modern consciousness and politics is a concern for historical narrative. Historical narrative has served two broad aims: to project a history and to prove or acknowledge that the existence of people of African descent has been worthy of text. As Frank Kirkland brilliantly and cogently writes in his essay "Modernity and Intellectual Life in Black," black intellectuals in the postemancipation period in the United States could not sidestep or underplay the momentous impact of slavery on black subjects.[10] Kirkland writes: "Whereas modernity in the West fosters the belief that a future-oriented present, severed from any sense of an historical past, can yield culturally distinctive and progressive innovations, modernity in black promotes the conviction that a

9. Jorge G. Castañeda, *Utopia Unarmed: The Latin American Left after the Cold War* (New York: Knopf, 1993).
10. Frank Kirkland, "Modernity and Intellectual Life in Black," *Philosophical Forum* 24 (1992–93), 136–65.

future oriented present can be the fortunate occasion in which culturally distinctive innovations are historically redemptive of a sense of past."[11] Through working within ruminations on the nexus of the black race and Western modernity of U.S. African Americans like Alexander Crummell, W. E. B. Du Bois, and Booker T. Washington, Kirkland's insights encapsulate the broader speculative problematic for Afro-Modernity writ large.

As the following analysis attests, many Afro-Modern peoples have rebutted the denial or diminished location of African-descended peoples in Western historical narratives. Here, a distinction between tabula rasa (erased slate) and tabula blanca (blank slate) provides a critical juncture from which to assess differences between Afro-Modern versus Western discourses of modernity. For Greco-Roman city-states as well as the French Republic after the revolution of 1789, history began with the body politic, not before. Tabula rasa, therefore, was an act of metaphorical violence, erasing historical narratives that acknowledged the roles of prior actors and agents in history.

For African and African-descended peoples, however, the equation of their past with an erased slate would deprive them of both past and history. As a people, they would be shorn of human time, not to mention humanity. Thus, David Hume's likening of a multilingual African to a parrot, Hegel's assertions that Africa was without history, and Kant's claims about the constitutional inferiority of African peoples can be viewed as the exclusion of African and African-derived people from the human family, and, consequently, any possibility of civilizational continuity, connection, or impression.[12] Their legacies, in short, were never on the slate in the first place, for no descendent of their family was capable of such inscription. The blank slate remained to be written upon, and when it was, its narrative would be composed by Western powers, or at the every least, dictated by them.

11. Kirkland, "Modernity and Intellectual Life," 159.
12. David Hume, *Essays: Moral, Political, and Literary,* ed. T. H. Green and T. H. Grose (London, 1875), vol. 1, 252. Georg Wilhelm Friedrich Hegel, *The Philosophy of History* (New York: Dover, 1956); Kant's writings on the hierarchies of races, including *Observations on the Feeling of the Beautiful and the Sublime,* trans. John T. Goldthwait (Berkeley: University of California Press, 1960) and Kant's 1775 essay, "The Different Races," are analyzed by Charles W. Mills in *The Racial Contract* (Ithaca, N.Y.: Cornell University Press, 1997), 70.

How does one respond to the claim that one's people are without history? Like other marginalized peoples, this question provided at least two distinct possibilities for rebuttal and reply. If one accepted the notion that African history did indeed exist but was forgotten, obscured or erased, then one could, as Martin Delany, Henry Highland Garnet, Ganga Zumba, and Bouckman have done, narrate a history of Africa and its peoples in accordance with the logic of tabula rasa: grand civilizations of centuries past, one continent and ocean away, in Africa.[13]

Black intellectuals throughout the New World shared the impulse to reach back across the epochal boundary between slavery and emancipation and the geographical boundary between Africa and points westward. In locales as diverse and disparate as Kwame Nkrumah's Ghana and Eric Williams's Trinidad, and in many black consciousness and black nationalist projects in white-dominated societies in the post–World War II period, a reconstruction of the past was one of the first pedagogical projects undertaken by Afro-Modern activists and intellectuals. These efforts are not solely (though they are significantly) an attempt to provide some sense of continuity with previous generations of people in distinct times and places, whether in Africa or on a New World plantation but an attempt at giving some coherence to their present, continuous lives. In this more comparative sense, Kirkland's notion of a "future past" is replicable across African diaspora populations.[14] Whether it is Afro-Centrism or Quilombismo, Negritude or a New Negro, each ideology and its attendant ideological subsets has a project of historical recovery that at the same time presupposes a new or, at minimum, distinctive, collective consciousness for African and African-derived peoples in the face of a perceived erasure of history by the West.

At the same time, however, a blank slate offered a critical distance and break from Africa if one accepted the premise that African–New World peoples were, in the main, New World or even European peoples. Both understandings of the past, however, whether implicitly or explic-

13. See Martin Delany, *Official Report of the Niger Valley Exploring Party* (New York: T. Hamilton, 1861); Henry Highland Garnet, *The Past and Present Condition and Destiny of the Colored Race* (Miami, Fla.: Mnemosyne, 1969); Ganga Zumba was the first leader of the *quilombo,* or outlaw slave society, of Palmares, in northeast Brazil. Bouckman was one of the early leaders of the Haitian Revolution.
14. See Kirkland, *Modernity and Intellectual Life.*

itly, would have to acknowledge the temporal disjuncture imposed on African-descended subjects. Even if black thinkers could affirm their historicity—that is, affirm that their pasts, however horrible, were worth knowing and writing about—they had to acknowledge the displacements and deferrals that racial slavery and imperialism imposed on them.

This is why Hume's cryptic commentary has dual significance, for it implies that the only civilizational possibilities for people of African descent were reactive and imitative. The act of mimicry itself, its subversive and infrapolitical implications notwithstanding, entails a temporal disjuncture. In historical and civilizational terms, Africans in the aggregate could—at best—aspire to caricature. They could only mimic the aggregate European.[15]

Herein lies the temporal disjuncture for African and African-derived peoples in their relationship with the modern West: As African and African-derived peoples had to sophisticate themselves through their relation to Western ideals and civilizations, they had to do so only after the West had. They could either "catch up" with the West by assuming certain practices and behaviors, or forever look across a civilizational chasm, stricken with a constitutional, genetic inability to forge societies that the West would stare upon with awe. The temporal consequences of racial inequality were to be experienced and felt across African and Afro-diasporic contexts wherever a person defined by their phenotypic proximity to the indigenous peoples of sub-Saharan Africa inhabited the same territorial realm with whites.

TEMPORALITY: RACIAL TIME

From this vantage point, it should not be difficult to consider the politics of human time affecting these populations. Consequently, what I call racial time became one of the disjunctive temporalities of both Western and Afro-Modernity, beginning with the emergence of racial slavery. Racial time is defined as the inequalities of temporality that result from power relations between racially dominant and subordinate groups. Unequal relationships between dominant and subordinate groups produce unequal temporal access to institutions, goods, ser-

15. See Mills, *Racial Contract.*

vices, resources, power, and knowledge, which members of both groups recognize. When coupled with the distinct temporal modalities that relations of dominance and subordination produce, racial time has operated as a structural effect on the politics of racial difference.[16] Its effects can be seen in the daily interactions — grand and quotidian — in multi-racial societies. If we are to understand racial politics and inequality in non-phenotypic, non-essentialized terms, then we must attempt to comprehend the meanings of race against the canvas of space, time, and history.

Time, when linked to relations of dominance and subordination, is another social construct that marks inequality between various social groups.[17] In phenomenologically rooted considerations of time, Alfred Schutz and Thomas Luckman characterized "waiting" as a "time structure that is imposed upon us."[18] Life-worlds, social being, and time as explicated by Henri Bergson, Schutz and Luckman, Martin Heidegger, and Emmanuel Levinas illuminate themes of otherness and temporality.[19]

16. My use of the term *structural effect* is derived from Timothy Mitchell's explication of the analytic distinctions between the state and civil society as a means of highlighting the difficulties in identifying the state as a concrete material entity. Mitchell suggests that a "boundary problem" exists in most accounts of the relationship between state and civil society, due to the absence of a neat distinction between state and civil society in real life. The effects of the state's activities can be seen and felt in civil society without the actual presence of the state itself. In this sense, the state has material effects without itself being material. See Timothy Mitchell, "The Limits of the State: Beyond Statist Approaches and their Critics," *American Political Science Review* 85 (1991): 77–96. By way of analogy, I would like to suggest that "race" or, more precisely, "racial difference" operates in a similar manner, as a structural effect on individual and group interaction. As a dynamic process, racial difference operates as an interpretive scheme in social, political, and cultural life. It serves to mediate the relationship between social structures and is neither a reified, static element of daily life nor a mere social construction that one can wish away merely by identifying its socially constructed nature.

17. Johannes Fabian, *Time and the Other: How Anthropology Makes its Object* (New York: Columbia University Press, 1983).

18. Alfred Schutz and Thomas Luckman, *The Structures of the Life-World*, trans. Richard M. Zaner and H. Tristam Engelhardt Jr. (Evanston, Ill.: Northwestern University Press, 1973).

19. Henri Bergson, *Time and Free Will*, trans. F. L. Pogson (New York: S. Sonnenschein, 1910); Schutz and Luckman, *Structures of the Life-World;* Martin Heideg-

From the beginning of their introduction to the New World, various populations of people of African descent were involved in struggles with slaveowners over their relative autonomy within the confines of slavery. For slaves, time management was an imposition of the slave master's construction of temporality divided along the axis of the master-slave relationship. This became increasingly apparent by the nineteenth century and is crucial for understanding what sorts of constraints slaves operated under within the "peculiar institution":

> The work extracted from slaves by their owner's occupied most of the slave's laboring time and thus inescapably circumscribed the lives of enslaved people. From the calories they expended to the music they played, no aspect of their lives was untouched by their work regimen—its physical and psychological demands, its organization, its seasonal rhythms, and its numerous divisions by skill, age and sex. Indeed, labor was so inseparable from life that, for most slaves, the two appeared to be one and the same.[20]

Students of both wage and slave labor in social history have analyzed time in relation to work levels—quality versus quantity of production.[21] With neither the structure of relationships that obtained between serfs and lords under feudalism nor that which held between labor and capital under capitalism, slaves could only struggle for the appropriation of time, such as the relative freedom to tend gardens on Saturdays or to shop independently at Sunday markets. Resistance to forced labor and time could be seen in work slowdowns, for example, by African–New World slaves. Tensions and social struggles arising from slave interactions with masters and whites in general, along with the resentments, anger, and fears associated with their interactions, became the sources

ger, *Being and Time,* trans. John Macquarrie and Edward Robinson (New York: Harper, 1962); Emmanuel Levinas, *Time and the Other and Additional Essays,* trans. Richard A. Cohen (Pittsburgh, Pa.: Duquesne University Press, 1987).

20. Ira Berlin and Philip D. Morgan, introduction to *Cultivation and Culture: Labor and the Shaping of Slave Life in the Americas* (Charlottesville: University Press of Virginia, 1993), 2.

21. See Eugene Genovese, *Roll Jordan Roll: The World the Slaves Made* (New York: Vintage, 1976); also Herbert G. Gutman, *The Black Family in Slavery and Freedom, 1750–1925* (New York: Vintage, 1976).

for collective consciousness and, ultimately, strategies for organized and individuated resistance.

"Free time" — or, rather, slave time that was not accounted for in slave labor — could and did have political consequences. After the Haitian Revolution (1791–1804), the control of slave time (both work and leisure) became a primary concern of slave owners throughout the New World. In the Caribbean, passes were issued to control movement of slaves. One slave owner in the U.S. South, for example, remarked: "I have ever maintained the doctrine that my negroes have no time whatever; that they are always liable to my call without questioning for a moment the propriety of it; and I adhere to this on the grounds of expediency and right." [22]

One glimpse of the desire for a new time for former slaves can be found in the observations of a Boston emissary who was sent to Orangeburg, South Carolina, to analyze political and economic conditions for cotton manufacturers in 1865, the year of slave emancipation in the United States:

> The sole ambition of the freedman . . . appears to be to become the owner of a little piece of land, there to erect a humble home, and to dwell in peace and security at his own free will, and pleasure. If he wishes, to cultivate the ground in cotton on his own account, to be able to do so without anyone to dictate to him hours or system of labor, if he wishes instead to plant corn or sorghum or sweet potatoes — to be able to do *that* free from any outside control, in one word to be *free*, to control his own time and efforts without anything that can remind him of his past sufferings in bondage. This is their idea, their desire and their hope.[23]

Former slaves, who recognized the direct correlation between their collective misery and white wealth, occupied the earthbound seat on the seesaw of modernity; their crouched weight enabled their masters to remain aloft. For them, emancipation, the rise of industrialization,

22. Quoted in Michael J. Mullin, *Africa in America: Slave Acculturation and Resistance in the American South and the British Caribbean, 1736–1831* (Urbana: University of Illinois Press, 1992), 119.
23. Quoted in Eric Foner, "The Meaning of Freedom in the Age of Emancipation," *The Journal of American History* (September 1994): 459.

sharecropping, tenant farming, and wage labor meant that one had to distinguish emancipation from sovereignty.

Temporal freedom meant not only an abolition of the temporal constraints slave labor placed on New World Africans but also the freedom to construct individual and collective temporality that existed autonomously from (albeit contemporaneously with) the temporality of their former masters. Thus, ensuing struggles between former slaves and their former masters produced what I shall call the second phase of racial time, beginning with the postemancipation period. Using E. P. Thompson's interpretation of the politics of labor time in English working-class formation, Philip S. Foner and David R. Roediger argue that the temporal politics of U.S. labor in the nineteenth century became one of the few common rallying points for workers of different skill and intraclass positions, distinct genders and races.[24] While they provide ample evidence of the verity of this assertion, less attention is paid to the manner in which various groups within working-class formations in the United States came to appreciate the temporal distinctiveness of their positions. Foner and Roediger persuasively argue that temporal politics encompassed ideas about freedom and citizenship, but a key distinction between the temporal politics involving labor and capital on the one hand and slaves and slave owners on the other is that while the former involved the politics of labor power under capitalism the latter was rooted in *total* labor. Theoretically, no time belonged solely to the slave. In order to radically transform the temporal inequities of their circumstances, slaves would have had to transform the mode of production and their position within it and would have had to transform themselves racially, an impossibility for the overwhelming majority of those considered black. Thus, racial time was a more "total" imposition of a dominant temporality than an abstract, acultural labor time.

There are three conceptual facets to racial time that can be used to analyze the unequal temporal dimensions of racial dynamics. Waiting, the first conceptualization, pertains to the first effect of the temporal disjunctures that result from racial difference. Members from subordi-

24. See Philip S. Foner and David R. Roediger, *Our Own Time: A History of American Labor and the Working Day* (New York: Verso, 1989).

nate groups objectively perceive the material consequences of social inequality, as they are literally made to wait for goods and services that are delivered first to members of the dominant group.

Time appropriation is the second conceptual innovation. It refers to the actual instance of social movement when group members who constitute a collective social formation decide to intervene in public debate for the purpose of affecting positive change in their overall position and location in society. For Afro-diasporic peoples, this has meant efforts to eradicate the chasm of racial time, not only in the nation-states where they reside but also in the nation-states where members of their epistemological community reside. While time seizure or appropriation operates on both collective and individual levels, it is collective action, I would argue, that often emboldens individuals to appropriate the time of a dominant racial subject and its related institutions for themselves. Time appropriation in racial politics mostly occurs during periods of social upheaval and transformation, whether locally, nationally, or transnationally. Sometimes starting in relative isolation, as in the Montgomery bus boycott, time appropriations can launch a series of events, propelling a single act into a series of acts, within the same location or well beyond its geographical realm.

The third conceptualization is concerned with the ethicopolitical relationship between temporality and notions of human progress. The belief that the future should or must be an improvement on the present is the underlying presumption of this idea, but it is also a notion with religious undertones. Millenarian movements, for example, contain ideas of "the last time" or a new time, either of which is the consequence of the encounter and arrival of God. Eschatological renderings of racial time can be found throughout the African diaspora, from the Voudoun of Boukman in the Haitian insurrection, to John Brown's and Nat Turner's invocations of a vengeful God who wreaks havoc on sinful whites, to James Baldwin's *The Fire Next Time:* The supernatural is summoned to leaven white privilege on earth, obliterating a temporality where evil in the form of racial prejudice, violence, and annihilation predominates. Religion provides the language for impending confrontation, but the spaces for confrontation were and are plantation societies, tenements, cities, rural areas, and nations — in short, any site where racial prejudice, socioeconomic exploitation, and violence are combined.

The term *New Negro* is invariably associated with the Harlem Renaissance and notions of cultural uplift proffered by Alain Locke and other black artists and intellectuals of 1920s Harlem.[25] The term *New Negro*, however, predates the Harlem Renaissance and was used by many African American communities outside of the United States. The very genealogy of the term is an instructive guide to how African-descended populations infused previously negative terms with newly transformed meanings. According to Michael J. Mullin, the term was first used by slaveowners in the seventeenth and eighteenth centuries to characterize enslaved Africans who required "seasoning"—acculturation in the linguistic, social, and laboring practices of their New World existence.[26] In parts of the Caribbean, New Negroes were assigned already "seasoned" slaves from their region or ethnicity to enable these new slaves to make the transition more rapidly and smoothly.

Afro-Cuban and Afro-Brazilian populations used *New Negro* to characterize their own postemancipation eras. In 1904, eighteen years after the abolition of slavery in Cuba, an Afro-Cuban civil rights activist created *El Nuevo Criollo* (New Creole in English), a newspaper devoted to the dismantling of myths of racial equality and ideologies of racial discrimination in Cuba. It is important to note that in the Cuban context, *creole* was meant to apply to first-generation whites born in the New World. Thus *El Nuevo Criollo* had a double meaning and was a variation on the theme of the New Negro: first as the new Cuban, second as the *gente de color* (black and mulatto) who sought to make the term *criollo* or *creole* encompass blacks and mulattos.[27]

A similar process of racial consciousness and recognition was occurring in Brazil, where an Afro-Brazilian vanguard emerged in the 1920s in São Paulo. They too would use the term *gente de color* to characterize blacks and mulattos as members of the same race (class was used interchangeably here). Like other Afro-diasporic communities in the New

25. See Henry Louis Gates, Jr., "The Trope of the New Negro and the Reconstruction of the Image of the Black," *Representations* 24 (1988): 129–155.
26. See Mullin, *Africa in America*.
27. See Aline Helg, *Our Rightful Share: The Afro-Cuban Struggle for Equality, 1886–1912* (Chapel Hill: University of North Carolina Press, 1995).

World, this vanguard viewed racial uplift as their principal responsibility. Little more than one generation removed from slavery, activists like Jose Correia Leite saw these and other tasks related to racial uplift as symptomatic of their epoch and phase of national/historical development: "The hearts of all sensible blacks have felt the sweetness of a new gentleness, as part of our compassionate temperament, when the rise of a new route [*rota despontar*] appears, guiding the successful fertile seeds that we have implanted within the breast of the race for the formation of our united front; for the rising of our column of resistance, securing the smiling, rising generation that comes in the future."[28] The rich, gendered symbolism of this passage conveys the hope of racial uplift and progress for Afro-Brazilians, with a clearly delineated understanding of the role of a black elite in making collective advances that would secure an improved future for the next generation of Afro-Brazilians.

Literate, possessed of some formal education, skilled or semiskilled in their professional occupations, the black elite were primed to exploit the meager resources and opportunities available to them for individual and collective advancement. The Afro-diasporic intelligentsia of the postemancipation period shared the presumption that they represented the vanguard — not necessarily the avant-garde — of their respective populations. In many ways, the U.S. African American W. E. B. Du Bois's concept of the "Talented Tenth," had its corollary in several African American populations.[29] Furthermore, they shared an abiding belief in the ability of black intelligentsia and ultimately, the "less talented" members of these communities to participate in and benefit from capitalist industrial development, mass communications, and modern technology.

These New Negroes, from Colombia to Cuba to the United States and Canada, were also conflicted about their relationship to their own cultural practices. While there is much literature celebrating the role of spirituals and "folk" practices and remedies in slave communities, the New Negro's evidenced discomfort with forms of behavior that could have been — and often were — negatively associated with slavery

28. Jose Correia Leite, "O Clarim d'Alvorada," in . . . *E Disse O Velho Militante Jose Correia Leite,* ed. Cuti (São Paulo: Secretaria Municipal de Cultura, 1992), 223–24 (my translation).

29. See W. E. B. Du Bois, *The Souls of Black Folk* (New York: Knopf, 1993).

by white and black alike would become the basis for a key dilemma of black aesthetics and cultural production throughout the diaspora.

Befitting their generation, the most significant leadership among African American elite of the late nineteenth and early twentieth centuries were journalists, writers, or those otherwise involved in mass communications and mass transport. Du Bois and Jose do Patroncino of Brazil were both journalists. Marcus Garvey was a printer by trade and training, a vocation that would be put to use in various newspaper and publishing ventures. In this sense, the invention of movable type had enormous consequences for former slaves who were among the last participants in the making of the modern world to be allowed to read and write in a dominant language.

Alain Locke and Garvey, like Martin Delany and Alexander Crummell before them, understood "the Negro condition" as a transnational phenomenon. Racism within the confines of the nation-state was a constitutive, rather than a secondary feature of national identity, Benedict Anderson's claims notwithstanding.[30] Alain Locke, who understood this, wrote that "as with the Jew, persecution is making the negro international."[31] These sentiments were echoed in other parts of the New World. In *Prevision,* another Afro-Cuban newspaper, founded in the first decade of the century, an Afro-Cuban activist for political independence wrote in 1928, "Let us make a circle, reconcentrate in it, and gather our race in its center. Let us make a stoic, strong, absorbing race; let us imitate the Jewish people, they are self-sufficient. . . . *Black comes before everything.*"[32]

Social and political movements toward national emancipation, in the cases of Haiti and Cuba, or toward racial equality, in the cases of Jamaica and the United States, were infused with the recognition of racial time and a desire for a new epoch for people of African descent. A new time for former slaves throughout the New World was emergent but contingent and highly precarious. In the United States, negative Southern reaction to black advances of Reconstruction (1865–77) led to disen-

30. Benedict Anderson, *Imagined Communities: Reflections on the Origin and Spread of Nationalism,* rev. ed. (London: Verso, 1991).

31. Alain Locke, ed., *The New Negro* (New York: Atheneum, 1992).

32. Juan Leon y Pimentel, "Adelante Prevision," *Prevision,* 15 September 1908, quoted in Helg, *Our Rightful Share,* 151.

franchisement and renewed racial terror.[33] In other parts of the New World, Western ideals of nation-statehood, civil society, and individual citizenship culminated in national independence for most colonies of the hemisphere by 1820. This process was complicated by other legacies of scientific racism, which would serve to resubordinate freemen and women after emancipation in newly minted Latin American polities.

It was a new time nonetheless, one that required an orientation toward the future and a rupture with the past. In this sense, the predicament of former slaves can be seen as the empirical referent for Jürgen Habermas's observation that claimants of modernity refuse to take "their orientation from the models supplied by another epoch." [34] In fact, the preoccupation of much of the vanguard of postemancipation periods in Brazil, Haiti, the United States, Cuba, and many other New World nations with African American populations was to rid themselves and their communities of any vestiges of enslavement, not only in collective memory but also in behavior and daily habits.

By the twentieth century in the United States, the term *New Negro* came to be associated with postemancipation Negroes who were bearers of new knowledge, values, and behaviors. Locke suggested that the New Negro's mission should be understood in two senses: as "the advance guard of the African peoples in their contact with twentieth-century civilization" and as "a mission of rehabilitating the race in world esteem from the loss of prestige for which the fate and conditions of slavery have been so largely responsible." [35]

AFRO-MODERNITY, MOTHER AFRICA: RACIAL TIME IN GHANA

The New Negro's calls for transnational solidarity were heard and acted on in Africa, further complicating the temporalities of Afro-Modernity. The emergence in 1957 of the first African country to achieve independence in the postwar period, the independent nation-state of

33. See W. E. B. Du Bois, *Black Reconstruction: An Essay Toward a History of the Part Which Black Folk Played in the Attempt to Reconstruct Democracy in America, 1860–1880* (New York: Atheneum, 1992).

34. Jürgen Habermas, *The Philosophical Discourses of Modernity: Twelve Lectures,* trans. Frederick Lawrence (Cambridge, Mass.: MIT Press, 1987), 7.

35. Locke, *The New Negro,* 14.

Ghana, and its first president, Kwame Nkrumah—two motivating forces behind Pan-Africanism—typified the transnational, anticolonial solidarity of the period.

The forces that would bring about independence, however, began much earlier, via the intersection of anticolonial struggle, Afro-diasporic politics, and the political evolution of Nkrumah. Like many aspiring African leaders, Nkrumah traveled abroad for his education, leaving Ghana to study at the all-black Lincoln University in Pennsylvania in 1935. This was in keeping with the crucial role historically black colleges such as Lincoln and Howard Universities played in educating a U.S. African American elite along with emergent political and cultural figures from the Caribbean and Africa.

Subsequently, Nkrumah traveled to London, where he was tutored by George Padmore, founder of the African News Bureau and mentor, with his childhood friend, C. L. R. James, to numerous African and Asian intellectuals who would become prominent in the emergence of Third World politics by the 1950s. Nkrumah returned to Ghana in the 1940s to become active in nationalist politics. In 1948, he was imprisoned, along with other nationalist leaders, for his activities in the United Gold Coast Convention (UGCC), which called for greater political autonomy from Britain. In that same year he founded the *Daily Mail,* a nationalist newspaper. He would later renounce his affiliation with the UGCC because of its lack of a popular base. Along with Komla Agbeli Gbedemah, Nkrumah helped form the Convention People's Party, an ambiguous mix of lower-middle-class, peasant, and working-class people, in 1951. Once again jailed in 1951 by colonial authorities for political agitation, Nkrumah became the party's leader from his jail cell, winning a parliamentary post in Accra, the nation's capital.

After achieving self-government in 1952, the republic of Ghana under Nkrumah's leadership became a matrix for Pan-Africanism. Nkrumah attempted to build a transnational Pan-African unity and relied on the political advice of people like Padmore, Du Bois and James.[36] Du Bois, Padmore, Alphaeus Hunton, Ras Makkonnen, and other Afro-diasporic

36. See C. L. R. James, *At the Rendezvous of Victory: Selected Writings* (London: Allison and Busby, 1984); Cedric Robinson, *Black Marxism: The Making of the Black Radical Tradition* (London: Zed Press, 1983); Manning Marable, *African and Caribbean Politics: From Kwame Nkrumah to Maurice Bishop* (London: Verso, 1987).

scholars passed through Ghana during this phase, providing strategic, technical, and other forms of support to the regime. Nkrumah, similarly, provided counsel to numerous African, Caribbean, and U.S. African American leaders.

In *Black Power*, Richard Wright's reflections on Ghana and Nkrumah in the heady days of independence, the U.S. African American expatriate found himself serving as a symbol of temporal disjuncture in an exchange with a British bank clerk in Accra.[37] After inquiring about Wright's opinion of Ghana on the eve of its independence, the clerk offered this almost fraternal, conspiratorial assertion: "You American chaps are three hundred years ahead of these Africans. It'll take a long time for them to catch up with you. I think that they are trying to go too fast, don't *you*? You see, you American chaps are used to living in a white man's country, and these fellows are not."[38] The banker's observations locate Wright's black identity under the rubric of American while placing him at a level of civilizational development superior to that of the African. The fact that the disparity is articulated in temporal terms shows one way in which the equation time = progress shaped the banker's thinking about the differences between Africans and U.S. African Americans. Instructive in their absence are the institutions and artifacts of modernity and modernization which Africans were presumably without. Thus, without engagement and familiarity with "the white man's country" Africans lived in a sort of empty time, one without a parallel Western history, which would require three hundred years to redress. But the years themselves would not redress their alleged underdevelopment; rather, it was the march toward technological, institutional, and normative sophistication, a sophistication which Wright himself concurred was needed to raise levels of national and continental accomplishment in Africa to those of Europe or North America.

Nkrumah, like other African vanguardist leaders of the era, struggled with the glaring inequalities in Ghanaian and African life that fell disproportionately on the shoulders of indigenous African peoples. Even under the constraints of limited political autonomy, Nkrumah saw through the veneer of a common fate and destiny for colonizer and

37. Richard Wright, *Black Power, a Record of Reactions in a Land of Pathos* (New York: Harper, 1954).
38. Wright, *Black Power*, 138.

colonized, to the direct linkages between European enrichment, African impoverishment, and the exploitation of African-derived peoples in other parts of the world. In characterizing the various forms of educational inequalities suffered by Ghanaian and other African peoples in 1951, Nkrumah provided the following overview of the confrontation between Convention Peoples Party (CPP) nationalists and colonial administrators in that year:

> When we confronted the colonial administration with this appalling situation on taking office at the beginning of 1951, they told us that the budget was limited and time was needed. Time, they said, was required to train the army of teachers needed for the education of all the children. They did not look very happy when we pointed out that they seemed to have time enough to allow the traders and shippers and mining companies to amass huge fortunes. As for the budget, we made the point that it did not seem improbable to use part of those fortunes to educate the children of the land from which they had been drawn.[39]

Nkrumah understood the temporal dimensions of inequality in his national experience. Time was the process through which British racism and imperialism moved in Ghana. These forces structured time to move more quickly for the extraction of capital, resources, and surplus value by the colonizers but less so for the educational development of Ghanaian children and the training of their teachers, or for the use of some of those extracted resources for positive national development.

Annihilating this temporal discrepancy would mean the annihilation of colonial underdevelopment itself, leading perhaps, to what Homi Bhabha has referred to as postcolonial time.[40] This discrepancy was recognized by African nationalists throughout the continent as the path toward unequal development, self-hatred, and dim esteem. What was required was an altering of the extant historical path toward a new time.

39. Kwame Nkrumah, *Africa Must Unite* (New York: International Publishers, 1970), 47.
40. Homi K. Bhabha, ed., *Nation and Narration* (London: Routledge, 1990).

In the United States, the inequalities and injustices of blacks had their own temporality. To be black in the United States meant that one had to wait for nearly everything. Legalized segregation, the maintenance of separate and largely unequal institutions, meant that blacks, as a consequence of prejudicial treatment, received health care, education, police protection, transportation, and a host of other services only *after* those same services were provided for whites. Above all, legalized apartheid in the United States represented an imposed disjunctive time structure within which U.S. African Americans were made to live.

On segregated public buses (such as the one ridden by Rosa Parks in Montgomery, Alabama, in 1955) standing black passengers were forced to wait for available seats in the black section, even if seats in the white section were available. In the era of legally segregated schools, it was common practice for black schools to receive teaching implements only after they had been used by white students in white schools. The following excerpt from an interview with Margaret Wright, a black Mississippian who attended segregated schools from the late 1950s to the late 1960s in the town of Hattiesburg, graphically illustrates the temporality of racial inequality under segregation:

> There was a cultural lag as far as receiving textbooks that white students used, about five years. It was a policy of the state that you could not order new books for 10 years. This put us (blacks) about 15 years behind the times in terms of textbook information. Teachers had a harder job because of this. They had to introduce more contemporary discussions because of this. By the time we got the books the information was outmoded and irrelevant. Three or four students' names would be in the book before we got them. By the time we received the books they were in either fair or poor condition, with the names crossed out and the previous condition of the book, "Good" or "Excellent," crossed out as well. Sometimes we would know the white children who owned the books previously, or we knew of them. We might have known someone who worked for them.[41]

Wright's reflections on her early years in segregated secondary schools encapsulates racial time for U.S. African Americans during this

41. Margaret Wright, interview by author, Cambridge, Mass., 6 July 1995.

epoch of "separate but equal." In this sense, what she characterizes as a "cultural lag" encompasses the temporal disjunctures of racial inequality. State government both structures and maintains the unequal and temporally distinct distribution of resources which, in turn, are given symbolic and human form through the mediated interaction between students and teachers of both races via used textbooks.

This procession of unequal transmission of data between whites and blacks represents what can be characterized as an institutionalized temporal disjuncture. Black students were low on the foodchain of disseminated information, and they received certain information only after it had been consumed and discarded by white students. It also suggested to black students that they did not deserve the education and information of their era — that the most up-to-date materials and training were not meant for them. Ideals of and aspirations toward racial equality could be juxtaposed by civil rights activists against the realities of anachronistic or obsolete goods, services, and even norms that were accepted by black communities because those communities had little or no choice.

Thus for blacks, waiting has encompassed the sense of human vitality that is harnessed because of racial time, the imposition of a time-structure that varies according to race. In *Why We Can't Wait*, Martin Luther King Jr. captures the frustration waiting produced among blacks and forcefully argues for the withdrawal of imposed time. Calling the movement of nonviolence the Revolution, King noted: "It is important to understand, first of all, that the Revolution is not indicative of a sudden loss of patience within the Negro. The Negro had never really been patient in the pure sense of the word. The posture of silent waiting was forced upon him psychologically because he was shackled physically." [42] In response, King argued that the movement sought to counteract the "go it slow approach" of many white liberals, who believed the Negro to be moving too fast: "We can, of course, try to *temporize,* negotiate small, inadequate changes and prolong the timetable of freedom in the hope that the narcotics of delay will dull the pain of progress. We can try, but we shall certainly fail. The shape of the world will not permit the luxury of gradualism and procrastination. Not only is it immoral. It will not

42. Martin Luther King, Jr., *Why We Can't Wait* (New York: Harper and Row, 1963), 25.

work."[43] Here, we glimpse Paul Virilio's synthesis of speed and politics, as the struggle for black civil rights can be conceived of as a movement to reduce waiting, to explode the differentials of human time.[44] Incrementalism was slow, therefore conservative. Acceleration of racial equality was temporally and politically emancipating and thereby good for the "race." In ameliorating the conditions that structured inequalities, time can be redirected toward the maximization of life-worlds. Schutz's phenomenology of time is again useful, as he distinguishes world-time— the time which transcends the life of an individual—from the life-world of individuals.

It could be said that the recognition by U.S. African Americans of the disparity of racialized time conveys the tension among the life-world of black people, whites, and world-time (the time which exists *after* individual lives have expired). Interestingly, even in his proposal for a Bill of Rights for the Disadvantaged, King posited that like veterans of the armed forces, blacks should be compensated for time lost.[45]

In this sense, racial and civil equality also meant the annihilation of racialized time. Thus, racialized time can be viewed as a negation of productive life. Blacks would no longer have to worry about hiding their ambitions, appearing as if they sought to move too fast in the world of whites. After all, waiting also denotes taking one's cues from somewhere or someone other than oneself; the end of waiting meant the beginning of a more autonomous existence.

With this obliteration of racialized time, the perception of temporality shifted from an axis of inequality to a potential era of racial equality. Again, emphasizing the political and social dimensions of time construction, memories of the period before inequality remind subaltern activists of the conditions they endured and the period in their lives that they do not want to return to.

Like Nkrumah, King understood the temporal dimensions of inequality. Though much maligned for its analytic—as opposed to its analogical—limitations, the parallels between colonialism in the Third World and racial oppression in the United States converge on the roles of violence and temporality. Violence, meted out by the state and by

43. King, Jr., *Why We Can't Wait*, 141.
44. Paul Virilio, *Speed and Politics* (New York: Semio(Text), 1977).
45. King, Jr., *Why We Can't Wait*, 150.

those whom the state vests with qualitatively superior citizenship, structures the process of temporal inequality. In both the colonial and postcolonial contexts, racial difference was the premise for maintaining inequality between U.S. whites and blacks, as well as between Africans and Europeans. Through a reversal of the predominant "race-centered" approaches, one can discern the "race" of subordinate subjects through their daily activities and institutionalized denials and not, as is commonly the interpretive scheme, through phenotype. The experiential knowledge of human time that is peculiar to certain groups in given situations is the actual basis of collective consciousness—whether of race, nationality, gender, or other forms of conscious collective activity.

Intellectuals of civil rights and black nationalist tendencies in the 1960s articulated this sense of *time appropriation,* seizing another's time and making it one's own. Bobby Seale's exhortation to "seize the time" affirms the need to appropriate a new temporality, wherein new values, freedoms, and forms of expression are operative.[46] Yet because struggles toward moments of equality are essentially power relations, the new era of equality is not something one can merely assume exists, and, as a result, "naturally" flow into. Seale does not want to halt the march of history, but to grasp it, seize it, and transform it for one's own use, an act which previously had been denied within the old time.

Time as ethical progress is contained in King's characterization of the delay, procrastination, and temporizing of racial equality in the United States as immoral and his equation of incrementalism with inconsequential change and conservatism.[47] Within the context of the United States, new time consisted of egalitarian relations between blacks and whites. The more powerful the imposition of one group's conception of time on another, the more a subordinate group will be forced to measure its hopes and aspirations against what is generally considered to be humanly possible within the context of their social and political circumstances. For critics of imposed time, there is the recognition of temporal distinctions between dominant and subordinate groups. For activists of subaltern groups, the question "What should we be doing with our time?" emerges from this recognition. In turn, activists

46. Bobby Seale, *Seize the Time: The Story of the Black Panther Party and Huey P. Newton* (New York: Random House, 1970).
47. King Jr., *Why We Can't Wait.*

spend part or all of their lives responding to this question in both word and deed.

CONCLUSION

The commentary, speeches, and social practices analyzed here provide glimpses of the temporal politics of racial inequality within the African diaspora and on the African continent itself. The transnational forms of political organization and community activism among Afrodiasporic peoples is a form of imagined community, in the sense in which Anderson conceptualizes this term but with two important qualifications.[48]

First, the glimpses of Afro-Modern politics provided here suggest that African and African-descended populations considered themselves part of a transnational "imagined community" but not premised on the territorial rudiments Anderson attributes to creole nationalism. Rather, their understanding of community had a distinct episteme, rooted as it was in a more epistemological, temporal sense of community.

Second, contrary to Anderson's claims that racism is merely the vehicle through which national chauvinism is expressed and implemented, the political histories of the African diaspora expose the role that racism has played as a constitutive — not an epiphenomenal — feature of national identity. This counterargument is in keeping with the work of Anthony Smith, Tom Nairn, and Ernest Gellner, whose research into the relationships between race, state, and nation have underscored how race and/or ethnicity have functioned as a foundational — though mythical — element of national identity.[49]

Like the movement of capital within the international political economy, Afro-Modern politics has treated national-state boundaries and territorial sovereignty as secondary considerations of their imagined community. Afro-Modernity is at once a part of and apart from the parameters of Western modernities. It has had its own rhythm, flux and

48. See Anderson, *Imagined Communities*.
49. Anthony Smith, *The Ethnic Origins of Nations* (Oxford: Oxford University Press, 1986); Tom Nairn, *The Breakup of Britain: Crisis and Neo-nationalism* (London: New Left Books, 1977); Ernest Gellner, *Nations and Nationalism* (Ithaca, N.Y.: Cornell University Press, 1983).

reflux, advances and setbacks—in the words of Langston Hughes, its dreams deferred. In conclusion, I have tried to suggest that the encounters between people of African descent and the West encompass questions of space, temporality, and modernity in addition to questions of slavery and culture. These encounters remind us, I believe, that there are many vantage points from which one can view and experience this thing known as modernity: as nightmare or utopia; as horrible past or future present. These contrasting views caution us against modernity's reification and implore us to view modernity as a process of lived experience, with winners and losers, as well as strivings for redemption, recovery, retribution, and revolution, each experience tumbling into another and becoming—dare I say—history.

Modes of Citizenship in Mexico

Claudio Lomnitz

One of the first cultural accounts of citizenship in Latin America was Roberto da Matta's (1979) effort to understand the specificity of Brazilian national culture. Da Matta identified the coexistence of two broad discourses in Brazilian urban society, calling them the discourse of the home and the discourse of the street.[1] He described "of the home" discourse as a hierarchical and familial register, where the subjects are "persons" in the Maussian sense—that is, they assume specific, differentiated, and complementary social roles. The discourse "of the street," by contrast, is the discourse of liberal citizenship: Subjects are individuals who are meant to be equal to one another and equal before the law.

The interesting twist in da Matta's analysis regards the relationship between these two discourses, a relationship that he synthesizes with the Brazilian adage that says "for my friends, everything; for my enemies, the law."[2] For da Matta, Brazilian society can be described as having

I am grateful to Carlos Forment for his help with sources on nineteenth-century patriotic speeches. I also wish to thank the students in my History of the Public Sphere in Latin America seminar at the University of Chicago, where I developed this essay, and Dilip Gaonkar for his encouragement.

1. Roberto da Matta, *Carnivals, Rogues and Heroes* (1979; reprint, South Bend, Ind.: University of Notre Dame Press, 1991), 137–97. For a more elaborated version, see *A casa e a rua: Espaço, cidadania, mulher e morte no Brasil* (São Paulo: Brasiliense, 1985). See also Marcel Mauss, "A Category of the Human Mind: The Notion of Person, the Notion of Self," in *The Category of the Person,* ed. Michael Carrithers, Steven Collins, and Steven Lukes (New York: Cambridge University Press, 1985), 1–25.

2. The same saying exists in Mexico and has been attributed to none other than Benito Juárez, Mexico's most famous liberal. See Fernando Escalante Gonzalbo, *Ciudadanos imaginarios: Memorial de los afanes y desventuras de la virtud, y apologia del vicio triunfante en la Republica Mexicana—tratado de moral publica* (Mexico City: Centro de Estudios Sociologicos, Colegio de Mexico, 1992).

"citizenship" as a degraded baseline, or zero degree, of relationship, a fact that is visible in the day-to-day management of social relations.

Specifically, da Matta focuses on an urban ritual that he called the *Voçe sabe com quem esta falando?* (Do you know who you are talking to?), a phrase used to interrupt the universal application of a rule — that is, to interrupt what he calls the discourse of the street — in order to gain exceptional status and to rise above the degradation reserved for all nobodies. So, for instance, a lady cuts in line to enter a parking lot; the attendant protests and points to the line, but she says "Do you know who you are talking to? I am the wife of so and so, member of the cabinet," and so on.

A similar dynamic has characterized modern Mexican citizenship. For instance, it has long been noted that in Mexico much of the censorship of the press has been "self-censorship" rather than direct governmental censorship.[3] Speaking to a journalist about this phenomenon, da Matta remarked that much of this self-censorship resulted from the fact that journalists, like all members of Mexican middle classes, depend to an unpredictable degree on their social relations. Reliance on personal relations generates a kind of sociability that avoids open attacks, except when corporate interests are involved. Thus, the censorship of the press is in part also a product of the dynamics of da Matta's degraded citizenship.

The logic that da Matta outlined for understanding the degradation of Brazilian citizenship could easily be used to guide an ethnography of civic culture and sociability in Mexico. The ease of application stems from similarities at both the cultural and structural levels: Familial idioms used to shape a "discourse of the home" have common Iberian elements in these two countries, due to related concepts and ideas of family and friendship, as well as to similar colonial discourses for the social whole.

In this essay I develop a historical discussion of the cultural dynamics of Mexican citizenship. I begin with a series of vignettes that explore what the application of da Matta's perspective to Mexico might reveal. I argue that the notion that citizenship is the baseline, or zero degree, of relationship needs to be complemented by a historical view of changes

3. See Petra María Secanella, *El periodismo político en México* (Barcelona: Editorial Mitre, 1983).

in the definition and political situation of citizenship. Without such a perspective on the changing definition of citizenship, a critical aspect of the politics of citizenship is lost. The bulk of this article is devoted to interpreting the dynamics of citizenship in modern Mexico, as it developed in the nineteenth and twentieth centuries. The conclusion argues against narratives of Mexican modernity that tell contemporary history as a simple "transition to democracy."

CULTURAL LOGIC AND HISTORY

Mexico City is a place of elaborate politeness, a quality epitomized by the people whose job is to mediate (for instance, secretaries and waiters) but also generally visible in the socialization of children and in the existence of elaborate registers of obsequiousness, attentiveness, and respect. All of these registers disappear in the anonymity of the crowd, however, where people will push, pull, shove, pinch, and cut in front of you. There is no social contract for the crowd; there are only gentlemen's pacts among persons. For instance, drivers in Mexico City tend to drive with their eyes pointed straight ahead and cast slightly downward, much like a waiter's. This way they need not make concessions and can drive by presocial Hobbesian rules: Don't give away an inch. If one's eye wanders even a little, it might catch another driver's eye, and that driver will gently and smilingly ask to be let into the flow of traffic. At this point, the world of personal relations often takes hold of the driver who had been trying to keep things anonymous, and he may gallantly let the other car through.

This dynamic contrasts with the culture of societies who have strong civic traditions, wherein citizenship is the place in which the social pact is manifested (England, for instance, where forming a queue is a sacrosanct rite of citizenship), but where personal relationships do not extend as far out. Thus, a British traveler to Mexico may be scandalized at the greedy and impolitic attitudes of the people on the street, whereas a Mexican will complain that no pleas or personal interjections were ever able to move an English bureaucrat to sympathy.

What are the mechanisms of socialization into this form of courtesy? Access to an alleged right or to a service in Mexico is very often not universal. Education, for instance, is meant to be available to all, but it is often difficult to register a child in a nearby school or to get him or

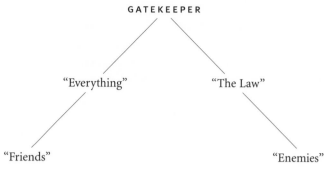

Figure 1. *"For my friends, everything; for my enemies, the law."*

her into a school at all. Public medicine exists, but it is always insufficient. Moving across the Mexico City traffic in an orderly fashion is often made difficult by the overuse of public space. In short, Mexico has never had a state that was strong enough to provide services universally. In this context, corruption and other market mechanisms easily emerge as selection criteria: If you pay money, the bureaucrat will see you first. The system has also generated forms of sociability that help shape a practical orientation that is well suited to the discretionary power that scarcity gives to bureaucrats and other gatekeepers.

One notable example of this is summed up in the very Mexican proverb that says "He who gets angry, loses" (*el que se enoja, pierde*). According to this principle, the wise person never explodes out of exasperation, because he or she can only lose by such an ex-abrupto. A service provider will only clam up when faced with an angry user and, since the service is a scarce resource, he or she will use politeness as a selection criterion.

Socialization into politeness, patience, and self-censorship thus has at least two significant social conditions. The first is a strong reliance on personal relations to activate, operate, and rely on any bureaucratic apparatus; the second is the reliance on personal relations to achieve positions in society. Both of these conditions would therefore appear to support da Matta's claim that citizenship is the zero-degree of relationship.

A difficulty is exposed by focusing closely on the implications of the saying "for my friends, everything; for my enemies, the law," however (see fig. 1). The saying is clearly a model for political action, yet it contains significant ambiguities in the proposed categories ("friends," "enemies," "the law," and "everything"), particularly if the saying is a recipe for a bureaucrat or a member of the political class—the "gatekeeper." Usually a bureaucrat does not deal with personal friends or personal enemies but with people to whom he or she is initially unrelated and indifferent. Some of these people will not receive the full service that the gatekeeper controls, while others will. Thus, an initially undifferentiated public gets shaped into "friends" and "enemies." "Everything" includes money (bribes) and prior personal connections—two routes to receiving exceptional treatment (as "friends"), and patience and politeness may at least keep you in the game. A breach of politeness or a burst of anger will in all likelihood place you in the "enemy" camp. The application of "the law" to differentiate the two is simply the use of bureaucratic procedure as a fundamental mechanism of exclusion.

We have, then, a logic that favors the development of personal relations, the elaboration of forms of obsequiousness and politeness, the cultural routinization of bribery, and the use of bureaucratic rules and procedure as mechanisms of exclusion. This logic is undergirded by structural conditions, of which I have stressed two—a relatively weak state and a large, poor population. Since these conditions have existed throughout Mexican history, one might expect that bribery, politeness, and a highly developed system of informal relationships have been equally constant practices and that they have been elaborated according to cultural idioms that apply a "discourse of the home" in order to create distinctions between potential users of a service. This is true at a general level.

However, while the cultural logic that I have outlined shows that citizenship is a degraded category, a "zero degree" of relationship, it also gives a false sense of continuity and constancy. I noted in the preceding discussion that the category of "friends" and "enemies" can be constructed in the process of applying a bureaucratic rule and that most of the population classified in these ways is initially indifferent to the bureaucrat. As a result, the definition of the pool that the bureaucrat is acting on is not determined by the cultural logic of social distance from the bureaucrat or gatekeeper. In other words, the gatekeeper is not actually ruling over a preselected group of friends and enemies but is instead culturally constructing "friends" and "enemies" out of a pool of people who are preselected not by him but by their theoretical relationship to a right.

As a result, although it is correct to say that—given a bureaucrat, a set of rules, and a pool of citizens—citizenship shall be the zero degree of relationship that needs to be complemented either by a prior personal claim, by a bribe, or by sympathy, the baseline of citizenship is not determined by this cultural logic, and it varies historically in important ways. These variations are not trivial, since they define the potential pool of users of a service that is being offered, an issue that also has critical significance for a long-standing history of the cultural forms of sociability that bear a connection to citizenship. A comprehensive view of modern Mexican citizenship therefore requires an interpretation of the relationship between legal and institutional definitions of citizenship and its cultural elaboration in social interaction. I shall attempt to sketch key elements of such a comprehensive view here.

EARLY REPUBLICANISM AND THE RISE OF THE IDEAL CITIZEN

The debates of Mexico's Junta Instituyente between Independence (1821) and the publication of the first Federal Constitution (1824) gave little sustained attention to citizenship. Laws governing who was a Mexican national and who was a Mexican citizen were vaguely inclusive, with attention lavished only on the question of patriotic inclusion/exclusion and with very little said about the qualities and characteristics of the citizen. Nevertheless, the process of independence had a critical role in shaping a field for a politics of citizenship.

So, for instance, in 1810 Miguel Hidalgo, the father of Mexican Independence, proclaimed the emancipation of slaves, the end to all forms of tribute and taxation levied against Indians and "castes," and the end of certain guild monopolies.[4] Although Hidalgo's revolt failed, his move to create a broad base for citizenship and to level differences between castes was preserved by leaders of subsequent movements. For example, Ignacio López Rayón's (also failed) attempt at a Mexican constitution (1811) abolished slavery (art. 24) and stated that "whoever is to be born after the happy independence of our nation will find no obstacle other than his personal defects. No opposition can stem from the class of his lineage; the same shall be observed with regard to those that represent

4. Bando de Hidalgo, 10 December 1810, quoted in Felipe Tena Ramírez, *Leyes fundamentales de México, 1808–1975* (Mexico City: Editorial Porrúa, 1975), 22.

the rank of Captain and above, or that render any special service to the country" (art. 25). The only fundamental exclusionary clause in this constitution, as in all early Mexican constitutions until that of 1857, regards the role of religion: "Catholic Religion shall be the only one, with no tolerance for any other" (art. 1).[5]

In addition to a common movement to broaden the base of citizenship such that lineage and race were abolished as (explicit) criteria of inclusion or exclusion, early proclamations and constitutions did tend to specify that only Mexicans—and often only Mexicans who had not betrayed the nation—could hold public positions (arts. 27 and 28 of López's constitutional project).[6] Thus, from the very beginning the idea was to create an ample citizenry and a social hierarchy based on merit: "The American people, forgotten by some, pitied by others, and disdained by the majority, shall appear with the splendor and dignity that it has earned through the unique fashion in which it has broken the chains of despotism. Cowardice and slothfulness shall be the only causes of infamy for the citizen, and the temple of honor shall open its doors indiscriminately to merit and virtue" (art. 38).[7]

Despite the general identification between early Mexican nationalism and the extension of citizenship rights in such a way as to include (former) slaves, Indians, and castes, there were a number of ambiguities and differences regarding the meaning of this extension. So, for instance, article 16 of the Mexican Empire's first provisional legal code states, tellingly, that "the various classes of the state shall be preserved with their respective distinction, but without prejudice to public employment, which is common to all citizens. Virtues, services, talents and capability are the only medium for achieving public employment of any kind."[8] By contrast, the Federal Constitution of 1824 does not even specify who is to be considered a citizen. Instead, it leaves to the individual states the definition of who shall be allowed to vote for their representatives in Congress (art. 9), while the selection of the president and vicepresident was left to Congress. Thus citizenship was to be determined by

5. López's constitution can be found in Tena, *Leyes fundamentales,* 24–27.
6. These strictures are repeated by Morelos in his *Sentimientos de la nación* (1813): "Article 9. "All [public] jobs shall only be obtained by Americans" (quoted in Tena, *Leyes fundamentales,* 29–31).
7. Tena, *Leyes fundamentales,* 27.
8. Tena, *Leyes fundamentales,* 27.

regional elites in conjunction with whomsoever they felt they needed to pay attention to, and access to federal power was mediated by a congress that represented these citizens.

It is worth noting that most of the distinctions between who was a Mexican citizen and who was merely a Mexican national are similar to the formulation found in the Spanish liberal constitution that was promulgated in Cadiz in 1812. Some of the early independent constitutions are a bit harsher than that of Cadiz on matters of religion (e.g., Father José María Morelos's Apatzingan constitution of 1814 sanctioned the Holy Office — that is, the Inquisition — and in article 15 it upheld heresy and apostasy as crimes punishable by loss of citizenship). In one matter, however, the constitution of Cadiz narrows citizenship beyond what is explicit in the earliest Mexican constitutions: Debtors, domestic servants, vagrants, the unemployed, and the illiterate all forfeited their rights as citizens (art. 25). This move was not explicitly embraced in the first Mexican constitutional projects, but neither was it entirely avoided. Agustine de Iturbide's *Plan de Iguala,* which was the first effective political charter of Independent Mexico, specified that until a constitution was formed, Mexico would operate according to the laws of the Spanish Cortes. The Federalist Constitution of 1824 left the door open for these mechanisms of exclusion by delegating the decision regarding who would be a citizen to the individual states. Finally, the Centralist and conservative constitution of 1836 reasserted the points of exclusion of Cadiz: The rights of citizenship were suspended for all minors, domestic servants, criminals, and illiterates; they were lost definitively to all traitors and debtors to the public coffers. All citizens had to have an annual income of 100 pesos, and substantially more if they wanted to be elected to office.

In short, early Mexican constitutions were involved in a double move: the elimination of criteria of caste and of slavery in order to create a broadly based nationality that included all people who were born in Mexico or who resided in the country, were members of the Catholic Church, and were willing to follow Mexico's laws; and the restriction of access to public office and to the public sphere to independent male property holders who could read and write. The category "citizen" was (and still is) not identical to that of "national" in legal discourse, though the two were tellingly conflated in political discourse. In fact, the relationship between the two was one of hierarchical encompassment. The Mexican citizen had the capacity to encompass Mexican nationals and to represent the whole of the nation in public.

INCLUSION AND EXCLUSION IN THE
ERA OF NATIONAL VULNERABILITY

At first glance, these early citizenship laws developed in a contested field in which the pressure to broaden the basis of citizenship coexisted with pressures to maintain political control in the hands of local notables.

Historian François-Xavier Guerra has argued that the urban patricians who had controlled the bureaucratic apparatus during the colonial period usually kept control over government despite these changes, relying on their power to manipulate local election processes.[9] However, Florencia E. Mallon has also shown that in the unstable context of mid-nineteenth-century Mexico, the need to mobilize popular constituencies, and the space that was available for spontaneous popular mobilization, led to the development of forms of liberalism and conservativism that catered to these popular groups.[10] It was, in part, the tensions that universal citizenship at times created for these local patricians and chieftains that fanned the development of a negative discourse about "the masses" in nineteenth-century Mexico: *la chusma, el populacho, la canalla, la plebe,* and other epithets portrayed masses as both dangerous and insufficiently civilized to manage political life.

Alongside these damning images of the plebe, a series of positive words referred to popular classes who were seen as ordered and civilized: *el pueblo, los ciudadanos, la gente buena,* and so on. To a large degree, the difference between positive and negative portrayals of the pueblo corresponded to whether the people in question were acting as dependents or whether they were difficult to control. Like the difference between the lumpen-proletariat and the proletariat, the distinction between a *canalla* and a *ciudadano* was that the latter either was a notable,

9. François-Xavier Guerra, "The Spanish-American Tradition of Representation and Its European Roots," *Journal of Latin American Studies* 26 (1994): 1–35.
10. Florencia E. Mallon, *Peasant and Nation: The Making of Postcolonial Mexico and Peru* (Berkeley: University of California Press, 1994), 129–33.

or at least depended on the same system as the notables who made the distinction, while the former had only loose connections of dependency to "good society."

So, for instance, in political speeches of the nineteenth century there are differences drawn between a lower class that may be described as "abject" and as an obstacle to progress, but that is also perceived as unthreatening and in need of state protection, and another lower class that is potentially or in fact violent and dangerous to civilization.

In a chronicle of his voyage to the United States published in 1834, Lorenzo de Zavala, a liberal from Yucatán who had been governor of the State of Mexico, a congressman, and an apologist for the U.S. colonization of Texas, tells his readers:

> Compare the moral condition of the people of the United States with that of one or two or our [federated] states and you will understand the true reason why it is impossible for us to raise our institutions to the level of our neighbor's, *especially in certain states*. In the State of Mexico and in that of Yucatan, which are the ones that I know best, of the million and two hundred thousand inhabitants of the former and the seven hundred thousand inhabitants of the latter, there is a proportion of, at the most, one in twenty [who know how to read and write]. [Of these] two fifths do not know arithmetic, three fifths do not even know the meaning of the words geography, history, astronomy, etc., and four fifths do not know what the Bible is. . . . To this we must add that at least one third of the inhabitants of Yucatan do not speak Spanish, and one fifth of the State of Mexico is in the same condition. Those who do not take into account the degree of civilization of the masses when they *make institutions for the people are either highly ignorant or extremely perverse* [his emphasis].[11]

Thus, the native population in particular was at the bottom of the heap and in need of elevation. A similar sentiment is echoed three decades later, after the French Intervention, when the 1857 Constitution was reinstated. There, in a session in Congress, representative Julio Zárate presented a proposal to prohibit private jails in haciendas and, more generally, to outlaw all punishment that was meted out in these

11. Lorenzo de Zavala, "Viaje a los Estados Unidos del Norte de América, 1834," in *Obras,* ed. Manuel González Ramírez (Mexico City: Editorial Porrúa, 1976), 156.

private institutions. He described the conditions of the Indian in the following terms:

> In the states of Mexico, Puebla, Tlaxcalla, Guerrero and Quere-taro, where the bulk of the indigenous population is concentrated, there is slavery, there is abjection, there is misery sustained by the great landowners. And this abject condition comprises close to four million men.
>
> It has been eleven years since the Constitution was ratified: private trials were prohibited, flogging and other degrading punishments were abolished; and authorities were given the right to establish jails for crimes . . . nonetheless, there are jails in the haciendas and stocks where the workers are sunk, and the Foreman gives lashes to the Indians, and debts are passed from father to son creating slavery, a succession of sold generations (15 February 1868).[12]

This view of the proto-citizen who needed to be elevated to true citizenship through state protection, miscegenation, or education, and whose condition was abject but not directly threatening to true and effective citizens contrasts with other portrayals of popular folk who are more difficult to redeem and more menacing. I shall offer two examples from the same congressional sessions that I have just cited.

On 9 January 1868 representative Jesús López brought to Congress a proposed law to banish bullfighting. This initiative was one of several attempts to isolate the causes of incivility and to transform the habits of a people who would not conform to the ideal of citizenship that the constitution granted them:

> The benefits of a democratic constitution, which raise the Mexi-can from the condition of slavery to the rank of the citizen, announce that Mexico marches toward greatness under the auspices of liberty. In contrast to this, as an obstacle that blocks Mexico's march toward prosperity, there exists in each community a place that symbolizes barbarism. . . .
>
> If we descend, sir, from these philosophical and moral consider-ations to search for material transcendental evils in society, we shall be confronted by the degradation of that class that, because of its

12. In Pantaleon Tovar, *Historia parlamentaria del cuarto congreso constitucional,* vol. 1. (Mexico City: Imprenta de I. Cumplido, 1872), 400–401.

ignorance, is called the lowliest class [*clase ínfima*], and that has been indelibly inoculated with a propensity to bloody acts. . . . This class, which has been disinherited from the benefits of illustration, does not know the goodness of virtue except by the harm it receives for being criminal; in it the noble sentiments that inhere in the human heart degenerate, because the government and the clergy, publicists and speakers, try to show them in abstract the matters of religion and of politics that their uncultivated intelligence cannot comprehend. All the while, the attractions of vice and the emotions that are produced by certain spectacles excite and move their passions. Since it is not possible to establish schools everywhere where this class can be well taught, remove at least those other [schools] where they learn evil, where the sight of blood easily fosters the savage instincts to which they have, by nature, a propensity. If we want good citizens, if we want brave soldiers who are animated in combat and humane in triumph, prohibit spectacles that inflate sentiments and that dull [*embrutecen*] reason.[13]

Readers would be incorrect, too, to think that the dangerous "lowliest" classes that are referred to here are strictly urban and that all rural Indians were thought to be safe for state or hacendado patronage. Rebellious Indians, usually labeled "savages," were highly dangerous. So, for instance, in his 1868 campaign against Indian rebels and a few remaining pro–Hapsburg Imperialists in Yucatán, President Juárez asked Congress to suspend a series of individual guarantees in Yucatán in order to carry out a military expedition there. One of the suspended rights was article 5 of the Constitution, which reads, "No one can be forced to render personal services without a fair retribution and without their full consent. The law cannot authorize any contract that has as its object the loss or irrevocable sacrifice of a man's liberty." In other words, slavery and corvée labor were authorized for the duration of the Yucatecan campaign, which was fought principally against the Indians.[14]

13. Tovar, *Historia parlamentaria*, 306–8.
14. The discussion occurs on 28 December 1867 (see Tovar, *Historia parlamentaria*, 122). In a related discussion a few days later, representative Zarco justifies the war in Yucatán by explaining that "From the days of Maximilian, it is well known that there were designs to create a viceroyalty in Yucatan, an asylum for reactionaries. These traitors toil to separate that territory from the republic and to instate it as a

Thus a discourse of the sort that da Matta called "discourse of the street," that is, an egalitarian and universalistic discourse of citizenship, could be applied to the "good pueblo." At the same time, the fact that in some nineteenth-century constitutions servants were not allowed to vote because they were dependents and therefore did not have control over their will was indicative of the fact that most of the good pueblo was made up of a kind of citizenry that was guarded not so much by the constitutional rights of individuals as by the claims that loyalty and dependency had on the conscience of Christian patriarchs.

Nevertheless, the image of a good pueblo was not simply that of the dependent masses, since this could be thought of either as a harmonious and progressive arrangement or (as we have seen) as a form of abject slavery. To comprehend ideological dynamics within this field better, two new elements need to be introduced: The first is the nation's position in a world of competing predatory powers, and the second is the question of national unity.

A sharp consciousness of national decline and of uncontrollable dangers for the nation can be found among Mexican political men almost from the time of the toppling of Iturbide (1822). References to decline and to danger abound both in the press and in discussions in Congress. So, for instance, deputy Hernández Chico claimed that the nation's situation was "deplorable" due to lack of public funds (14 June 1824).[15] On 12 June of that same year, deputy Cañedo warned of the need to guard against a full civil war, in light of secessionist movements in the state of Jalisco. The image of the Republic being split apart by rival factions is almost always seen as the cause of this decline or imminent disaster, as in the case of a speech read in Congress by the minister of war against a pro-Iturbide uprising in Jalisco on 8 June 1824: "Yes sir, there are vehement indications that these two generals are plotting against the republic, that they desire its ruin, that it is they who move those implacable assassins that afflict the states of Puebla and Mexico; they who

---

principality so that they can sell the Indians off as slaves" (quoted in Tovar, *Historia parlamentaria*, 137). Interestingly, to combat these reactionaries and the Maya rebels, Juárez and his liberals essentially legalized corvée labor and slavery in the peninsula.

15. All citations of discussions of the First Constitutional Congress are from the facsimile edition, *Actas constitucionales mexicanas (1821–1824)*, 10 vols. (Mexico City: Universidad Nacional Autónoma de México, 1980). Dates of discussion will be cited rather than pagination, which is not entirely sequential.

propagate that deadly division, that confrontation between parties, it is they who are behind the conspirators who cause our unease and who make life so difficult."[16]

This feeling of pending or actual disaster caused by lack of union increased and became pervasive in political discourse as the country indeed became unstable, economically ruinous, and subject to a number of humiliations by foreign powers.

In a remarkably frank, if not entirely extraordinary, "Civic Oration" proffered on the anniversary of Independence in the city of Durango in 1841, Licenciado Jesus Arellano recapped the history of political divisions and fraternal struggle in the following terms:

> Let's go back in time to September 27, 1821 [the day Independence was achieved]. . . . That day, my fellow citizens, the very day of our greatest fortune, also initiates the era of our greatest woes. It is from that day that a horrible discord began to exert its deadly influence. Unleashed from the abysmal depths where it resides, it flung itself furiously in the midst of our newly born society and destroyed it in its crib. . . . There in the shadows of that frightful darkness we can hear the roar of the monster that spilled in Padilla the blood of general Iturbide: the blood of the hero who finished the work of Hidalgo and Morelos. There, too, you can hear the horrible cry of that malicious and treacherous spirit that sold the life of the great (*benemérito*) and innocent general Guerrero to the firing squad.[17]

The heroes who had initiated the Revolution — Hidalgo, Allende, Aldama, Morelos — had all been martyred by Spaniards, but the two who actually achieved Independence — Iturbide and Guerrero — were both murdered by factious Mexicans. This was to stand symbolically in a position analogous to Original Sin, wherein Mexicans are denied their entry to National Happiness because of their internal vices and divisions: "Woe is you, unfortunate Mexico! Woe is you because not having yet fully entered the age of infancy, you decline in a precocious decrepitude that brings you close to the grave! Woe is you because you

---

16. Minister of War, *Actas constitucionales,* 8 June 1824.

17. *Oración cívica que en el aniversario del grito de independencia se pronunció en el palacio de govierno de Durango el 16 de septiembre de 1841 por el Lic. Jesus Arellano* (Colección Lafragua, Biblioteca Nacional, Mexico City). Hereafter Arellano, "Civic Oration."

are like the female of those venomous insects that thrive in our climate, and of whom it is said that it gives birth to its children only to be eaten by them!"[18] Decline was caused by personal ambition and folly among leaders and would-be leaders of government, so much so that Arellano begins his remarkable speech distancing himself from any sort of political activity: "I have not yet traveled—and God spare me from ever taking—the murky paths of the politics that dominate us; of that science whose principles are the whim of those who profess it, where the most obvious truths are put in doubt, and where he who is best at cheating and who is best at disguising his deceptions is considered wise."[19]

The ultimate results of vice, selfishness, and ambition have been the ruination of Mexico, its decline, its inability to reap the benefits of freedom and independence. For some speakers, these vices were typical of one party: monarchical interests of conservatives, for instance; or Catholic fanaticism that led to blocking the doors to colonization from northern Europe and the United States; or to Federalist folly in delegating too much power and autonomy to states. For all, they reflected a lack of virtue and the fall of public morality. To quote again from Arellano: "We must acknowledge that our vices have grown and that public morality is every day extenuated, that our country has been a constant prey of ambition, of jealousy, of fratricidal tendencies, of atrocious vendettas, of insatiable usury, of fanaticism and superstition, of ineptitude and perversity, and of clumsy and inhumane mandarins."[20]

In synthesis, it is mistaken to imagine that in its origins the discourse of citizenship was in any simple way about settling a "zero degree of relationship." On the contrary, early legal codes had quite significant strictures regarding who could be a citizen. These restrictions readily allowed for the emergence of one specific discourse about the good and the bad pueblo: Good pueblo was the pueblo that was obedient, the portion of Mexican nationals who allowed themselves peacefully to be represented by Mexican citizens; bad pueblo was the pueblo that was not governed by the class of local notables, and this included rebellious Indians (like those cited in Yucatán or in Durango) as much as the feared clases ínfimas that were not assimilable through public education.

18. Arellano, "Civic Oration," 11. Curiously, the scorpion would later go on to become emblematic of the state of Durango.
19. Arellano, "Civic Oration," 6.
20. Arellano, "Civic Oration," 16.

At the same time, the tendency to conflate nationality and citizenship, at least as a utopian idea, existed from the very beginning, and this allowed for another kind of distinction between good and bad citizens. This distinction focused on the "petty tyrants." Some of these were perceived, particularly after the Constitution of 1857, as local caciques or hacendados who kept Indians in a slavelike position and away from their individual rights as Mexicans and as citizens, as was the case in the speech, cited earlier, against jails in haciendas. Others, and this was particularly prevalent in the earlier period, were tyrants in their selfish appropriation of what was public.

This latter form of dividing between virtuous and vicious elites readily allowed for the consolidation of a discourse of messianism around a virtuous caudillo, as is illustrated in another patriotic speech, pronounced on 11 September 1842 (anniversary of the triumph against the Spanish invasion of 1829) in the city of Orizaba: "The political regeneration of Anahuac [Mexico] was reserved *ab initio* to a singular Veracruzano: an entrepreneurial genius, an animated soldier, a keen statesman, a profound politician or, in sum, to Santa Anna the great, who like another Alcides and Tesco, will purify the precious ground of the Aztecs and rid it of that disgusting and criminal riffraff (*canalla*) of tyrants of all species and conditions."[21]

In short, the political field around the definition of citizenship involved three kinds of distinctions: one between a pueblo that would be encompassed by a group of notables and a pueblo that would not; another between selfish and false citizens who sought private gain from their public position as citizens and those who equated citizenship to public service and sacrifice; and a third between citizens who strove to open the way for the extension of citizenship rights and those who strove to block them in order to enhance their own petty-tyrannical authority.

In some contexts, these views could be articulated to one another. For example, the situation of the bad pueblo was compared to that of a young woman who was not under the tutelage of a man—it was fodder for "seduction" by bandits or by factious aspiring politicians. The bad pueblo was fodder for the vicious politician, as much as it was

21. *Opúsculo patriótico, que pronunció el ciudadano teniente coronel graduado Francisco Santoyo, como miembro de la junta patriótica de esta ciudad [de Orizaba] el dia 11 de septiembre de 1842* (Colección Lafragua, Biblioteca Nacional, Mexico City), 16.

the principal challenge for enlightened liberal governments that sought to expand public education, eliminate the obscurantist influence of the Church, and prohibit bullfights, cockfights, and other forms of barbaric diversions.

The description of citizenship as a zero degree of relationship, then, is misleading from the very entry of Mexico to modernity because it emphasizes only one aspect of the phenomenon, which is the fact that familial discourses have always been used to supersede the universalism of the legal order. Moreover, the notion of the citizen as the baseline of all political relationships is historically incorrect, since in the early national period it was clearly a sign of distinction to be a citizen, and even after the Constitution of 1857 and the Revolutionary Constitution of 1917, it still excluded minors and women. Having established this general point, let us return to our evolutionary panorama of the development of citizenship in Mexico.

THE DEMISE OF EARLY LIBERAL CITIZENSHIP

The first truly liberal constitution of Mexico (1857) develops an inclusive and relatively unproblematic identification between citizenship and nationality: To be a citizen, all you need is to be a Mexican over 18 (if you are married; over 21 if you are not) and to earn an honest living (art. 34). Simplicity, however, is sometimes misleading.

Because in theory everyone was a citizen if they were of age (the article does not even specify that you need to be male to be a citizen, though this apparently went without saying, since female suffrage in Mexico did not exist until 1957), the Constitution and the congresses that met after its ratification were very much concerned with giving moral shape to the citizen.

Fernando Escalante ends his pathbreaking book on politics and citizenship in Mexico's nineteenth century arguing that "there were no citizens because there were no individuals. Security, business, and politics were collective affairs. But never, or only very rarely, could they be resolved by a general formula that was at once efficacious, convincing and presentable." [22] His book demonstrates that there was a high degree of pragmatic accord between liberals and conservatives on the matter of

22. Escalante, *Ciudadanos imaginarios,* 372.

laws and institutions not being applicable in a systematic fashion because consolidating state power was more fundamental and urgent, and
neither group could adequately resolve the contradiction between creating an effective and exclusive group of citizens and the actual politics
of inclusion and exclusion demanded by the society's numerous corporations.

Despite this pragmatic agreement regarding the priority that consolidating state power had over citizenship rights, the ideal of citizenship was about as obsessively pervasive in Mexican political discourse
as was the rejection of politics as a site of vice. Part of this obsession was
a result of the fact that, until Juárez's triumph over Maximilian in the
late 1860s, political instability and economic decline raised realistic fears
that Mexico could be swallowed up by foreign powers or split apart by
internal rifts. Collective mobilization seemed the only way forward in
all of this, and there is a sense in which Mexican history between Independence and the French Intervention (1821–67) can be seen as a process
of increasing polarization. In the end it was this process, in conjunction
with emerging capitalist development and the construction of the first
railroads in the 1870s, that allowed for the first successful centralized
governments of Juárez and, especially, of Diaz, to operate.

Escalante has demonstrated that the old idea, championed by Cosío
Villegas, that Juárez's restored republic was a genuine experiment in
liberal democracy is simply wrong, and that the consolidation of the
central state under Juárez needed to sidestep the legal order and to create informal networks of power as much as the Diaz dictatorship that
followed it.[23]

I have no space here to go into details concerning the evolution of
citizenship under the Porfirio Diaz regime (1876–1910), but a few remarks are necessary. Certainly, the achievement of governmental stability and material progress pushed earlier recurrent obsession over
citizenship to the background. A plausible hypothesis is that a strong
unified state and the concomitant process of economic growth led by
foreign investment was a more valued goal for the political classes than
citizenship. In fact, the earlier fixation on citizenship was due, in large
part, to the fact that regional elites needed to call on altruism in order

23. Escalante, *Ciudadanos imaginarios,* 375–76.

to try to hold the Mexican state together; once the state could not hold its own, this motivation disappeared.[24] A discourse on "order and progress" quickly superseded the earlier emphasis on citizenship and the universal application of laws as the only way to progress; a strong state that could guarantee foreign investment was the key to that progress.

Thus, during the Porfirian dictatorship it was the state, and its power to arrange space and to regiment an order, that was the subject of political ritual and myth; the masses, it was hoped, might eventually catch up to progress or — if they opposed the national state, as the Yaqui, Apache, and Maya Indians did — they would be eliminated. In short, whereas the law and the citizen were the ultimate fetishes of the era of national instability,[25] progress, urban boulevards, railroads, and the mounted police (*rurales*) were the key fetishes of a Porfirian era that upheld the state as the promoter of that progress, and the vehicle for the ultimate improvement of Mexico's abject rural masses.[26]

24. In the case of Texas and New Mexico, altruistic appeals to national identity and shared religion were the principal resources used by Mexico to try to keep those territories in the republic. See Andrés Reséndez, "Caught between Profits and Rituals: National Contestation in Texas and New Mexico, 1821–1848" (Ph.D. diss., University of Chicago, 1997).

25. On 7 February 1868, just a few months after the execution of Maximilian von Hapsburg, the project for a law trying to ritually enshrine the 1857 Constitution was presented to Congress. The justification for this proposal is significant: "It is unquestionable that this *talisman* [the Constitution of 1857] that is so loved by the Mexican people, was the cause of the prodigious valor that distinguished us in the bloody war that has just passed" (cited in Tovar, *Historia parlamentaria,* 398; emphasis in original).

26. Descriptions of Porfirian state theater are plentiful; for the boulevards, see Barbara Tenenbaum, "Streetwise History: The Pase de la Reforma and the Porfirian State, 1876–1910," in *Rituals of Rule, Rituals of Resistance: Public Celebrations and Popular Culture in Mexico,* ed. William H. Beezley, Cheryl English Martin, and William E. French (Wilmington, Del.: SR Books, 1994), 127–50; for the rurales, see Paul J. Vanderwood, *Disorder and Progress: Bandits, Police, and Mexican Development* (1981; reprint, Wilmington, Del.: SR Books, 1992); for a general appreciation of Porfirian state theater, see Mauricio Tenorio-Trillo, *Mexico at the World's Fairs: Crafting a Modern Nation* (Berkeley: University of California Press, 1996).

If this were the end of the story, however, how could we come to terms with the fact that in the 1930s Samuel Ramos, the famous founder of a philosophy about the Mexican as a social subject, identified the *pelado* (urban scoundrel), that is, the subject who had been considered beyond the pale of citizenship since Independence — as the quintessential Mexican? Ramos argued that Mexican national character was marked by a collective inferiority complex. This inferiority complex was exemplified in the attitude of the pelado who is so wounded by the other's gaze that he replies to it aggressively with the challenge of *Qué me ves?* (What are you looking at?).[27] Thus, where the driver of our earlier Mexico City example seeks anonymity in order to act like a wolf, but becomes a gentleman with eye contact, the pelado rejects eye contact with a threat of violence. But while the nineteenth-century politician would not have hesitated in identifying the true citizen with the (unconstantly) amiable driver and the pelado as an enemy of all good society and an individual lacking in love and respect for his patria, post-Revolutionary intellectuals like Ramos made the urban rabble into the Ur-Mexicans. Why the change?

Before the Revolutionary Constitution of 1917, Mexican citizens had the right to vote and very little else. The right of education existed in theory, but as historical studies of education have shown, public education during the Porfiriato was controlled to a large extent by urban notables, a fact that was reflected in extremely low literacy rates.[28] Moreover, as I mentioned earlier, the right to vote was often nullified by the machinery of local bosses, who controlled voting as a matter of routine.

The 1917 Constitution and the regimes following the Revolution changed this in a couple of significant ways. First, under the leadership of José Vasconcelos in the 1920s, and in an effort to wrench the formation of citizens from the hands of the Church, public education went on a crusade to reach out to the popular classes. This effort was successful to a significant degree, and schools were built even in re-

27. Samuel Ramos, *El perfil del hombre y la cultura en México* (1938); reprinted in *Samuel Ramos; Trayectoria filosófica y antología de textos por Agustín Basave Fernandez del Valle* (Monterrey: Centro de Estudios Humanísticos de la Universidad de Nuevo Leon, 1965), 131–35.
28. Mary Kay Vaughan, "The Construction of the Patriotic Festival in Tecamachalco, Puebla, 1900–1946," in Beezley et al., *Rituals of Rule*, 213–46.

mote agrarian communities. Second, the 1917 Constitution established the right of access to land. The land, in this constitution, belonged to the nation, as did the subsoil and territorial waters. Correspondingly, citizens had rights to portions of that national wealth under certain conditions. Third, the 1917 Constitution specified a series of workers' rights, including minimum wages, the prohibition of child labor, the prohibition of debt peonage, maximum working hours, and the like. Thus, being a citizen promised rights of access to certain forms of protection against the predatory practices of capitalists who, significantly, were often identified as foreign.

Identifying members of the urban rabble as the prototypical Mexicans was, in this context, consonant with the state's expansive project. The modal citizen should, indeed, be the affable and reasonable member of the middle classes—and Ramos's portrayal of the pelado was in no way laudatory—however, Mexico's backwardness and the challenge of its present made it useful to identify the typical subject as being off center from that ideal.

At the same time, the Revolutionary state, like the Porfirian state, did not concern itself so much with producing citizens. Instead, the goal was to create and to harness corporate groups and sectors into the state apparatus. Although Presidents Álvaro Obregón and Plutarco Elías Calles upheld the ideal of the private farmer in the 1920s and thought it a much more desirable goal than that of the communitarian peasant, the task of building up the state was more important to them than that of establishing the citizen.

The principal shift between the Porfirian and the post-Revolutionary state is that the latter consolidated a political idiom of inclusive corporativism that could be used to complement the Porfirian (but still current and useful) theme of the enlightened and progressive state. By the time President Lázaro Cárdenas nationalized the oil industry (1938), political discourse in the Mexican press by and large lacked any reference to the ideal citizen and portrayed, instead, a harmonious interconnection between popular classes under the protection of the Revolutionary state.[29]

In short, early republican obsession with citizenship was primarily due to the extreme vulnerability of Mexico's central state. It was not

29. Martin Welsh, "Citizenship in Crisis: Oil, Banks, and the Public Sphere, 1938–1982" (unpublished manuscript, Department of History, University of Chicago).

produced by an existing equality among citizens, but rather by existing divisions among the elites. As soon as a central state was consolidated, citizenship went from being seen as an urgent and supreme ideal to being a long-term goal that could be achieved only after the enlightened, scientific state had done its job. In turn, this perspective was transformed by the post-Revolutionary state, which complemented it with the organization of the pueblo into corporations that were regulated and protected by the state.

These broad shifts have had their corresponding counterparts in the history of the private sphere. The private sphere of citizens in Mexico has never been very fully guaranteed. In the early republican period, liberals identified corporate forms of property as a central obstacle to citizenship: Specifically, they targeted the property of Indian communities and of the Church. However, the expropriation of both communal and ecclesiastical corporate holdings in 1856 did not lead to the desired end, which was to create a propertied citizenry but, instead, to even greater concentration of landed wealth in the hands of an oligarchy. As a result, enormous proportions of the population lacked a secure private sphere and lived either as dependents or as members of communities whose rights could only be defended collectively.

After the 1910 Revolution the state sought to protect individuals from slavelike dependence on the oligarchy; however, the relations of production that it fostered were equally problematic from the point of view of the consolidation of a private sphere. Agrarian reform failed to build a Lockean citizenry in the countryside because *ejidatarios* (land grantees) are not legal owners of their land. Moreover, they depend on local governmental support for many aspects of production, and so are feeble participants in the construction of a bourgeois public sphere. Similarly, the numerous indigent peoples of Mexico lack a secure private sphere, as ethnographies of the so-called informal sector have amply attested. People in the informal sector lead lives that are largely outside of the law; as a result, they need to negotiate with state institutions to keep tapping into illegal sources of electricity, to keep vending in restricted zones, to keep living in property that is not formally theirs, and so on.[30]

30. See, for example, Larissa Lomnitz, *Networks and Marginality: Life in a Mexican Shantytown* (New York: Academic Press, 1975); Carlos Vélez-Ibáñez, *Rituals of Mar-*

Thus, although incorporation to a modern sector was one of the critical goals of post-Revolutionary governments, the modalities of incorporation retained significant sectors of the population that not only did not benefit from access to a private sphere that was immune from government intervention but in fact depended on government intervention in order to eke out a living in a legally insecure environment. Of the three sectors that made up Mexico's state party, two — the peasant sector and the popular sector — had no sacrosanct private sphere from which to criticize the state, and therefore no protected basis for liberal citizenship.

This situation, which of course does not exist in Brazil in the same way, complicates the vision of citizenship as a debased category, for it is through claims of citizenship that the peasantry and the informal sector have negotiated with the post-Revolutionary state — exchanging votes and participation in Revolutionary national discourse for access to lands, to credits, to electricity, or to urban services. At the same time, this citizenship belongs to a faceless mass, not to a collection of private individuals. The pelado who in Ramos's account felt wounded by the mere gaze of the erstwhile modal citizen, and who asserted his right to nationality by his involvement in Revolutionary violence, is harnessed back into nationality not through patron-client ties to private elites but through a series of exchanges with state agencies through which he receives the status of massified citizen.

Let me illustrate what the shape of official citizenry was like in the era of single-party rule. In the PRI's 1988 presidential campaign, which was in many respects the last traditional PRI campaign, public rallies and events were divided into several types.[31] First, there were events targeted to specific portions of the party's tripartite sectorial organization (Peasant Sector, Labor Sector, and Popular Sector); second, there

---

ginality: Politics, Process, and Culture Change in Urban Central Mexico, 1969–1974 (Berkeley: University of California Press, 1981); Antonio Azuela, ed., *La Urbanización popular y el orden jurídico en América Latina* (Mexico City: Universidad Nacional Autónoma de México, 1993).

31. For a full description of these campaign rituals, see Larissa Lomnitz, Claudio Lomnitz, and Ilya Adler, "The Function of the Form: Power, Play and Ritual in the 1988 Mexican Presidential Campaign," in *Constructing Culture and Power in Latin America,* ed. Daniel Levine (Ann Arbor: University of Michigan Press, 1993), 357–402.

were meetings with regional and national groups of experts who organized problem-focused discussions with the candidate and an audience
(CEPES and IEPES); third, there were massive public rallies that were
meant to show the party's muscle by uniting the whole pueblo in a single
square; and fourth (this was an innovation for the 1988 campaign), there
were talk show–like events where the candidate fielded questions from
callers who were not identified as members of a party sector.

The image of the nation as it was generated in the massive public
rallies was that of a corporate organism. Like public displays of the social
whole since the colonial period, the public of these rallies was divided
internally by sectors, each of which signaled its corporate presence with
electoral paraphernalia (sheets painted with the candidate's name and
the name of the supporting sector; flags, T-shirts, tags, or hats printed
with the candidate's initials and those of the party or sector), but also
with a certain uniformity of look: peasants in their hats and sandals,
railroad workers in their blue hats, schoolteachers in their middle-class
garb, and so on.

Alongside this hierarchical and organic image of the nation as composed of complementary, unequal, and interdependent masses, campaign rituals also presented certain modal images of citizenry. This is
apparent in the use of dress in the various rallies, for although the presidential candidate often dressed up as a member of the sector that he was
visiting (dressing as a rancher when in a rally of the peasant sector, as
well-dressed worker in a rally of the labor sector, and in a suit in a discussion with the experts), the relationship between "the suit" and other
costumes is not one of equality. Rather, the suit is the highest formal
garb, the one that the candidate will use on a daily basis when he is in
the presidency, and the one that he has daily used as a government official prior to becoming a presidential candidate. The suit is the modal
uniform of the public sphere. Public sessions devoted to the discussion
of regional and national problems are attended almost exclusively by
suits, even when their inhabitants are representing interests associated
with labor or agriculture. Thus, the image of the citizen with a voice
stands in contrast to the massified citizen.

This situation has been identified by Mexican democrats as a lack of
a civil society, and these same democrats have been building a narrative of Mexican democracy that has the heyday of the corporate party
(the 1940s and 1950s) as the zero-point in Mexican citizenship. Ac-

cording to this view, the corporate state effectively funneled Mexican society into its mass party until the 1960s, when certain groups, especially middle-class groups—but also some peasants and urban poor—no longer found a comfortable spot in the state's mechanisms of representation and of resource management, producing the 1968 student movement.[32] The violent suppression of this movement, and the expansion of state intervention in the economy in the 1970s, gave a second wind to the corporativist state. However, an unemcompassable civil society would keep growing during this period and would reemerge politically in the mid-1980s, when the state's fiscal crisis weakened its hold on society. This situation has been leading inexorably to the end of the one-party system and the rise of Mexican democracy.

During the period of state party rule, political classes in Mexico had a pretty clear mission, which was to tap into resources by mediating between state institutions and local constituencies. It was in this period that a clever politician coined the phrase *vivir fuera del presupuesto es vivir en el error* (to live outside of the [state's] budget is to live in error). The expansion of the state for several decades was a process of ever-incorporating political middlemen as new social movements emerged. So, in the 1970s and 1980s positions were created for leaders of squatters' movements, for leaders of urban gangs, for student movement leaders, for teachers' movement leaders, and others. The fiscal crisis of the state that began in 1982 severely limited its possibility of engaging in this co-optive strategy, and so the numbers of nongovernmental organizations in active service rose dramatically, as indeed did opposition parties. During the 1990s, the disenfranchisement of these groups was reflected in the growing political clout of the opposition, a tendency that culminated in the elections of July, 2000, when the PRI lost the presidential election.

There has undoubtedly been an intensification of citizen activity in this period, with vast numbers of people rejecting massified corporate forms of political participation that are no longer providing real benefits and with strong voter participation, as well as a huge increase in participation in political rallies, demonstrations, and the like. The press, too, has broken with the unspoken rule of preserving the figure of the

32. Today this version is common wisdom, but for a succinct synthesis of this perspective, see Lorenzo Meyer, *Liberalismo autoritario: Las contradicciones del sistema político mexicano* (Mexico City: Oceano, 1996).

national president from direct attack, and its criticisms of government have become much louder.

At the same time, the fact that many political leaders and mediators are now living outside of the fiscal budget may also mean that a new form of massified citizenship is being constructed. The economic costs of democracy and democratization are so far very high in Mexico, and a lot of money is going to all political parties, as well as to running electoral processes. Elections and electoral processes have become a source of revenue in their own right, and the jockeying between party leaderships could become divorced from the ever-growing needs of the country's poorest, particularly because the middle and proletarian classes are now large enough to sustain such an apparatus. This situation is illustrated by the fact that today there is undoubtedly more democracy in Mexico than at any time in recent memory; however, the extent of urban insecurity, the numbers of fences and walls, and the presence of the military and of private security guards are also at their highest levels in recent memory.

In this junction, like in the post-Revolutionary years in which Ramos was writing, there is an increasing number of people who are unprotected by relations of private patronage, unprotected by the state, and with insufficient private possessions to participate as reliable citizens. By contrast, as in the unstable years of the early and mid-nineteenth century, there is an increasingly large class of lumpen-politicians that seeks to funnel the "bad pueblo" into "factious" movements. And the passage from unruly anonymity to amicable personal contact may become more strained as the capacity to claim that "the one who gets angry first, loses" itself loses credibility.

CONCLUSION

Da Matta's analysis of the relationship between liberal and Catholic-hierarchical discourses in the negotiation of citizenship is a useful entry-point for the description of debased forms of citizenship as they have existed in Iberoamerica. However, his strategy is best suited to highlight the micropolitics of access to state institutions and does not clarify the specific ways in which citizenship is filled and emptied of contents; it therefore misses a critical dimension of the culture of citizenship, including how, when, and by whom it is politicized.

In this essay I have sketched out a rough outline of the politics surrounding citizenship in modern Mexico. There have been two periods when discussions of citizenship have been truly central to political discourse. The first period, which I analyzed in some detail, is the era of political instability and economic decline that followed Mexican Independence; the second is the contemporary, post-1982 debt crisis period of privatization and decline of single-party hegemony. The view that I developed suggests that the intensity of discussions surrounding citizenship in the first five decades after Independence reflected both the complex politics of including or excluding popular classes from the political field and the fact that national unity seemed unattainable by any means other than through unity among citizens and violence against traitors (be these indigenous groups or fractious "tyrants" with their clientele of *canallas*). In other words, citizenship was continually invoked as the first and foremost need of the nation at a time when the country had no effective central state, had a declining economy, and was threatened by both imperial powers and internal regional dissidents.

Beginning with President Juárez, but especially under President Diaz, the national state was consolidated and a national economy was articulated, thanks to the state's capacity to guarantee both foreign investment and national sovereignty. As a result, the "bad pueblo" was slowly neutralized and substituted only by the growth and expansion of what I have called the "abject pueblo," or the people who were not fit for citizenship (not knowing how to read or write, not speaking Spanish, and living in conditions of servitude that effectively preempted participation as full independent citizens). In the process, the national obsession with citizenship diminished even as the celebration and fetishization of the state as the depositary of rationality, order, and progress grew. The combination of national consolidation, rapid modernization, and the extension of a truly degraded form of citizenship to the vast majority is part of the backdrop of the Mexican Revolution of 1910.

The constitutional order that emerged from the Revolution allowed Mexicans access to a series of benefits, including land and protection against employers. Nevertheless, the post-Revolutionary order did not either achieve the ancient liberal goal of turning the majority of the population into property holders. In fact, the fragility of the private sphere for large sections of the population has been one of the constants in modern Mexican history. As a result, the revolutionary state combined the Porfirian cult of enlightened, state-led progress with an organicist construction of the people.

This Revolution gave citizenship another kind of valence. Instead of attacking communal lands and trying to transform every Mexican into a private owner, post-Revolutionary governments gave out land and protection as forms of citizenship, but they retained ultimate control over those resources. As a result, citizenship in the post-Revolutionary era (up to the mid- or late 1980s) can be thought of in part as massified and sectorialized, since peasants and workers of the so-called informal sector received benefits on the force of their citizenship, and yet lacked independence from the state. Thus, the debased citizen that da Matta speaks of is clearly different in the pre-Revolutionary and the post-Revolutionary periods since, in the latter, "nobodies" could make claims for state benefits on the basis of their collective identity as part of a revolutionary pueblo, whereas in the former they could not.

Part of the current difficulty in Mexican citizenship is that social critics acknowledge that state paternalism and control over production led to unacceptably undemocratic forms of rule and, indeed, to policies that led to the bankruptcy of the country. Still, at least the 1917 Constitution envisaged parceling out some benefits to people by virtue of the fact that they were citizens. The contraction of the state has produced massive social movements and a very strong push around democratization and the category of the citizen, but the current emphasis on electoral rights risks emptying the category of its social contents once again, and given the fact that Mexico still has a large mass of poor people with little legally private property or stable and legally sanctioned work, and given, too, that Mexico's state is still incapable of extending rights universally, we may yet see the reemergence of a pernicious dialectic between the good pueblo and the bad pueblo.

Modernist Ruins: National Narratives and Architectural Forms

Beatriz Jaguaribe

Rio de Janeiro is a city that enacts a continuous dialogue between its architectural constructions and natural surroundings. The sheer exuberance of the tropical vegetation casts into perspective architectural aspirations and contrasts to the neglect of its urban infrastructure. The vitality of Rio's urban culture is mirrored not only in monumental stone but also in the constant creation and recreation of musical forms, dance rhythms, bodily configurations, and new artistic expressions. Yet at the end of the nineteenth century and the beginning of the twentieth, the tourists that visited what was then the federal capital from the backlands of Brazil were only moderately concerned with the tropical scenery. Instead, they were eagerly purchasing postcards that depicted the emblems of national progress.[1] Postcards of trolley cars, monuments, and technical installations embedded with the mythologizing force of the modern were sent to relatives and friends stranded in the remote and provincial expanses of a largely unexplored Brazil.

Capital cities tend to exhibit a deliberate architectural symbology that distinguishes them from other cities. They symbolize the construction or the several constructions of a national pantheon. In contrast to Brasília, which was specifically planned as a modernist capital in

This essay is a modified English translation of a version that was published in Portuguese as "Ruínas Modernistas," *Lugar-Comum* 1 (1997): 99–115.

1. See Gilberto Freyre's comments: "Throughout Brazil thousands of postcards were spread . . . postcards that depicted less the Corcovado or the forest of Tijuca or the palm trees of the Jardim Botânico—marvels that were more for Englishmen rather than Brazilians to see. . . . In these postcards, the provincials visiting Brazil insistently spoke to relatives or old acquaintances of their families of the urban and industrial progress of what was now called the Capital of the Republic." Gilberto Freyre, *Ordem e progresso* (Rio de Janeiro: Editora Record, 1990), 476; my translation.

Interiors of Palace Gustavo Capanema

the late 1950s, Rio de Janeiro accumulated a varied symbolic repertoire as capital of the colony in 1763, capital of the independent empire of Brazil under the regency of Pedro I in 1822, and finally capital of the newly proclaimed republic in 1889. Under the positivist motto of "order and progress," which is slashed across the national flag, modernity and nationhood were closely linked in the consolidation of the republic.

By tearing down the crumbling colonial mansions of the downtown area, razing topographical obstacles that interfered with the opening of new avenues adorned with modern buildings of eclectic architecture, Mayor Francisco Pereira Passos from 1902 to 1906 sought to transform the antiquated capital into a modest version of the Parisian ideal.

Supported by the hygienist endeavors of doctors and engineers, Pereira Passos, in the guise of a local Haussmann, attempted to instill a model of modernity that reproduced in the tropical scenario what was deemed to be the utmost modernity of urban planning forged by French cultural models and, to a lesser extent, American innovations.

Getúlio Vargas's rise to power in the 1930s signaled a rupture with previous cosmopolitan aspirations of the Old Republic. During his reign as supreme dictator of Brazil, Vargas commissioned the construction of several public buildings that were to reflect the edification of the nation according to an assortment of notions concerning the nature of the modern and its linkage to a national ethos. The construction of the Ministry of Education and Health (Ministério da Educação e da Saúde [MES]) in the 1930s and 1940s represented the triumph of the modernist canon—a triumph that was later reflected in the architectural plans for the university campus of the Federal University of Rio de Janeiro in the vicinity of the Fundão, built from 1949 to 1962.[2]

With the shifting of the federal capital from Rio de Janeiro to Brasília in the 1960s, modernist architecture came to directly convey the fabrication of a new national ethos.[3] The modernist canon was exemplarily

2. In this essay I use both the current name—Palace Gustavo Capanema, named after the minister that enabled its construction—and its former name, the Ministry of Education and Health (Ministério da Educação e Saúde [MES]). The archival material contained in the excellent article of Maurício Lissovsky and Paulo Sérgio de Moraes de Sá, "O novo em construção: O edifício-sede do Ministério da Educação e Saúde e a disputa do espaço arquiteturável nos anos 30," in their As colunas da educação: A construção do Ministério da Educação e Saúde, 1935–1945 (Rio de Janeiro: Edições do Patrimônio, 1996), xi–xxvii, served as my main source of documentation for the historical elaboration of this essay. Their article also details the plans for the construction of a university campus at the Fundão. See also Donato Mello Jr., "Um campus universitário para a cidade do Rio de Janeiro," Arquitetura Revista 2 (1985): 52–72.

3. The complete triumph of modernist architecture was fully consolidated with the invention of Brasília in the late 1950s. The international attention that Brasília's construction attracted placed this immense peripheral nation at the vanguard of modernist architecture. Internally, the construction of the capital city in the desertic heart of Brazil emblematized the utopia of a modernity that would irradiate its modernity by the mimetic means of a new national foundation. The modernist city, the new capital of the peripheral country, signaled the possibility of staging the modern outside of its central axis. The remarkable feat of constructing a capital in the tabula rasa of the central plateau of Brazil was the initial signature of an inaugural

embodied in the architect and urban planner Lucio Costa. Costa was the leading figure of the group of architects that constructed the Ministry of Education and Health in the 1930s and 1940s and was responsible for Brasília's urbanistic pilot plan in the 1950s. When in the late 1960s the governor of Rio de Janeiro decided to overcome Rio's demise as an ex-capital by promoting urban expansion in what was then the vast expanse of beaches of the Barra da Tijuca, he summoned Costa to be the fore-most urban planner. Yet the presence of the state became increasingly muted as Rio de Janeiro underwent construction booms fomented by the real estate market. The neighborhood of the Barra da Tijuca initially idealized by governmental agencies soon became a zone of massive real estate speculation. It grew rapidly in the 1970s and became the cultural landmark of a new urban style in the 1990s.

In the implementation of these urban reforms, the modernizing em-blem shifted from urban constructions attempting to emulate cosmo-politan models influenced by nineteenth- and early-twentieth-century French architecture, to the nationalist and internationalist modernist architecture of the 1930s and 1960s, and then to the globalized scenario of the 1990s.

In this essay, I wish to insert the urban strategies of these modern-izing endeavors as background references to a discussion that seeks to uncover the relation between the construction of modernist architec-tural icons in Brazil in the 1930s and the narration of a national moder-nity. In particular, I am interested in exploring how temporality and differing historical perspectives alter both physically and symbolically the validation of a previous national ethos embodied in this case by the modernist building. The decay of the Palace Gustavo Capanema, known in the 1930s and 1940s as the Ministry of Education and Health, and to a lesser extent the decrepitude of the buildings that make up the uni-versity campus of the Federal University of Rio de Janeiro, highlight the conflicting relations of these modernist constructions to their own tem-porality. These modernist architectural forms previously triumphed as

---

history that projected itself into the new architectural shapes. Confronted by regional discrepancies, violent social inequality, and incongruous patterns of premoderniza-tion and modernization, the capital city of glass and concrete emerged as a utopia of a standardized and egalitarian modernity. For a discussion of Brasília's modernist symbology, see James Holston, *The Modernist City* (Chicago: University of Chicago Press, 1989).

the emblematization of national narratives of modernity or projections of the nation on a path to modernity. Nonetheless, as embodiments of the national modern ethos, these state-sponsored constructions decayed. Still, crucial architectural principles instilled by modernist architecture and urban planning continue to subsist in the currents of Brazilian urban real estate markets.

One perspective on these former national icons of modernity is that of the contemporary viewer who contemplates the wreckage of decayed modernist architecture at the end of the twentieth century. By acknowledging the decrepitude of these public buildings, one negates their utopian premises. Built to convey a sense of the new and the ethos of the modern nation, these buildings were constructed under the sign of the future. They anticipated the trajectory of the nation by being the avantgarde of modernity. At the closing of the twentieth century, we glance at the outmoded structure of what was once the future projection of our present.

Although currently being renovated and despite the fact that it never ceased to function as a government office, the building of the Palace Gustavo Capanema suggests in the dismantlement of its structure the paradoxical figure of the modernist ruin. The notion of the modernist ruin, therefore, is not to be taken literally. Yet, neither is it a subjective projection of the nostalgic viewer. These buildings become modernist ruins within a specific moment and context of contemplation. A moment positioned between their former newness and their ultimate implosion — or restoration. In their fractured materials, they translate into ruin the fragility of former utopian projections. What is foregrounded by the decay of these edifices is the contradiction between the purpose of the modernist structure as the embodiment of the new and the tangible display of its datedness in the midst of the cultural transformations of the city.

Built to be both symbolically modern and overtly functional, these buildings lost their newness not only because of their material erosion but also due to the fragmentation of the modernist national ethos that shaped them. The modernist ruin condenses the contradictions of how the objects of modernity, while positing themselves as the new, inevitably bear their own demise and yet deny their aging process. As the emblematization of modernity's newness, the modernist building negotiated a projection of a future that has now become outmoded.

The representations of the national, the experiences of the urban, and the staging of different notions of modernity are also encapsulated in the paradoxical figure of the modernist ruin. In the case of some of the buildings that I will refer to in this essay, the dialogue between modernity and history is further dramatized by the encroachment of natural tropical vegetation on the cultural buildings of functionalist architecture.

In contrast to the modernist ruins, the real estate boom of the new beachfront neighborhood of the Barra da Tijuca in Rio de Janeiro offers the spectacle of globalized consumerism under the full sway of the market. The apparent opposition between the former avant-garde buildings now transfigured into modernist ruins and the triumph of the contemporary towers of the Barra da Tijuca narrates an important aspect of the cultural trajectory of the city of Rio de Janeiro. While discussing this trajectory, I am interested in exploring the specificity of a tropical modernity in a city that was not only once the capital of Brazil but also a synecdoche for a Brazilian cultural ethos.

In discussing together these buildings that belong to different layers of modernization, I have attempted to construct an imaginary maquette where several concepts of the city are staged: the city as polis, the city as the locus of citizens and the state, the city as the market habitat of consumers, and the city as an imaginary community forged by contrasting multicultural heritages. In piecing together this maquette, I have made use of Aldo Rossi's notion of the analogous city and, more fundamentally, of Walter Benjamin's concept of the dialectical image.[4]

Rossi suggests that each city unfolds into several other cities. These analogous cities take shape from repertoires of associations that include the collective memories of history, personalized remembrances of the past, and subjective fluctuations of the wanderer within the urban maze.

4. For references to the notion of the analogous city, see Aldo Rossi, *A Scientific Autobiography* (Cambridge, Mass.: MIT Press, 1981). See also Patrizia Lombardo, "Plaza d'Italia," in *Tre Citta*, ed. Aldo Rossi (Milan: Electra, 1984), and Beatriz Jaguaribe, "Os passos perdidos: Cidade e mito," *Revista do Patrimônio Histórico Artístico e Nacional* 23 (1994): 247–61. For a discussion of Aldo Rossi's interpretation of the monument, see David Harvey, *The Condition of Postmodernity: An Enquiry into the Origins of Cultural Change* (Oxford: Basil Blackwell, 1989). For an interpretation of Benjamin's arcades project and his concept of the dialectical image, see Susan Buck-Morss, *The Dialectics of Seeing: Walter Benjamin and the Arcades Project* (Cambridge, Mass.: MIT Press, 1993).

In the midst of the turbulent transformations of the modern metropolis, monuments withstand as promises of a collective memory that can be activated by the architect or urban planner.

While recapturing the memories of modernity of the Paris arcades in the nineteenth century, Benjamin evoked the discarded consumer items of the past with a construction of the dialectical image. Akin to the allegorical gaze, the dialectical image effects a juxtaposition of meanings, a montage that unsettles mythical interpretations by estranging its elements and demonstrating its incongruities. By recasting the notion of the analogous city within that dialectical image, one allows monuments to become not merely the architectural support for a historical collectivity but an allegorical construction of historical interfaces.

In the arcades project, Benjamin collected the debris of old splendors. Dusty mannequins, rusty machines, aged photographs, frayed corsets, and moth-eaten top hats became artifacts of the outdatedness of modernity's former newness, archeological fossils of fashion that represented the perpetuation of the image of the ephemeral. The memories of modernity posit a discrete paradox. The modern projects itself as the new, the actual, the contemporary. While remembering former modernities, we evoke their pastness to authenticate the newness of "what's new" and yet filter the contemporary through a gauze of the particles of the past. The relation of negation and affirmation modern objects perpetuate with their historical trajectory and durability promotes a juxtaposition of opposing temporalities. The patina of age coats discarded fashions with the aura of past experiences, and monuments weathered by time or disfigured by graffiti reveal their perishability.

In the mutations of a historical ethos and by means of the very erosion wrought by time, monuments become ruins. The monument as ruin either acquires a different symbolic aura on the rubble of its very deconstruction or is refunctionalized to project something distinct from its initial architectonic purpose. The monument as ruin transforms itself into a dialectical image in the varied repertoires of the analogous city.

Examples of modernist ruins (such as the buildings of the former Ministry of Education and Health and the edifices of the Federal University) reveal by their decomposition not only their architectural perishability but also the evanescence of a modern national project erected according to the totalizing parameters of the modernist pantheon. The ruins of classical empires expressed the invincibility of time and the resisting grandeur of human constructions. The romantic appraisal of gothic or Roman ruins enshrouded them in the melancholic acknowledgment of past greatness deterred by natural forces.[5] Modernist ruins express the decrepitude of the new. In their rebellion against the action of time, they manifest a denial of death and a negation of history. But the natural realm covers the writings of history as sure as vegetation smothers concrete. Paradoxically, history is once again reaffirmed in the inevitable ephemerality of constructions that supersede one another. The modernist ruin as the defeat of the new and as the debunkment of a future utopia offers no exemplary redemption.

THE TROPICAL BELLE ÉPOQUE AND THE MODERNIST INVENTION

An enduring trait of the modernizing urban strategies of Rio de Janeiro was an obsessive promotion of the new and the modern. The vogue mirage of modernity fomented the construction of eclectic architecture in Rio's Belle Époque. Stylized techniques of ornamentation that recalled the past were incorporated not because they nostalgically signaled the opulence of former eras in the bleakness of modernity but because they were the newest trend in France.

In the late nineteenth and early twentieth centuries, the imitative efforts of local urbanists who sought to transform Rio de Janeiro into a tropical Paris gave rise to a vast assortment of marble muses, colored glass reproductions of European landscapes, revivalist gargoyles, and other Parisian replicas. Set against the tropical vegetation and in the torrid heat of Rio de Janeiro, these European replicas, often made in cheaper materials than their European models, decayed quickly, offering the spectacle that Claude Lévi-Strauss would summarize in his famous axiom, "Les tropiques sont moins exotiques que démodés." Clothed in English cashmere or encased in velvets and corsets, the local elite of the Belle Époque attempted to keep, despite its being somewhat beaded with sweat, a civilized stiff upper lip as they paraded the slogan, "Rio is becoming civilized." But one of the enduring features of Rio de

---

5. For a discussion of the meaning of classical ruins in romantic literature, see Laurence Goldstein, *Ruins and Empire: The Evolution of a Theme in Augustan and Romantic Literature* (Pittsburgh, Pa.: University of Pittsburgh Press, 1977).

Janeiro was the strength of its multicultural urban heritage that would not be obliterated by the maintenance of a European facade.

Machado de Assis, Lima Barreto, João do Rio, and other writers of the late nineteenth and early twentieth centuries focused their attention on the contradictory social experiences of the modernization of the federal capital. Whether in the ironic prose of Machado that subtly detected the incongruities of a slave-owning society that outwardly endorsed bourgeois patterns of citizenship; in the social protest of the excluded articulated in Barreto's novels; or in the exotic decadentist scenarios of João do Rio's opium dens and religious sites, Rio de Janeiro unfolded as a variegated multiracial society of transcultural practices.

With the modernist movement of 1922, the transcultural legacy of Brazil was consolidated, and the nation was reinaugurated under a mestizo pantheon. Contact with the European avant-garde, the valorization of the primitive, and the desire to seek the specificity of cultural interactions outside the European norm led to a severe critique of the cosmopolitanism of the Belle Époque. Oswald de Andrade's "Anthropophagic manifesto" (1928) offered a satirical model of cultural appropriation: No longer imitators or subservient colonial subjects, Brazilians were now cultural cannibals who devoured the more savory bits of European culture and cooked them together with African and Indian ingredients into an overwhelming cultural concoction.[6] Modernist innovations in literature and the arts forged under the impact of the Semana de Arte Moderna movement in 1922 contrasted to the predominant architectural forms of the 1920s that either reproduced eclectic buildings or recultivated colonial roots with a neocolonial architecture.

Modernist architectural consciousness in Brazil decidedly breached the public sphere in 1925 when the Russian émigré Gregori Warchavchik wrote a newspaper article that became the first Brazilian "Manifesto of Functional Architecture." And in 1929, Le Corbusier's meteoric arrival in Rio shook the very foundations of previous architectural paradigms. During the 1930s, Getúlio Vargas rose to power in a revolutionary struggle that left a cleavage between elite bastions of the formerly oligarchic Brazil and a new, tentatively urban, Brazil with an incipient middle class. By 1937, Vargas, now entrenched as the supreme dictator

6. Oswald de Andrade's *Manifesto antropófago,* in *Vanguarda Européia e modernismo Brasileiro* ed. Gilberto Mendonça Teles (Petrópolis: Editora Vozes, 1983), 353–60.

of the Estado Novo, had established cultural ties with the most important sectors of the modernist intelligentsia, and it was by means of the prominent writers of this modernist group—among whom were Carlos Drummond de Andrade, Manuel Bandeira, and Mário de Andrade— that modernist architecture found expression in Brazil, chiefly by way of the Minister Gustavo Capanema's sponsorship of Lucio Costa.

In 1935, a public competition for the contract to design the new Ministry of Education and Health was undertaken. Although the official winners of the competition were awarded monetary prizes, their design was never implemented. Instead, a parallel committee was set up that awarded the design to Lucio Costa and a group of modernist architects including Oscar Niemeyer. The MES they constructed was the first modernist functionalist public building in Brazil.[7] Its design was directly influenced by Le Corbusier, and it became a hallmark of a new foundational ethos.

MODERNIST ICONS: THE MINISTRY OF EDUCATION AND HEALTH AND THE FEDERAL UNIVERSITY

In the 1930s, Vargas inaugurated the construction of a series of monumental government buildings: the famously modernist MES, the Ministry of Finance (Department of the Treasury), and the Ministry of Labor.

In these architectonic undertakings, one senses that the implementation of the new was not merely a question of formal constructions but a reappraisal of Brazilian history. The official modernist gesture aligned with the modernist intelligentsia tried to reorder national history to renegotiate the vestiges of the past that the ornamental and imitative architecture of the Belle Époque had protagonized. But it was an incomplete project because while culture, education, and health were contained within a modernist building of the utmost avant-garde spirit, both the Ministry of Finance and the Ministry of Labor were erected according to conventional, monumental, and eclectic architectural principles.[8]

7. See Alberto Xavier, Alfredo Britto, and Ana Luiza Nobre, *Arquitetura moderna no Rio de Janeiro* (Rio de Janeiro: Rioarte, 1991).
8. For a discussion concerning the symbolic and ideological disputes between the modernism of the MES and the symbology of the Ministry of Finance, see Lauro Cavalcanti, *As preocupações do belo* (Rio de Janeiro: Taurus, 1995).

Ministry of Finance

In contrast to the imposing, monumental marble architecture of the Ministry of Finance—an architecture that is reminiscent both of Albert Speer's Nazi colossus and the grandiose revivalist constructions of the Italian fascists—the symbology of the MES is discrete, oblique, and abstract.

In the interaction between government agencies and the modernist intelligentsia, the construction of the MES anticipated the invention of Brasília, which they would collaborate on in the 1950s. The cost of these undertakings made it clear that the invention of a new vision of architecture would have to be espoused by an ideological ethos that could be contained within the parameters of government projects. This ethos fluctuated according to the political currents and variously embraced concepts such as modernization, egalitarianism, developmentalism, and civic-mindedness. At stake in each undertaking—be it the construction of the MES during the Estado Novo or the invention of Brasília during Juscelino Kubitschek's democratic regime—was a reordering of Brazilian history encapsulated by the mythic resonance of the notion of modernization.

The dispute vis-à-vis strategies of modernization was waged between factions of the modernist literati seeking to define themselves against the progressivist, positivist modernism endorsed by the scientistic elite of the Belle Époque. The struggle for the acceptance of new modernist ideals implied not only their gradual institutionalization but also a battle with previously institutionalized canons. In this saga, the role of arbiter of the modern was delegated to the foreign architect whose presence contributed validity and authority to the implementation of local modernism. In the dispute that followed the construction of the MES, the interaction between Le Corbusier, the minister Gustavo Capanema, and the dictator Getúlio Vargas revealed the ambiguities between institutional power, international modernism, and peripheral nations.

Only in relatively young peripheral countries would it be possible to create a new historical horizon based on a new architectural mythology—an architectural mythology dependent on the approval of the foreign architect-as-arbiter who would guarantee the international relevance of national architectonic projects. Yet the notion of the modern fabricated by the promotion of the new, a newness invented in Europe, was not necessarily synonymous with the eradication of the past. The "new" modernity of the MES was inserted into a pattern of allegorical prefigurations wherein the "new" referred to the past in order to project the future.

The new modern Brazilian architecture sought to encompass a multicultural heritage not by folklorist appropriation but by means of the evocation of atemporal universal forms that expressed its historical process. The international neutrality of the glass façades, brise-soleil, and pilotis was attenuated by the presence of a mosaic of blue tiles tinged with the same nuance of blue as the tiles of the baroque churches in Rio. Portinari's mural paintings describing the economic cycles of sugarcane and coffee and other episodes of Brazilian history reinforced a national epic narrative.

Maurício Lissovsky and Paulo Moraes suggest that an indispensable quality of the "new" was contained in the criteria of durability, monumentality, and functionality.[9] The criteria of functionality was the unquestionable basis of modernist architecture. The principles of circulation, hygienization, and flexible compartmentalization, principles that urbanists at the beginnings of the century also espoused, seemed to encounter their ideal translation in the spacious functionality of modernist

9. See Lissovsky and Moraes, *O novo em construção*, 3.

Palace Gustavo Capanema

architecture. Le Corbusier's notion of the house as "a machine to live in" and Mies van der Rohe's minimalist axiom of "less is more" also constituted the architectural vocabulary of the MES.

The modernist building's claim to monumentality and durability, however, was undermined by objections. Contrary to the Ministry of Finance building's ornamental eclecticism stuffed with historical references, noble materials, and folkloric murals depicting indigenous costumes, the MES's allusions to the past are ecliptic and lack authority. The colossal statue of the "Brazilian man" who was to be depicted standing upright and stark naked finally was never undertaken because the minister Capanema and the sculptor Celso Antonio could not come to an agreement as to what kind of Caucasian or mestizo features the statue should have.[10] The discrete symbology of the MES was directed against the eclectic and leaned toward the valorization of a baroque colonial memory. As several researchers have stated, the modernists laid claim to being the arbiters of the past and of the future. The past, as represented in the eclectic ornamental architecture of the Belle Époque, which was

10. For a discussion of the Brazilian colossus see Cavalcanti, *As preocupações do belo,* 8, and Lissovsky and Moraes, *O novo em construção,* 3.

considered the height of modernity at the beginning of the century, was transformed via contrast to authentic baroque and the new modern into kitsch.

In a visit to Rio de Janeiro in 1926, Gilberto Freyre noted the discrepancies between the tropical milieu and the horrid architectural constructions that uglified the natural surroundings. Upon visiting the newly constructed Legislative House, Freyre commented:

> The frontispiece of the building is adorned with sculptured figures. National figures. Figures from Brazilian history. And these Brazilian figures by means of a most comical criterion of harmony or classicism are garbed in Roman style. It is as a character out of a vaudeville show—and the subject has already been represented in a theatrical spectacle—that the figure of Colonel Benjamin Constant emerges. A Benjamin Constant with goatee and pince-nez, dressed in a Roman skirt, with bare arms and legs holding the reins of General Deodoro's fiery horse. The General is also dressed in Roman fashion. He holds a sword the size of a kitchen knife. Everything of an amazing ridicule.[11]

Yet this model of the Belle Époque had been considered the highest vogue of modernization in the urbanistic reforms of Pereira Passos, reforms that evicted the poor from crumbling colonial houses in the center of Rio and opened new suburbs, fomenting the division between the northern and southern zones of the city and the encircling shantytowns. However, at the time of Freyre's visit to the Legislative House, even in the Europeanized center designed for the elegant promenade of the local elite, the intermingling of social classes and racial groups was part of the urban spectacle and of the commotion of the urban street scene. Bars, bookstores, street vendors, bahianas in turbans, immigrants with their national rural costumes, and the local elite in their English cashmere jostled one another in the parks and squares. The pulsation of street life in Rio was largely a mixture of multicultural practices. Despite repressive measures, African cults and Afro-Brazilian music had a strong presence in the Belle Époque: In the 1920s and 1930s, at the intersection of Belle Époque buildings, baroque churches, and modern-

11. See Gilberto Freyre, *Tempo de aprendiz,* vol. 2 (São Paulo: Instituicao Brasileira de Difusao Cultural, 1978), 275; my translation.

ist skyscrapers, the tunes of the samba descended from the *favelas*.[12] In favor of the preservation of the street ambiance, Freyre argued in vain against models of urbanization that privileged the automobile and condemned to oblivion the subtle joys of flanerie.

The obliteration of the street scene, a crucial element of Le Corbusier's urban planning, was enacted in Brasília by means of Costa's functionalist compartmentalization of recreational and working areas and the construction of the "super-blocks."[13] Although the MES was constructed during Vargas's authoritarian regime and Brasília was erected during Kubitschek's democratic regime, the modernist city would later be incarcerated by authoritarian symbolic appropriations. Interpreted by the modernist supporters as a monument of intelligence against obscurantism and baptized by Roquette Pinto as the "Crystal Palace of the Guanabara," the MES in the transparency of its architecture could not but dialogue with the contrasting images of the surrounding polis.

According to Lissovsky and Moraes, the MES's most vulnerable point was its precarious durability.[14] The abundance of glass, the frailty of the pilotis, and the open spaces that could be appropriated by beggars or excluded outsiders were deposed against an architecture that had as its base the principles of functionality. These objections were tossed aside by means of analogies between modernist architectonic principles and classicism. Le Corbusier's pilotis conveyed the eternal aura of Greek columns in antiquity.

During the period in which the MES was being projected, another grandiose modernist project was also germinating. The University of Brazil, the contemporary Federal University of Rio de Janeiro, demanded a new campus and academic installations. In the struggle between contending factions, there arose a dispute between the followers of Le Corbusier and the admirers of Marcello Piacentini, the renowned Italian architect. Piacentini had been responsible for the new build-

12. See Hermano Vianna, *O mistério do samba* (Rio de Janeiro: Jorge Zahar and Universidade Federal do Rio de Janeiro Editora, 1995).

13. A key design element in suburban real estate development starting in the 1920s, the "super-block" featured prominently in the planning of numerous suburbias and "new towns" in Great Britain and the United States, including Radburn, New Jersey, "town for the motor age."

14. See Lissovsky and Moraes, *O novo em construção*, 3.

ings of the University of Rome. He was admired by the fascist regime for his ability to fabricate new buildings with the auratic monumentality of classical antiquity. Piacentini and Le Corbusier represented distinct ideological factions and disputes, although some of the collectivizing traits of internationalist architecture closely resembled those of fascist inspiration. The European strife between international modernist architecture and the architecture of totalitarian regimes had clear repercussions in Vargas's authoritarian nationalist policy. In Germany, Speer, Hitler's favorite architect, emphasized the notion that Nazi constructions should anticipate their future ruins, ruins that should inspire heroic thoughts for future millennia.[15]

Although it also sought to construct its own brand of monumentality, modernist internationalist architecture was not directly linked to a recaptured monumentalization of the past. The modernist monument primarily designated a future that was already contained in its own inaugural design. The "new" escaped historical temporality, rebelled against its inevitable aging, did not intend to see itself as a ruin, and did not aspire to the same heroic thoughts of the fascist architects. History was a progressive becoming which the modernist structure should always anticipate. Even the Brazilian MES, with its tenuous linkages to the past, was built to be a building that would appear to have been inaugurated daily. Time should not count in the congealed space of the future. But the modernist architectural solution shaped on the premises of the new inevitably invited its own dethronement by yet another, newer newness. As a monument to the creation of the *new,* modernist architecture would have to mythically immobilize itself in the eternal new in order to escape the ravages of time.

*

Shards of glass, peeling plaster, rusty steel, shattered brise-soleil, broken tiles, humidity stains, and the abundant growth of weeds are part of the repertoire of decadence that until recently enshrouded the MES, the former icon of modernist architecture in Brazil.

At the other extreme of the city, the modernist campus of the Federal University of Rio de Janeiro, a project that emerged in the contentions between Piacentini and Le Corbusier in the 1930s and finally

15. See Albert Speer, *Inside the Third Reich* (New York: Macmillan, 1970), 56, 154.

broke ground in 1949, offers a desolate spectacle. Le Corbusier's modernist principles triumphed, but the actual buildings have been transformed into dysfunctional masses of decaying concrete. The modernist buildings rise like standardized blocks of concrete in the midst of deadened vegetation and scalding asphalt lanes. The decentralization of the constructions that Vargas had deliberately chosen to be a part of the university's urban planning in order to deter possible student protests has in fact served its purpose: Each department is an isolated bunker. Precarious public transportation induces students to agglutinate frantically around the main exits in a desperate attempt to escape from the functionalist maze.

In addition to mismanagement stemming from bureaucratic ineptitude, these buildings are also imploding under the weight of their material deterioration. Patios and corridors suffocate beneath the debris of discarded papers and broken materials. Benches and sculptures are embraced by weeds and fungi. If in Walter Benjamin's poetic evocation "allegories are in the realm of thought what ruins are in the realm of things," the eroding campus of the Federal University and the decadence of the former Ministry of Education and Health are allegorical ruins of the modernist collapse.[16] The material recuperation of these buildings points to how very urgent the promotion of their functional premises becomes. Made to be functional, they cannot age gracefully because the very notion of aging is incompatible with their functionality as architectural machines.

BARRA DA TIJUCA AND THE AESTHETICS OF CONSUMPTION

The vision of modernist ruins or of former icons of now decadent modernist buildings are part of a symbolic mapping that includes contemporary skyscrapers and postmodern luxury high-rises and condominiums in the Barra da Tijuca. The modernist ruin is therefore not merely a matter of the actual physical decadence of the buildings but also of the fracturing of a previous ethos that was never fulfilled and has already become dated.

In the high-rise buildings of the hypermodern Barra da Tijuca in

16. See Walter Benjamin, *The Origin of German Tragic Drama,* trans. John Osborne (London: Verso, 1977), 178.

Rio de Janeiro, modernist functionality becomes kitsch ostentation by means of a showy paraphernalia of gadgets and technical devices ornamentally strewn to emphasize the overwhelming presence of the contemporary.

Contemporary modernist skyscrapers and exclusive condominiums constructed according to derivative modernist paradigms or postmodern citations are fenced off in a rigid isolation, fortifying and arming themselves against the intrusion of the impoverished city. The condominiums of the Barra da Tijuca in particular aspire to be high- or middle-class havens from the swelling slums. Centered on standardized patterns of what a contemporary upper-middle-class lifestyle is supposed to be, the Barra da Tijuca enacts an ambiguous dilemma vis-à-vis the rest of Rio de Janeiro.

Costa had initially planned the Barra da Tijuca according to Le Corbusier's urbanistic design of megatowers enclosed in green gardens and interconnected by high-speed avenues. Similarly to the standardized super-blocks of Brasília, the apartment buildings of New Ipanema and New Leblon built by the architects Edmundo and Edison Musa according to Costa's concepts were intended to correct the urban chaos of neighborhoods such as Copacabana and to promote family living in a secure and neighborly ambiance.

Ironically, the design of Brasília's super-blocks—initially projected as a means of promoting social egalitarianism and solidarity—became in the Barra da Tijuca the design of enclosed condominiums that expel any outsider who does not pass the surveillance of the guarded community. In these fortified anticities, alongside lower- and middle-class sectors, the nouveau riche have found a congenial habitat. Coined by newspaper social columns as the "emergents," the newly wealthy of the Barra da Tijuca are eager to extol the qualities of their lifestyle, a lifestyle that emphasizes ostentatious displays of kitsch such as Persian carpets covering the interiors of Mercedes Benz automobiles, golden helicopters, and high-tech gadgetry, as well as "authentic" baroque saints strategically placed beside canvasses of the "emergent" painter Romanelli, who paints pictures on order to match upholstery. In their eagerness to emulate California wealth and Miami lifestyles, the real estate advertisements of the Barra da Tijuca also emphasize a paradoxical relation to Rio de Janeiro. On the one hand, the Barra da Tijuca is the quintessence of the new: a "newness" that is continuously spectacularized in real estate propaganda, in the inauguration of mega shopping malls, in the construction of new facilities; a "newness" that attempts to create an amnesiac utopia of consumerism crystallized in the globalized scenario of the shopping mall and protected by an architecture of fear that seeks to privilege the existence of the city as a market, the privileged space of consumers who have a right to citizenship according to their purchasing power. In its lack of historical density, however, the Barra da Tijuca attempts to create its own mythology as a former Rio that never quite existed but that is now being repackaged. Not only are the architectural landmarks of Rio de Janeiro reconstructed inside the protected sphere of the shopping mall, but also the model condominiums are suggestively named New Leblon and New Ipanema. A new Leblon and Ipanema that promote the actualization of a former mythic moment where the beach was the public garden of the "girls from Ipanema," and social tension and unrest were nonexistent.[17] Faced with the increasing violence and menace of the explosive city, the New Leblon and New Ipanema condominiums offer a secluded protective space, a suburban retreat that offers the mythology of a false past while canceling what Baudelaire used to call the commotion of the modern: the vision of the modern city with its assortment of strangers, buildings, and unexpected encounters.

Between the utopia contained in the modernist ruin-monument, the super-block of Brasília, and the contemporary condominium lies a trajectory of the architectural projections and failed state projects that sought to imprint an exemplary and totalizing transformation of Brazilian society.

RENOVATED RUINS

The eighteenth-century mania for ruins centered on a theatrical spectacularization of the contrast between the decay of human constructions set against the natural environment. Ruins were especially

---

17. "A Garota de Ipanema" was cowritten by composer Antônio Carlos Jobim and poet and lyricist Vinícius de Morais. An adherent of the 1930s Brazilian Modernism, Vinícius's career saw him assume the vice-consulate of Brazil in Los Angeles from 1947 to 1950, around the same time that Jobim's transformations of the Brazilian samba into the bossa nova earned him worldwide success and shortly before Stan Getz's rendering, "The Girl from Ipanema," became the most successful vehicle for circulating bossa nova in the United States.

valued by the later Romantics when their death-bearing silhouettes were framed by live natural overgrowth, when the embrace of ivies and leaves covered the monumental stone. The debunking of past eras was as much a testimony of the civilizing efforts to make history and a demonstration of the need to deposit a cultural signature on the natural as it was a sign of the impossibility of overcoming the devastations of time. Ruins were so impregnated with historical aura that in the eighteenth century the fashion of creating artificial ruins became highly prized.[18] Whether authentic or artificial, the ruin mania of the eighteenth and the nineteenth centuries suggests the need of the modern present to ground and contrast itself to a previous historical trajectory.

In *England's Ruins: Poetic Purpose and Natural Landscape,* Anne Janowitz remarks that in Britain the romantic penchant for ruins was part of a more extensive process of imaginary nation-building.[19] The expansion of the British empire was further reinforced by the vision of its lengthy history. The trail of ruins littering the natural landscape fostered a sense of empire being nurtured by the naturalization of the ruin transformed into a token of mythic origins.

In contrast, the sense of nation-building in Brazil was upheld by the promise of the modern rather than by the ruins of a relatively recent colonial past. Paradoxically, the modernist building of the former MES reflected in its decadence a unique "aura" of a past modernity that is expressed in the memory of unfulfilled utopias, in an evocation of an imagined national modernity, in failed aspirations that speak to us of an era of public intellectuals, educational projects, and the construction of a modern mestizo national pantheon. The modernist ruin of the

18. See Carlo Carena, "Ruína/Restaura," in *Einaudi Encyclopedia,* vol. 1 (Lisbon: Imprensa Nacional-Casa da Moeda, 1984), 107–29. Carena reveals that the French specialist Delille admonished against the trendy fondness for false ruins. He cautioned readers that real historical value could only be found in those ruins that had been effectively destroyed by time. In Benjamin's terminology, one could say that Delille was protesting against the "deauratization" of the ruin by means of an artificial reproduction that abolished the veracity of its uniqueness. While the historical ruin projected a sentiment of the sublime, the artificial ruin was a mere commodity. See Walter Benjamin, "The Work of Art in the Age of Mechanical Reproduction," in *Illuminations: Essays and Reflections,* ed. Hannah Arendt, trans. Harry Zohn (New York: Schocken, 1969), 217–51.

19. Anne Janowitz, *England's Ruins: Poetic Purpose and the National Landscape* (London: Basil Blackwell, 1990).

MES expressed also the transitory nature of its own functionality. The physical recuperation of the building marks its passage from modernist monument to modernist ruin and to an ultimately reconstructed icon.

The modernist building in Rio de Janeiro symbolized a dream of reason in what was perceived to be the city of chaos. As a modernist ruin it can be bathed in the nostalgic light of past illusions. It is now being renovated as a souvenir of the modernist past in the contemporary scenario of the postmodern. It can be subjected to naturalized neutrality as a mere office building that is functional or dysfunctional according to the fluctuations of the political and economic circumstances. Yet, in the contradictory pulses of the city, the modernist ruin dismantles its utopian project and becomes a monument that resymbolizes our historical trajectories by fabricating a myriad of dialogues with the recent past. The aged functionalized building projects its dismantling silhouette against the changing city. Modernist tiles contrast to the kitsch trinkets sold by street vendors. The unconfined city transforms architectural forms and national narrations into a plurality of histories.

Contributors

Homi Bhabha is Chester D. Tripp Professor in the Humanities at the University of Chicago, where he teaches English and art history. His publications include *The Location of Culture* (1994) and the edited volume *Nation and Narration* (1990).

William Cunningham Bissell is finishing his Ph.D. in anthropology at the University of Chicago on conservation, colonialism, and the city in Zanzibar.

Dipesh Chakrabarty teaches South Asian history and history of culture at the University of Chicago. He is the author of *Rethinking Working-Class History: Bengal, 1890–1940* (1989); *Provincializing Europe: Postcolonial Thought and Historical Difference* (2000); and *History as Critique: Debating the Pasts of Modernity in India* (forthcoming).

Dilip Parameshwar Gaonkar teaches rhetoric and cultural studies at Northwestern University. His recent publications include "The Idea of Rhetoric in the Rhetoric of Science" in *Rhetorical Hermeneutics* (1996) and a coedited volume, *Disciplinarity and Dissent in Cultural Studies* (1996).

Michael Hanchard teaches political science at Northwestern University. His recent publications include "Jody" (*Critical Inquiry*, Winter 1998) and *Orpheus and Power* (1994).

Beatriz Jaguaribe teaches communications at the Federal University of Rio de Janeiro. Her publications include *Fins de século: cidade e cultura no Rio de Janeiro* (1998) and, with Nizia Villaça, *Rio de Janeiro: cartografias simbolicas* (1994).

Leo Ou-fan Lee teaches Chinese literature at Harvard University. His publications include *Voices from the Iron House: A Study of Lu Xun* (1987) and *Shanghai Modern* (1999).

Claudio Lomnitz teaches history and anthropology at the University of Chicago. His publications include *Exits from the Labyrinth: Culture and Ideology in Mexican National Space* (1992), "An Intellectual's Stock in the Factory of Mexican Ruins" (*Journal of American Sociology*, 1998), and the forthcoming *Deep Mexico, Silent Mexico: Nationalism and the Public Sphere.*

Thomas McCarthy teaches philosophy at Northwestern University. His recent publications include *Ideals and Illusions: Reconstruction and Deconstruction in Contemporary Critical Theory* (1991) and, with David Couzens Hoy, *Critical Theory* (1994).

Tejaswini Niranjana is a Senior Fellow at the Centre for the Study of Culture and Society in Bangalore. Her publications include *Siting Translation: History, Poststructuralism, and the Colonial Context* (1992) and the coedited volume *Interrogating Modernity: Culture and Colonialism in India* (1993).

Elizabeth A. Povinelli teaches anthropology at the University of Chicago. Her recent publications include "The State of Shame: Australian Multiculturalism and the Crisis of Indigenous Citizenship" (*Critical Inquiry*, Winter 1998) and "Reading Ruptures, Rupturing Readings: Mabo and the Cultural Politics of Activism" (*Social Analysis*, 1997).

Shahzia Sikander attended the National College of Art in Lahore, Pakistan, and the Rhode Island School of Design before holding a residency in the Core Program at the Museum of Fine Arts in Houston. She now lives and paints in New York City.

Charles Taylor teaches philosophy at McGill University. He is the author of *Sources of the Self: The Making of Modern Identity* (1989) and *The Ethics of Authenticity* (1992).

Andrew Wachtel teaches Slavic languages and literatures at Northwestern University. His recent publications include *Making a Nation, Breaking a Nation: Literature and Cultural Politics in Yugoslavia* (1998) and an edited volume, *Petrushka: Sources and Contexts* (1998).

Index

Costa, Lucio, 330, 336, 341, 344
Creative adaptation, 18, 20, 21, 22, 23, 183, 184, 185, 229
Creolization, 265, 268
Crowd, 108, 301; urban, 111
Cultural assimilation, 41
Cultural nationalists, 18
Cultural performance, 54
Cultural politics, 250
Cultural production, 113, 115
Culture: adversary, 13, 16; "African," 252; of circulation, 119; civic, 224; indigenous, 28; mass-mediated, 224, 225; material, 96; metropolitan, 5; modern, 233; mono, 237; non-Western, 17; patriarchal, 235; political, 219, 220, 221, 224, 225, 226, 232; popular, 19, 121, 224, 225; public, 220; subculture, 146; traditional, 36, 55; urban material, 103; Western, 105, 116; Western material, 106; world, 181

DaMatta, Roberto, 299, 302, 324
Dafu, Yu, 99, 110
Dandy, 13, 110; Bengali, 151
Darnton, Robert, 115
Davidson, Basil, 273
Day, Lal Behari, 134
de Iturbide, Agustine, 306
Democracy, 136, 139, 140, 146, 216, 219, 221, 222, 223, 301, 341; democractic society, 200, 201; democratic speech, 138; democractic theory, 224; democratic thought, 228; democratization of literary taste, 143; liberal, 316; Mexican, 322–326; modern, 196
Deosaran, Ramesh, 270
Department stores, in Shanghai, 95–97
Derrida, Jacques, 73
Devi, Sarala, 142
Dialectical image, 332, 333
Diaspora, 249, 275, 288; African, 273, 274, 280, 285, 297; global, 36; subaltern, 250, 252

Diasporic: Afro-diasporic people, 276; artists, 167; Indians, 256
Diaz, Porfirio, 316, 325
Difference, 15, 23, 44, 55, 171, 182, 183, 188, 276, 233, 262; colonial, 262; cultural, 167, 216, 232, 234, 264; ethnic difference, 214, 264; racial, 264, 284, 296; social, 35
Dignity, 49, 188, 194, 305
Discourse, 111; of home, 299, 300; political, 217; public, 220; of street, 299, 300, 311
Diversity, 202, 204, 205; cultural, 212, 224, 225
Divergence, 23, 234
Dostoevsky, Fyodor, 67, 68, 69, 71, 75, 85
Double consciousness, 3
Douglas, Ann, 95
Dover Beach, 185, 188
Du Bois, W. E. B., 287, 288, 290
Durkheim, Emile, 174
Dutt, Michael Madhusudan, 141, 144
Duxiu, Chen, 112
Dzhabaev, Dzhambul, 81, 82

Eliot, T. S., 7
Emancipation, 258, 283, 288, 304
Emblems, 327, 331; modernizing, 330
Emigration, 19, 255, 256, 258, 260; indentured, 256, 257
Emundo, 344
Enemies, 299, 302, 303
Enlightenment, 6, 7, 8, 9, 10, 11, 13, 115, 275; package, 180; Western post-Enlightenment tradition, 112
Entertainment, 89, 95, 97
Entrepreneurship, 184
Equality, 202, 221, 223, 296, 320, 321; legal, 223; racial, 288, 294; substantive, 213
Escalante, Fernando, 315
Essentialism, 34
Ethnic, 27, 199, 200, 239; cleansing, 199; groups, 44
Ethnicity, 206, 250, 270

John, Saint, 68
Johnston, Tess, 92
Juarez, 310, 316, 325
Justice, 225; economic and social, 45; natural, 39
Justification, 229; rational, 191

Kant, Immanuel, 11, 12, 13, 194, 197, 198, 203, 204–16, 217, 222, 223, 226, 234, 234, 278
Keating, Paul John, 41, 42
Kelly, John, 259
Kenesbayev, S. K., 80
Keynesianism, 224
Khlebnikov, Velimir, 72, 73, 74, 75
King, Martin Luther, 294, 295, 296
Kirkland, Frank, 277, 278, 279
Kitsch, 340, 344, 347
Kubitschek, Juscelino, 337, 341
Kymlicka, Will, 220

Language: protolanguages, 72, 73; Russian, 65; universal, 65, 72, 75, 82, 83; universal language theories, 71
Law, 39, 57, 207, 217, 221, 231, 299, 302, 303, 317; aboriginal, 28, 43, 48; ancient, 27, 32, 33, 37, 40, 41, 42, 44, 53; coercive, 209; common, 26, 32, 39, 41, 42, 49, 55; constitutional, 218; cosmopolitan, 213, 214; customary, 27, 34, 39; indigenous, 26, 28, 31, 39; international, 208, 209, 212, 213, 216; modern, 18, 229, 231; national, 213; natural, 218; positive, 217; public coercive, 207, 209, 210; sacred, 56; social, 40; statutory, 218; traditional, 26, 29, 39, 49, 55; universal, 213
Law of peoples, the, 212, 225, 230
Le Corbusier, 335, 336, 338, 339, 341, 342, 343, 344
Lee, Leo Ou-fan, 21
Lefebvre, François-Joseph, 161, 162
Legal pacificism, 212, 216
Leite, Jose Correia, 287

Lenin, Vladimir Ilyich, 79
Lermontov, Mikhail Yuryevich, 67
Lévi-Strauss, Claude, 334
Liang Qichao, 111–14
Liberal, 308; capital, 43; nation, 27; nationalism, 27, 203; nation-state, 27; parliament, 29; political theorists, 197; power, 28; principles, 197; state, 41; theorists, 27, 201, 203; theory, 197; universalism, 197
Liberalism, 43, 197, 203, 307
Life-world, 4, 8, 295
Linguistics: universalist thought, 82; universality, 84
Lipkin, Semen, 81
Lissovsky, Maurício, 338, 341
Literature: Chinese leftist, 119; French, 98; global, 147; modern, 99, Western, 114, 120; world, 79, 80, 107, 145, 147
Locke, Alain, 286, 288, 289
Locke, John, 228
Lomnitz, Claudio, 16
Lomonosov, Mikhail, 64, 65
Lopez, Ignacio Rayon, 305
Lopez, Jesus, 309
Luckman, Thomas, 281
Lukács, Georg, 10
Luther, Martin, 133
Lyall, Alfred, 260
Lyotard, Jean-François, 14

Majlish and *majlishi*, 133–37, 143
Major, Ernest, 113
Makkonnen, Ras, 290
Mallon, Florencia E., 307
Manifest destiny, 63, 64, 67, 70
Mann, Sonny, 267
Mao Dun, 87, 88, 104, 121
Marr, Nikolai, 82, 83
Marx, Karl, 3, 7, 15, 273
Mass media, 28, 40
Masses, the, 307, 308, 311, 317, 322
Maussian, 299
Maximilian, 316

Plantations, and plantation system, 252, 255, 257
Plato, 194
Plekhanov, Georgy Valentinovich, 138
Pluralism, 216, 219, 234; cultural, 177, 204, 232
Politeness, 301, 302, 303
Political community/communities, 197, 198, 199, 202, 215, 217, 220, 221, 234
Political economy, 125
Political theory, 205, 222
Political identity, 198
Political integration, 202, 219, 220, 221, 223, 228
Political unification, 199
Popular: constituencies, 307; music, 251; press, 114; rule, 229
Porfirian state, 319
Porfiriato, 318
Postcolonial, 117, 249; contexts, 296; discourse, 116; space, 271
Postcolonialism, 118
Postmodernism; globalism, 118; theorists, 112
Postnational system, 201
Povinelli, Elizabeth A., 20
Power, 11, 12, 178, 182, 209, 212; power/ knowledge, 10; power relations, 296
Primitivism, 71
Private sphere, 320, 321, 325
Privatization, 325
Proletariat, 307, 324; industrial proletariat, 273; lumpen-proletariat, 307, 324
Protestant ethics, 175
Pueblo, 16, 307, 308, 314, 320, 322; abject, 16, 324; bad, 16, 313, 314, 324, 326; good, 16, 311, 313, 325, 326; revolutionary, 326
Public, 314; arena, 103; buildings, 129; discourses, 55; education, 313; life, 158, 160; office, 306; opinion, 47; parks, 103, 104; places, 137; rallies, 321, 322; relations, 46; spaces, 89; sphere, 34, 39, 98, 113, 114, 163, 180, 189, 190, 193, 194, 220, 221,

261, 267, 306, 320, 322, 335; testimony, 49; transportation, 343
Pushkin, Alexander Sergeyevich, 66, 67, 69, 70

Race, 34, 206, 250, 264, 284, 287, 296; biracial society, 270; multiracial societies, 281; racial consciouness, 286; racial identity, 271; racial inequaliity, 296, 297; racial politics, 281; racial slavery, 275, 277, 280; racial terror, 289; racial theory, 214; racial uplift, 286
Racism, 40, 288; scientific racism, 289
Ramgoonai, Drupatee, 266
Ramos, Samuel, 318, 319, 321, 324
Rampersad, Indarani, 269
Rastafarianism, 261
Rationality, 8, 10, 16; instrumental, 2, 10, 11, 114, 173, 174, 176, 177, 178, 181, 191, 193; means-ends, 8; purposive, 8
Rationalization, 8, 10, 174, 175
Rawls, John, 202, 219, 220, 225, 226, 229, 230, 231
Ray, Charu, 143
Ray, Hemendrakumar, 154
Ray, Jibendra Singha, 146
Ray, Nisithranjan, 124
Ray, Satyajit, 145, 148
Ray, Sukumar, 145, 154, 155
Reason, 10, 11, 191, 209, 214, 308, 309; human, 8, 112; political-practical, 208, 211; practical, 208, 217, 218; subject-centered, 10
Recognition, 28, 29, 41, 195, 296; cultural, 28, 39; legal, 39; mutual, 219; national, 28
Reddock, Rhoda, 254, 264
Reification, 10, 298
Reinvention, 165
Republicanism, 215, 216; civic republican-ism, 222
Ressentiment, 60
Return passage, 254

Rights, 38, 43, 39, 207, 223, 225, 227, 228, 230, 303, 310, 319, 326; basic, 218, 219, 220; civil, 8; citizenship, 305, 306, 316; common law, 41; communal, 204; constitutional, 27, 311; cultural, 262; of education, 318; electoral and voting, 30, 318, 326; equal, 219, 222, 231; fundamental, 203; human, 27, 203, 212, 223, 227, 228, 229, 230, 232, 272; individual, 203, 204, 223, 231, 314; land, 48, 49; Native Title, in Australia, 31, 32; special, 45; system of, 218, 219, 225, 226, 234; transcultural human, 229

Rio, Joao do, 335

Ritual, 46, 90, 96, 98, 187, 188, 300, 317

Rodney, Walter, 255

Roediger, David R., 284

Rohlehr, Gordon, 267

Rome, 7, 63, 64; imperial, 91; "the third," 20

Rorty, Richard, 27

Rossi, Aldo, 332

Rousseau, Jean-Jacques, 110, 207

Roy, D. L., 144

Ruins, 22, 237, 245, 332, 342, 345, 346; allegorical, 343; artificial, 346; Gothic and Roman, 334; modernist, 22, 331, 332, 333, 334, 343, 345, 346, 347; renovated, 345; and ruin mania, 346

Rule of law: 197, 203, 207, 202, 212, 219, 222; global, 216; international, 208–9

Russian culture and civilization, 61; as Eurasian culture, 76; as Eurasian synthesis, 78; as mediating civilization between East and West, 77; Russian cultural theory, 63, 70

Russian nationalism, 60; and foreign policy, 62; ideal, 69; national identity, 64; national ideology, 60, 67; nationalist projects, 60, 61, 64, 66, 67; nationalist thought, 59, 77, 79

Russian universalism, 69, 84; Russian as universal language, 71

Sabba, 131

Sakar, Susobhan, 150

Santa Anna, Antonio López de, 314

Sanyal, Hirankumar, 145, 150, 153, 154, 155

Sarkar, Benoy, 124

Schutz, Alfred, 281

Schwartz, Benjamin, 112

Science, 179, 180, 193, 179; scientific attitude, 191; scientific consciousnes, 173; scientific reason, 175; scientific thinking, 173

Seale, Bobby, 296

Secular, 58; secularism, 250; secularists in Trinidad, 268; secularization, 17, 59, 173, 180; secular outlook, 181

Self-determination, 29, 30, 198, 199

Settler nation, 20, 27, 31, 44

Settler state, 34

Shakespeare, William, 70

Shorty, Lord, 265

Shostakovich, 81

Sikander, Shahzia, 165

Silverman, Kaja, 28

Simmel, Georg, 3

Simulacra and simulacrum, 36, 94

Sinha, Kaliprasanna, 135

Slavery, 252, 255, 261, 282, 287, 304, 306, 309, 310, 311; racial, 275, 277, 280

Slavophiles, 59, 60, 63, 68

Social contract, 194, 215, 301

Social hierarchy, 305

Sociality, 129

Social movements, 323, 326

Sociability, 128, 184, 300

Solov'ev, Vladimir, 76

Solzhenitsyn, Aleksandr, 63

Somov, Orest, 66, 67

Sovereignty, 115, 198, 210, 212, 275, 276, 277, 284, 325

Space, 89, 141; allegorical, 107; domestic, 161; homosocial, 161; hybrid, 163; public, 89, 149, 302; social, 127, 186, 187; spatial location, 35

Library of Congress Cataloging-in-Publication Data

Alternative modernities / edited by Dilip Parameshwar Gaonkar.

p. cm. — (Public culture)   Includes index.

I S B N 0-8223-2703-1 (cloth : alk. paper)

I S B N 0-8223-2714-7 (pbk. : alk. paper)

1. Pluralism (Social sciences)   2. International relations and
culture.   3. Civilization, Modern.   4. East and West.   5. North and
south.   I. Gaonkar, Dilip Parameshwar.   II. Series.

HM1271 .A44   2001   306 — dc21   00-046659